HONORING THE TRUST

HONORING THE TRUST

Quality and Cost Containment in Higher Education

William F. Massy

President, The Jackson Hole Higher Education Group, Inc.
Professor Emeritus, Stanford University

ANKER PUBLISHING COMPANY, INC.
Bolton, Massachusetts

Honoring the Trust
Quality and Cost Containment in Higher Education

ISBN 1-882982-56-8

Composition by Deerfoot Studios
Cover design by Red Brick Design

Anker Publishing Company, Inc.
176 Ballville Road
P.O. Box 249
Bolton, MA 01740-0249 USA

www.ankerpub.com

To Sally

About the Author

William F. Massy is President of the Jackson Hole Higher Education Group, Inc., and Professor Emeritus at Stanford University. He earned tenure at Stanford's Graduate School of Business and later entered university administration as Vice Provost and Dean of Research. As Stanford's Vice President for Business and Finance he pioneered financial management and planning tools that have become standards in the field.

In 1987, Dr. Massy founded the Stanford Institute for Higher Education Research where he currently directs the Project on Educational Quality and Productivity as part of the U.S. Department of Education's National Center for Postsecondary Improvement.

Dr. Massy is the author of several previous books and consults internationally in the areas of resource management, academic quality improvement, and mathematical modeling of higher education institutions.

Contents

Preface

The public trust in colleges and universities has eroded significantly in recent years and will continue to do so unless considerable reforms are undertaken. For the past six years, I have worked with colleagues at the National Center for Postsecondary Improvement (NCPI) on research aimed at effecting such reforms. This book represents a main product of that research. Its title asserts that improvements in quality and cost containment are required not only for the well being of individual institutions, but more importantly, to honor the trust placed in academe by the broader society.

This assessment from NCPI's *Postsecondary Research Priorities: Improving Institutional Practice and Public Policy* (2002) sums up my point of departure: First, higher education is not perceived by the public to be in a state of crisis. Yet when measured in terms of students' educational achievement, higher education institutions' performance falls significantly short of its capacity. Perhaps as a consequence of the shortfalls, higher education has become less of a priority for financial support from both public and private sources.

The performance shortfalls are troubling even in the absence of crisis. They should motivate improvement in an enterprise that prides itself on being the envy of the world. Failure to address these problems has led many who know higher education to question its cost and quality, even as the general public has remained complacent. Institutions should feel challenged to remedy the shortfalls despite constrained resources. Continued failure to address them will jeopardize the nation's investment in higher education and our preeminent position internationally. Such failure would represent a breach of trust.

This book is no jeremiad. Instead of simply listing higher education's flaws, it presents a practical program for improvement—what faculty, institutional leaders, trustees, and oversight bodies can do now to improve the quality of education without spending more or abandoning other priorities. The diagnosis could have been written five or ten years ago, but it took until now to identify and try out the interventions.

The book's genesis lies in five events that shaped my career between 1987 and 1995. The first was Stanford University President Donald Kennedy's suggestion, circa 1987, that I turn to higher education research after finishing my tour as the university's vice president for business and finance. That suggestion initiated a three-year transition from vice president to a professor in the School of Education (I had previously been a business school professor), to my founding of the Stanford Institute for Higher Education Research (SIHER), and to the 15 years of work that has culminated in these pages.

The second event was Professor Robert Zemsky's invitation to join him in keynoting the first Pew Higher Education Roundtable, which he was initiating at the University of Pennsylvania in 1988, and then to become a permanent member of the roundtable. My talk, "A Paradigm for Research in Higher Education," began by describing the context in which colleges and universities operate and how that context has changed over time; i.e., the main subject matter of Chapter 1. It went on to cite the practical importance of an overall mental model of how colleges and universities operate. The nonprofit enterprise model, markets, production functions, cross-subsidies, and the other constructs that comprise the subject matter of Chapters 2 and 3 build on this theme. Subsequent discussions at the roundtable and research with Bob helped develop my ideas about the teaching-research balance (including the so-called "academic ratchet"), the impact of information technology on teaching and learning, and the related subjects covered in Chapters 4 and 5.

The third event came when Richard Chait and Richard Anderson, professors at the University of Maryland and Columbia Teachers College and cochairs of the National Center for Postsecondary Governance and Finance's Forum for College Financing, came to Stanford to suggest that I develop a "think-piece on productivity in higher education." I had been interested in the subject for years. Indeed, my book with David S. P. Hopkins, *Planning Models for Colleges and Universities* (Stanford University Press, 1981), had explored the underlying concepts as part of an overall model for higher education. My training as an economist taught me that the relation between costs and benefits is important for *all* activities, even those that can properly be characterized as academic. My experience as a Stanford professor, vice provost, and vice president had sensitized me to the possibilities for productivity improvement even in well-managed universities. So I accepted the challenge, and began a 15-year association with three successive national centers for the improvement of higher education.

In 1990 I teamed with professor Alan Odden of the University of Southern California (later the University of Wisconsin) on a proposal to the United States Department of Education's Office of Education Research and Improvement to add a finance center to the Consortium for Policy Research in Education (CPRE). We won the competition and, as specified in the proposal, I resigned my vice presidency to establish the finance center's higher education division at Stanford. Our main project was a field research study of how faculty view productivity, the teaching-research balance, incentives and rewards, and other subjects related to the academic production function as seen on the ground within departments. This study provided extensive empirical descriptions of the traditional faculty view as cited throughout this book. A second project resulted in *Resource Allocation in Higher Education* (University of Michigan Press, 1996). Chapters 2, 3, and 10 build on some of the ideas presented there.

The last chapter in the national center chronology began with the 1995 recompetition, which was won by the National Center for Postsecondary Improvement, a research consortium of Stanford University, the University of Pennsylvania, and the University of Michigan. Professor Patricia Gumport, who took over as SIHER director when I moved to Jackson Hole in 1996, chaired the center. I was responsible for the center's project on faculty roles and responsibilities and served on its executive committee with Bob Zemsky and Peter Capelli, Mike Nettles, Marv Peterson, Rich Shavelson, and (until he became president of the Carnegie Foundation for the Advancement of Teaching) Lee Schulman. NCPI funded my continuing analysis of the field interview data (referred to here as the NCPI interview data), the research on quality assurance in Scandinavia described in Chapter 8, and much of the time needed to write this manuscript. In addition, work on the aforementioned research agenda during 2001 and 2002 at NCPI national forums and within the executive committee helped inform the conclusions in Chapter 11 and last-minute revisions throughout the book.

The final event occurred in Hong Kong, circa 1995, when the University Grants Committee asked me to chair its first ever Teaching and

Learning Quality Process Review (TLQPR). A variant of academic audit as described in Chapter 8, the TLQPR propelled me into the worldwide higher education quality assurance network. The work began with a review of international practice, continued through the development of design concepts, and ended with implementation across the Territory's (then) seven colleges and universities. The TLQPR was regarded as an important success, and the second round is being implemented as this book goes to press. In addition to informing Chapter 8, it helped jell the ideas about education quality processes that are presented in Chapters 6 and 7. Testing in the context of on-the-record academic audits sharpened these concepts and made them more robust than if they had remained abstract research propositions.

ACKNOWLEDGMENTS

Now it's time to thank the many people who helped bring my ideas to fruition. First come those who shaped the events mentioned above: Don Kennedy for suggesting a higher education research career, Bob Zemsky for getting me into the roundtable and being a steadfast friend and colleague these past 15 years, Richard Chait and Richard Anderson for getting me started on productivity, Alan Odden for supporting my work with CPRE, and Patti Gumport (whom I hired as a Stanford assistant professor and now has moved on to succeed me) and fellow executive committee members for their support and help at NCPI. I'm grateful as well to Greg Henschel of the Department of Education who went to bat for this project at a number of important junctures.

Andrea Wilger, research associate at SIHER and project director for the faculty interview study, deserves a special word of thanks. Her efforts contributed mightily to the study and the publications that came out of it, and I wish her well in her current career as mother of two robust young boys. Let me thank, as well, our graduate students, especially Carol Colbeck, Ted Fu, John Jennings, Alex McCormick, and Jean Prinvalle. Thanks also to Roberta Callaway, SIHER's administrative manager and my long-time assistant, for her cheerful countenance and for keeping the office wheels turning.

Nigel French, former Secretary General of the University Grants Committee, also deserves special thanks for his support as a friend and colleague before, during, and after the first TLQPR, and for his coauthorship of several papers on quality and accountability. I doubt if the review could have succeeded without his organizing and negotiating skills, or his abiding faith in academic audit as the preferred method of higher education quality assurance. Nigel has caught the academic bug and now is pursuing his doctorate in higher education at the Institute of Education, London. Thanks, too, to Antony Leung, then chairman of the University Grants Committee (UGC) and now Financial Secretary of the Hong Kong Government, for trusting me to run the program and backing me when the going got tough. I'd also like to thank the 18 members of the first TLQPR panel and the other UGC members involved in the review and its aftermath, particularly Al George, Inga-Stina Ewbank, Ron Oxburgh, Ted Parks, Helen Siu, Brian Smith, Stewart Sutherland, Frans van Vught, Ann Wright, Wee Chou Hou, Richard Wong, and Kenneth Young. Back in the United States, Dean Hubbard, President of Northwest Missouri State University, introduced me to Baldrige and helped marry the ideas to activity-based costing as described in Chapter 9. Dean has been a steadfast friend and supporter throughout my journey through quality and productivity.

Let me again gratefully acknowledge financial support from the three aforementioned national centers: most recently the National Center for Postsecondary Improvement, funded under the Educational Research and Development Center program, agreement number R309A600001, CDFA 84.309A, as administered by the Office of Educational Research and Improvement (OERI), and the United States Department of Education. Of course the findings and opinions expressed herein do not reflect the position or policies of OERI or the United States Department of Education.

I would also like to thank the team at Anker Publishing, who did such a good job of editing the manuscript. All remaining errors, whether substantive or editorial, are mine.

William F. Massy
Jackson Hole, Wyoming
July 2002

PART ONE:
THE CASE FOR CHANGE

1

THE EROSION OF TRUST

"Americans continue to enjoy the most envied, most copied system of post-secondary education in the world." And yet, "American colleges and universities are openly troubled by a sense of diminished opportunities and lessened capacities. Fundamental questions about the quality, content, and cost of colleges and universities are rife, both within and without the academy."[1]

These words did not represent an attack on the academy, but rather a thoughtful voice from within—from 19 scholars and observers of higher education, myself included, who had convened during the spring of 1988 for the inaugural Pew Higher Education Roundtable.[2] Our conversation was spirited, and sometimes the disagreements were intense, but in the end a consensus emerged: US colleges and universities may be good, but they could be a great deal better. And because the world is changing, being good enough today risks trouble in the future. Peter Drucker may have overstated the case when he said that "Universities will be relics in 30 years,"[3] but higher education can no longer take its values and privileges for granted. Settling for good enough erodes the public's trust in higher education and puts institutions and faculty at risk.

Fifteen years after Drucker's prediction, the American public characterizes higher education as getting a "respectable B": good enough, indeed better than elementary and secondary schools, but hardly excellent.[4] Survey respondents said that attracting the best possible teachers and researchers and ensuring that students work hard to achieve high academic standards represent the enterprise's most important goals. When asked what should be done to improve colleges and universities, they cited

3

efficiency improvement and lower prices as being most important. Perhaps of most concern, the proportion of respondents who feel that higher education is wasteful increases with the level of degree attained—in other words, familiarity with the academy.

While such opinions don't signal a crisis in American higher education, they should not be used to justify complacency. The nation's colleges and universities are no longer held in awe, but rather are seen as just another industry with good and bad elements of performance. College may be the ticket to the good life, but its benefits for democracy and culture no longer command a top priority for the public purse. Higher education increasingly is viewed as a private rather than a public good: very important for those who get it, but something most government officials can safely take for granted. As a private good, one can argue that the economic benefits college confers on individuals are sufficient to offset tuition payments—even if costs are higher than they need to be. It is no wonder, then, that higher education gets a smaller share of public expenditures and that even foundations, traditionally an important source of support for institutional development, are refocusing their priorities elsewhere. While these symptoms don't mean colleges and universities are on the road to becoming relics, they do imply an erosion of the academy's previous high trust levels.

One can reasonably ask whether a "B" performance will be good enough to meet the challenges of the 21st century. The knowledge economy places ever-larger demands on the American workforce, and this can only increase as other nations build technological prowess and competitiveness. Political and social issues become ever more complex—for example, in the areas of organizational ethics, social justice, the environment, and now international terrorism. Such issues require thoughtful and informed deliberation, not the narrow pursuit of self-interest and dogma. Personal value and lifestyle issues become similarly complex as the available options increase geometrically. And arching over everything is this overwhelming truth: Whatever one learns in college can only be the starting point for lifelong learning. Students must learn fact-finding and problem-solving skills as well as mastering specific areas of knowledge. Will "B" performance produce the needed results?

Access for disadvantaged groups remains a major priority for colleges and universities, for the foundations that remain active in the field, and for many political constituencies. Yet solutions to the access problem are couched mainly in financial terms: how to fund poor students so they can eventually partake in the economic benefits associated with a college degree. But while the very fact of access improves social justice, one can reasonably ask "Access to what?" Dropout rates are alarmingly high, and anecdotal evidence suggests that many institutions don't fully understand the needs of the disadvantaged. Surely this is another manifestation of "B" performance.

This book takes the view that universities and colleges can be a great deal better than they are—that their "respectable B" can be transformed into a "solid A" without massive infusions of funds. The case in a nutshell is this: Participation rates have soared, but schools have not fully embraced the educational needs and competencies of their broadened constituencies. Institutional behavior has become increasingly market driven, but the markets generally reward prestige—they don't gauge the true quality of education, and therefore they produce a perverse set of incentives. Policymakers don't understand the economic behavior of universities, and the universities themselves know too little about their costs and the degree of cross subsidy among programs. Faculty lack needed understanding of education quality and how to produce it at optimal cost levels, they don't know how to measure it, and their incentive system doesn't reward efforts to improve. Finally, technology is disrupting the status quo by changing everything from the production of education to the scope and intensity of competition. Each of these themes, and many subthemes, will be taken up in later chapters. Only by examining the problem's root causes can one see how to improve education quality and contain cost.

One thinks of universities as excelling at higher education, research and scholarship, and public service. Yet there is reason to doubt the academy's core competency in education. Such competency means the ability to deliver the best education possible given the resources invested. This book argues that colleges and universities are not all they can be, that they can improve the quality of education without spending more, dismantling the research enterprise, or undermining essential academic values. Its title asserts that the gap represents a breach of trust that needs to be repaired.

This book concentrates on undergraduate education, although the ideas also apply to professional and master's programs that are not steppingstones to the PhD. Part One examines how higher education's environment and institutional policies have led to shortfalls in education competency, and how such shortfalls reinforce the status quo. We'll review the academy's position in the modern world, analyze universities as economic enterprises, consider how accounting ambiguities obscure important information about costs and cross subsidies, evaluate the tension between teaching and research, and consider the disruptive influence of information technology.

Part Two presents a practical program for improving education quality while containing costs. We'll address the processes by which institutions and faculty improve and assure education quality, the adoption of para-digm-changing technology, and the introduction of methodologies to analyze and contain costs. Imagining what more could be accomplished if such a program were implemented helps demonstrate the existence of competency shortfalls. The last chapter sums up the recommendations in an action agenda: what academic leaders and board members can do to rebuild their institution's core competency in education. I am under no illusions about the difficulties that would-be change agents will face. I have faced many such difficulties myself. However, the potential gains make arduous efforts worthwhile. I hope this book will encourage and guide those who wish to undertake the task.

My critique of higher education's costs and educational quality could have been written some years ago, but I waited until I could include tangible recommendations about the way forward. Ten years of research, consulting, and responsibility for the implementation of reforms, built upon almost 20 years as a university officer and earlier years of experience as a professor, have informed these results. What I did not foresee was the degree of change spurred by competition and the information technology revolution. This has increased the urgency of what I am trying to say.

QUESTIONS OF COMPETENCY

Close examination reveals the traditional university's core competency to lie in knowledge creation and dissemination, not in educating students at the highest quality possible given available resources. Professors do research and scholarship and make knowledge available to their students, but most spend little time on the processes of teaching and learning. They don't focus sufficiently on student needs or the backgrounds and learning styles presented by would-be learners. They don't think deeply enough about the assessment of learning outcomes. They don't try regularly to substitute lower-cost for higher-cost processes while maintaining quality. A true core competency in education would include all of these things.

Traditional universities possess one element of education competency, but they fall short on the others.

One-dimensional competency appeared sufficient until recently. First, the boom of research following World War II placed knowledge creation on a pedestal—not only for the nation's 100 or so major research universities, but also for nearly all four-year institutions. Academic prestige and perceptions about education quality came to depend on research. This drove up cost and eroded faculty teaching effort, but the local content monopolies enjoyed by colleges and universities and the difficulty of measuring educational value added shielded institutions and professors from the consequences of their actions. Applicant pools depended on prestige. and prestige depended on research. Faculty jobs also depended on research, as did a significant fraction of institutional funding—even funding provided in the name of education. Why look beyond content given these circumstances?

The difficulty of conceiving alternatives provided another reason for defining content as synonymous with education competency. There was no systematic protocol for assuring and improving education quality. Great teaching was viewed mainly in terms of classroom performance, which could be discounted by saying that some professors have more standup talent than others. Such talent was believed to be less important than content knowledge and the ability to publish, and in any case little could be done to improve it. Moreover, the traditional methods of teaching had been in place for decades or centuries. Aside from spurring research, people thought the only way to boost education quality was to improve faculty-student ratios and spend more on educational support functions. Few could imagine paradigm-changing innovations.

Dissatisfaction with the conventional model has been brewing for some time, but advances in information technology and quality assurance brought things to a boil. Technology opens many new options, and content knowledge isn't sufficient for choosing among them. Instead, one must understand the process of student learning and how to make cost-saving tradeoffs. Moving into uncharted territory also puts a premium on student assessment—absent such feedback, technological change might do serious harm without one's knowing it. Good assessment depends on clear decisions about objectives, which should be informed by an understanding of student needs. In other words, the design and implementation of paradigm-changing technology requires well-developed education quality protocols and cost management methodologies as well as content knowledge and technological prowess.

Quality assurance methodologies have been spurred by the rising participation rates and the drive to improve educational value for money, but mostly overseas. Many innovations in this arena are largely unknown in the United States—a fact that is discussed with increasing openness at international meetings on education quality.[5] America achieved mass participation before such methodologies had been invented, and like many successful innovators we became self-satisfied with our accomplishments. However, a new wave is sweeping the world. As the new methodologies prove themselves, prospective students and national quality evaluators from overseas will ask American institutions to support their quality claims with data rather than reputation.

Even now, US universities appear to be losing market share in the export of higher education services. Competition is especially fierce in Southeast Asia, which has accounted for nearly 60% of the business in recent years. For example, 90% of Australian universities now run some 500 offshore programs, mainly in China, Japan, Malaysia, Singapore, and Vietnam.[6] Australia also reports a massive increase in its foreign student population, including a significant rise in students from the United States and Canada. Higher education guru Rosabeth Moss Kantor sums up the problem this way:

> The global economy sets in motion forces that shift power to consumers. The ability to bypass the establishment because new choices across borders and technologies means that dominant players that once monopolized a channel are losing power.[7]

America's traditional hegemony in higher education may not be in immediate jeopardy, but given the new economy our universities cannot afford to rest on their laurels.

The Chinese ideogram for "crisis" consists of two characters: "problem" and "opportunity." The juxtaposition of problem and opportunity aptly characterizes American higher education at the beginning of the 21st century. US higher education has not reached the crisis stage yet, but failure to attend to the issues could put us there. We have some serious problems, but also some real opportunities. Closing the education competency gap represents the biggest opportunity.

CRITICAL VOICES

Many will recall the emergence of doubt about the academy's core competency in education. In 1986, for example, the nation's governors formally charged that their states' graduates were not as well educated as students of past decades. The influential *Integrity in the College Curriculum,*[8] published by the Association of American Colleges, declared that "America's colleges and universities no longer have a 'firm grasp of their goals and missions,' partly because the faculty's 'allegiance to academic disciplines [is] stronger than their commitment to teaching or the life of the institutions where they are employed.'"[9] And then, addressing work in the disciplines themselves as well as in teaching, Allan Bloom's *The Closing of the American Mind* asserted that faculty had relinquished, for reasons of politics and self-interest, their roles as scholar-mentors.[10] His attack struck a responsive cord with the American public: The book sold some 800,000 copies.

Bloom's book opened the floodgates. For example, journalist Charles Sykes asserted in *Profscam* that "professors have destroyed the university as a center of learning . . ."[11] More seriously, academics Paul Gross and Norman Levitt argued in *Higher Superstition: The Academic Left and Its Quarrels with Science*[12] that the academy has not maintained objectivity in teaching and scholarship—that academic quality could no longer be taken for granted. Although these writers were politically conservative, we shall see that the root of their concerns went beyond politics.[13]

The emergent concerns were not limited to quality. They included the cost of education as well. During October 1986, in an address at Harvard University, then-Secretary of Education William Bennett challenged institutions' tuition hikes and their protestations about financial stringency. "The old church," he said, "fell into some disrepute because its exhortations to poverty and holiness were too often belied by the worldliness and sumptuousness of its clerics. Similarly, American higher education simply refuses to acknowledge the obvious fact that, in general, it is rich."[14] Furthermore, echoing the concerns of the quality critics, ". . . more money has given many in our universities the opportunity to avoid doing one thing above all—actually teaching large numbers of students, or, in some cases, any students. Bennett's axiom: After a certain point, the more money you have, the fewer distinguished professors you will have in the classroom."

Reflecting on the accumulating evidence, the Pew Roundtable concluded, "American colleges and universities must make a fundamental investment in quality control."[15] We considered the nontraditional student and said that institutions ought to be doing more to adapt their curricula and methods of service to this "new majority" of learners.[16] We described how institutions solve problems by elaborating staff functions (the "administrative lattice") and how professors shift their time toward research (the "academic ratchet").[17] Rather than narrowing blame, we argued that the overemphasis on research was everyone's problem: "It is not just the faculty, but their institutions and, at least indirectly, the consuming public, that contribute to the ethos that places a premium on research and publication at the expense of teaching effectiveness."[18]

Further testimony followed. Page Smith, longtime UCLA professor and founding provost at the University of California at Santa Cruz, decried in *Killing the Spirit* the professorial tendency to shun teaching in the name of research. In an even more telling indictment, he asserted that "the routine and pedestrian [research] far outweighs the brilliant and original; that routine and pedestrian research is not merely a very expensive nullity but a moral and spiritual drag on the institutions in which it takes place and a serious distortion of the nature of both the intellectual and scholarly life . . . [and] the economic cost is also scandalously high . . ."[19] Richard Huber's *How Professors Play the Cat Guarding the Cream* echoed these concerns and challenged "administrators and faculty to begin to think about the *unthinkable—how does the faculty spend its time.*"[20]

Perhaps the most sobering testimony came from Henry Rosovsky, longtime dean of the faculty of arts and sciences at Harvard University and in no way predisposed to criticize higher education. In *The University: An Owners Manual* (1990), he discussed the pros and cons of professors' outside activities—for example, professional service and consulting—and the tendency of some to be absent from campus for purposes of research.[21] But during the spring of 1991, in his last annual report to the faculty, he became unequivocally critical. "The crux of the matter," he wrote, is that the faculty of Arts and Sciences "has become a society largely without rules, or to put it slightly differently, the tenured members of the faculty—frequently as *individuals*—make their own rules."[22] But rather than blame the faculty, he pointed out that "faculty behavior has been quite rational and understandable, given the absence of constraints." Furthermore, as he describes the feelings of a senior colleague, "the administration should assume most of the blame precisely because of our manifest unwillingness to set clear tasks and clear limits."

Lest anyone think these criticisms are dated, consider this recent assessment by Stanford President Emeritus Donald Kennedy.

> Yet public criticism of higher education has become increasingly more strident. The assault comes from various sources, Left as well as Right. It sounds a variety of themes: the failure of science and policy studies to provide answers we desperately need (why isn't AIDS a thing of the past, and why is K–12 education in such bad shape?); inadequacies in the quality of undergraduate instruction (why can't Susie's calculus teacher speak English as well as Susie can?); failure to respond adequately to economic stringency (corporations everywhere are downsizing; why isn't productivity in higher education improving?). The attacks are being felt, and morale in the academy is as low as those inside it can remember.[23]

The idea that the academy is a system without rules raises serious questions about its core competency in education. Unruliness also threatens institutions' ability to adapt to the sweeping changes now confronting colleges and universities. The critics' voices—I have described only a few—are sufficiently numerous and credible that no thoughtful person should dismiss them out of hand. Where there's so much smoke, there's likely to be at least some fire. Yet most people within the academy believe they are not at fault—that somehow the problems would go away if only their case could be more effectively made and if only people would listen.

Not so. The problems are real, and the academy's advocates are increasingly being viewed as nothing more than self-interested spinners.[24] In "An End to Sanctuary," the Pew Roundtable argued that "In the face of such adversity, higher education could well be expected to decry the unfairness of it all. We have in mind, however, a much different accounting—one that *reexamines the assumptions* that underlie higher education's growth and hence its prospects and opportunities."[25] Simply restating the assumptions in more forceful terms would no longer suffice. An informed and objective reexamination would be required. As President Clara Lovett of Northern Arizona University put it in her recent paper, "Cracks in the Bedrock: Can U.S. Higher Education Remain Number One?":

It is time to focus on the resources we have, including the public funds for instruction, research, and financial aid, and rebuild the foundation of our higher education system on different premises.[26]

THE CLASSIC UNIVERSITY

To understand higher education's current state, one must start with the classic ideal of a university or college. The ideal probably originated in the first half of the 20th century, when America was assimilating the German research university along with the English liberal arts college traditions, but its roots go back much further. The classic university may never have existed in pure form, but the ideal has had a profound influence on how the academy views itself and how others view it.

The Faculty

I'll never forget the admonition of a thoughtful colleague when, as a vice president of Stanford, I proposed an action that seemed to go against faculty self-interest. "The faculty *are* the university," he said, "so how could such an action further the university's well being?" We worked the problem out, but the reminder stuck. "The faculty are the university" lies at the core of the classic university ideal. Professors are not employees hired to perform particular tasks; they represent the very essence of academe. They create, preserve, retrieve, interpret, and transmit knowledge. They pursue knowledge for its own sake, and they consider teaching to be a calling— not a job or even a profession. Faculty embody what it means to be teacher-scholars and, therefore, members of the academic community.

At the dawn of the university age, groups of scholars came together to interact with each other and with students. Infrastructures and employment relationships came later. So did the creation of departments, the organization of knowledge into disciplines and of instruction into courses, and the formal certification of degrees. Money and the trappings of organization have been important for universities since the 12th century, but in the beginning came the faculty.

The Students

Next, of course, came the students. Scholars want to propagate and expand their disciplines, and this requires a constant stream of new disciples. In the classic university, students share their professors' scholarly goals and—except for the lack of training and experience that defines them as students—they are competent to pursue these goals. Students sit at the feet of scholars in order to absorb knowledge and methods of thought defined in terms of the academic disciplines, not the needs of the outside world. (Professors tend to define their disciplines in terms of the structure of knowledge, which they view as more fundamental than transitory worldly needs.) The best students will become teacher-scholars, and the others will benefit from exposure to scholarship after they leave the ivory tower. While in the academy, however, all students are expected to behave as academics—that is, to devote the best of their time and effort to the pursuit of knowledge for its own sake.

The Library

The library represents the classic university's third essential element. Although faculty content experts and student content recipients represent major knowledge repositories, human memory does not provide a sufficient basis for archiving and organizing knowledge. The library provides that function, and also the reference infrastructure needed to access the information. Without a good on-site library, it was said, faculty and students cannot pursue their scholarly goals effectively.

Scholarship

While faculty, students, and libraries represent the classic university's quintessential elements, scholarship is where the three come together. Scholarship was valued for its own sake in the classic university. It probably furthered education as well as or better than other approaches that were available at the time—for example, having students memorize predetermined canons. Engaging in scholarly inquiry and vigorous debate with peers and professors reflect active learning, which we now know to be more effective than the passive absorption of facts. Face-to-face interaction around scholarly issues was a good way to get student involvement. Because scholarship was fairly general compared to today's research, bright, motivated undergraduates could get to the frontier and feel the thrill of knowledge creation. Finally, shared cultural literacy increased the value of scholarly knowledge, even for those who would not pursue careers as scholars. Being viewed as literate by peers didn't hurt one's job prospects or social standing.

One might say the academy defined "relevance" according to its own criteria and then exported the criteria to the broader society. Society accepted the academy's definition of an "educated person," then closed the loop by evaluating universities according to the same criteria. This comfortable and self-reinforcing process persisted for centuries, until challenged by research specialization and mass student participation in the years following World War II. In its day, it reflected a powerful core competency in education.

Classic universities also came to be defined as "places"—campus settings where students learn and professors teach and pursue scholarship. Campuses provide space for contemplation, interaction, and safe experimentation with different ideas and lifestyles. They are supposed to be inspiring as well as functional, as witnessed by the Gothic- and Georgian-style buildings found at many traditional colleges and universities. The best campuses are designed with propinquity in mind. For example, the arrangement of disciplines and individual faculty offices can spur or inhibit certain kinds of intellectual activity. Finally, today's campuses include substantial supporting infrastructures: from classrooms and laboratories, to student services, athletics facilities, maintenance shops, administrative offices, and that perennial focus of attention—parking.

Substantial barriers to entry protected the classic university. It's not easy to get high-quality professors together with top-rated students and supply them with a world-class library and an inspiring and functional campus. Institutions have worked for decades and spent huge sums without achieving real success. But for those that succeeded came substantial monopoly power that let them perpetuate the classic university ideal. In the original classic university, before air travel and telecommunications, the monopolies were substantially local. Later the markets for students and faculty became national or global. Now, with the advent of information technology, the academic production process is becoming global as well. But the classic university ideal remains campus-centric. It continues to assume the historic barriers to entry and the local monopoly power they confer.

Classic universities are strongly associated with handicraft processes: that is, one-off production like teaching a particular class or performing a specific piece of research. There are two reasons for this. First, knowledge work is complicated. Until the advent of information technology, there weren't good alternatives to handcrafting each act of teaching and scholarship. Second, in teaching especially, one-off production has come to be associated with intimacy. Consider the classic gold standard for education: Mark Hopkins and his student on a log. By delivering education through one-on-one dialog, it is said, the Williams College president could tailor content to his student's needs, interests, and capacities. He could draw the student into an active learning posture, assess her progress, and make corrections in real time. Mass production, the perceived alternative to handicraft, is regarded as dehumanizing and thus not appropriate for the classic university. Yet many of today's lecture courses don't begin to meet the gold standard.

Autonomy

Autonomy represents the classic university's final essential element. Professors should be free to study and teach what they wish, for example, and the university should be free to set its own policies for governance, performance evaluation, degree certification, and the like. Autonomy also requires a certain level of resource independence—i.e., that the university has sufficient discretionary resources to enable it to exercise judgment in pursuit of academic goals. Without discretionary resources, institutions and professors would be slaves to the market. The classic university ideal assumes substantial financial autonomy: e.g., through gifts and endowments, selectivity, and "no-strings" governmental appropriations.

"Autonomy" means freedom, the right of self-governance. But while most observers agree on the need for academic autonomy, they differ as to whether it is a true right or simply a delegation. To take a specific and often controversial example, peer review can be justified on either ground: as a delegation because only peers have the necessary expertise, or as a right because only peers have the standing to sit in judgment (as a "jury of one's peers"). The argument is important because it colors one's view of how the modern environment impinges on the classic university ideal and whether higher education is responding appropriately.

The rights argument holds that because the faculty are the university, they should be free to decide important academic issues just as citizens' votes should be decisive in a democracy. In other words, academic freedom should be valued intrinsically, not simply as a means to an end. Each professor is entitled to his or her system of values and priorities, and no authority should be able to say that one system is better or worse than another. The intrinsic justification for autonomy holds that, like individual political freedom, academic freedom represents more than privilege. According to this view, any abridgement is a breech of trust by the larger society.

Autonomy also can be defended on instrumental grounds—that is, as a means to an end rather than an end in itself. Who, for example, is in a better position to gauge the benefits of this or that intellectual activity than the professors involved? Micromanagement would prevent these professionals from doing their jobs, to the detriment of both scholarship and teaching. This may sound like the intrinsic case for academic freedom, but it's not. Intrinsic academic freedom is unconditional: Barring unprofessional activity or moral turpitude, professors are not accountable for the competent exercise of their freedoms. One can be called to account for poor methodology or failure to consider prior work, but not for the choice of topic or the ends eventually achieved. Delegated responsibility, on the other hand, does carry accountability for achieving particular ends even when those receiving the delegations are the only ones with the requisite know-how.

The difference represents more than word play. The language of delegation and accountability used by many of higher education's external stakeholders, especially those who pay the bills, threatens adherents to the classic university ideal. Likewise, the language of rights (even when leavened with duty) sounds self-serving to many outside the academy. The two sides talk past each other, and in the process they erode the trust between higher education and the general society.

FROM IVORY TOWER TO ECONOMIC MAINSTREAM

The classic university ideal came about for good reasons. However, certain myths and confusions have grown up over the years. They didn't matter as long as the conditions that spawned and protected the classic university remained in place, but now those conditions are changing. The changes started 50 years ago, when higher education began moving into the economic mainstream.

Prior to World War II, higher education operated on a small scale as compared to the modern-day enterprise. This derived from low participation rates—only the elite could afford college and appeared well prepared to benefit from the college experience. Most institutions were controlled privately, student populations were not very diverse, and institutional cultures were fairly homogeneous. The values of students, faculty, and those who paid for education and supported scholarship tended to be consistent with the classic university ideals. Most people defined the classic university in scholarly terms—particularly those associated with the liberal arts.

The result was a self-fulfilling cycle of success. Low participation rates meant that only the elite got college degrees. The resulting degree-holders did well in later life, which reinforced the classic university's approach to education. Conflicts between teaching and research were minimal because educators, students, and payers all agreed that better scholarship produced better education. Academic autonomy meant the community of scholars could define its own goals and determine for itself how well individual professors and students achieved them. The academy's noble goals and monopoly on expertise forestalled calls for accountability or even independent evaluation. In effect, good performance was whatever the academy defined it to be.

One such definition held that the university was above the market—that, somehow, markets should bend to academic values whenever the two came into conflict. Many professors continue to hold this view, which they associate with the classic university. I'll return frequently to the conflict between values and market forces. For now, let me note simply that the conflict is not new.

Clark Kerr, president of the University of California during its major growth period and noted writer on higher education, describes this tension in terms of the classical polarity between the Agora (the market) and the Acropolis (which represents scholarship). He points out that universities have always served the labor market (and by extension, the market for research).

> In fact, universities began in Europe in early modern times precisely for that purpose... The cherished academic view that higher education started out on the Acropolis and was desecrated by descent into the Agora led by ungodly commercial interests and scheming public officials and venal academic leaders is just not true. If anything, higher education started in the Agora, the market, at the bottom of the hill and ascended to the Acropolis at the top of the hill. ... Mostly it has lived in tension, at one and the same time at the bottom of the hill, at the top of the hill, and on the many pathways in between.[27]

Post-War Changes

Two seismic shifts intensified the conflict during the post-war era: educational massification and massively funded research. Massification stemmed from a desire to extend the benefits of higher education to more segments of the population. The research largesse applied wartime lessons to strengthening the nation's science and technology base. Initially the two shifts reinforced the classic university ideal. Eventually, however, they generated a powerful impetus for change.

Educational Massification

Massification meant shifting higher education from an elite to a broad-based enterprise. Fueled by the GI Bill, state investment, and the Great Society programs, participation rates grew from 10% in 1940 to 50% in 1975. The states invested heavily in new campuses, in converting teacher-education colleges to mainstream universities, and in expanding the traditional institutional base. Private universities enjoyed a period of buoyant demand and, after a time, unprecedented flows of gifts and endowment investment returns. As college degrees became tickets to the good life, professors, their institutions, and the arcane processes of university education were all the more held in awe.

With massification and the perceived economic value of the degree came concerns about education for the disadvantaged, especially minorities. Universities came to be viewed, and viewed themselves, as engines for redressing the wrongs of prior generations and bringing minorities into the social and economic mainstream. Admissions and financial aid offices catered to the needs of the disadvantaged. Student services professionals grappled with the cultural problems faced by these groups, who tended to drop out at greater rates than the traditional majority. Unfortunately, however, the educational dimension of college life did not change a great deal. Institutions grudgingly added remedial work where necessary, but few professors asked whether the content needs and learning styles of the new populations were materially different from those of the classic student.

Funding of Research

The watershed for research came in 1945, when Vannevar Bush, provost at MIT and wartime national science advisor, made the case for federally funded science in the public interest. Bush and his supporters were

"... convinced that science was distinct from other kinds of government programs, that it must be free from political control, and that, to be successful, scientists should be free to direct their own affairs."[28] The resulting partnership between the universities and the federal government provided the impetus for US scientific hegemony. The partnership aided universities financially while at the same time shifting their priorities from teaching toward research.

The increased importance of research "cast a long shadow on undergraduate education at many large universities."[29] The 1988 National Survey of Postsecondary Faculty indicated that, at all kinds of institutions, teaching performance had become "at best a neutral influence on faculty income."[30] At the institutional level, colleges as well as universities followed what sociologist David Reisman in 1958 had called a "snake-like procession" as they vied for the prestige conferred by research and graduate programs.[31] Although the research game was becoming more and more competitive, the rewards were seen as worth the effort. This perception was amplified by the propagation across the sector of faculty trained in the research-oriented doctoral programs of prestigious universities.

The drive for research unleashed a set of dynamics that soon became self-amplifying. Research success confers prestige as well as immediate and long-term financial benefit, but the path to success is unforgiving. One can cut corners in teaching and suffer few if any consequences, but to do so in research means failure to publish and loss of grant and contract support. Furthermore, the traditional though largely unexamined assumption that good research represents a necessary and sufficient condition for teaching quality produced powerful benefits in the educational marketplace. Universities could have their cake and eat it too. They could stress research, if necessary at the expense of time devoted to undergraduate teaching, while simultaneously improving selectivity and student quality. Small wonder, then, that research became the coin of the realm, the best way to get one's ticket punched for institutions and professors alike. That core competencies in education were eroding, or at least not keeping up with massification and the demands of diversity, did not even appear on the radar screen.

The massive increases in enrollment and research meant that the universities would enter the nation's economic and political mainstream, but the consequences of mainstream participation took some time to emerge. The interim represented a golden age of expansion without strong market discipline or political accountability—in effect, a 20-year honeymoon. This was long enough for a whole generation of professors, myself included, to mature in an environment of affluence and autonomy that many came to regard as an academic birthright.

END OF THE HONEYMOON

The honeymoon ended during the waning years of the Johnson administration, when the Vietnam War diverted resources from the Great Society, fueled inflation, and propagated questions about the academy's values. Following Vietnam, the energy crisis and the resulting stagflation trimmed governmental and private purchasing power, and the end of the baby boom weakened student demand in relation to the recently expanded educational capacity. For the first time in decades, real faculty salaries fell and academically worthy programs had to be cut for purely financial reasons. Internal competition for scarce resources and the culture wars of the 1960s and 1970s fragmented the professoriate and undermined the authority of institutional leaders. Trust eroded within the academy and between the academy and the outside world. Many within higher education came to resent the outside influences, and many outsiders came to mistrust the academy. Universities and professors began a long slide from objects of awe to subjects of accountability.

Accountability also reared its head in research. Reacting to alleged abuses in Department of Defense (DOD) university research funding, the Mansfield Amendment to the Military Authorization Act of 1970 prohibited the DOD from sponsoring research unless it had a "direct or apparent relationship to a specific military function."[32] While faculty usually found ways to justify their research, however basic, in terms of specific military function, the mere fact of having to do so raised questions about the university-government research partnership. Congress did not trust university investigators to make scientific judgments in the national interest as Vannevar Bush had envisioned 25 years earlier, and skepticism about professors' claims about military relevance further eroded trust in the academy.

Governmental regulation on a massive scale soon became another sign of the times. Universities were brought under the National Labor Relations Board (NLRB), the Occupational Safety and Health Administration (OSHA), and many other state and federal regulatory bodies. The fact that businesses had for years been subject to such regulations was scant comfort when compliance costs, which totaled many millions of dollars, were tallied against higher education's newly constrained financial base. Other regulations affected colleges and universities even more directly. Affirmative action goals and timetables forced their way into student admissions and faculty hiring decisions—further eroding autonomy as well as adding to cost. Title IX forced institutions to spend additional millions to equalize athletic expenditures for men and women. The point is not that these requirements were inappropriate—indeed, most were desirable and some were welcomed. It is that higher education now was in the economic mainstream and subject to the obligations as well as the benefits of mainstream participation

ASCENDANCY OF MARKET FORCES

The ascendancy of market forces and the unleashing of competition completed the transition from ivory tower to economic mainstream. Financial stringency led universities to search more aggressively for new income sources. Schools put enrollment management on a more professional basis and sought to expand student markets by creating new degree and continuing education programs. Outreach to nontraditional populations—for example, part-time students outside the post–high school age group—intensified. Fundraising became more widespread and highly organized, with dedicated professional staffs and recognized methodologies and consultants. More institutions entered the competition for sponsored research, and many developed sophisticated programs for aiding would-be faculty investigators.

Market forces brought schools into head-to-head competition as they jostled for the same scarce dollars. For example, the conventional wisdom of the Golden Age, that students' choices should be as economically neutral as possible and that financial aid should be based purely on need, was undermined as institution after institution embraced high-volume merit-based aid as a competitive tool. Students, in turn, learned to play one school off against another—for example, by "dialing for dollars" to augment financial aid offers.[33] In research, more and more would-be investigators at a broader array of schools vied for a constrained funding pie. The trend toward spreading the research wealth, which accelerated during the 1980s, drove the success rate for proposals to federal agencies substantially downward.[34] Reputation still mattered, but many more institutions and investigators were being allowed into the game.

IN PURSUIT OF PRESTIGE

One might think that competition would pressure universities to demonstrate and then steadily improve their education competency, but this was not the case. Instead, competition boosted the importance of prestige, which in turn came to be associated with performance in research. Research performance is easier to measure than educational performance, and its pursuit is eminently consistent with the classic university ideals. In time, prestige became the chief arbiter of market power.

Researchers at RAND, a nonprofit institution long noted for its analytical prowess, have documented the dominant role of prestige. They met with administrators, students, and faculty at 26 colleges and universities spanning all regions of the country and all four-year institutional types. After reviewing the data, the researchers classified institutions in terms of their posture on prestige:[35]

1) **Prestige based** institutions seek to maintain or enhance their current high level of prestige and the market power that goes with it. They define themselves in terms of academic values rather than market needs and exploit their market power to pursue research and scholarship, boost salaries, and enhance the quality of institutional life.

2) **Prestige seeking** institutions are not highly prestigious currently but want to become so. They invest heavily in activities they think will confer prestige—for the most part in research-related activities and enhancements such as athletics that will increase institutional prominence. These investments may come at the expense of other priorities like faculty salaries (except for research stars) and the quality of institutional life.

3) **Reputation focused** institutions are not prestigious and are not trying to become so. They invest in meeting the identifiable demands of customers and building a customer-based reputation. These institutions have embraced the market and are trying to do as well as possible in market terms.

The RAND researchers described the three types of institutions in ways that are highly relevant for this book.

1) **Prestige-based** institutions tend to be inward-looking, preoccupied with what they are, what they value, and what they have by way of human, financial, and physical resources. Faculty governance and traditional academic values powerfully influence their decisions.

2) **Prestige-seeking** institutions have similar characteristics, except for their acceptance of delayed gratification and a more powerful management capable of moving the institution toward its goal.

3) **Reputation-focused** institutions are more outward looking. They are customer rather than faculty driven, they generally have strong management, and they measure themselves by outcomes that have been identified as valuable to customers.

RAND's sample of 26 institutions was insufficient for estimating the size of the three segments. However, as described in Chapter 2, the University of Pennsylvania's Institute for Research on Higher Education used quantitative data on a sample of 1,200 institutions to segment the market. The segmentation differs from RAND's scheme, but the data have allowed me to conclude that about half the nation's universities, which represent three-quarters of collective financial commitment to higher education, appear to enjoy or be seeking prestige.[36]

The RAND researchers argue that the sacrifices required for building prestige may not pay off in the current market environment. What a Stanford could do in the 1950s, before the sponsored research market had matured, now is beyond the capacity of most institutions. For nonelite institutions, prestige-seeking behavior means trying to force-fit the classic university model onto a massified educational mission or else trying to escape from massification altogether. Institutions that already enjoy prestige may be using it to shield themselves from accountability for education quality. Neither strategy is socially advantageous in the long run.

The ascendancy of market forces also produced a fundamental shift in how governments viewed public universities. Traditionally, governments had supported and protected "their" universities as precious resources for education, research, and public service. Now the role became procurement of essential services for their populations at the least possible cost in relation to quality.[37] Like medical doctors, university professors became viewed less as custodians of a precious flame and more as providers of services—services whose production requires a high degree of training and professionalism, but services nevertheless. Arguments rooted in classic university values began to fall on deaf ears. While most governments recognize the dangers of micromanagement, they now insist on getting value for money. Complaints that accountability initiatives compromise academic values are met with the admonition "adapt, or suffer the consequences." Increasingly, adaptation is seen as rebuilding the academy's core competency in education.

WHAT SHOULD BE PRESERVED?

What are the core values of the university? How can they be protected while higher education—now characterized by massive scale, specialized research, and high technology—does the things necessary to rebuild its core competency? I have described the need for change. Now it's time to recount what should be preserved.

Academic Freedom

Academic freedom should be high on the list. This means freedom from political interference in the academy's intellectual work. Intellectual work that is driven by political forces is not intellectual at all: It seeks simply to win arguments and influence the distribution of power. The academy has the professionalism, internal discipline, and tradition needed to rise above politics. The world needs this kind of voice, and few institutions other than the academy can provide it. While the programs advocated in subsequent chapters may abridge some purist definitions of academic freedom, they preserve its essence because the faculty remains in charge.

Autonomy

Other manifestations of autonomy also should be protected. I'll show in Chapter 3 that when universities are starved for funds they behave just like for-profit entities. That curtails the exercise of academic values and makes the institution a slave to the market. Put another way, universities need the flexibility to maintain certain activities, including humanistic and cultural ones, even when the market won't support their full costs. Micromanagement of funding also undermines academic values and prevents the institution from operating efficiently. Hence, public funds should come mainly in the form of block grants. Institutions should be free to manage their internal affairs without undue regulation or interference, subject to ex post performance accountability.

Empowerment

The sense of empowerment felt by most professors represents another priceless asset that should be protected. Pushing universities to adopt "managerialism" (that is, the top-down direction of academic activities) would kill the goose that lays the golden eggs. Most businesses would pay dearly for the self-starting professionalism that is the hallmark of the professoriate. Universities have it already. The challenge is to help professors, department chairs, deans, provosts, and presidents find ways to channel and support this energy in ways that are most productive for the institution and its students.

My colleague at Stanford, Professor Patricia Gumport, speaks of the "social charter for higher education." It is this charter that provides the justification for preserving the academy's core values. Here is her list.

- Produce an educated citizenry.

- Serve in a compensatory capacity by assisting those who are poor and disadvantaged to have a better life.

- Contribute to economic development by training and retraining workers, and by supporting industry's interests with advancements and applications of knowledge.

- Conduct research for national, state, and local interests.

- Provide a place apart for faculty and students to have academic freedom, to foster cultural critique and dissent.

- Serve local community settings as a good neighbor or partner.

- Provide health care or support through teaching hospitals and medical centers.

- Provide entertainment, sports, and high culture.

Academic freedom, institutional autonomy, and faculty empowerment are necessary conditions for fulfilling the social charter. But neither the academy nor the public should forget that these represent means to ends rather than ends in themselves.

Colleges and universities are, at root, ethical and public-spirited enterprises. They strive to exemplify what is best for society, including but not limited to the generation of economic value. Confusion and self-interest sometimes get in the way, but this provides no reason to doubt the fundamentals. The academy's moral compass points in the right direction most of the time, and no element of society can claim more than that. Higher education should be held accountable for improvement, but institutions that are genuinely trying to improve should be supported even if their current performance is less than perfect. The challenge is to stimulate improvement and document its achievement without stripping away the autonomy institutions need in order to function effectively.

Endnotes

1. Knight Higher Education Collaborative (September 1988), p.1A.

2. Participation in and association with the Pew program has profoundly affected my view of higher education. Members of the initial roundtable, most of whom continued to meet four times a year for the next several years, consisted of: Patrick Callan (Vice President, Education Commission of the States); K. Patricia Cross (Professor of Education, University of California at Berkeley); Darryl Greer (Executive Director, The New Jersey State College Governing Board Association); John Wells Gould (Vice President for Programs, The Pew Charitable Trusts); D. Bruce Johnstone (Chancellor, the State University of New York); Henry Levin (Professor of Education, Stanford University); Arthur E. Levine (President, Bradford College); Arturo Madrid (President, The Thomas Rivera Center); William Massy (Professor of Education and Business Administration and Vice President for Finance, Stanford University); Mary Patterson McPherson (President, Bryn Mawr College); James A. Norton (Interim President, Hiram College); Virginia Smith (President Emeritus, Vassar College); Lewis C. Solomon (Professor and Dean of the Graduate School of Education, UCLA); Glen R. Stine (Executive Director, Resource Planning and Budget, University of Pennsylvania); Susan B. Stine (Program Officer, The Pew Charitable Trusts); Ursula Wagener (Director of Policy Studies, University of Pennsylvania); Timothy Warner (Associate Provost and Director of University Budgets, Stanford University); Marna Whittington (Vice President for Finance, University of Pennsylvania); and Robert Zemsky (Professor and Director, Institute for Research on Higher Education, University of Pennsylvania). The Pew Higher Education Program was led by Robert Zemsky.

3. Peter F. Drucker (Forbes cover story, March 1997, p. 22).

4. Based on a random sample of 1,000 adults who felt they knew their state's institutions of higher education well enough to make an assessment. The Landscape (2001).

5. The 6th biennial conference of the International Network of Quality Assurance Agencies in Higher Education (INQAAHE), held in March 2001 in Bangalore, India, was attended by some 300 delegates from 46 countries. Of these, only three were involved in US domestic higher education quality assurance. (One of these, the author, was representing Hong Kong.) This is only a small indicator, but it suggests the relative paucity of concern about international developments in quality assurance.

6. Campbell and van der Wende (2000), p. 11.

7. Quoted by Marjorie Peace Lenn at the INQAAHE Bangalore conference.

8. Association of American Colleges (1985).

9. Knight Higher Education Collaborative (September 1988), p. 1A.

10. Bloom (1987).

11. Sykes (1987), quoted in Smith (1990), p. 3.

12. Gross & Levitt (1994).

13. Rosovsky and Kennedy, cited later, can hardly be called conservative. The basic tenet of this book—apolitical in terms of left versus right—supports the root concerns of all these authors.

14. William Bennett, Secretary of Education, "Address at Harvard University," October 1986; excerpted in Pew Higher Education Research Program (September 1988), p.1.

15. Knight Higher Education Collaborative (May 1989), p. 3A.

16. Knight Higher Education Collaborative (January 1990).

17. Knight Higher Education Collaborative (June 1990).

18. Knight Higher Education Collaborative (June 1990).

19. Smith (1990), p. 179.

20. Huber (1992), p. 4.

21. Rosovsky (1990), Chapter 9.

22. Henry Rosovsky, "Annual Report of the Dean of the Faculty of Arts and Sciences [Harvard University], 1990–91"; excerpted in Knight Higher Education Collaborative (September 1992), pp. B1–B2.

23. Kennedy (1997), p. 2. His Chapter 1 eloquently describes the current criticism of the academy.

24. Kennedy (1997), p. 11 cites an example where young Congressional staff members, including their own alumni, said that universities were viewed as "just another interest group, like Big Oil." Many of us in higher education have encountered similar sentiments.

25. Knight Higher Education Collaborative (September 1991), "Distillations," p. 1 (emphasis added).

26. Lovett (2002), p. 13.

27. Clark Kerr, "A General Perspective on Higher Education and Service to the Labor Market." Unpublished paper excerpted in Knight Higher Education Collaborative (September 1988), "Distillations," p. 1.

28. Office of Technology Assessment (OTA) (1986), pp. 15–16.

29. Glassick, Huber, and Maeroff (1997), p. 8.

30. Fairweather (1993), p. 35.

31. Reisman (1958), p. 35.

32. See Graham and Diamond (1997), pp. 92–95, for interpretation.

33. Students phone around to describe aid offers in hopes of eliciting a counteroffer. See The Institute for Research on Higher Education (1994).

34. The figure dropped from 38% to 31%, whereas the fraction of would-be principal investigators funded remained constant at about 40%. This implies that the available resources were being spread more widely and that the most successful investigators were getting fewer projects funded. Office of Technology Assessment (OTA) (1991), p. 249.

35. Brewer, Gates, and Goldman (2001).

36. All the institutions in NCPI's highly selective segment and many in the name-brand segment qualify as prestigious by RAND's definition. (See Chapter 2 for the segment definitions.) The rest of the name-brand schools and at least half the core schools seem to be actively pursuing prestige. The resources figure excludes sponsored research, auxiliaries, medical facilities, and the like.

37. Knight Higher Education Collaborative (September 1993).

2
Universities As Economic Enterprises

Misunderstandings about how universities function as economic enterprises make change agency extraordinarily difficult. They also help to explain the erosion of trust. For example, some defenders of the academy believe that its nonprofit status guarantees socially responsible performance. This includes educational excellence and effective cost management as well as access and diversity, research, and public service. However, critics think the same nonprofit status shelters inefficiency, the pursuit of idiosyncratic academic values, and competency gaps.

Neither view is correct, and neither is wholly incorrect. Nonprofit universities exist to produce value rather than money, but the enterprise must face marketplace realities every day. Some universities are larger and more complex than most businesses, and most are vulnerable to market forces. They must obey the laws of economics and deal with price, cost, efficiency, and finance. Williams College economist Gordon Winston has described the juxtaposition of academic values and market forces as pitting "university as church" against "university as car dealer." I described it in Chapter 1 as the Acropolis versus the Agora.

University performance depends on its production processes as well as academic values and market forces. ("Production" refers to the methods universities use to accomplish their education, research, and public service goals—one should not think of assembly lines.) Performance also depends on resource availability, that is, on the institution's financial condition.

This chapter begins by discussing how academic values, market forces, production processes, and financial constraints interact to drive the behavior of universities as nonprofit enterprises. Then we'll examine market power, tuition and financial aid, and the incentives for efficiency improvement and productivity. Some observers say higher education is too complicated to understand in economic terms, but we'll see that is not the case. Although a lack of critical data limits our ability to quantify key aspects of performance, it is indeed possible to understand university behavior from a qualitative standpoint. Perhaps this will provide a stone in the shoe for better data collection.[1]

NONPROFIT ENTERPRISES

"Why can't a college be more like a firm?" Posed by Gordon Winston, the question's conflicting answers to this question lie at the root of much misunderstanding about higher education. Trustees and university financial officers think their institutions should be more business-like, a view that is shared by many of the academy's external stakeholders. Professors, on the other hand, argue strenuously that the academy is not a business and shouldn't behave like one. Presidents, provosts, and deans often feel caught in between. To quote Winston:

> There's some urgency to [the above] question because the changes sweeping over higher education are going to be very hard to evaluate and harder to predict and control if we aren't clear about how to understand these institutions and this "industry." In his 1994 Nobel lecture, Doug North described the importance of the "shared mental models" we use to make sense out of the world because they go far to determine what we see and what we don't see and what we make of it all. An inaccurate mental model of higher education disserves us all. If we think colleges are just like firms when they're importantly different from firms, we will make a hash of it.[2]

We'll also make a hash of it if we view colleges as being too different from firms.

Traditional colleges and universities are not-for-profit enterprises.[3] At the simplest level, such enterprises exist to "do good" while for-profit ones exist to make money. But like many issues addressed in this book, the reality is more complicated. Economists since Adam Smith have pointed out that, by competing in the marketplace, for-profit companies further the public good even as they maximize private returns. What, then, is the not-for-profit's particular role?

Yale economist and law professor Henry Hansmann, who has written extensively on this subject, emphasizes that the main difference between for-profit and not-for-profit enterprises is that the latter can't distribute profits to shareholders.[4] Nonprofits can and sometimes do accumulate substantial surpluses. However, the surpluses must be saved or reinvested in some aspect of the enterprise's work rather than distributed to owners in the form of dividends.[5]

Three conditions determine whether the not-for-profit form of organization should be preferred in any particular situation.

1) The output of the enterprise is important to society—a "social good," so to speak. People need it, and no substitutes are readily available.

2) It's difficult to evaluate quality, so buyers have to rely on the supplier to create value for money on their behalf rather than in the interest of owners who might line their pockets by shortchanging quality.

3) The output costs so much to produce that it would not be affordable if the enterprise had to recover its full costs. Broad access requires a public subsidy in this case, and nonprofits can't siphon off subsidy payments for the benefit of shareholders.

Industries that meet criterion 1, and either or both of criteria 2 and 3, present fertile ground for the development of nonprofit enterprises.

Consider the classic university in its traditional setting. Higher education is important and few substitutes are thought to exist, the quality of education is difficult to evaluate, and costs are high enough that subsidies appear desirable. All three criteria are satisfied, which is why universities have most often been organized as nonprofits. The public relies on academic traditions and values to safeguard quality. Favorable tax treatment, for donors and for the enterprise itself, and direct state support (in the case of public universities) provide the needed subsidies.

Unfortunately, the university's nonprofit status doesn't ensure that quality will in fact be safeguarded and that the subsidies will go where intended. One must go beyond the aforementioned criteria to see what's really happening. The nonprofit enterprise model provides the tools needed to analyze why such anomalies arise.

THE NONPROFIT MODEL

Beginning in the late 1970s, economist Estelle James and I separately developed the economic model for describing how nonprofit enterprises work.[6] Figure 2.1 depicts the model in graphical form. (The symbol $\Leftarrow$ means "depends on.") It describes universities as maximizing the amount of value they create, subject to reality checks based on the marketplace, production processes, and finance.

Figure 2.1

The Nonprofit Economic Model as Applied to Universities

Universities strive to maximize:		
Degree of value fulfillment	$\Leftarrow$	Quantity and quality of academic activities and each type of output produced (e.g., teaching and research in various fields)
Subject to three reality checks:		
1. Demand for outputs	$\Leftarrow$	Quality in relation to "price" (e.g., tuition net of financial aid)
2. Activities needed to produce the outputs	$\Leftarrow$	The processes of production and the desired output quality and quantity
3. Total revenue (depends on output quantity and price)	$\geq$	Total expenditure (depends on the activities and the cost of performing them)

Value

Like all nonprofits, universities want to do good. More and better output will improve their degree of value fulfillment. Using the shorthand of modeling, "value fulfillment" sums up the "Acropolis-like" or "churchy" part of the university's decision-making equation.

How value is defined represents the key difference between the nonprofit and for-profit enterprise models. "Degree of value fulfillment" sums up all the academic and social values the university and its faculty care about. For example, the Forum for the Future of Higher Education recently commissioned a research paper on "good work" in universities. Based on earlier interviews with professionals in journalism and genetics, the authors define "good work" as "work that is deemed [to be of] high quality by those knowledgeable about the domain; ... and work that takes into account, one way or another, some conception of the broader public good."[7] In short, good work means "excellence in the public interest."

By this criterion, high-quality education and research represent value for their own sake, not simply outputs that can be sold. Diversity reflects another intrinsic value, as does the advancement of academic disciplines. The list of outcomes that need to be protected, presented near the end of Chapter 1, provides good candidates for value attribution. Some items represent public benefits and some private benefits: Either way, they qualify as being socially valuable.

Value fulfillment need not depend on quantification—anything the academy cares about can be accommodated under the value rubric. But quantification can help focus attention. Prestige is intangible, for example, but rankings like those published by the National Academy of Sciences and *U.S. News & World Report* operationalize the concept.

James's summary of the literature identified the following variables as possessing value for institutions and professors.[8]

1) **Research and low teaching loads:** Professors tend to prefer research to teaching. Research contributes to the discipline and to individual visibility as well as to institutional prestige.

2) **Numbers of enrollments and degrees:** Graduate students are valued because of their contributions to research and propagation of the discipline. Undergraduate numbers are most valued in colleges that specialize in teaching and may actually be negatively valued "at the margin" in research universities. ("At the margin" means that while the overall value is positive, additions to student numbers actually reduce value.)

3) **Student quality:** Better students are more satisfying to teach and do better at teaching each other. Students with good test scores also show better in public announcements of admissions statistics and tend to do better after graduation, so they contribute more to university prestige.

4) **Teaching quality:** Professors want to provide good quality teaching, even though they aren't able to measure it very well.

5) **Small class sizes and good teaching support services:** Because independent assessments of education outcomes are difficult, class sizes

and teaching support services may be viewed as proxies for quality. Smaller classes and better support services also reduce faculty workloads and thus contribute to research.

Certain fields may be valued more highly than others, as when liberal arts colleges value the core academic disciplines more highly than applied fields like business and technology. Individuals and disciplines also may differ in value orientation. What matters is that university leaders can identify the value implications of different choices and make their decisions accordingly. In principle, value differences are thrashed out as part of the university's governance process.[9]

While the aforementioned variables certainly reflect the public interest, we'll see that it's possible to have too much of a good thing. For example, Chapter 4 argues that the extra social value achieved by boosting research and lowering teaching loads declines and may even turn negative as the production of these "goods" increases. Moreover, value as seen by institutions and professors may diverge from value as seen by the broader society—for example, research and low teaching loads may be valued by academics well beyond the point of social optimality.

Contrast these examples with the for-profit case, where value is defined mainly as profit. Profit equals total revenue minus total expenditure, so performance reflects a financial common denominator that means the same thing to everyone. Businesses do consider other dimensions of value, but the obligation to create financial returns for shareholders, and the ability of shareholders to oust management if the company under-performs financially, limits their ability to do so. Because nonprofits don't distribute financial returns, they can work with a broader definition of value.

In an ideal world, a university's ability to create value would be unbounded. Unfortunately for academic ideals, however, the pursuit of value confronts some serious constraints. First among them comes the need to obtain revenue—which brings in market forces and the car dealer phenomenon.

Markets

Most colleges and universities depend heavily on revenue-producing transactions. In private liberal arts colleges, for example, almost 80% of revenue comes from net tuition.[10] Private research universities get about 55% of revenue from tuition and another 30% from research grants and contracts. Public research universities get about 22% of revenue from tuition and another 20% from research. Tuition accounts for about 28% of revenue at other public universities. The people who supply these funds have a variety of motives, including a desire to build institutions and support academic work generally, but their immediate goal is to fund specific activities or obtain particular services at reasonable prices. In other words, they respond to "customer value," as opposed to academic value.

Although rank and file professors have yet to embrace the marketing concept, many university leaders have mastered the so-called Four Ps of marketing: product, price, promotion, and place. Schools try to design programs that will sell, and then they promote them aggressively. New undergraduate majors, niche master's programs, and continuing education reflect a growing focus on product, for example, and enrollment management offices spend a great deal of time on promotion. Provosts analyze tuition rates and financial aid policies at peer institutions and consider enrollment trends before setting their own prices. Finally, "place" strategy is becoming more important as distance learning breaks down the natural barriers of time and space.

Markets impinge on nonprofit enterprises the same as they do on business firms. Willingness and ability to pay determine whether potential students accept or reject a university's admission offers and whether potential sponsors accept or reject its research proposals. Willingness to pay depends on the prospect's perceptions about quality in relation to price and the offerings of competing institutions—in other words, on relative value for money. Universities can cite their lofty values when trying to persuade prospects to buy, but in the end the prospects are free to accept the arguments or not—or try to negotiate a better deal if that appears possible.

Production

The types and levels of activity needed to produce the university's outputs provide a second reality check (box 2 in Figure 2.1). For example, people can accomplish only so much in a day and computers will run only so fast. The needed activity levels depend on the processes of teaching and research, on the amount of support they get, and on the desired quantity and quality of outputs. In contrast to markets, which involve external stakeholders, organizing the production of academic and customer value is mainly a university responsibility. How universities discharge this responsibility and how they can improve their performance represent the main subjects of this book.

Finance

Box 3 in Figure 2.1 says that revenues must at least equal expenditures—that universities cannot afford to run deficits indefinitely if they want to stay alive. This brings financial performance into the model, not as the university's primary goal but as a constraint that prevents insolvency. Most universities spend right up to their budget limits after allowing for reserves.[11] Why? Because spending increases value fulfillment. Hence, we could view box 3 as containing an equals sign without really changing the model.

Revenue depends on the amount of output demanded by buyers and the net price they pay, that is, on the demand function represented in box 1. Cost depends on the activities needed to produce the outputs (on the production function shown in box 2) and their prices or unit costs. Then box 3 closes the system by determining how much value fulfillment is affordable given the demand and production functions. For example, price hikes enabled by stronger student demand allow a university to spend more on teaching and thus climb higher on its value curve. Lower-cost teaching (at the same quality) might allow more spending on research, which again would boost value fulfillment.

Revenue and cost each consist of a fixed and variable component. "Fixed" means that the amounts don't vary significantly with output, at least within the ranges the university is likely to encounter.[12]

Fixed cost includes the university's central administration, library collections, and maintenance of plant. These costs would change if enrollments or research activities were to shift dramatically, but not if the changes are modest or represent redistributions among programs.

Variable cost picks up everything else, for example, the direct costs of teaching and of library services (which vary with the number of patrons, not collection size). Unit cost equals variable cost per unit of output.

Fixed revenue includes public universities' state appropriations where determined as a lump sum rather than by an enrollment formula, plus income from unrestricted gifts and endowments. Such revenues are fixed in the sense that they don't vary with enrollment or research activity, at least over short periods of time. They can and do vary for their own reasons, however—for example, due to politics and stock market swings.

Variable revenue includes tuition and student fees, direct and indirect cost recovery on grants and contracts, state appropriations when linked to enrollment, and other income from the sales of services. Price equals variable revenue per unit.

Universities don't usually parse their revenues and costs into fixed and variable components, but the task isn't difficult if one seeks approximations useful for decision making rather than exact accounting results. Contribution margins, which loom large in decisions to expand or contract departments or programs, depend on the variable components of cost and revenue. The university's ability to resist market forces depends heavily on the fixed component of revenue. Parsing and contribution margins will be addressed in Chapter 3, and the importance of fixed revenue will be addressed later in this chapter.

INSTITUTIONAL SEGMENTS

There are more than 2,000 four-year colleges and universities in the United States. All share the traditional academic values to one degree or another, but they differ dramatically in terms of market position. One cannot explain the dynamics of the higher education marketplace without analyzing these differences.

Researchers at the National Center for Postsecondary Improvement (NCPI) have mapped the market using data from government, associations, and publishers for some 1,200 four-year institutions.[13] The mapping depends on admission and yield rates, the percentage of freshmen that graduate with a bachelor's degree in five years, the percentage of undergraduate enrollment that is part-time, and the ratio of bachelor's degrees to total undergraduate enrollment. It produced the following broad groupings.[14]

- **Highly selective institutions** (about 4% of the total) comprise the most competitive market segment. Their undergraduates usually get their degrees within five years, and they provide the best path to graduate and professional study. A baccalaureate from one of these schools opens the way to substantial salary increments, especially when combined with a postgraduate degree.

- **Name-brand institutions** (about 14%) are selective enough for their degrees to carry significant prestige value, but graduate admissions

rates and labor market rewards lag those of the highly selective segment. They graduate a large proportion, but not necessarily a majority, of their undergraduates within five years. The name-brand schools
are well regarded in the marketplace, but many are vulnerable to competition.

• **Core institutions** (about 70%) serve mainly state-level and metropol-
  itan markets. Some students aspire to a name-brand experience, while
  others attend on a part-time or intermittent basis. Many core institutions owe their existence to massification. Many of them are tilting
  toward name-brand status while the rest are undecided or have begun
  to tilt toward the user-friendly segment.

• **Convenience/user-friendly institutions** (about 12%) teach large
  numbers of part-time and intermittent students who may or may not
  be seeking a degree. Being closest to the market, these schools are
  often the most innovative in program design and teaching methods.

The NCPI scheme maps the terrain between the Acropolis and the
Agora. It also challenges the traditional academic view that the journey
represents "descent." For example, the missions of convenience/user-
friendly schools are no less important than those of their more prestigious
cousins. Such schools cater to students—including disproportionate numbers of blacks and Hispanics—who can't afford the time and money needed for full-time attendance. This mission is worthy, not the consequence
of "ungodly commercial interests and scheming public officials and venal
academic leaders."[15] The convenience/user-friendly and core institutions
may also be more innovative than the more traditional name-brand and
selective schools. The convenience/user-friendly institutions, in particular,
focus on educational value added for their target student populations
rather than on abstract conceptions of what it means to be "academic."

Universities nearer the Acropolis also find ways to engage the market,
even as they continue to espouse the traditional academic values. Robert
Zemsky and I described this phenomenon in a 1995 article entitled
"Expanding Perimeters, Melting Cores, and Sticky Functions: Toward an
Understanding of Our Current Predicaments."[16] By "expanding perimeters" we meant the entrepreneurial activities of faculty, research centers,
intellectual property licensing, continuing education, and similar programs. During the last few years, for example, even the most prestigious

institutions have begun pursuing e-learning and other ways of exporting educational content. Some are doing so on a massive scale, to the point of creating for-profit subsidiaries to exploit the market opportunities.

Yet the traditional university's heart retains its grip on the Acropolis. The humanities and social sciences, in particular, resist the entrepreneurial temptations. But they pay a price. "Melting cores" alludes to the squeezing of their resource base. The perimeter expands while the core struggles to break even. As the core's influence on the perimeter decreases, academic coherence becomes strained and it becomes harder to agree on values and strategies. Some observers believe that, in the interest of academic cohesion and collegiality, the perimeter should cross-subsidize the core at ever-increasing rates. Most, however, hold that while cross subsidies may be necessary, the core has an obligation to help itself. This means improving its responsiveness to markets, cost effectiveness, and educational competency.

COST ESCALATION

The cost of higher education has received much attention in recent years, but little has been learned about how to contain it. Two national commissions studied cost and financial aid issues since 1993, for example, and Congress holds periodic hearings on the subject.[17] Yet tuition rates continue to rise and there is no agreement about whether federal financial aid dollars stimulate the escalation even as they mitigate its effects for individual students.[18] The ever-rising costs erode the public's trust in higher education. Why, then, are they are they so difficult to rein in?

Universities press their pricing to the limits that markets, regulators, and public opinion will allow. They justify their actions in terms of the rising cost of excellence and other factors beyond their control, but that is only part of the story. The impetus for price hikes stems from the university's own choices—in particular, from the way it defines "excellence."

Universities don't seek profits, but they do strive for value fulfillment. Because value fulfillment is open ended, no respectable university will run out of worthwhile things to do. Higher prices boost revenue, other things being equal, which enables more worthwhile activity and thus more value fulfillment. University president and higher education scholar Howard Bowen summed this up in what is now known as Bowen's Law: "Universities will raise all the money they can and spend all the money they raise."[19]

Because universities define "excellence" as producing as much value as they can, justifying price hikes by the high cost of excellence is circular.

Bowen's Law follows immediately from the nonprofit enterprise model. Higher tuition allows more spending, and more spending improves value fulfillment, which is what the university is trying to maximize. In other words, expenditure levels are determined by revenue, not by the cost of production. (That's why Bowen's Law is sometimes called the "Revenue Theory of Budgeting.") Covering one's costs becomes a moving target because cost will quickly rise to equal revenue. I used to chide my Stanford colleagues by saying that the provost's job was to spend as much as possible, while my job as chief financial officer was to define "possible" and assure the trustees that he wasn't spending more than our revenues could sustain. In terms of the nonprofit model, the provost pursued value fulfillment while I enforced the financial constraint.

Gordon Winston offers a variation on Bowen's Law. He says universities want to maximize the subsidy, defined as spending minus net tuition, that they provide for their students. For example, if a school gets $3,000 per student in net tuition revenue and spends $10,500, it provides a subsidy of $7,500.[20] Maximizing the subsidy provides students with the greatest possible value over and above what they pay in tuition, which, Winston argues, represents intrinsic value for the institution and also boosts demand. He goes on to say that, in maximizing the subsidy, universities are more likely to push up spending rather than hold price below market levels. This amounts to Bowen's Law as I have defined it.

Winston also explains the spending pressure by what he calls a "positional arms race" in higher education, with student quality as the prize. "In an arms race, there's a lot of action, a lot of spending, a lot of worry but, if it's a successful arms race, nothing much changes. It's the purist case of Alice and the Red Queen where 'it takes all the running you can do, to keep in the same place.'" The arms race drives institutions to maximize all revenue sources, including tuition, in order to match others' spending increases. It's a race that "has no end—no finish line to get to first—instead, it's a process that can go on and on and on…"[21]

Some people think that improved operational efficiency would arrest the growth of tuition and perhaps even allow universities to roll back prices. But as desirable as they are, such efficiencies won't solve the tuition problem. Schools reallocate most efficiency savings to other activities rather than passing them along to students. Schools cut their overall budget when necessary to deal with revenue shortfalls, but they rarely pass savings along voluntarily.

Things work differently when costs go up. For example, escalation in salaries and the prices of energy, library materials, and the like spurs quick action by tuition-setters. Because they expect other institutions to act as well, passing along the increases isn't likely to bring competitive disadvantage. Hence the effect of cost upon tuition is asymmetric. Cost escalation tends to drive up tuition rates but efficiency gains aren't likely to reduce them.

Nor are new gifts and endowments likely to reduce tuition. For example, most high-priced institutions also enjoy extraordinary levels of gift and endowment support.[22] None of them have low tuitions—if anything, their extra prestige enables them to charge more. Institutions charge the going tuition rate for schools of their type. Gifts and endowment income produce higher levels of spending, not financial offsets that are passed on to students.

MARKET POWER

Granted that Bowen's Law motivates universities to boost tuition, what is it about the higher education marketplace that lets them do so year after year by amounts that significantly exceed inflation? Most businesses would be delighted with a more than doubling of constant-dollar prices as posted by colleges and universities during the last 20 years, but few enjoy this kind of market power.[23] Higher education can indulge itself because the market power enjoyed by its highly selective and name-brand segments provides a pricing umbrella for other institutions.

Enterprises develop market power by differentiating their offerings and improving the prestige and visibility of their brands. Market power brings control in the marketplace. For example, it permits universities to boost tuition while maintaining or expanding their enrollments. Such market power would be defendable if it was education competency that conferred the advantage. RAND's "reputational" and NCPI's "convenience/user-friendly" segments compete on competency, but most institutions compete on prestige. Prestige brings revenue, which can be spent to produce more prestige, which generates more market power—not to mention additional research funding and gift support. Market power confers self-reinforcing advantages, and the circle is not necessarily virtuous.

Difficulties in the evaluation of education quality present the first big problem. Deciding among schools by comparing price in relation to quality becomes problematic when relative quality is unknown. Absent direct information on quality, prospective students must use surrogates like selectivity, faculty-student ratios, research prowess, and even price itself. The surrogates define prestige, but they don't describe education quality. Worse, they tend to reinforce rather than inhibit price escalation. Selectivity correlates with prestige, which depends heavily on research. Research and faculty-student ratios depend on expenditures, which are enabled by higher prices. For highly selective and name-brand institutions, price-quality associations reinforce the circularity and the positional arms race. Economists consider markets where information shortfalls preclude informed decision-making to be "inefficient." The higher education marketplace appears very inefficient by this criterion.

Some readers may dispute my assertion that prestige does not describe an institution's core competency in education. To them I say, "read on." This book's central thrust holds that selectivity, research, and the richness of inputs do not necessarily predict the value added by education. A further thrust holds that rebuilding educational competency in highly selective and name-brand institutions represents a necessary condition for improving market information and efficiency. I hope the skeptics will suspend their disbelief until all the evidence and arguments have been presented.

COMPETITION

Critics might also point out that price competition among colleges and universities is growing despite the market's preoccupation with prestige.[24] The nation's small under-endowed private colleges think twice before raising tuition, and even then they must discount their sticker prices at ever-increasing rates. Mid-level private universities also must wheel out the discounts lest they lose students to the low-priced (and highly subsidized) public sector. Even the nation's most prestigious private universities find ways to discount—indeed, some have announced major increases in their financial aid offers.[25] Obviously, market inefficiency does not preclude price competition.

The apparent contradiction can be resolved by examining the price leadership of the highly selective and name-brand institutions. The market for higher education tends to be inelastic, especially in the high-end market segments.[26] That is, demand doesn't fall off very much when price goes up. People want degrees from the prestigious schools, and although they may complain about the cost, most end up being willing to make the sacrifice. Institutional aid discounts the price for students with financial need and other desired attributes. The discounts enhance access and help schools shape their enrollment profiles, but enrollment caps limit student numbers in the prestigious institutions. The sticker price at elite private institutions goes up and up, and tuitions at public ones rise as fast as the politics of their situations allow.

For years the highly selective private institutions functioned as "800-pound gorillas" on the pricing scene: "The less-wealthy schools have been able to charge high tuitions only because those at the top charged even more."[27] Driven by Bowen's Law and, except for targeted financial aid, largely immune from market pressures, the highly selective and name-brand private institutions have provided a pricing umbrella for the rest of the four-year higher education sector. Core and convenience/user-friendly schools compete fiercely with their peers, but the rising tuition tide has been raising all the ships.

Highly selective institutions don't charge as much as their markets would appear to allow. Selectivity means that demand exceeds the number of places the university is willing to make available. Because the market-clearing price is bound to be higher than the sticker price, the gap appears to represent a voluntary discount provided even to full-pay students.

What limits the pricing umbrella in this way? Why don't the highly selective universities do as a Stanford Nobel laureate in economics once urged me to do: increase tuition to the point where demand equals supply and provide financial aid for worthy students who can't or won't pay the price? Such a strategy would extract as much money as possible from those willing and able to pay. In the language of economists, it would appropriate all consumer surplus (the area under the demand curve) for the institution's benefit. It represents Bowen's Law carried to the limit.

Such a strategy might be workable. At Stanford we routinely tested our need-based aid program by calculating yield rates by income category for students who applied for aid. We wanted the rate to remain constant across income classes. For example, if middle-income students turned down our admissions offer more often than low-income students, this was evidence of a "middle-income gap" that should be mitigated by sweetening the aid package for middle-income students. We might also have used merit aid to tune the composition of the entering class, for example, to get desired numbers of scholars, athletes, musicians, etc. One might question our ability to manage things so precisely, but in principle it should be possible.

More problematic was the chance that a high sticker price would deter qualified but less-than-affluent students from applying in the first place. Generous aid packages won't help if prospective students don't get close enough learn about them. The political and public relations fallout from an extraordinarily high tuition also were problematic. We didn't want to stand apart from peer institutions in terms of media or governmental scrutiny any more than we wanted to appear unusually expensive in the eyes of prospective applicants.

The example illustrates that nonprofit model's "market constraint" embodies more than current applicants' willingness and ability to pay. Public opinion and the perceptions of future applicants are important too. By this argument, the highly selective institutions are not abridging their market power for altruistic reasons. They're just recognizing a broader market constraint. At the same time, most university leaders do care about the financial burdens that tuition places on parents, even those who have the ability to pay.

FINANCIAL AID

Nothing illustrates the juxtaposition of academic values and market forces better than financial aid. The so-called Robin Hood principle, by which universities charge those who can pay more than those who can't, represents an intrinsic or "churchy" value. No-need aid, on the other hand, is a market response—the kind of price discounting one associates with car dealerships.

A 1994 study of five liberal arts colleges showed that less than 50% of entering students were paying full tuition. The colleges certainly cared about financial burdens, but market reasons weren't hard to uncover: Yield rates for aided students were about twice as high as those for unaided students. In some cases prospective students would phone around to get the best offer. In the words of the researchers, "Aid was clearly a condition of enrollment for a substantial proportion of each institution's freshman students."[28] It is hard to separate altruism from self-interest in cases like this.

National data show that about a third of gross tuition receipts are returned to students in the form of institutional financial aid.[29] Public institutions distribute almost 80% of their aid according to need, but the figure is only 44% in the private sector. The difference reflects a combination of public policy and the growing price competition being faced by the weaker private institutions. Despite the commitment to need-based aid, however, the variation in college participation rates by income class has increased by one-third since 1980.[30] Low-income students are not keeping up.

Higher education leaders lament the drop-off of need-based aid. For example, Claire Gaudiani, president of Connecticut College, asks us to "imagine what America would be like if all the recipients of need-based financial aid disappeared from Wall Street, government agencies, laboratories, board rooms, nonprofits, and academia."[31] I don't have to imagine: Without four years of need-based aid from Yale, I almost surely wouldn't be writing this book. But while need-based aid is desirable, this doesn't mean that no-need aid should be discouraged. In fact, the nonprofit model suggests that despite their propinquity in budget and financial statements, need and no-need aid arise from different motivations and may not directly compete with each other in university decision making.

No-need aid is a fact of life for many private colleges and universities. Failure to meet admissions goals means empty seats in the classroom and empty beds in the dormitory. The empty seats and beds represent sunk costs. Such costs can't be scaled back quickly in response to enrollment shortfalls, and at small institutions serious cost-cutting efforts may undermine viability. Like airlines that discount fares to fill empty seats, financially pressured colleges do so to gain enrollments. This makes sense as long as the discounted price is greater than the program's variable cost.

Achieving a target student profile provides another reason for offering no-need aid. The target profile depends partly on the university's value system (for example, as in the case of diversity goals), but favorable profiles also produce economic consequences. Good test scores boost prestige and top-notch athletes win games. Moreover, higher education depends on what is called "customer-input technology."[32] Students learn from other students, so an institution's student profile affects the amount and kind of learning it provides. Hence the motivation to shape the profile of incoming students is very strong. Need-based aid can help because it removes income from the factors that affect demand. However, need aid does not address the full range of diversity objectives.[33]

Despite the skepticism of many in higher education, merit-based aid has some desirable social effects. It broadens the scope of price competition, which many outside the academy believe to be desirable. Some need-aid advocates argue that price should be removed from the student's decision-making equation, but this seems both impractical and inconsistent with the idea that students should have the largest possible array of choices—including ones at discounted price levels.

Public policy favors price competition, including competitive financial aid. The so-called overlap case provides an example. The federal government applied the Sherman Act to a group of private colleges and universities that were meeting regularly to "coordinate" individual students' need-based awards—and, by extension, to deter no-need aid. The group defended itself by saying that because need-based aid is socially virtuous they were doing the country a service rather than engaging in price-fixing. The government disagreed, and eventually all but one institution (MIT) signed a cease and desist order.[34] MIT went to trial and lost on the merits. Although the verdict eventually was reversed on technical grounds, the judge's finding that setting need levels was tantamount to setting price and his ringing statement that "few aspects of higher education are more commercial than the price charged to students"[35] have deterred further actions of this kind.

Critics also worry that merit aid may draw funds away from need-based aid. We've seen, however, that need-based aid depends mainly on values and no-need aid depends mainly on markets. No-need aid will increase as markets become more competitive, which is exactly what one observes. But need-based aid won't necessarily fall. If the intrinsic values associated with need-based aid compete successfully with the institution's other values, such aid will continue. If not, the problem lies with the institution's spending priorities rather than with its need to respond to the market. A university may meet demonstrated need at the same time it addresses market pressures with no-need aid. Turning the issue around, an institution may offer merit aid to fill its classrooms and use some of the extra income to provide need-based aid.

EFFICIENCY AND PRODUCTIVITY

Bowen's Law says universities will spend as much as they can, but does this motivate inefficiency? The answer is an emphatic "no." But efficiency and its close cousin, productivity, are not as straightforward in higher education as in business.

Constraint 2 of the nonprofit model implies that a university's productivity limits its ability to produce value. Better efficiency allows universities to produce more value, just as it boosts business profits. The complications arise because external stakeholders find it hard to hold nonprofit managers accountable for performance, because universities tend to value faculty intrinsically, because value can't be measured as precisely as profit, and because the academy has only a fuzzy understanding of its teaching and learning processes. For these reasons universities don't address efficiency as energetically as they respond to market forces. I'll elaborate on them shortly, but first we'll explore the meaning of efficiency in higher education.

The common-sense definition of efficiency holds that the enterprise produces its products or services at the least cost possible given the state of the art. Productivity improvement means enhancing the state of the art with better processes and technology. Efficiency presents a moving target. A process may be efficient in one era but then becomes inefficient as the state of the art progresses. Given the rise of technology, education stands on just such a threshold at the present time.

Universities maximize enterprise-wide spending, but they don't maximize spending for every academic activity and program. Some programs produce surpluses that can be used to fund other activities or the university's fixed costs. To use a term familiar from business, we call these surpluses contribution margins. In terms of the nonprofit model, a program's contribution margin equals the difference between its variable revenue and variable cost. Boosting efficiency means reducing variable cost, which will increase the contribution other things being equal. Bowen's Law turns out not to be problematic because the bigger a given program's financial contribution the more the university can spend on other things it values.

Efficiency implies a certain minimum cost of production. For example, one can think of the minimum cost for "producing" an undergraduate degree of a given quality in a particular major for students who enter with particular preparation levels. It's hard to measure minimum cost, but one can easily imagine actions that drive actual cost above the minimum, for example, classes that are smaller than needed for effective learning or unnecessary student failures caused by poor teaching.

Efficiency depends on the effectiveness of resource usage in relation to one's objectives. Dartmouth emeritus professor James Brian Quinn, a recognized authority on strategic planning and the impact of technology in the service sector, advocates the criterion of "best in world" as an effectiveness measure.[36] If a given operation isn't "best in world" one should strive to improve it or consider outsourcing to someone who does meet the criterion. "Best in world" implies cost-effectiveness, that is, efficiency in the pursuit of objectives. An academic department that doesn't optimize class sizes or deliver good teaching can't be "best in world." Either it should improve or its programs should be considered for outsourcing—an increasingly practical option given the Internet. Quinn recognizes that valid reasons may exist for keeping the unit, for example, protection of essential academic values or the transaction costs of outsourcing. Even when such reasons exist, however, inefficient units should be pressed to improve.

Turning again to the nonprofit model, efficiency implies that the cost of the activities set out in box 2 in Figure 2.1 (the production function) has been driven as low as possible. That is, an efficient program is one where cost cannot be reduced without hurting quality. At the enterprise level, an efficient university is one where overall value fulfillment cannot be increased without spending more.

I mentioned four complications, or impediments, that limit a university's pursuit of efficiency. The first stems from the absence of external owners. In business, shareholders can hold managers accountable for financial performance without fear of negating core values or risk of reprisal. In the limit, the company's stock price simply falls far enough to trigger a hostile takeover, at which point a new broom sweeps the inefficiencies away. Nonprofits have no stockholders, for the good reasons discussed earlier. "With no profits to distribute, neither stockholders or corporate raiders can put a fear of inefficiency into nonprofit managers."[37]

The second impediment concerns the academy's tendency to value inputs as well as outputs.[38] For example, Robert Zemsky tells the story of how as associate provost for planning he once asked the dean of the Wharton School why he was investing so much in support staff as opposed to faculty. "Professors are costly," the dean replied, "so I'm leveraging their time as much as possible. I'm trying to maximize efficiency. What do you maximize?" Zemsky was originally a history professor. He thought for a moment, then replied, "*Monks*—that is, *professors*. I want to maximize the number of professors, just like the medieval monasteries wanted to maximize the number of monks—for the good of the order. I value professors intrinsically, for the good of the academy." The concepts of leverage and efficiency meant little to the monasteries because they valued their monks intrinsically. To the extent that professors are valued for what they are rather than for what they produce, the same is true in the university.

Having spent my life in the academy, I share Zemsky's view that professors are more than mere employees. It's reasonable to value professors intrinsically, because they are the custodians of important intellectual and cultural values. However, there's a tension here, just as there is a tension between the university as church and as car dealer. Many who pay the university's bills don't share its love of "monks." They want teaching and research to be produced as efficiently as possible, and if this means reducing faculty numbers by leveraging their time with support staff—and, now, with information technology—so be it. The tension will get worse as competition increases.

The third impediment stems from the difficulty of measuring value fulfillment, and hence of determining whether cost cutting will reduce value or not. Businesses measure profits with considerable precision, which allows them to reward executives and employees for efficiency improvement. Things are different in the academy. Would a new round of cost cutting boost efficiency or would it diminish educational and scholarly quality? How can one identify minimum cost benchmarks without knowing what value is being produced? The ability to answer such questions represents an important dimension of educational competency, to which I'll return in later chapters.

The final impediment to higher education's pursuit of efficiency arises from fuzzy knowledge about teaching and learning processes, another manifestation of the education competency gap. Because such processes have traditionally been taken for granted, most professors know surprisingly little about how to improve educational efficiency. This is another topic to which I'll return later.

Cost-per-student figures can't settle the question of whether a given university is efficient—either in absolute terms of relative to its peers. Such ratios can raise questions, but on-site evaluation is required to provide answers. For example, without local knowledge one cannot judge whether the observed variations stem from efficiency or quality differences. If a department is expensive, moreover, does this mean it's inefficient or does it reflect more money being spent on research? Only by analyzing the individual activities that create value in education and research can one assess a department's level of efficiency and what might be done to improve it.

While there's no direct evidence about whether universities are efficient, indirect evidence indicates that the answer is "no." For example, universities usually "bundle" teaching and research in ways that seem likely to limit efficiency.[39] Every professor is supposed to participate heavily in both activities, regardless of his or her comparative advantage. Because research time is considered to be an entitlement regardless of performance or prospects, expensive and scarce faculty resources aren't used with full effectiveness. The academy argues that such entitlements are necessary for good teaching but external stakeholders believe they add cost for no good reason—that better targeting of faculty research effort would significantly improve efficiency.

The aforementioned impediments provide additional indirect evidence. Better accountability to trustees, oversight boards, and the public can compensate for the absence of external shareholders. Improving the clarity of goals and objectives can mitigate the input valuation and value measurement problems. Better competency can improve education process knowledge. All such improvements can enhance an institution's ability to subsidize highly valued activities, the subject to which we turn next.

Endnotes

1. Siegfried (2000) discusses the reasons for this lack of attention.

2. Winston (1997), pp. 1–2.

3. "Not-for-profit" is technically better than "nonprofit," since many not-for-profit enterprises do make profits and many for-profit ones fail to do so. "Nonprofit" flows more naturally, however, so it's generally my term of choice.

4. Hansmann (1981, 1986).

5. Nonprofits that wind up their affairs must designate another nonprofit as the recipient of residual assets or sacrifice the assets to the state.

6. Hopkins and Massy (1981), Chapter 3; James and Neuberger (1981); James (1986, 1990); Massy (1996), Chapter 3.

7. Damon, et al. (2000), p. 2.

8. Adapted from Massy (1996), pp. 61–62. The source was James (1990).

9. So-called agency problems occur when value differences go underground—for example, if deans, chairs, or professors secretly pursue values that conflict with the university's values. This certainly occurs, but well-managed institutions work hard to minimize the problem. See Hoenack (1983) for a detailed discussion of agency problems.

10. McPherson and Schapiro (1994b), Table 10. "Net tuition" means tuition minus institutional scholarships.

11. How to allow for reserves and future inflation need not concern the general reader. See, for example, Massy (1981, 1990), and also Chapter 4.

12. The operational definitions of "fixed" as opposed to "variable" cost and revenue are highly context-specific. For example, teaching costs are fixed in the short run due to faculty contracts but variable in the longer run because of attrition. The policy elements of research administration and student services don't depend on output (assuming there will be research and students in the first place), whereas the services component (e.g., the cost of proposal preparation and student counseling) is variable. Chapter 3 contains some additional discussion and examples.

13. The Institute for Research on Higher Education (1997). The work was performed by Professor Zemsky and his colleagues at the University of Pennsylvania's Institute for Research on Higher Education, a member of the NCPI consortium. Neither they nor the RAND team cited in Chapter 1 knew of each others work in progress until after their basic findings had been developed.

14. NCPI breaks up the first, third, and fourth segments into two sub-segments each, but this degree of refinement is not needed here.

15. Clark Kerr, "A General Perspective on Higher Education and Service to the Labor Market." Unpublished paper excerpted in Pew Higher Education Research Program (September 1988), "Distillations," p. 1.

16. Zemsky and Massy (1995).

17. National Commission on Responsibilities for Financing Postsecondary Education (1993); National Commission on the Cost of Higher Education (1998); United States Senate Committee on Governmental Affairs, Hearings in the Rising Cost of College Tuition and the Effectiveness of Government Financial Aid, February 9–10, 2000.

18. The argument for stimulation holds that by injecting more buying power into the system, aid providers shift the demand curve to the right—which makes price increases easier, other things being equal. The empirical picture is mixed, however. McPherson, Schapiro, and Winston (1993, p. 11) could not find statistical evidence that increases in federal aid increased gross tuition in private colleges and universities, but they did find such effects for public institutions. It's also likely that federal aid offsets some institutional aid, which effectively boosts net price.

19. Bowen (1980).

20. These approximate the actual figures as calculated by Winston and Yen (1995, Table 1) for all the schools in his sample.

21. Both quotations are from Winston (2000), p. 1. Ehrenberg (2000) describes the arms race as a "dysfunctional competition for students."

22. See, for example, Zemsky, et al. (1999), to be discussed in Chapter 4.

23. Johnstone (2000), Table 3, reports that between 1980 and 2000 private institutions posted average annual real tuition increases of 3.7% and public ones 3.9%, which compound to 2.07 and 2.15, respectively.

24. See, for example, Winston and Zimmerman (2000).

25. See, for example, Winston and Zimmerman (2000). They mention Princeton, Yale, and Swarthmore, and there have been others.

26. Kane (2000) reports that demand declines about 5% for every $1,000 increase in tuition. (At public institutions, where some 80% of the students are, $1,000 represents much more than a 5% percentage of base price. Hence the demand is inelastic.) Other authors report that price has a "discernable but small effect" on the overall demand for higher education. See, for example, Leslie and Brinkman (1989) and McPherson and Schapiro (1998). The effect of relative price on institutional market share is likely to be larger, however.

27. Winston and Zimmerman (2000), p. 17.

28. The Institute for Research on Higher Education (1994), p. 35. The data come from Charts 1 and 2.

29. McPherson and Schapiro (1994a). Reproduced in Winston and Yen (1995), Table 7.

30. Kane (2000).

31. Gaudiani (2000).

32. The term was coined by Winston (1997), p. 5.

33. See Cook and Frank (1993) and Hansmann (2000) for an elaboration of the arguments for mixing on the basis of talent and other non-economic variables.

34. Stanford was not a member of the overlap group, although we were frequently invited to join. Our general counsel believed from the outset that the coordination was illegal. My colleagues and I avoided meetings when such issues were on the agenda. If they arose unexpectedly, we were instructed to depart—spilling our coffee or making some other commotion on the way out so people would remember our refusal to participate.

35. *United States v. Brown University,* 805 F. Supp. 228 (E.D. Pa. 1992).

36. Quinn (2000).

37. Winston (1997), p. 3.

38. Hopkins and Massy (1981, p. 91) describe how input valuation affects the nonprofit model.

39. Zemsky and Massy (1995) explore these ideas. See also Chapters 3 and 8 herein.

3
Subsidies and Contribution Margins

No subject generates more heat and less light than the question of subsidies in higher education. Some observers argue that nearly all students receive subsidies, while others believe that full-pay students at private institutions subsidize scholarship students. Researchers may argue that overhead on grants and contracts subsidizes teaching, whereas some financial analysts insist that educational funds subsidize research. Many people mistrust cross subsidies as a matter of principle. Others, myself among them, believe that cross subsidies represent a defining feature of nonprofit enterprises.

Solid answers to these questions would go a long way toward resolving the disputes that plague analysts, university leaders, and the public. This is important not only for restoring trust, but for removing a major roadblock to the improvement of education competency. We'll see that while the data aren't sufficient to clear up the ambiguities, the available indirect evidence, reasoning based on principle, and some rough and ready modeling yield enough insight to inform decision making.

I'll begin by extending the nonprofit enterprise model to address subsidies and contribution margins. Then I'll review the industry data on revenues and costs and identify certain accounting ambiguities that make the conventional margin and subsidy calculations suspect. The chapter concludes by describing undergraduate education's contribution margins at selective private institutions and asking whether students get what they pay for. The appendix presents a crude model for explaining who and what gets subsidized.

CROSS SUBSIDIES ARE US

Cross subsidies are a way of life in colleges and universities. For example, teaching may subsidize research or one teaching program may subsidize another. Anyone who doubts the pervasiveness of cross subsidies should consider this: Studies show that science majors cost up to twice as much as liberal arts or business majors, yet traditional undergraduates pay substantially the same regardless of program. Such cross subsidies reflect the university's value system—in this case the conviction that students should not be deterred from science study for financial reasons. We'll see that the nonprofit model shows how cross subsidies reflect values and how they distinguish nonprofit from profit-making enterprises.

"Cross subsidy" means using revenue obtained from one kind of output to pay for activities that produce something else. The term "contribution margin," introduced in Chapter 2, represents a program's contribution to the enterprise's fixed costs and, in the case of nonprofit enterprises, to the pool of funds available for cross subsidies. Subsidized programs have negative contribution margins. Positive contributions bolster the university's ability to provide cross subsidies.

The most important cross subsidy issue involves teaching and research, but there are many others. For example, a certain private university sustains its divinity school with surpluses from other schools. Why? Because the program dates from the founding of the university and represents a core institutional value. That divinity loses money does not mean it should be eliminated or even downsized. If this university has made its judgments carefully, and I believe it has, divinity's continuing subsidy represents a reaffirmation of value rather than a reflection of inefficiency or a sign of trouble ahead.

Cross subsidies are not unheard of in the for-profit world, but they tend to be transitory. For example, a company may subsidize entry into a new market with profits from old markets or defend itself from especially aggressive competitors by setting price below cost. Such cross subsidies disappear after a while, either because the driving circumstances pass or because the company abandons the money-losing product or market. Not so in the nonprofit world. As with divinity, cross subsidies in universities can persist for decades or even centuries.

A Conceptual Decision Rule

Suppose we could see inside a provost's mind as she ponders next year's enrollment targets for her university's business and divinity schools. Divinity loses money and business produces surpluses. But divinity lies at the core of the university's value system, she reasons, and the dean believes that extra divinity students would boost value fulfillment handsomely—provided, of course, that the school's budget incorporates the extra students' variable cost. Business isn't as central to the university's traditional values, so it generates less value fulfillment per student. In fact, certain humanities professors claim that business has too many students already, to the detriment of the university's traditions and core values.

Some provosts would key on the academic values, and tell divinity to expand and business to hold its enrollment constant, or perhaps even to contract. Other provosts, and most chief financial officers, would follow the money and tell business to expand and divinity to contract. Our provost is an economist, however, and she knows that the nonprofit model requires a more complex calculus. And because she's a mathematical economist, she formulates this "conceptual decision rule."[1]

Conceptual Decision Rule

Let $M_i = (1/k)$(change in value fulfillment)$_i$ + (variable revenue)$_i$ − (variable cost)$_i$ where M stands for "incremental net gain," i stands for program (divinity or business in this case), k is a normalizing constant, and "change" refers to what happens if the program adds some extra students.

Rule: Expand program i if M_i is positive, contract it if M_i is negative, and leave it the same if M_i is zero—always making sure that the budget is balanced.

Recognizing that equations don't convey meaning for most of her audience, she also offers the following plain-language explanation.

> Every program produces two "goods"—value fulfillment and revenue. One might say these represent "love" and "money." I'll expand a program if the extra love plus the extra money exceeds the cost of expansion, and conversely, I'll continue expanding or contracting until the sum of love and money

just equals variable cost. By doing this I'll produce more value overall than if I considered love alone.

This simple statement speaks volumes. To maximize one's own values, one must take money as well as love into account. So much for the argument that money should be a dirty word in academe.

Extra divinity students produce high value fulfillment but little extra tuition revenue after needed levels of financial aid are deducted. If net tuition is far less than direct cost, divinity might have to be contracted even though its value fulfillment is high. Business students produce more net tuition but less value fulfillment than do divinity students in this case. If business's net tuition exceeds direct cost by a sufficient amount, the provost might expand it even as she contracts divinity. The expected challenge from the divinity dean might be met with this provostial rejoinder:

> No, I've not debased the university's values by "putting money above love," as you put it. The "profits" obtained by expanding business will be used to boost value fulfillment elsewhere, which will leave the university better off overall. Without business's positive contribution margin I would have to contract divinity even more. All the money eventually will be converted to value fulfillment because, as a nonprofit enterprise, we don't pay dividends to shareholders.

The conceptual decision rule works as long as each student added to a given program generates less value fulfillment (maybe only a little less) than the previous one, program revenue remains the same or declines as students are added, and variable cost per student remains the same or rises.[2] If these reasonable conditions are met, expanding programs for which marginal net gain is positive and contracting those with negative net gain will boost the university's value fulfillment. By finding the configuration where all the M- values equal zero and the budget is balanced, the provost obtains the best value possible given market conditions, teaching and learning processes, and the university's financial situation. The rule applies not only at the school level (and to individual departments and interdisciplinary programs), but also for broad categories of activity like teaching and research.

A Practical Decision Rule

A real-world provost wouldn't be able to apply the conceptual decision rule directly, despite its power. The problem lies in the first term: "$(1/k)$(change in value fulfillment)." What is k and how does one measure "change in value fulfillment"? For now, let's think of k as converting dollars to value units. We'll see that it plays an important role, but not one that's relevant now. The immediate problem lies with measuring value fulfillment. Provosts and other academics can sense when they feel better or worse about the value implications of a decision, but few can imagine quantifying their feelings. Therefore, we need to transform the decision rule to something practical.

"Variable revenue" and "variable cost" represent the rule's observable quantities. They can be approximated by net tuition per student and unit cost, multiplied by the number of enrollments.[3] Making this substitution produces the practical decision rule.

Practical Decision Rule

Contribution margin$_i$ = (net price$_i$ – unit cost$_i$) • N_i
    where i stands for program and N_i stands for enrollment, and

Surplus (deficit) = Sum of all the contributions + fixed revenue – fixed cost.

Rule: Adjust enrollments until the surplus (deficit) equals zero (or another agreed-upon value) and the relative contributions seem consistent with the university's values.

This may look a bit complicated, but it reflects the kinds of reports that accountants produce routinely. The first statement defines the programs' contribution margins and the second defines the university's overall financial balance. Programs with negative contribution margins receive cross subsidies as noted earlier, and we'll see in a moment that cross subsidies are proportional to value fulfillment.

The rule requires two conditions for a good decision. First, the budget must be balanced or produce a surplus or deficit that is consistent with the university's strategic financial plan. Second, the array of contribution margins must be consistent with the university's values—for example, the relative contributions of business and divinity must feel right to decision makers.

The rule doesn't tell the provost what to do, but it provides a framework for systematic judgment. Suppose a trial calculation predicts that the university would run a deficit with the student numbers tentatively planned. She might consider adding enrollments to programs with positive contribution margins, which would boost revenue, or subtracting them from programs that are receiving cross subsidies. She might also increase net price or fixed revenue, or cut variable or fixed costs. Each move will reconfigure the array of contributions and cross subsidies, so the provost must ask whether each new array is consistent with her value system. Eventually she will find a solution that feels reasonable in value terms while at the same time balancing the budget.

I don't claim that provosts actually do these calculations. However, the laws of economics tell us that careful resource allocations approximate them. The model also allows us to gain qualitative insight about university values and behavior.

Values and Financial Contributions

The practical decision rule uncovers a surprising and powerful relation between intrinsic value and financial contribution: When value fulfillment is maximized, programs with positive contribution margins will have negative incremental values and conversely:[4]

$$(1/k)(\text{change in value fulfillment})_i = -(\text{financial contribution}_i)$$

Providing the practical decision rule is satisfied, one can infer a program's incremental value fulfillment, expressed in dollar equivalents, simply by calculating its contribution margin.

We now know that our hypothetical provost believes divinity has positive incremental value—otherwise she would not give it a cross subsidy. Likewise, she must assign business a negative incremental value because she won't let it expand further despite its positive financial contribution. Does this mean she thinks business makes no intrinsic contribution to the university's value fulfillment—that its sole reason for being is to produce financial returns? Probably not. While academic purists might push this view, few provosts (or business professors like myself) would give it a moment's consideration. Business schools *do* produce positive value in absolute terms, but that doesn't preclude negative *incremental* value. By way of analogy, I like my work, but working too much drives out other activities and thus reduces value fulfillment. I stop working when value fulfillment starts dropping off, but that doesn't mean I dislike my work overall.

The prevailing view of undergraduates in research universities provides further insight into the relation between financial contributions and changes in value fulfillment. Recall the second item in Estelle James's list of university values, presented in Chapter 2: "Undergraduate numbers are most valued in colleges that specialize in teaching and may actually be negatively valued 'at the margin' [that is, incrementally] in research universities." Universities are committed to undergraduate education, but they may value it negatively at the margin because more students would take faculty time away from research. Colleges, on the other hand, may value undergraduates positively at the margin but be deterred from expanding enrollment because of financial or market constraints.

If certain universities value undergraduates negatively at the margin, why do they sustain enrollments at their present levels? The answer is they need the money. This implies that contribution margins for undergraduate education are positive, which would mean that undergraduates cross-subsidize research.

The relation between financial contributions and value fulfillment also applies to interdepartmental cross subsidies. When Stanford produced its first department-by-department analysis of contribution margins, for example, the dean of engineering looked at the result and within a month had imposed a departmental merger. The cross subsidy going to one of the departments was too big to be justified by the department's value to the school. The merger strengthened both departments and saved enough money to produce an acceptable array of cross subsidies.

Other cross subsidy examples can be found among the growing number of universities that practice responsibility center budgeting.[5] Such universities mitigate the adverse effect of market forces by imposing a participation fee on each school's revenue and providing subventions based on the value generated by each school in relation to its earning power. ("Participation" means being part of the university—in effect, these fees represent internal franchise taxes.) The aforementioned divinity school subvention provides a good example.

Participation fees generate money for cross subsidies, but are they really necessary? Can universities subsidize some schools and departments *without* taxing others? Can they subsidize all departments simultaneously? The answers lie in the nonprofit model's fixed revenue term. If there is enough fixed revenue—for example, if the university has a large endowment—all programs can be subsidized without participation fees. Fixed revenues don't preclude cross subsidies among programs; they just give the university more flexibility in exercising its value judgments. Conversely, when fixed revenue is smaller than fixed cost, the university must "tax Peter to pay Paul," or else leave Paul to the tender mercies of the market.

Financial Stringency

The nonprofit model also explains what happens when a university faces financial stringency, that is, when most or all of its contribution margins are negative and there is little fixed revenue. Financial stringency increases the conceptual decision rule's normalizing constant, k, which can now be defined as the "incremental value of money." Incremental dollars become more valuable as money gets tighter, so k grows and the rule's value term, "$(1/k)$(change in value fulfillment)," declines. Eventually k may grow so much that the value term becomes negligible, in which case the equation reduces to "(change in revenue)$_i$ = (change in cost)$_i$." Elementary economics teaches that this formula is precisely the one used by business firms to maximize their profit.[6] The conclusion is inescapable: Universities with serious financial problems behave just like businesses; they are driven strictly by the market.

What does it mean to be driven strictly by the market? It means no cross subsidies. The university cannot tax Peter to pay Paul because no program has the wherewithal to be taxed. It cannot exercise its academic values because it has no money to do so. In the language of Chapter 1, the university cannot afford the Acropolis so it must embrace the Agora. In Gordon Winston's words, it must abandon the church and become a car dealer. The virtues we associate with being nonprofit thus are revealed as requiring a certain level of affluence. Poor nonprofits behave like for-profits.

Market forces also put pressure on professors. We've seen how positive contribution margins, which provide the wherewithal for cross subsidies, must be associated with negative marginal value fulfillment. This means the university's value-maximizing strategy may require professors to do things they don't want to do, such as teach in financially remunerative programs with low academic content. Such programs aren't generating intrinsic value, but their positive contribution margins help keep the university afloat. When financial stringency drives up the incremental value of money, professors may be asked to sacrifice intrinsic values to achieve financial gains. For a generation of senior faculty raised in relative affluence, such requests will seem to violate academic principles. This helps explain the angst expressed by many academics today.

The Case for Cross Subsidies

The nonprofit model demonstrates that cross subsidies are intrinsically good, not intrinsically bad as some critics would have it. Cross subsidies reflect the legitimate exercise of academic judgment. Therefore, efforts to make universities more market-responsive by cutting their discretionary revenue can be overdone. A certain level of market responsiveness is desirable, but there should be scope for value-based judgments.

Too much market pressure can erode a university's sense of what constitutes "good work." For example, research on good work in journalism describes how market pressures are squeezing professional standards.[7] While stars like Tom Brokaw can resist such influence, local anchors experience constant pressure to popularize, trivialize, or sensationalize their stories in order to gain ratings. In higher education there are documented examples where liberal arts colleges adopted whole new definitions of good work in order to survive in the marketplace.[8]

Finally, the model highlights the fundamental difference between for-profit higher education enterprises and most nonprofit ones: The for-profits don't cross-subsidize on a long-term basis. For-profits play an important role in education markets where quality can be evaluated and is affordable without direct public subsidy. However, they can't be expected to sustain less popular programs with the proceeds from more popular ones, or to subsidize faculty research and scholarship. Society will continue to rely on the nonprofit sector for these outcomes. But what happens if the for-profits compete away the contribution margins that the nonprofit universities rely on to provide these subsidies? This already is happening as the for-profits enter high-margin programs like the MBA. To counter this threat, nonprofit universities will have to improve their core competencies. Failure to do so will undermine their ability to compete and thus erode the very values the academy seeks to protect by defending the status quo.

FLOWS OF FUNDS WITHIN UNIVERSITIES

Where does a university's money come from and where does it go? All empirical questions pertaining to subsidies and cross subsidies hang on the answer.

Gordon Winston's Economics 101 model of university finance calculates the student subsidy by subtracting net tuition from the university's education and general expenditures. According to this model:

> College students pay only a fraction of the cost of their education. Large student subsidies—paying two-thirds of the cost at the average U.S. college or university—are the central fact of the economics of higher education.[9]

"Economics 101" means keeping things simple. As Winston says, "Until recently, we've had an oddly fragmented picture of the economic workings of colleges and universities, mainly because of a long tradition of 'fund accounting.' It had its virtues, but clarity about economic structure wasn't one of them."[10] Fund accounting separates donor and other special-purpose accounts in the university's financial statements. This is required for legal reasons, but it makes the statements hard to interpret. Economics 101 rises above fund accounting to highlight the underlying economic relationships.

Figure 3.1 describes where a university's income comes from and where it goes. Bars (a) and (b) depict the sources and uses of funds. Bar (c) subtracts auxiliary expense and saving from total uses to get the cost of producing academic outputs, and bar (d) subtracts funded research to get what appears to be educational cost.[11] ("Auxiliary expense" refers to nonacademic functions like dormitories and food services, and patient care by medical school faculty.) Bar (e) subtracts net tuition and fees from educational cost to obtain the apparent student subsidy, which then is separated into scholarships targeted to individuals and the general subsidy that goes to all students. Finally, bar (f) shows the sticker price and the average net price paid by students on financial aid.

Figure 3.1

Where the Money Comes From and Where It Goes

Sources	Uses	Cost of academic outputs	Educational cost	Apparent student subsidy	Gross and net tuition
Auxiliary income	Auxiliary expense				
Grants & contracts	Saving				
	Funded research	Funded research			Sticker price
Gifts & endow. income	Admin. & support		Apparent subsidy	General	
	Instruction & unfunded research	Education		Individual	Net price
Net tuition & fees			Net tuition & fees		
(a)	(b)	(c)	(d)	(e)	(f)

The term "apparent subsidy" signals that the results don't necessarily mean what one might think. We'll see, for example, that educational cost includes unfunded research. But before getting to that, let's look at the data on apparent subsidies.

Table 3.1 presents revenue and expense data for US four-year institutions, scaled to percentages of total revenue in order to facilitate comparisons.[12] As defined in the table, public and private universities generally have substantial amounts of funded research, whereas private colleges are mostly of the liberal arts variety. Like their private counterparts, the public colleges (which are mostly called comprehensive universities) do relatively little funded research. The table's format follows Figure 3.1 except that public service has been added and no data are presented for auxiliary revenue and expense. (Auxiliary income and expense usually are about equal, so their omission doesn't affect the analysis.) Readers may note that the bars in Table 3.1 are roughly proportional to the figures for private universities.

Private universities receive more money from gifts and endowment income than they do from net tuition and fees, whereas private colleges get more income from tuition. Public institutions show large percentages for state and local appropriations. Befitting their mission, they also do more funded public service work. Not surprisingly, the public and private colleges have much less grant and contract revenue than the universities.

Table 3.1

Income, Cost, Apparent Student Subsidy, and Financial Aid (1989, by institutional type)

| | *Percentages of Total Revenue* | | | |
| | Private | | Public | |
	Universities	Colleges	Universities	Colleges
(a) Sources of funds				
Net tuition and fees	31%	55%	16%	19%
Gifts and endowment income	43%	36%	21%	10%
State & local appropriations	1%	1%	48%	62%
Grants & contracts	26%	7%	16%	8%
Total sources of funds	100%	100%	100%	100%
(b) Uses of funds				
Instruction & unfunded research	36%	34%	37%	45%
Funded research	19%	2%	19%	6%
Funded public service	3%	2%	8%	3%
Administration & support services	31%	46%	29%	39%
Saving	11%	14%	7%	8%
Total uses of funds	100%	100%	100%	100%
(c) Output mix				
Instruction & unfunded research	67%	81%	66%	84%
Funded research & public service	23%	5%	27%	8%
Saving	11%	14%	7%	8%
Total uses of funds	100%	100%	100%	100%
(d) "Instructional" cost				
Net tuition & fees	31%	55%	16%	19%
Apparent student subsidy	36%	25%	50%	64%
Total "instructional" cost	67%	81%	66%	84%
(e) Apparent subsidy				
Targeted to individuals	10%	24%	19%	33%
General	26%	1%	32%	32%
Institutional subsidy	36%	25%	50%	64%
Federal financial aid	1%	2%	2%	3%
Total subsidy	37%	27%	52%	67%

Source: Blasdell, McPherson, and Schapiro (1993), Tables 1–4.

Savings percentages run from 7% to 14%, which seems high given the institutional proclivity for spending. Probably this is due to anomalies in the data. Even if the savings figures are anomalous, they don't materially affect the subsidy calculations.

Private universities subsidize students to the extent of 36% of revenue. More than two-thirds of the 36% represents a general subsidy that goes even to full-pay students, with the remainder being financial aid awards to individual students. The private colleges subsidize to the extent of 25% revenue. Most of this goes to financial aid, probably because hundreds of small nonselective colleges must offer merit scholarships in order to survive. Not surprisingly, subsidies at public colleges and universities are larger than those in the private sector. These subsidies, which come more from state and local appropriations than gifts and endowments, range from 50% to 64% with between one-third and one-half targeted to individuals.

These results appear to support the contention that most undergraduates receive subsidies. Counting federal scholarships, shown in the last line of the table, the apparent subsidies range from 27% to 37% in the private sector and 52% to 67% in the public sector.[13] Furthermore, the "apparent general subsidy," the amount received even by full-pay students, exceeds 25% of revenue or more in all but the private colleges.

These are substantial figures, but do they demonstrate that undergraduates are in fact getting more education than they pay for? Unfortunately, the answer is "no." Before concluding that students enjoy handsome subsidies, we had better explore the true meaning of "educational cost" as used in the calculations. Hidden cross subsidies from education to research may eat up the apparent subsidy, possibly to the point where tuition rates exceed the true cost of education.

ACCOUNTING AMBIGUITIES

Given their importance, one might expect cross subsidies to be well defined and carefully measured by university accounting systems. Not so. Some institutions have learned to measure cross subsidies among schools and departments, but their accounting systems shed little light on the cross subsidies between education and research. Few schools ask the hard questions or tell their stakeholders the full story about cross subsidies.

Moreover, accounting ambiguities prevent third parties from understanding where the money really comes from and where it really goes.

Figure 3.2 outlines the flows of funds within colleges and universities. The shaded boxes list revenue sources: money intended for education on the left and money intended for research on the right. The three main categories of expense, which appear down the middle of the diagram, are defined as follows.

• Instruction and unfunded research includes three kinds of activities: instruction, unfunded research, and departmental administration, including the cost of deans' offices, department chairs and secretaries, and faculty time devoted to hiring, tenure review, and other aspects of departmental governance.

Figure 3.2

Flows of Funds in Colleges and Universities

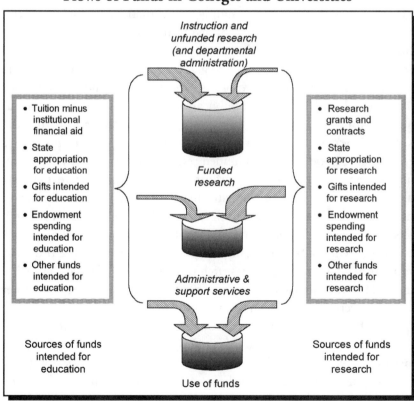

- Funded research consists of project work where costs are accounted for separately. Usually such projects are funded by grants or contracts, but university funds also appear frequently.

- Administrative and support services include the university's central administration, libraries and information resources, and building operation and maintenance.

The arrows reflect the relative size of the funds flows in a typical institution. Most education-related money goes to instruction and unfunded research and to administrative and support services. The so-called direct portion of grant and contract revenue, that which investigators can spend, shows up in funded research. The indirect portion, that which the university collects as overhead, goes to administrative and support services except for sums that flow to instruction and unfunded research to cover departmental administration.

Ambiguity begins with the instruction and unfunded research expense category. Often this gets labeled simply as "instruction," but such a label is inaccurate when professors are expected to produce research and scholarship. Consider a research-active social science professor with a teaching load of two courses per term and no grants or contracts, for example. He may spend a quarter or a third of his time doing unfunded research or preparing scholarly articles for publication, yet all his time is counted as "instruction." Or consider a physics professor with a grant from the National Science Foundation (NSF). One might expect this professor's research time to be charged to funded research and paid for by the grant, but that isn't likely. Most NSF grants don't pay academic-year faculty salaries, even though the investigator may work as much as half time on the project. The grant pays the professor's summer salary and for research assistants, travel, equipment, and supplies, but NSF considers the academic-year salary to be the university's responsibility because "the professor would be paid anyway." Such research time usually is charged to instruction.[14] This includes large amounts of time that, as we will see in Chapter 4, don't materially benefit education.

But that's not the end of the ambiguity, even for instruction and unfunded research. Recall that this expense category actually includes the cost of department- and school-level administration. Decanal and departmental staffs don't come cheap, nor does the faculty time required for governance and the hiring and evaluation of colleagues. The federal government recognizes that extra costs are incurred when the department or school must support substantial numbers of grants and contracts, so it includes departmental administration in its allowance for overhead. But while the government recognizes departmental administration as a separate expenditure category, most universities do not. They count it as "instruction," even when the government pays them substantial sums to cover departmental administration's contributions to research.

The growing importance of research and more intense competition for sponsored research dollars makes the misrepresentation of instructional expenditures ever more serious. Chapter 4 describes how professors feel pressured to do research, even in universities and colleges that are not generally considered to be research intensive. More time for research means lower teaching loads, less preparation time, and less out-of-class student contact, that is, a shift of effort from teaching to research. On the funding side, competition leads federal research officers to drive down overhead rates and academic-year faculty salary payments, so that universities get less reimbursement for faculty time and other resources expended on behalf of research. The sums involved are very large. For example, a recent RAND study estimates that universities may recover as little as 70% of the facilities and administrative costs associated with federal projects and that universities contribute about $5 billion of research support from their own funds. This sum, which represents about one-fifth of all funding for research in universities, comes mostly as unfunded contributions to facilities and administration and the subsidizing of faculty research time.[15]

A third ambiguity concerns the intent of revenue providers. Do they mean to support education (especially undergraduate education), do they mean to support research, or don't they care? The intent of tuition payers and research sponsors is clear: They are buying a service at a market price. However, what about state governments, current donors, and prior donors whose funds helped build the endowment? Restricted gifts and endowments often include clear directions, for example, that the money is to be spent for a particular research project or educational program. But what about unrestricted gifts and gifts restricted only to the level of a school or department? Do undergraduate and professional-school alumni who give in small amounts, which usually are unrestricted, believe they are helping educate the next generation of students or supporting faculty research, possibly at the expense of education? Do state legislators intend that their general appropriations should support mainly education, or are they happy to contribute handsomely to research as well?

Universities don't know the intent of many revenue providers. Once they have met legal restrictions, they are free to spend the money any way they wish. Combine that with the ambiguity of accounting reports on "instruction" expenditures and one has a potentially corrosive situation. The university doesn't know the providers' intent and neither the providers nor the university knows whether the funds are being spent on education or research. Lacking data, there can be no natural correcting forces. Universities continue their rhetoric about the huge subsidies enjoyed by students, while critics continue to harbor suspicions that the emperor's clothes are, well, scanty.

THE CASE FOR FULL DISCLOSURE

Does the disconnect further the academy's long-term best interest? Former Harvard President Derek Bok once offered this wry comment: "To be so admired in other parts of the world while being so roundly criticized at home [has been] a singular achievement of our institutions of higher learning."[16] How deeply do critics resent the fact that they're not getting the full story about cross subsidies? Might it be better to collect and disclose accurate data and then debate any cross subsidies on their merits? There is danger in such a strategy: What if state legislators, for example, were to declare that their money should go for education rather than research? But this is precisely the kind of question that *should* be debated in a democracy. Disclosure would be painful in the short run, but it would clear the air. It would be more consistent with the university's fundamental commitment to knowledge and openness.

Better disclosure also would remove some major impediments that stand in the way of cost containment. It would enable universities to better understand their cost structures, monitor meaningful cost trends, and benchmark themselves against other institutions. The universities are being held hostage by their own policies. Today's ambiguities forefend controversy about cross subsidies, but at a high cost. By not probing into cross subsidies, universities deprive themselves of data they need to optimize resource allocation and improve their production processes.

Of course there are measurement problems. University accounting systems don't record the time professors spend on administration and unfunded research, and for good reason. Professors don't punch time clocks, so there is no audit trail to distinguish the time spent on one task versus another. It's hard to imagine such a trail even in principle, because the faculty's job is so complex and the nature of intellectual work so varied. To do the job right, one would have to distinguish among teaching and other education-based activities, keeping up with one's field, scholarship in support of teaching, and research oriented mainly to grants and publications—not to mention the tasks required for departmental administration. Often these activities are entwined with each other in mixes that vary minute by minute throughout the day, and in the evenings and on weekends as well. These are the classic reasons for not differentiating unfunded research from instruction in the university's accounting system, and they are correct in my opinion.

But these problems don't preclude estimating the amount of time professors spend on research. Current accounting standards grew from historical circumstances, before the advent of big research, when most "instruction" expenditures really went for education. The ambiguity didn't matter before research became big business, but now it obscures a key element of institutional performance. MIT's Jay Forester, inventor of the systems dynamics approach to decision-support modeling, taught that if you're sure a phenomenon exists, the one value you know it does not have is zero. Yet that's the value you've assigned if you leave it out of the model. To ignore unfunded research and the research component of departmental administration is to assert they are insignificant, but this is not consistent with known facts. Any informed estimate will be better than simply assuming the value is zero.

Universities could estimate the amount of faculty time spent on research if they were motivated to do so.[17] Their accounting systems can't measure departmental administration either, but they use periodic sample surveys to estimate the fraction of departmental expense that goes to administration. They do so because the estimates increase overhead recovery on grants and contracts. Surely they could estimate the fraction representing unfunded research if they wanted to. Some first-rate universities in the United Kingdom use diary studies to do just that.

Unraveling the intent of funds providers would be more difficult. However, an analysis of stratified samples of unrestricted gift, endowment, and governmental subsidy accounts would provide substantial insight. Such accounts might be classified as funding mainly for education or for research. An undecided category could be included, but I believe that in most cases the provider's predilections would be fairly clear. For example, the classification could be informed by examining the university's donor appeals and by interviewing people in state government. If the academy doesn't want to perform these tasks, or if its ability to make disinterested classifications is suspect, they could be undertaken by a neutral third party with university cooperation. Precise quantitative estimates are neither possible nor necessary. A rough qualitative assessment of government and donor intent would be sufficient.

The concerns about cross subsidies won't go away on their own. Most informed commentators agree that research continues to drive the academic enterprise. Therefore, if education does not now cross-subsidize research, it may well do so soon. The National Association of College and University Business Officers recently developed a common methodology for allocating administrative and support costs between education and research, thus producing better estimates of the cost of education.[18] The methodology goes a long way toward clearing up the ambiguities described here, and I believe it should be adopted widely. However, it does not address unfunded research or government and donor intent. Further work on these issues will be needed before higher education can claim to be fully disclosing its economic performance.

MARGINS AT SELECTIVE PRIVATE INSTITUTIONS

Absent data on the cross subsidy between education and research, analysts must resort to indirect measures and inferences. One approach involves the measurement of institutions' overall contribution margins from undergraduate education. The methodology is not without its own ambiguities, but it does provide some provocative results.

I recently joined Robert Zemsky and his colleagues at the University of Pennsylvania in a study of contribution margins from undergraduate education at 48 selective private institutions (30 colleges and 18 research universities).[19] Normally, margins reflect the excess of direct revenue over direct expenditures for particular departments, schools, and programs. However, because cross subsidies recycle program-level margins into expenditures elsewhere in the university, the margins don't drop to the bottom line as institutional surpluses. Therefore, our study defined "margin" not as an excess of revenue over expense, but as the excess of "instructional" spending and student financial aid over the expenditure levels needed to maintain the institution's educational quality and market position.[20] The definition implies that institutions need not use these margins to maintain themselves competitively in the student marketplace. Hence, they can cross-subsidize activities, such as research, that other stakeholders value highly.

The only data available for comparing margins among institutions combines expenditures for undergraduate education with those for graduate education and unfunded research. Therefore, we used a technique called frontier analysis to disentangle the various kinds of spending.[21] The analysis identified the institutions that spend the least, taking into account the numbers and types of degrees produced, enrollments, undergraduate market position as measured by admit and yield rates for the freshman class, and reputation as measured by the *U.S. News & World Report* and other survey data. Economists would say these institutions operate on the efficient frontier because no school produces similar outputs in similar circumstances at lower cost. We define the efficient institutions as those with zero contribution margins.

The analysis proceeded in three steps.

1) Reasoning that many liberal arts colleges do not have large graduate and research programs, we used them to benchmark the cost of undergraduate education. To get the benchmarks we applied frontier analysis to all 48 institutions using total spending, but only undergraduate enrollments and degrees.[22] This produced a set of efficient liberal arts colleges and their associated unit costs, and contribution margin figures for the other liberal arts colleges.

2) Using the unit costs determined in step 1, we estimated the costs of efficient undergraduate education in the research universities. Subtracting these from the universities' actual costs produced figures for spending on graduate education and research. (This measure probably is conservative because elite liberal arts colleges offer more student-faculty contact than research universities.)

3) Then we estimated the cost of efficient graduate education by performing a second frontier analysis, this time relating the spending for graduate education and research obtained in step 2 to graduate degrees and enrollments. This produced a set of efficient research

universities and their estimated unit costs, and contribution margins for the remaining universities.

The results were striking. As shown in Table 3.2, the margins for the top three universities average 68% and those for 12 of the 18 exceed 30%. Margins at the colleges are lower but still substantial, for example, half are above 15%. At the bottom end of the list, two universities and four colleges are on the efficient frontier.

What does it mean to have a 68% margin? If the analysis can be taken literally, it means that the institution spends 68% more than can be accounted for by its size, enrollment mix, market position, and reputation. Critics may argue that the quality of education is better at the high-margin institutions than at the lower-margin ones, but there is no hard evidence to this effect. All the institutions are name brand or highly selective, and the analysis took the available surrogates for quality into account. The strongest argument that the quality of education is better in the high-margin schools is that they spend more, but this argument is circular. In any case, what unbiased observer would claim that the value added by undergraduate education at the University of Chicago, Yale, and Harvard (the three highest-margin universities) is two-thirds better than at Brown and Tufts, which are on the efficient frontier?

Table 3.2

Average Contribution Margins at
Selective Colleges and Universities

Universities	Average margin	Colleges	Average margin
1–3	68%	1–5	30%
4–6	54%	6–10	20%
7–9	44%	11–15	16%
10–12	32%	16–20	9%
13–15	7%	21–25	2%
16–18	1%	26–30	0%

Computed from Zemsky, et al. (1999), Tables 2.2 and 2.3.

How the high-margin institutions spend their discretionary funds casts additional doubt on the alleged proportionality between cost and quality. To get at this question, we looked at the relation between margins and expenditure patterns.

The results "indicate what most critics and many long-time observers of the nation's selective and name-brand colleges and universities have long suspected: the greater the margin that an institution earns, the more it spends on research, full professor salaries, instruction (including unfunded research), and academic support."[23] In this case, "research" means separately budgeted research paid for from the institution's own resources. Higher salaries mean the institution can attract research stars. More money for "instruction" (and unfunded research) allows lower teaching loads and smaller and more specialized classes. Such changes would benefit students if faculty time commitments remained the same, but faculty may well seize the opportunity to reduce the time they spend on teaching.[24] Spending more on academic support further leverages professors' time and improves the quality of their work life.

Financial aid represents an exception to the generalization that most of an institution's earned margin is spent in pursuit of faculty interests. Institutions with more discretionary funds are likely to spend a significant portion of them pursuing more diversified classes through need and merit scholarships. On the other hand, we found no evidence that extra discretionary funds are spent on student services, libraries, or administration. Our overall conclusion: "What you get is what you see: better-paid faculty performing more research, and greater allotments for student financial aid."[25]

DO STUDENTS GET WHAT THEY PAY FOR?

Whether students get what they pay for is a complicated question. Selective private colleges and universities earn big margins and spend them on activities that may or may not produce much educational value added. We also know that cross subsidies reflect institutional values, which run strongly toward research. Students may get what they pay for in a direct sense through positive general subsidies, even if some funds donated or appropriated on their behalf are used to cross subsidize research.

The Economics 101 model suggests that students not only get what they pay for, but that full-pay students are heavily subsidized even in private institutions. But this ignores the data ambiguities discussed earlier. The more complicated model described in the appendix to this chapter takes these considerations into account. This model yields only rough estimates based on the sparse data now available. These data suggest that while students almost surely get subsidized in public institutions the situation is mixed in private ones. Looking at all sources and uses of funds, education appears to cross-subsidize research in the research universities and conversely in the liberal arts colleges. Perhaps most important, the model allows an institution, or its trustees or oversight board, to evaluate the direction of subsidy in its own particular case.

Another approach focuses on the economic value of a college degree. The baccalaureate has become a virtual prerequisite for high-paying jobs. Whether the economic advantages reflect the value of screening or the value added by education is an open question, but the fact remains that they exist. As long as private rates of return remain high, one can say that college students get what they pay for.

But that's not all. Students from highly selective and name-brand schools have better job prospects than those from less-prestigious schools. They also have a better chance of getting prestigious graduate degrees, which confer extraordinary economic benefits.[26] Whatever mechanism produces the benefits, people are willing to pay high prices to get them. Again, they seem to get what they pay for.

These observations aren't entirely satisfying. They leave the delivered quality of education off the table. Imagine two scenarios. In the first, universities deliver a full measure of educational competency to the task of educating undergraduates while at the same time scoring research successes. In the second, universities leave many educational tasks undone and rely on research-generated prestige to maintain their market position. Given today's lack of data on the delivered quality of education, either scenario can work in the marketplace. However, the two are not equivalent to students or to the society at large.

The first scenario delivers better education than the second. To claim that the second produces more benefits overall, one would have to show that the research lost by going from the first scenario to the second is more valuable than the educational quality gained. Even then, there would be equity questions. How should the private benefits forgone by students in the second scenario be balanced against the public benefits of the extra research? Even if the students retain their salary advantage, based on the university's prestige, they have lost important benefits related to lifelong learning and quality of life. They, and the stakeholders that defend their interests, would eagerly trade off a little research-based prestige for significant educational gain.

These are, of course, just hypotheticals. But the mind experiment raises important questions.

- Does research prowess guarantee or strongly imply a "full measure of educational competency"? The first scenario cannot occur if the answer is "yes." However, Chapter 4 presents the case for a "no" answer.

- Can universities sustain selectivity on the basis of prestige that is largely powered by research rather than demonstrated educational competency? The second scenario cannot occur unless this is true. Chapter 2 presented the case that it is, and the case will be buttressed in later chapters.

- Would it be possible for universities operating according to the second scenario to move to the first without decimating their research? In other words, is trading off "a little research-based prestige for significant educational gain" a realistic possibility? Subsequent chapters build the case that the answer is "yes."

- Would the value of research lost by the tradeoff be greater than the value of educational quality gained? Chapter 4 argues that the answer is "yes" for today's universities and faculty, given their reward and incentive systems. However, the case is doubtful for the society at large. Sustaining it requires that the value of research given up at the margin exceeds the incremental education gain. Many voices have argued that some research done at universities is of low value; this book shows how large education quality gains can be achieved with modest incremental effort.

- Which scenario best describes higher education today? Again, a major thrust of this book holds that many of America's colleges and universities tilt more toward the second scenario than the first. These, of course, are the ones with market power. But they exert disproportionate influence on all institutions because they define what it means to be a university and socialize subsequent generations of faculty.

The aforementioned discussion does not depend on the direction of cross subsidy between education and research. Providing the greatest good for the greatest numbers argues for improving education quality even if research does subsidize education—though, of course, this would raise its own equity issues. The case for improving quality becomes overwhelming if education does in fact cross subsidize research. How could one justify siphoning off resources that would give students what they pay for if spent on education? If the subsidization is substantially neutral, and would remain so even after a modest shift of resources toward education, the problem becomes one of efficiency. By not delivering the best education possible given the resources spent, universities would be operating inefficiently. Improvements would benefit everyone.

Appendix

SUBSIDY CALCULATIONS

We begin by calculating the apparent student subsidy. The subsidy depends on "educational cost," which we now understand to be the sum of instruction and unfunded research. What if unfunded research is significant? Suppose, for example, that only three-fourths of educational cost truly goes for teaching. Do students still receive subsidies in this case?

Table 3A shows the breakeven educational effort required to produce a general subsidy. For example, at least 61% of all apparent educational spending in private universities must actually go to education before a general subsidy emerges. Values below the breakeven produce negative subsidies, which imply that full-pay students are subsidizing research or other university activities, whereas they get exactly what they pay for at breakeven.

Spending three-fourths of apparent educational cost on education would put a private research university above its breakeven point. (Table 3.1 assumed that 100% of educational expenditures goes for teaching, which produces an even larger subsidy.) The same is true for public colleges and universities, but not for private colleges. Their breakeven is 98%, which means that virtually all the educational spending must go for teaching. This is a consequence of their tiny general subsidy (1%). Doubtless the selective colleges have a larger general subsidy and thus a lower breakeven point. Row 2 of the table calculates the breakeven percentage in a different way. This calculation allocates the expenditures for administration and support services in two steps: first in proportion to instruction and unfunded research versus funded research and public service, and then according to the fraction of educational cost that truly goes to education.[27] This comes closer to the way institutions actually allocate costs for purposes of federal reimbursement, but there are enough ambiguities to preclude claiming it as the only correct method. However, it appears safe to say the true breakevens fall somewhere between the two calculations, for example, at the averages presented in the table's third row.

Table 3A

Breakeven Educational Effort Required to Produce a General Subsidy

	Private		*Public*	
	Universities	*Colleges*	*Universities*	*Colleges*
Apparent educational spending	61%	98%	52%	62%
Two-step overhead allocation	74%	100%	64%	67%
Average	68%	99%	58%	65%

The breakevens can be compared with the percentage of effort faculty reported in Chapter 4 as going to research.[28] For research universities, the comparable breakeven figure is about 32% (100% minus the 68% shown in the table). Larger faculty effort percentages would indicate that students cross-subsidize research, and smaller ones that students receive subsidies. The 32% is about equal to the 30% of reported faculty research time in research universities, although more than the 19% reported for doctoral universities. For private colleges, the breakeven is 1% as compared to the 11% of reported research time at such colleges. These figures suggest that full-pay students may cross-subsidize research at private colleges. Breakeven in public universities is 42%, which is well above the aforementioned 30% reported research time in research universities and 19% in doctoral universities. Finally, the 35% breakeven for public colleges far exceeds the 14% research time in comprehensive universities.

These figures suggest that the more research-intensive private universities run close to breakeven, that liberal arts colleges may subsidize research to some extent, and that the remaining institutions do in fact subsidize full-pay students. I want to emphasize, however, that both sides of the comparisons involve gross approximations. About all one can say for sure is that the public universities do provide subsidies, whereas the picture is not clear for private institutions.

The breakeven analysis provides information about the general student subsidy, but it doesn't answer all the questions about cross subsidies. Negative general subsidies imply that education cross-subsidizes research, but do positive ones mean the cross subsidy goes the other way?

The answer depends on the intent of donors and those who provide state and local appropriations. Figure 3A brings intent into the model.[29] The vertical axes display the fraction of gift, endowment, and appropriations income intended for education, and the horizontal axes display the fraction of educational cost that actually goes there. The graph's four panels use data for private universities to highlight different aspects of the model.

The first panel depicts the student subsidy, starting with the breakeven point. The vertical dashed line at 68% on the horizontal axis represents the average breakeven figure for private universities given in row 3 of Table 3A and the narrow shaded area represents the upper and lower bounds given in rows 1 and 2. Points to the left of breakeven produce negative general subsidies and points to the right produce positive ones. The horizontal line labeled "financial aid" expresses the individually targeted subsidies as a percentage of gift, endowment, and appropriations income (GEA). Table 3.1 showed that private universities spend 30% of revenue on financial aid.[30]

Moving to panel 2, points above and to the left of the diagonals represent cross subsidies for research paid from educational funds while those below and to the right represent the opposite. It is no accident that the breakeven and financial aid lines come together at the diagonal. At this point, general income providers want to devote 30% of their money to education and that is exactly what is needed to fund financial aid. Nothing is left for other aspects of education or to fund research. Hence there can be no cross subsidy and the university must be at breakeven on the general student subsidy.

Figure 3A

A Model for Subsidies and Cross Subsidies

(Illustrated for Private Research Universities)

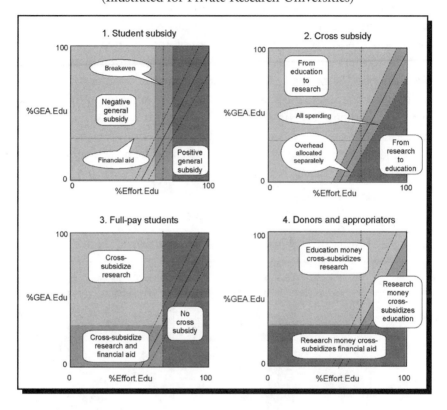

Panel 3 depicts the subsidy situation as viewed by full-pay students. Such students receive subsidies when the university operates to the right of breakeven, and because they are subsidized they can pay no cross subsidy to anyone else. Points to the left of breakeven represent negative general subsidies, so full-pay students must be cross-subsidizing someone. In the upper-left quadrant, donors and appropriators supply enough educational funds to cover financial aid. Hence one can reasonably claim that full-pay students cross-subsidize only research. Below the financial-aid line they fund scholarships for fellow students as well as research.

Panel 4 describes the subsidy situation as seen by donors and appropriators. In the upper quadrant, money intended for education turns out to cross-subsidize research. Moving downward and to the right eventually reverses the cross subsidy. Points in the rightmost quadrant represent cross subsidies from research to education (including financial aid). Points in the bottom quadrant represent subsidies to financial aid alone.

Figure 3B extends the results to all four institutional types. The patterns are similar, but the locations of the breakeven and financial aid lines, the slopes of the diagonals, and the regions of uncertainty vary.

The results paint a provocative picture of cross subsidies in universities. Suppose, for example, that private universities operate at breakeven with respect to the general student subsidy. This would mean they expend one-third of their effort on research. Donor funds would cross-subsidize research in this case if the percentage intended for education exceeds about 30%, the amount needed to cover financial aid. The percentage climbs to 44% if research drops to a quarter of effort and it climbs to 54% if

Figure 3B

The Model Applied to All Institutional Types

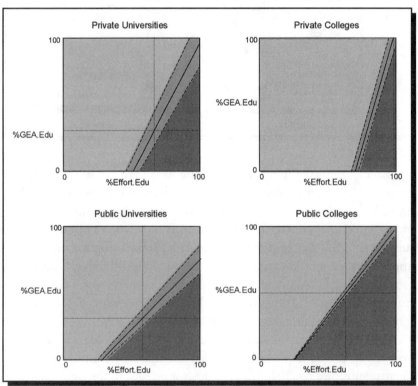

research drops to one-fifth of effort. While one can't rule out smaller percentages, these figures seem low given that they include money given for financial aid and exclude contracts and grants, and that most universities position themselves as supporting education as their central mission. It seems to me that the direction of the cross subsidies runs from education to research.

The situation is even more dramatic for the public universities. If they put a third of their effort into research, appropriators and donors will find themselves cross-subsidizing research if the percentage of GEA income intended for education exceeds about 40%. The figure climbs to 48% if research drops to one-fourth of effort, to 53% if the figure is one-fifth, and to 63% if research drops all the way to one-tenth of effort. I believe that research surely accounts for more than one-tenth of university effort and that appropriators and donors want more than 63% of their funding to go for education. This result appears to explain the widespread concerns about cross subsidies in public higher education.

In private colleges, research is unlikely to average more than a few percent of effort—so little, in fact, that the model appears to have little meaning. Research counts for more in the public colleges. At 95% effort applied to research (an absurdly large level), the model predicts that donors and appropriators would be happy if 90% of their funds were designated for education. Not surprisingly, the cross subsidy problem in the colleges doesn't seem as significant as in the universities.

In closing, let me reiterate that the figures presented are broad aggregates and that the model's results don't apply to any particular institution or the schools within any particular state. Hence they should be used with caution. On the other hand, the model could easily be applied to data for particular institutions and jurisdictions. Perhaps colleges and universities will decide to answer the questions posed by the model before their external stakeholders begin to ask them. They can estimate the fraction of effort that goes to research and the percentage of gifts, endowments, and appropriations that is intended to support education. Getting these data and debating any cross subsidies on their merits could go a long way toward clearing the air. Crude as it is, the cross subsidy model presented here can help get these issues discussed effectively.

Endnotes

1. For the rule's precise statement and derivation, see Chapter 3 of Hopkins and Massy (1981).

2. The first condition says that the university values "earlier" units of output more than later ones—for example, having 50 as opposed to no divinity students would contribute more to value than going from 200 to 250, which is surely a reasonable way to view the matter. The second condition says that getting more students requires larger tuition discounts, since the first students to enroll are the ones with greater willingness and ability to pay. The third condition, which says that each increment to output costs the same or more than the preceding one, is the most problematic. However, the assumption probably isn't violated significantly because the model deals only with the variable cost of production—not the spreading of fixed cost. Taken together, the three conditions ensure that the decision rule maximizes rather than minimizes value fulfillment.

3. The approximation assumes that net price and unit cost don't change significantly as enrollment varies by small amounts.

4. To prove the relation, simply substitute the practical decision rule's definition of contribution margin into the conceptual rule and rearrange terms. The constant k converts value units to dollar equivalents, as noted earlier.

5. Responsibility center budgeting devolves all revenue to the schools, which are free to spend as they wish subject to overhead charges and participation fees. See Whalen (1991), Massy (1996), and also Chapter 9.

6. "Change in revenue = change in cost" has the same meaning as "marginal revenue = marginal cost," which is the for-profit enterprise decision rule taught in elementary economics courses.

7. The research was mentioned in Chapter 3: Damon, et al. (2000).

8. Bartels (1993).

9. Winston (1997), in the Abstract.

10. Winston (1997), p. 1.

11. Funded research in bar (c) is larger than in bar (b) because the former includes the overhead portion of grant and contract income.

12. The table uses Gordon Winston's "global revenue" concept except for the omission of auxiliaries and the cost of capital tied up in facilities. The data come from Blasdell, McPherson, and Schapiro (1993), who developed it from government sources (mainly IPEDS).

13. Winston calculates the subsidies by deciles and analyzes their incidence by type of institution, but this refinement is beyond our scope. See Winston and Yen (1995).

14. Formal cost sharing would shift the time to funded research. However, universities resist such cost sharing because of its adverse effects on overhead recovery. In fact, most cost sharing is of the informal variety: that is, it is not separately budgeted and thus is included in instruction and unfunded research.

15. Goldman and Williams (2000), p. xii.

16. Quoted in Graham, Lyman, and Trow (1995), p. 3.

17. See Cox, et al. (2001), for a recent example that demonstrates the feasibility of such estimation.

18. National Association of College and University Business Officers (NACUBO) (2002).

19. Zemsky, et al. (1999), Chapter 2.

20. The financial aid variable includes aid for undergraduate and graduate students combined. In the selective name-brand institutions that constitute our sample, "most student aid is a discretionary expense rather than a price discount—that is, these institutions had sufficient surplus, but not enough admitted applicants who were able to pay the stated price to matriculate." Zemsky, et al. (1999), p. 55.

21. We used a type of frontier analysis called "Data Envelopment Analysis," which has been applied to colleges and universities by a number of authors with generally good results: see, for example, Ahn, Charnes, and Cooper (1989), Tomkins and Green (1988), and Beasley (1995). We defined the DEA's input variable as the costs of instruction and unfunded research, academic support, student services, library, and institutional financial aid. The output variables were the numbers of degrees and enrollments by program level (undergraduate, master's, and PhD), market position, and reputation (the *U.S. News & World Report* rankings and data from a survey of institutional presidents and other educational leaders).

22. Because some liberal arts colleges do have small graduate enrollments, we used total full-time equivalents for them in the colleges but only undergraduates in the case of research universities. The analysis allowed us to estimate the unit cost of an undergraduate degree in each research university, adjusted for selectivity and reputation.

23. Zemsky, et al. (1999), p. 66.

24. Massy and Wilger (1992).

25. Zemsky, et al. (1999), p. 67.

26. The Institute for Research on Higher Education (1997).

27. The first-step calculation takes instruction and funded research as a percentage of the first three rows of Part *b* of Table 3.1. This is roughly similar to the way universities allocate overhead to grants and contracts per federal OMB Circular A-21.

28. Based on Milem, Berger, and Dey (2000). See endnote 15 in Chapter 4 for detail.

29. The model uses the breakeven points from Table 3A and the financial aid percentages from Table 3.1 to solve for *a* and *b* in the equation for the diagonals: %GEA.Edu = $a + b$ %Effort.Edu. The resulting parameters are as follows.

	Lower bound		Average		Upper bound	
	a	b	a	b	a	b
Private universities	−0.975	0.0188	−0.938	0.0203	−0.938	0.0167
Private colleges	−2.233	0.0322	−2.416	0.0352	−2.416	0.0329
Public universities	−0.272	0.0100	−0.258	0.0108	−0.258	0.0088
Public colleges	−0.306	0.0126	−0.303	0.0130	−0.303	0.0121

30. The model assumes that financial aid gets first call on GEA funds. This is a requirement rather than an assumption when funds are restricted to financial aid. The assumption is reasonable for other funds because most universities position the spending on aid as coming from gifts and appropriations rather than tuition.

4

Research, Teaching, and the Quality of Education

M ost academics believe that research begets good teaching and that good teaching begets educational quality. This chapter examines both propositions. We'll see that research does boost educational quality, but that it's possible to have too much of a good thing. This issue is particularly important for institutions where cross subsidies run in favor of research. We'll also begin to distinguish between good teaching and the broader array of activities required for core competency in education.

Chapters 2 and 3 ended with discussions of efficiency. We saw that the concept applies to colleges and universities no less than to business firms, but that certain impediments limit its impact in universities. The imbalance between teaching and research creates a further problem. The problem stems not from the quantity and quality of inputs or the desire to perform, but rather from the goals that drive the enterprise. This chapter addresses the faculty's view of productivity. Then it reviews the teaching-research balance and the academic incentive and reward structure. It closes with some ideas about how to broaden the definition of productivity to include more of what's important for education.

HOW FACULTY VIEW PRODUCTIVITY

"Productivity" means "Having the power of producing: creative, generative, *a productive effort.*"[1] For economists, productivity adds the dimension of efficiency—the quantity and quality of output produced per unit of resource expended. Although "creative" and "generative" certainly describe a university, the academic culture expresses ambivalence about the idea of productivity. The real questions are "Producing what?" and "How should cost enter the equation?" How do faculty feel about these questions?

To answer this and other questions pertinent to this book, my research team at the National Center for Postsecondary Education (NCPI) conducted extensive interviews with 378 faculty members at eight research universities, three doctoral-granting universities, four comprehensive universities, and four liberal arts colleges.[2] Most of the interviewees were asked for their views about productivity.

While defining "productivity" did not come naturally to these respondents, the concept was not foreign to them either. Most accepted their obligation to be productive, but they did not always agree on the meaning of productivity.

> Does the word "productivity" mean anything to you?

> Yes, of course it does. But there are many gauges of productivity. As far as teaching is concerned, I don't like the word productivity because it sounds like a factory or something. Excellence in teaching is a better word ... But I think we can certainly talk about productivity in terms of one's research, how many students one produces, and things like that. (Professor, physics, research university)

> I think a measure of productivity would be one's success with publications and bringing in grants. In this setting [at the college], one might include one's success with teaching endeavors. But typically we would be thinking about research productivity. (Assistant professor, biology, liberal arts college)

> I have a very elitist opinion about productivity in higher education ... If we turn out one person per year who can do better-than-average, good research, that is a very, very important contribution to society—just that fraction, that tiny number. (Professor, physics, doctorate-granting institution)

> [Productivity] tends to refer to one's writing. That's the ordinary connotation of the word. So saying someone is a productive scholar or a productive colleague in this department means they write things. (Professor, English, research university)

Most professors believe that "productivity" is synonymous with "results," the dictionary definition. Few define it as economists do: as results per unit of input. When asked about improving productivity, they think about garnering more dollars so they can produce more results, or at least holding dollars constant and producing more. The idea of producing the same or more results with fewer dollars almost never arises spontaneously.

When professors are asked what kinds of results are important, research comes to mind most often. In fact, the quantity and quality of research represents the defining characteristic of productive behavior for many professors. Numbers of students taught comes up occasionally, though usually in the context of pejorative statements about the evils of nose counting. Excellence in teaching comes up more often, though some respondents questioned how well excellence is measured. Sometimes, as in the third example above, productivity is defined as producing a single outstanding graduate or changing a student's life.

Logically, institutional mission should dominate the faculty's definition of productive behavior. One might think the definition should include a balance of research and teaching in research universities, and that in liberal arts colleges and comprehensive universities it should stress teaching. While this is true to some extent, the NCPI research found a good deal of commonality across institutional types. Specifically, respondents at all kinds of institutions defined productivity in terms similar to the views of these research university professors.

> What does productivity mean to you?

> It means the number of articles published per year. In terms of what I've been hired to do, productivity is the number of good articles I put out in a year. (Assistant professor, economics, research university)

> Every faculty member must be productive. There's no room to have a few who aren't bringing in big grants. (Professor, chemistry, research university)

Even respondents who defined productivity partly in terms of teaching often coupled this with consideration of research. For example:

> Well, our professors score very high on student evaluations. We have a good track record of students going on to good graduate programs... As for our research productivity, we have a very good record in both applied and basic research: The people in the public administration area have produced a number of manuals and reports that are used by state agencies, and the people in the more basic area of research have published in the best journals in the discipline. As a department, we have produced a number of books published by reputable publishers, and done well in outside evaluations of the department. (Professor, political science, comprehensive university)

Notice, too, that the definition of teaching productivity refers to student evaluations and the record of students going on to graduate school. Neither addresses the modern requirements, described in later chapters, for core competency in education.

The tuition payers and government agencies that provide higher education's core funding usually view education quality as their highest priority, but almost three times as many quotations in the NCPI database deal with the centrality of research as with the importance of teaching. We observed a fundamental tension between the philosophy of faculty and the stated goals of mass public higher education, for example, in this argument for the classical faculty value system:

> I think the state should support a university as a center of intellectual activity. It shouldn't just concentrate on how many courses somebody teaches. It should concentrate on the nature of the entire intellectual activity that's going on in the area. I think our university does a lot more in society than educate kids. It plays a role in society that's greater than education. (Professor, physics, research university)

Most external stakeholders would agree with these sentiments in broad terms, but they want to hold universities accountable for productivity in education as well as research and public service.

Why do most professors define productivity in terms of research? Because that's where the rewards are. Intrinsic motivations and institutional rewards combine to drive professors' preoccupation with research.

Research is inherently satisfying. Moreover, successful research leads to publication, and publications produce rewards within and outside the institution. Rewards like tenure, salary increments, and recognition join with the joy of discovery in driving the research-based definition of "productive behavior."

The NCPI interviews confirm that professors try to use their own time and other departmental resources as productively as possible. For example:

> Everyone is interested in productivity around here. We're trying to cope with the paper onslaught, the electronic onslaught—making the department more productive, spending more time on things that are really creative. (Professor, physics, research university)

Professors leverage their time with graduate student assistants, with secretaries and technicians, and, in some cases, with technology. Indeed, some of the pressures on departmental budgets come from faculty seeking resources to leverage their time more effectively. Just as in allocating their own time, professors spend departmental discretionary funds—which can be used for things like equipment, supplies, and travel—as effectively as possible.

The efforts to economize take different forms in teaching and research. Professors do not hesitate to reengineer research processes when new ideas and technologies come along. Computers and electronic communication aids, for example, have been quickly assimilated. Professors are quick to form research partnerships—both within their own departments and with colleagues at other institutions—in order to maximize research performance. They often do more with less in research: boosting the output from particular tasks while simultaneously cutting their costs. Most of our faculty respondents believe in doing whatever is necessary to maximize research productivity. In the words of the quality movement, professors strive to continuously improve their research performance and they reengineer their approach to research whenever necessary.

Reengineering and continuous improvement are far less common in teaching. Professors understand how to do more with more, for example, and if necessary they will do less with less. But they usually can't imagine doing more with less. By default, research improvement becomes the main tool by which professors and institutions try to boost education quality.

PRODUCTIVITY FROM AN EDUCATIONAL PERSPECTIVE

At a common sense level, educational productivity must reflect both numbers and quality. For example, teaching more students at dramatically lower quality levels will reduce productivity. But how should one define "quality"? Does it mean graduates who demonstrate higher levels of knowledge and skill? Not necessarily, since this could reflect lackluster educational performance following on highly selective admissions. Educational quality should reflect the amount and relevance of learning that actually takes place within the institution. Economists call this value added. Creating value added represents the essence of educational competency.

Value added can be parsed into two components. "Value" implies benefit for the student, while "added" implies a cause-effect relation between the educational experience and the value achieved. Value added requires what quality gurus call "fitness for purpose"—that the education be tailored to student needs. What should a student who successfully completes the course or program know and be able to do, for example? How does the course or program build on the student's prior knowledge and capability? How will it contribute to the student's future employment opportunities, capacity to make social contributions, and quality of life? All this applies to the students actually being taught, not some ideal student with the same values and mental capacity as the faculty. And, as noted above, the value needs to be produced in the institution itself, not brought in via admissions selectivity. Selective admissions may broaden the options available to produce value, but they provide no excuse for easing up because the graduates will do well in any case.

Educational productivity means value added for all or at least most of a program's students. Producing a future scientist or professor is fine, but this should not overshadow the need to serve the broader student population. Professors should research the needs of their students and translate the knowledge into curricular design. They should study their students' learning capacities and styles, and design educational processes accordingly. This is particularly important for disadvantaged students. "Leaving no one behind" should be a key goal of educational competency.

But value added isn't the only thing. Educational productivity also includes an efficiency dimension. Formally, this translates to "value added per unit of resource expended." Boosting value added without spending more would improve productivity, for example, and maintaining value added while spending less would do the same. (Spending less allows resources to be deployed elsewhere, which boosts value added overall.) Adding the efficiency dimension means that faculty bear a responsibility for cost as well as quality. How they can discharge this responsibility will be taken up in Chapter 8.

DOES RESEARCH ENHANCE EDUCATION?

Most professors believe that research is a necessary condition for educational quality, and many believe that it's a sufficient condition as well. Neither the NCPI interviews nor my experience as a Stanford professor and vice provost for research casts any doubt on the proposition that research contributes to educational quality. However, it is possible to have too much of a good thing. For many institutions, the balance between research and education has tilted too far toward research. To understand why, we need to examine the contribution of research to teaching and how it can hurt as well as help the undergraduate educational experience.

The standard of accomplishment for students achieving an undergraduate degree provides a good place to start. Responding to worldwide demand to define the meaning of bachelors, masters, and doctoral degrees, the UK Quality Assurance Agency for Higher Education recently developed a "National Qualification Framework." The Framework includes the following statements:

> *Bachelor's degrees with honours* [the most common undergraduate degree in the UK] are awarded to students . . . who have demonstrated a systematic understanding of *key aspects of their field* of study, including acquisition of coherent and detailed knowledge, *at least some of which* is at, or informed by the forefront of defined aspects of a discipline.

> *Master's degrees* are awarded to students who have demonstrated . . . a systematic awareness of knowledge, and a critical awareness of current problems and/or new insights, *much of which* is at, or informed by, the forefront of their academic discipline, field of study, or area of professional practice.[3]

The statements illustrate the role of research in undergraduate education: important but not dominant. Fitness for purpose requires that faculty select and utilize research materials according to student need, preparation, interest, and learning ability. State-of-the-art knowledge is important only some of the time, and traditional disciplinary standards may be less important than detailed knowledge about one's students.

Figure 4.1, also from the UK Quality Assurance Agency, illustrates how departments can accomplish the above. In economics, for example, an instructor might engage students on how to abstract essential features from complex systems as well as teaching the conventional content of economic theory. Such skills may be more important for most undergraduates than the theoretical formalities, yet they often are viewed as byproducts to be discovered by the students themselves instead of central educational objectives.

Figure 4.1

Excerpts from the UK's Economics, Philosophy, and Biology Benchmark Statements

Economics. From the study of economic principles and models, students see how one can abstract the essential features of complex systems and provide a usable framework for evaluation and assessment of the effects of policy or other exogenous events. Through this, the typical student will acquire proficiency in how to simplify while retaining relevance. This is an approach that they can then apply in other contexts, thereby becoming more effective problem-solvers and decision makers.

Philosophy. [Students will acquire the] ability to recognize methodological errors, rhetorical devices, unexamined conventional wisdom, unnoticed assumptions, vagueness and superficiality.

Biology. [The biologist learns to] interpret data from living systems, in which many variables cannot be held constant. That skill is readily applicable to decision making in work environments that are dynamic, with many variables that are changing simultaneously.

Source: The Quality Assurance Agency for Higher Education, UK

Professors often cite the direct involvement of undergraduates in research as an important benefit for undergraduate teaching. But while such involvement is valuable for students who get to work closely with faculty, the numbers invariably are small. First, many students aren't very interested in research and would rather spend their time taking advantage of other learning resources. This doesn't represent laziness, but rather a different kind of motivation, for example, a desire for development other than that leading to an academic or scientific career. Second, real undergraduate research involvement is time-consuming for professors as well as students. Graduate students are much more productive, so they get the lion's share of faculty attention in doctorate-granting universities. Much undergraduate research involvement turns out to involve relatively routine or even menial tasks, like crunching numbers or running rats through mazes, that have limited educational value.

Research also benefits education in other ways. Consider what happens as one successfully injects research into a department without prior research or scholarly prowess, for example. The first step usually involves hiring recent PhDs: people who have been trained in research and who are up to date on the latest thinking in their fields.[4] The new assistant professors write papers and begin to put the department on the research map. They also revitalize the department's education programs by injecting new energy and new course content. They stimulate existing faculty members and they provide students with new kinds of mentors and role models.

Having a core group of published researchers makes it easier to attract better faculty at both the junior and senior ranks, so over time the average quality of the faculty as measured by talent and performance will tend to increase. The new professors compete successfully for grants and contracts that further the research program and contribute to the university's fixed costs through overhead recovery. Better faculty, more publications, and generous sponsored research funding build institutional prestige, and prestige boosts gift receipts and the quality and quantity of admission applications. More money and better students allow professors to further enhance the school's educational programs and reputation. Unfortunately, however, these benefits are not costless. Eventually they come at the expense of time and effort that otherwise would be devoted to educating undergraduates.

THE ACADEMIC RATCHET

Faculty time represents the university's most important asset, and time pressures escalate as research becomes more and more central to a department's value system. We saw how the first increments of research and scholarship can energize previously unproductive faculty time. However, there are only so many hours in a day and even the most highly motivated professors have finite amounts of energy. Therefore, increases in research activity will, sooner or later, come at the expense of time devoted to educational tasks.

Time substitution does not diminish teaching quality immediately. Research enables professors to "work smarter"—to accomplish more with the time they do spend on teaching. Professors report many examples of how research enhances curricular content, and research-oriented teachers bring more "presence" to the classroom. Yet time on task does matter. For example, consider the time spent preparing lectures, developing classroom and presentation material, grading and providing feedback on exams and papers, and meeting or emailing students to discuss their work. These are time-consuming activities, especially when done well, and they compete directly with the demands of research. The same is true for activities like advising, mentoring, and tutoring. As researchers Albert Hood and Catherine Arceneaux have said, "Student services developed because faculty involvement in the development of the whole student declined as emphasis on research and knowledge creation increased."[5] The "long shadow"[6] cast by research on undergraduate education refers to such substitutions writ large.

Figure 4.2 depicts what happens as research demands squeeze time from educational tasks.[7] Improvements in research increase the quality of education as indicated by the curve's initial upward slope. An economist would say that research complements the production of education. ("Complement" denotes positive synergies.) However, increases in the amount of research also draw faculty time away from educational tasks. Hence the curve rises less steeply and eventually becomes horizontal. Beyond this point the extra time lost is more important than the extra synergies, so greater research intensity actually reduces education quality. Economists would say that research increments substitute for educational quality in this part of the diagram.

The gray dot depicts a situation where research and teaching are complements on average but substitutes at the margin. The quality of education is better with the indicated amount of research than it would be with none, but increments to research reduce educational quality. It's hard to determine a given department's position on the curve, but there's no reason to believe that universities always, or even usually, operate in the upward-sloping range where more research improves education quality. In fact, the typical research-oriented department seems to operate somewhere near the gray dot, that is, in the region of substitution. It appears that liberal arts colleges and some comprehensive universities operate in the region of complementarity, but that may not persist given the pressures to increase research.

Figure 4.2

The Teaching-Research Tradeoff

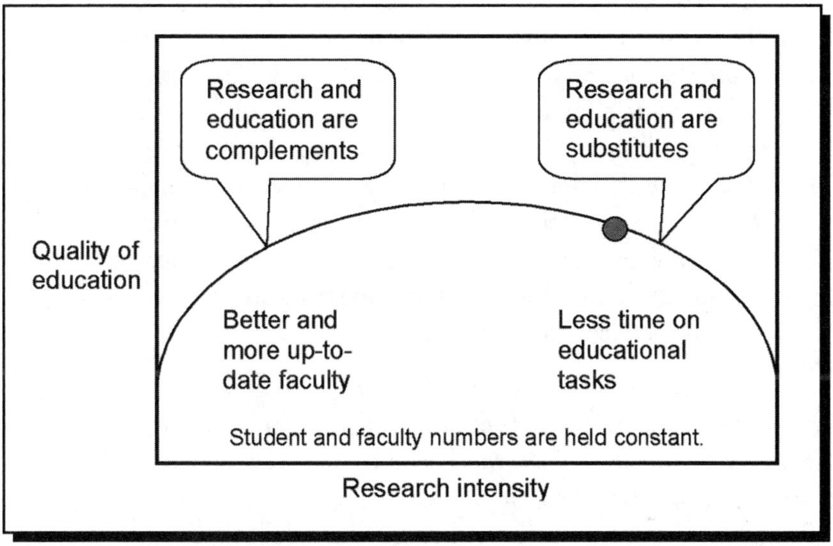

Robert Zemsky and I have described how the so-called academic ratchet pushes an institution inexorably rightward in Figure 4.2.

> *The academic ratchet.* A term to describe the steady, irreversible shift of faculty allegiance away from the goals of a given institution, toward those of an academic specialty. The ratchet denotes the advance of an independent, entrepreneurial spirit among faculty nationwide, leading to increased emphasis on research and on publication and on teaching one's specialty in favor of general introduction courses, often at the expense of coherence in an academic curriculum. Institutions seeking to enhance their own prestige may contribute to the ratchet effect by reducing faculty teaching and advising responsibilities across the board, thus enabling faculty to pursue

their individual research and publication with fewer distractions. The academic ratchet raises an institution's costs, and it results in undergraduates paying more to attend institutions in which they receive less faculty attention than in previous decades.[8]

An article in *The Chronicle of Higher Education* cites this continuing evidence that the ratchet continues to click away.

> The bar for tenure is rising at major research universities and teaching institutions alike. Most departments demand more published research—either articles or books, or both. Some institutions even accelerate the whole procedure, sizing up young scholars years before tenure time and showing them the door if it looks like they won't eventually measure up.... The most significant change, people say, is the overwhelming pressure to publish early and publish frequently. At some institutions, that shift has come at the expense of teaching and service, professors say.[9]

The ratchet mechanism depends on departmental norms: that is, on strongly held, shared beliefs about professors' relations with their colleagues and institution.[10] Norms become embedded in departmental routines and are mostly taken for granted by the individuals involved.[11] Deviations from norms are subject to simple rules of appropriateness based on past experience and comparisons with accepted behavior in similar organizations.[12] For example, professors will accept a certain range of teaching loads, but larger loads require a quid pro quo like summer salary or time off in a subsequent semester. Similar norms operate in the areas of class preparation and grading, advising and mentoring, and systematic work on improving and assuring education quality. Unfortunately, the norm for the latter currently is rather low.

The ratchet's dynamic property stems from an asymmetry in professors' reactions to deviations from the norms.[13] Deviations in the wrong direction trigger concern or even active opposition, so chairs and program directors minimize them to the extent possible. Favorable deviations are welcomed whenever resources permit. They trigger envy and emulation if their occurrence becomes widespread and visible, for example, "She got teaching relief in order to do research, but what about me?" Favorable deviations will become enacted as new norms if they occur frequently enough, such as "the teaching norm for all researchers now is two courses a semester instead of three" or "researchers can teach one course each semester in their specialties." Enactment of a new norm means the ratchet has clicked over. Then process starts again from the new, more favorable level. The result is a steady drift of the norms in directions viewed as desirable by faculty, that is, directions that further research.

The speed of drift depends on the amount of energy in the system. "Energy" reflects the passion of faculty to do research. Departments add energy when they hire faculty with strong research talent and provide powerful rewards for publishing and getting grants. Institutions' quest for prestige and the fact that virtually all PhD programs stress research have boosted energy levels enormously during the last 40 years. More energy means more pressure to move rightward in Figure 4.2.

How fast the ratchet clicks also depends on the availability of discretionary resources. More resources allow administrators to satisfy professors' desires more frequently, which accelerates the enactment of new norms. For example, enlarging the faculty roster spreads teaching responsibilities over more professors and thus reduces teaching loads. Adding student services professionals can relieve faculty workloads in advising and student life.[14] It's easier to add faculty and support staff when resources are plentiful. Over time, higher education's market power has generated enough new money to power the ratchet.

The NCPI faculty interviews show that professors usually find ways to protect their research time, even at the expense of cutting corners in undergraduate education when resources become scarce. For example:

> Yes, class sizes have increased a lot. We have eliminated all undergraduate seminars. We have a couple of optional lab classes, but those are only small classes we have left. Our average undergraduate class size last fall was 125. I go over and over this and nobody disputes the numbers. [What about educational quality?] Crummy. Let me back up. It's not all crummy. We have some wonderful teachers. But how much can you do with that kind of class size... When I first came here, a lot more classes had papers and essay exams and people have just had to eliminate, eliminate, eliminate because how can we possibly do all this. So there are many more

classes with multiple-choice exams and very little writing. (Professor, psychology, research university)

Class sizes have increased dramatically. In this department, we've managed to keep upper division class sizes somewhat manageable. They've increased but I'd say by about 25% to 30%. But the lower division classes, the introductory classes have in some cases doubled or tripled in size. And now we have classes that are over 100, close to 200 in some cases. And that is new for us... Well, it's hard to argue that a class with 150 or 175 is as good as a class with 50 or 75. We give more multiple-choice type of tests than we used to. And assigning a paper is impossible in some cases. But we really don't have much choice. The state won't give us money for additional faculty. We're in a bind. (Professor, philosophy, doctoral granting institution)

Two conclusions emerge from these commentaries. First, professors don't like to shortchange educational quality by increasing class size or cutting the amount of feedback given to students, but they will do so if the alternative is heavier teaching loads or more time spent on grading. Such responses should come as no surprise given the faculty's intrinsic sense of priorities and the academic incentive and reward structure. Second, university administrators seem oblivious to these quality degradations. Our respondents didn't describe pointed discussions with chairs, deans, and provosts about larger class sizes or multiple-choice examinations, and the literature fails to report much internal accountability for even these rather rudimentary drivers of education quality. No wonder external constituents are concerned about the academy's quality assurance processes.

Quantitative data on the effects of the ratchet are scarce, but some information does exist. For example, researchers Jeffrey Milem, Joseph Berger, and Eric Dey report "a general and [statistically] significant increase in time spent engaged in research at all four-year institutions" over the 20 years ending in 1992. Furthermore:

Faculty at research universities report the greatest amount of time spent in research, followed by faculty at doctoral universities, comprehensive universities, liberal arts colleges, and two-year colleges. Though faculty at research universities maintained their "advantage" in the time they report allocating to research, the gap is closed somewhat between them and the faculty at doctoral institutions. The greatest proportional change between 1971 and 1989/92 was seen at the comprehensive universities and doctoral universities (20% and 15%, respectively).[15]

My rough calculations based on these data suggest that research accounts for about 30% of the time reported by faculty at research universities, about 19% at doctoral universities, 14% at comprehensive universities, and 11% at liberal arts colleges.[16]

Additional evidence for the ratchet comes from Zemsky's and my model of how faculty view deviations from teaching load and class size norms.[17] We documented quantitatively what many would consider a common-sense conclusion: Professors bias their planning so that, when enrollments become known, class sizes and teaching loads are more likely to be below the norms than above them. Perhaps more compelling are the reactions of experts on faculty behavior. For example, when asked whether verification of the ratchet phenomenon should be a prime goal of the NCPI faculty interview project, our advisory committee unanimously recommended that we not dwell on that question because the ratchet's existence was obvious.[18] (We asked questions about the ratchet anyway and did get the expected corroboration.)

Few informed commentators now question the proposition that the rightward pressure depicted in Figure 4.2 becomes self-reinforcing once research has become a significant priority. This is happening in all kinds of institutions. For example, the NCPI interviews unearthed ratchet-based behavior at comprehensive universities and liberal arts colleges as well as at research and doctoral-granting universities. One can argue about where a given department sits on the curve and how far over the top the most extreme departments in the research-intensive universities have gone, but there is no doubt about the pervasive pressure to boost research. To reiterate, the ratchet's steady, irreversible shift of faculty effort toward research and scholarship is occurring at all kinds of four-year institutions, not just at doctorate-granting schools. At best this inhibits the improvement of core educational competency; at worst it represents a corrosive force.

INCENTIVES AND REWARDS

With a nearly-unanimous voice, the NCPI faculty respondents stressed the importance of research in hiring, tenure, promotion, and salary decisions. Even at liberal arts institutions that have tried to emphasize undergraduate education, professors still view research as the activity their institution rewards the most. Many respondents reported that their institutions define "research" almost solely in terms of external funding and number of publications. One summed the situation up this way: "I would not criticize a faculty member who comes here and devotes his time to research. That's sensible. He's doing the job we're paying him to do."

Statistical analysis of the NCPI survey data produce the results shown in Figure 4.3.[19] Not surprisingly, more than 90% of faculty cite tenure and promotion as their number-one priority. Salary and merit increases come next, followed closely by release time/sabbatical. We know that tenure and promotion are dominated by research in most institutions, and research surely is important for salary setting as well. Release time/sabbatical benefits all aspects of faculty life, not the least research, and startup funds are more likely to further research than teaching. These three incentives are cited particularly often by faculty in research universities, which

Figure 4.3

Percentage of Faculty Reporting
Reward or Incentive as Important

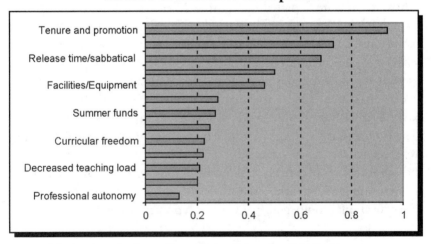

Source: The Institute for Research on Higher Education (2000), Chart 1

reinforces their relevance for research. However, faculty in liberal arts colleges and doctorate-granting and comprehensive institutions also cite them more often than most other items. They cite facilities/equipment, travel/conferences, and summer funds more often than their brethren in research universities—probably because the latter get these from their grants instead of their institutions. Again not surprisingly, the research university faculty mention working with students only one-sixth as often as liberal arts faculty and only one-third as often as faculty in doctorate-granting and comprehensive universities.

These figures confirm the great importance of research in the professorial reward and incentive system. Liberal arts colleges present the lone exception, and it is only a partial one. Almost 60% of liberal arts faculty cite working with students as an important reward or incentive, a figure that is exceeded for these faculty only by tenure/promotion, salary and merit increases, and release time/sabbatical. Faculty in other institutional types cite research-related incentives and rewards more often than, say, working with students. No wonder, then, that the academic ratchet clicks steadily along.

While most institutions in the NCPI sample have mounted initiatives to re-emphasize the importance of undergraduate teaching, professors remain skeptical. Our respondents reported no real changes in the reward system as a result of these initiatives. One respondent related the painful lesson he had learned when denied tenure at his first institution—a school ostensibly committed to undergraduate education. Because his undergraduate teaching efforts went unrewarded before, he now concentrates almost exclusively on research as he works for tenure. He pointed out that teaching awards which carry bonuses or small salary increments are just a few "prizes for people at the top" and "give virtually no incentive for most people to do better." Many respondents echoed the thought that success in teaching usually goes unrewarded. For example, a former department chair told us that, with one exception, all the faculty in his department who had won major teaching awards were below the 50th percentile of the departmental salary scale.

All this reflects what has become a common theme in the academic literature: Research, not teaching, gets the lion's share of the rewards conferred by institutions and colleagues, and that these incentives and rewards are not necessarily consistent with the institution's mission.[20]

There are two kinds of rewards: intrinsic and extrinsic. Intrinsic rewards stem from the professor's own value system—psychological pay-offs based on what he or she thinks is important or enjoys doing. Extrinsic rewards are conferred by others. Such rewards may be financial in nature, as in salary increases, or intangible as in acts of private or public recognition. Intrinsic rewards are very important for university professors.[21] Many professors consider academe as a "calling" rather than a way to make money, a fact that is reflected in the relatively low salary levels that persist in many nonelite colleges and universities. Some authors go so far as to say that extrinsic rewards, especially financial ones, may "cheapen" the activity in question and thus undermine the efficacy of intrinsic rewards.[22] Others argue that extrinsic rewards do not necessarily undermine intrinsic motivation, but that fears about being manipulated and resistance to the intrusive measurement regimens that often accompany extrinsic reward systems may well do so.[23] In most cases, though, faculty respond to both kinds of rewards.

Figure 4.4 describes how the attributes of research and teaching drive the faculty incentive and reward system. Research offers positive intrinsic rewards, such as new, challenging experiences and the joy of discovery. (Plus signs indicate that professors are motivated to spend more time and effort.) The majority of our faculty respondents cited such values—in fact, they represent the reasons why most of today's professors got a PhD and entered academic life in the first place. Research also produces outputs that can be peer reviewed, and favorable reviews confer financial and non-financial rewards that are highly valued by faculty.

Being principal investigator on a grant also confers important perquisites like independence, a reduced teaching load, and money to pay one's summer salary, support graduate students, travel, and buy equipment. Academics pooh pooh the idea of bonuses, but successful grants-manship usually confers a "bonus" in the range of one-ninth to three-ninths of base salary for doing what one would like to do anyway during the summer.

Compare these with the rewards for teaching. Many respondents cited the joy of working with students and the thrill of shaping young minds. Beyond that it's hard to find compelling rewards. Professors don't like negative teaching ratings, and they will expend a reasonable amount of effort to avoid them. However, the possibility of negative ratings is an issue only for a minority, and the ratings tend to be discounted in any case. While

Figure 4.4

Faculty Incentives and Rewards

	Intrinsic drivers	Extrinsic drivers
For research	+ Intellectually challenging work + The joy of discovery + Travel and working with colleagues	+ Outputs that can be peer reviewed provide the basis for internal rewards and external market value + Money and perquisites that come with grants
For teaching	+ Working with students, shaping young minds – Dull and repetitive work	+ Avoidance of poor teaching ratings and student problems and complaints + The occasional teaching award
– Inadequate measures of educational performance		

rating systems have become ubiquitous and are now generally accepted by professors, they do little to motivate the pursuit of excellence in teaching. Most professors support the idea of teaching awards, but they are skeptical about their effects on behavior. Some respondents characterized teaching awards as "the kiss of death" for assistant professors: The correlation with gaining tenure is negative, perhaps because the winners put so much time into their teaching.

Respondents also cited some negative aspects of teaching. One is dull and repetitive work, such as preparing to present material one has presented many times before, grading, office hours, and emails back and forth with students. Another is the lack of truly effective measures of educational performance. The literature on incentives shows that motivation depends on one's ability to form reasonable expectations about the effects of effort on performance.[24] Forming such expectations requires feedback, but few professors can gauge what happens to learning when they commit more effort. This undermines the intrinsic rewards associated with such commitments and blocks the application of most extrinsic rewards as well; hence, this item spans both columns of the table. This contrasts with the clear effects of research effort on performance.

Broadening the Definition of "Research"

The disparity in rewards between research and teaching wouldn't matter so much if the academy defined "research" more broadly. A broader definition would tighten the linkage between research and educational competency. It would stretch the curve in Figure 4.2, thus extending the range of complementarity between teaching and research.

Ernest Boyer proposed just such a broadening in his influential book *Scholarship Reconsidered.*[25] The book and its sequel, *Scholarship Assessed,*[26] identified four distinct types of scholarship: the scholarship of discovery (traditional research), the scholarship of integration, the scholarship of engagement (originally known as the scholarship of application), and the scholarship of teaching. The books argue that the typical research agenda is too narrow, that a disproportionate focus on the scholarship of discovery inhibits progress in the other three areas. The other areas are not only important in their own right, they also offer great promise for the improvement of undergraduate education.

Figure 4.5 depicts how the four types of scholarship interact to produce different kinds of knowledge.[27] The scholarship of discovery (research) develops new theories and facts, that is, new ways of understanding the world. Such results often take the form of "abstract analytical knowledge"—powerful concepts, but ones that are difficult for students and other nonexperts to grasp. The scholarship of engagement applies research findings to real-world problems. In addition to producing practical results, such "active practice" brings the abstract analytical knowledge down to earth so broader audiences can understand it. The scholarship of integration provides reflective observations on both basic and applied research. In addition to their intrinsic value, such reflections can translate abstract, analytical, and highly specialized research reports into more accessible language and provide the context and perspective needed for broad understanding.

The scholarship of teaching, and teaching itself, should draw heavily on the other three kinds of scholarship. Because the scholarship of discovery looms so large in the academic mind, however, teaching has focused disproportionately on abstract analytical knowledge. A broadened scholarship would bring more reflective observation to the teaching agenda. It would place more emphasis on active practice, which is directly relevant to many fields and can provide contextual examples for others. Active

Figure 4.5

The Four Kinds of Scholarship

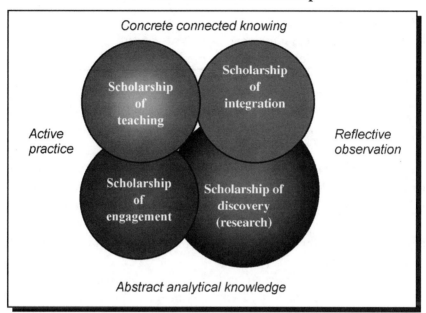

practice also reflects "concrete connected knowledge," which means more to many students than the abstract analytical knowledge of traditional research.

A broader view of scholarship also would benefit undergraduate education in other ways. For example, the scholarship of teaching includes research and development on new teaching and learning methods and assessment instruments that can inform such work. The scholarship of integration—for example, writings that sum up and interpret available knowledge and current issues in a particular field—can inform the development of curricula and be assigned as student readings. Such writings counterbalance the tendency toward specialization and the problems it poses for undergraduates. The scholarship of engagement gets faculty into real-world problem solving. University technology transfer programs facilitate the scholarship of engagement, as do case-writing projects and many kinds of public service assignments. Such experiences help faculty design teaching programs and connect the students' education to the real world.

Last but not least, a broadened scholarship would bring faculty incentives more in line with the needs of undergraduate education. Faculty time spent on the three new categories of scholarship would be more directly relevant to education. Spending too much time on scholarship would still hurt, but the crossover point would be moved outward.

While the broadening of scholarship has attracted much attention, traditional research still holds sway on most campuses. First, the specialization represented by the scholarship of discovery remains deeply rooted in disciplinary norms. Each specialty develops a set of terms—a code, so to speak—that is largely undecipherable outside the specialty.[28] It's hard to work at the state of the art without using the code. Moreover, peer review relies upon and enforces the code. It is dangerous to drop the code and write articles and books for nonexperts, even though the nonexpert audience is most relevant for the scholarships of integration, engagement, and teaching. As a result, even the best publications outside the traditional research realm tend to be discounted for purposes of promotion, tenure, and salary setting.

The scholarship of integration is further disadvantaged by the academy's narrow view of "novelty." Exemplary integrative works often are discounted because they contain "nothing new"—because each item of covered material was previously published in traditional research reports. Reviewers don't recognize that integrative works should be judged according to whether the whole is novel, not whether the individual parts are new. The scholarship of engagement suffers from the same bias because applying knowledge to practical problems usually means relying on basic research that has already been published. The application may be intellectually challenging and the results may be very important, but since practitioners who can attest to its novelty and importance rarely are represented on peer review councils, the traditional criteria hold sway.

The scholarship of teaching also suffers from the academy's narrow view of novelty, but confusion about whether such scholarship is synonymous with the teaching and the development of educational materials has proved to be an even greater difficulty. Critics argued that if the scholarship of teaching equals teaching, then nearly everything professors do should be counted as scholarship—in which case the definition of scholarship would be weakened beyond all recognition.

Pat Hutchings and Lee Shulman recently clarified matters.[29] According to the new definition, all scholarship must address an important problem or issue and produce generalizable results that can be made public and reviewed by peers. In particular:

> A scholarship of teaching will entail a public account of some or all of the full act of teaching—vision, design, enactment, outcomes, and analysis—in a manner susceptible to critical review by the teacher's professional peers and amenable to productive employment in future work by members of that same community.[30]

They go on to say that the act of teaching is neither public nor generalizable, does not advance the field, and is rarely reviewed by peers. The act of teaching depends on scholarship, but it is not scholarship. In their words, "The scholarship of teaching requires a kind of 'going meta,' in which professors frame and systematically investigate questions related to student learning."[31] The ability to generalize is the *sine qua non* of all scholarship, including the scholarship of teaching.

MOTIVATING EDUCATIONAL COMPETENCY

For 50 years now, the academic ratchet has been compressing the amount of time professors spend on educational tasks and specialization has been making research less relevant to the needs of most undergraduates. Broadening the definition of research can mitigate the latter problem, but that won't arrest the ratchet.

Unfortunately, efforts to improve the incentives and rewards associated with good teaching have proved insufficient to counterbalance the rewards for research. The disparities discussed in earlier sections make me pessimistic about finding a magic bullet that will make teaching as attractive as research. Improving educational competency will require a new approach. The action program introduced in Chapter 1 and elaborated in Chapter 11 presents just such an approach. While the program's underpinnings have yet to be presented, enough can be said now to demonstrate its effects on incentives.

The program centers on the processes by which institutions and faculty improve and assure education quality—what in Chapter 6 we will dub "education quality processes." Such processes apply the faculty's talent and expertise to build their institution's "local capital" in education. They include determining student needs and learning styles, designing better curricula and learning processes, developing and using learning assessment measures, and assuring that teaching gets its fair share of faculty attention despite distractions and competing priorities.

Quality process work falls between the scholarship of teaching and teaching itself. It guides and motivates the teaching function, but it is not teaching. Quality processes draw upon and in some cases contribute to the scholarship of teaching, but the results need not be generalizable enough to qualify as scholarship. Such processes aim to build local intellectual capital rather than that of a field or discipline. Producing publishable results represents a bonus, but what really matters are the benefits to department and institution. When done well, quality processes make the university a learning organization with respect to educational competency.

Quality process work does share some important attributes with scholarship, however. It results in documents, designs, measuring instruments, computer programs, and other artifacts that can be disseminated and reviewed by peers. It can be done collaboratively with colleagues, who thus will gain visibility about one's work. (In contrast, the act of teaching is perishable and usually done in isolation from colleagues.) The work products and collegial visibility enable the concrete feedback that is so important for intrinsic motivation. They also demonstrate a professor's performance and can be considered systematically in promotion/tenure and in dispensing the other rewards and incentives listed in Figure 4.3. Looking externally, one can imagine a growing market for professors with exemplary quality process experience as departments strive to improve their educational competency. This would boost the legitimacy of such work and provide further incentives for good performance.

These contributions to institutional capital definitely should be reflected in salary setting. Failure to do so sends a strong signal that the institution doesn't care about educational competency. Some of the categories cited less frequently in Figure 4.3—for example, summer support, graduate assistants, internal grants, and travel to conferences to present results—also present prime reward and incentive opportunities. When Frank Turner was provost at Yale University, he reminded me how few such dollars it takes to provide incentives in the humanities and other areas lacking sponsored research support—even at an affluent research university. More money will be required in well-funded disciplines, but even here some faculty can be moved with relatively few institutional dollars.

Figure 4.6 positions improved educational competency within the broader system that animates academic behavior. Work on education quality processes represents the desired behavior for purposes of this discussion, although improved cost consciousness and the introduction of paradigm-changing technology could well have been included. Presidents, provosts, governing boards, and external agencies can press for improved competency, partly by arm-twisting and partly by revising the reward and incentive environment. Intrinsic rewards also are important, as is success in the marketplace.

Figure 4.6

Motivators of Improved Educational Competency

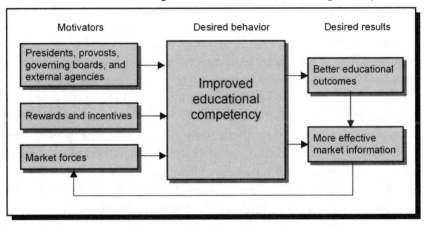

Improved educational competency will produce better outcomes. Students will be served more effectively and the public objectives of higher education will be advanced. But that is not all. Because educational competency includes an ability to assess student learning, better performance databases are likely to develop. Once it becomes known that departments and institutions routinely collect data on educational value added, ways will be found to get at least some of this information into the public domain. Suppose *Peterson's Guides, U.S. News & World Report,* and other media began publishing this kind of information, for example. Institutions with a good story to tell would soon cooperate, and laggard institutions eventually would be pressured to follow. Better information would enable applicants to consider educational performance along with price, prestige, and other factors, and governing board members would press their institution to do better even if prestige currently protected its selection ratio. In the language of Chapter 2, the market would become more efficient.

Unfortunately, the operation of markets presents us with a chicken–egg problem. Markets can't motivate improvement without good information, yet getting the information depends on having gotten improvement in the first place. The traditional behavioral patterns, which do not include much emphasis on quality processes, depend on a system of internal and external values and incentives that reinforces the status quo. Market forces can help change the incentives once quality process work has gained a foothold, but they have proved insufficient to start the process. That's why presidents, provosts, governing boards, and external agencies need to become proactive in stimulating the educational competency agenda.

Such efforts should address professors, department chairs, and deans as partners, not as adversaries. The improved quality processes need to be embedded in the institution's ongoing routines, not imposed through top-down accountability. Experience shows that once work on quality processes has been legitimized, significant numbers of professors will step forward to embrace it. I have heard professors say, "At last someone cares." They are willing to invest time in competency improvement even if this means taking some time away from research. These may not be the research stars, but that doesn't matter. As long as a critical mass of faculty are willing to invest, and the necessary rewards are forthcoming, the job will get done.

Endnotes

1. *Random House Dictionary of the English Language,* second edition unabridged (New York: Random House, 1987): definition of "productive," of which "productivity" is the adverbial form.

2. The sample included faculty from a subset of the 19 institutions for which we had significant amounts of curricular data, as well as doctorate-granting and comprehensive institutions selected randomly from the *1988 Higher Education Directory.* Departments were selected from the set of departments that formed the core of undergraduate education in the arts, sciences, business, and engineering within each institution. Department chairs were asked to identify a balanced group of faculty at the assistant, associate, and full professor levels, without regard to their performance or views. All quotes and data from "NCPI faculty interviews" reported in the book come from this sample. Much of the

material about productivity was first published in Massy and Wilger (1995), pp. 11–15.

3. Randall (2001), p. 54, emphasis added.

4. Sometimes a school will recruit an established faculty member to build its research program, but the chronic overproduction of PhDs usually makes it easier to hire junior people than established researchers. See Goldman and Massy (2001) for documentation of the overproduction of PhDs in science and engineering. The situation tends to be even worse in the humanities and social sciences.

5. Hood and Arceneaux (1990), pp. 17–18.

6. Glassick, Huber, and Maeroff (1997), p. 8.

7. Adapted from Nerlov (1972).

8. Zemsky and Massy (1990), p. 22.

9. *The Chronicle of Higher Education,* "A Higher Bar for Earning Tenure" (January 5, 2001, p. A12.)

10. Such norms are central to "Resource Dependence Theory" (Pfeffer and Salancik, 1978) and "Institutional Theory" (Meyer and Rowan, 1977).

11. March (1981).

12. Steinbruner (1974).

13. Massy and Wilger (1992), p. 371.

14. Hood and Arceneaux (1990); Fenske (1989); Smith (1990).

15. Milem, et al. (2000), pp. 465–466. They use data from national surveys conducted in 1971 by the American Council on Education and in 1989 and 1992 by the Higher Education Research Institute. Fairweather (1996) also uses national surveys of faculty activity to document the research drift in all types of academic institutions except community colleges.

16. The surveys use a nonlinear nine-point coding scheme. I translated the codes into hours spent on research and educational tasks using a model based on the normal distribution, then converted the results into percentages. The model produced workweek estimates in the 40- to 50-hour range.

17. Massy and Zemsky (1994).

18. This was an advisory committee for the Center for Higher Education Policy Studies, precursor to NCPI, circa 1992.

19. See The Institute for Research on Higher Education (2000) for the full set of results. Among other things, the data of Figure 4.3 are broken out by institutional

type: research universities, doctorate-granting institutions, comprehensive institutions, and liberal arts colleges.

20. See for example, Diamond (1999).

21. Staw (1983).

22. Deci and Ryan (1982); Bess (1977); McKeachie (1979); Csikszentmihalyi (1982).

23. Berman and Skeff (1988); Cook, et al. (1990).

24. Needham (1982). See also the discussion in Chapter 3.

25. Boyer (1991).

26. Glassick, Huber, and Maeroff (1997).

27. Adapted from a presentation by Gene Rice of the American Association for Higher Education: Hong Kong University Grants Committee training session on research assessment, September 1999. These views are consistent with Laurillard (1993).

28. The material in this and the following two paragraphs are based on the presentation by Gene Rice that was cited above.

29. Hutchings and Shulman (1999). Shulman is Boyer's successor as president of the Carnegie Foundation for the Advancement of Teaching, which is now located near Stanford University in Menlo Park, California.

30. Hutchings and Shulman (1999), p. 13.

31. Same reference and page as above.

5

Technology's Misunderstood Potential

"Information technology will change everything, and that worries me because 'everything' covers a lot." This statement by Cornell Senior Vice President Fred Rogers to the 1998 Forum for the Future of Higher Education sums up both the excitement and the angst generated by the information revolution. Historian Tom Hughes speaks of "disruptive technologies"—ones that upset the established order of things.[1] That surely applies to information technology in higher education.

Technology is changing how information is created, stored, retrieved, and transmitted—in other words, it is shaking the very foundations of the academy. Technology already has transformed university administrative functions, and the changes continue as institutions adopt enterprise systems in finance, human resources, fund raising, and student data management. Technology has transformed libraries by automating acquisition and circulation, making card catalogs virtual, and providing online access to electronic journals and other materials. Now it's transforming "the business of the business"—how teachers teach and students learn. Learning to use technology with the maximum degree of effectiveness surely represents a core educational competency.

This chapter explores technology's impact on education and explains why the potential is widely misunderstood. We'll begin by looking at history. What happened to other industries when their underlying technologies were upended? One cannot accurately predict the consequences of such upheavals, but it's possible to reason by analogy. Such reasoning confirms that technology will indeed transform higher education. The chapter's second section looks at how technology affects teaching and learning

115

processes and how experts in the field extrapolate the trends. Next we'll examine how innovations get adopted and apply this knowledge to colleges, universities, and professors. Using technology to change how teachers and students interact emerges as a key results area. Therefore, the chapter's fourth section describes how a course might be reconfigured to use the new tools with maximum effectiveness. The last section asks whether technology will continue to push up educational costs or whether it can reduce them over the long run. An appendix presents two case studies of paradigm-changing technology applications: Northwest Missouri State University and Rensselaer Polytechnic Institute.

TECHNOLOGICAL CHANGE

"History reveals technology as value laden and human shaped," wrote Hughes in the introduction to his paper, "Through a Glass Darkly: The Future of Technology-Enabled Education." That's why "technological change is as difficult to fathom and predict as political and social history."[2] Technological advancement creates opportunities but it doesn't dictate how the opportunities will be used. That depends on people, and on the contexts and organizations in which they operate. There is no such thing as "technological determinism." However, some kind of change becomes inevitable once innovation lets the genie out of the bottle. The results may be good or not so good, but there will be change.

Individuals can choose whether to adopt a given innovation or not. For example, they may judge that it won't work, or that its costs exceed its benefits. And if they do decide to adopt it, they can implement effectively or foul things up. Yet broad forces drive the application of technology forward despite individual discretion. If one person rejects a potentially useful innovation, someone else eventually will try it. If innovators implement a new technology badly, others will learn from the experience and eventually get it right. Early missteps can delay the diffusion of an innovation, but they are unlikely to block it forever.

One shouldn't be surprised if the first uses of a new technology seem less than earthshaking. For example, the first railroad in the United States, which operated over the 13 miles from Schenectady to Albany in 1836, used the revolutionary DeWitt-Clinton engine, "but someone forgot to invent the railroad car."[3] The engine pulled stagecoaches with wheels modified to run on tracks—as odd a picture as some of today's efforts to use technology in education may look to future generations.

Innovation can be viewed as relaxing constraints that stand in the way of progress. For example, professors might like to reach more students with their lectures but be constrained by the size of the lecture room or the on-campus student population. Conventional television relieves these problems, but other constraints such as inflexibility and loss of interaction with students limit its application. There is a powerful lesson here: Innovation relieves constraints but other constraints almost surely will lurk close by. But these, too, may eventually be overcome. In the case of television, two-way circuits now make interaction possible and compressed video provides flexibility through distribution on the Internet.

How the electric motor flattened the factory illustrates the successive elimination of constraints.

> The factory of the mid-nineteenth century was a multistoried affair, expensive to build and inefficient in organizational structure and materials handling. One had to live with these constraints because economies of scale in energy dictated a single prime mover—a steam engine which, given the bearing technology of the time, had to be linked to machines mainly by vertical rather than horizontal drive shafts. The first electric motors simply replaced central steam engines, leaving the other constraints in place. In time, however, it became possible to distribute the motors to individual workplaces. This provided much greater flexibility. Eventually people learned to restructure the whole manufacturing enterprise, to "flatten the factory," and thus eliminate the inefficiencies of the multistory mills.[4]

A similar scenario can be written about computers. Forty years ago, economies of scale dictated a single mainframe to which people had to bring their work. Technological advances enabled remote input-output and timesharing on the mainframe. Further advances led to minicomputers and eventually to personal computers and laptops. However, real distributed processing didn't happen until ubiquitous connectivity was achieved via the Internet. Colleges and universities are learning that distributed computational power confers huge advantages, just like power distributed to the workplace in factories. One should not be surprised that the full potential of these advantages has yet to be realized. Major paradigm changes take time, and the Internet came of age only in the mid-1990s. It took decades to flatten the factory.

Huge changes are overtaking higher education: new possibilities but also new competition, including that from the for-profit sector. Much of the new competition is being driven by technology. For example, for-profit educators now can reach large numbers of people via the Internet, particularly in lucrative markets like business and software engineering. Information technology also generates new student needs and learning styles, for example, the expectation of any-time any-place learning and short attention spans as fostered by MTV. Faculty roles change as students learn to access knowledge via technology and universities lose their local monopolies on content expertise. The fundamentals of education—the transformation of students by teachers and knowledge—may remain the same, but the processes, their interaction in the marketplace, and even our perceptions about them are changing dramatically.

Such transformations have happened before. The rise of the railroads transformed the movement of people and goods, for example, but it did more than that. The railroads enabled the growth of cities. They broadened markets, enabled economies of scale in manufacturing, and expanded the scope of competition. They also broadened peoples' horizons: Imagine traveling from New York to California in less than a week! They even led to the standardization of time. One couldn't operate minute-by-minute schedules with a plethora of local times, so in 1883 the railroads got together and established the United States' four standard time zones.[5] The processes of transportation, their interaction in the marketplace, and peoples' perceptions about them all had changed. Many established industries and modes of thought fell by the wayside as the changes unfolded, and new ones emerged and prospered. The railroads truly were a disruptive technology.

Economist Joseph Schumpeter, writing early in the last century, described capitalism as a process of creative destruction. The system gives entrepreneurs the freedom to innovate and access to the resources they need to do so effectively. Innovations are driven forward by the desire of individuals and firms to better themselves, and if they disadvantage others in the process, so be it. (Governments can ensure a level playing field and provide a social safety net, but they can't insulate people from change without stifling innovation.) The result is a series of "long cycles" of progress, each driven by a major technological breakthrough: the steam engine and the first industrial revolution, the railroads, the Bessemer converter and efficient steel production, electricity, the telephone and telegraph, the automobile, reliable air travel, and now the information revolution. Each innovation transformed society as it transformed the industries involved.

The creation, storage, retrieval, and transmission of information are the core technologies of colleges and universities. Therefore, it should come as no surprise that the information revolution is transforming higher education even as it fuels a long cycle of economic prosperity. Other industries changed fundamentally when their core technologies were upended. Now it's our turn. We don't know where the changes will lead or how long they will take, but we should plan on an interesting ride.

THE PROMISE FOR EDUCATION

Shared interest in technology's promise for education brought 30 thought leaders from academe, business, policy, and philanthropy together at Stanford in the spring of 1995 to participate in the Forum for the Future of Higher Education's Technology and Restructuring Roundtable. The roundtable asked whether information technology can "significantly improve education quality and productivity." The affirmative answer is summed up by the title of the publication that summarized the roundtable's deliberations: "Leveraged Learning."[6] Technology won't replace the human element in education; it will leverage faculty and student effort. This early and sober assessment presents a useful contrast to the hype that has emerged in recent years.

The discussion began on a sober note: Leveraging technologies have appeared before in education and most have been met with opposition or indifference. Patrick Suppes, professor emeritus of philosophy at Stanford and noted for his work on learning theory applications as well as technology, pointed out in his conference keynote that:

> ... the use of written records for teaching—a practice well established by the fifth century B.C.—[was] education's first great technological innovation. As Plato recounts in *Phaedrus*, however, many thought written materials made learning impersonal and destroyed the intimate relationship between

student and tutor.... Mass printing, the next great technological milestone, enabled educational documents to be distributed widely and cheaply for the first time. Ironically, although this capability developed by the mid-1400s—and
earlier in Eastern cultures—the use of textbooks did not
emerge until the end of the eighteenth century, demonstrating the slow pace at which innovation's important effects
sometimes develop.[7]

While sobering, this message was not discouraging. The innovations
did eventually take root and the written materials did not destroy the intimate relationship between teacher and student. But the most important
message was that education's core technology has been known to change.
Therefore, it can change again.

Ways to Leverage

The roundtable identified seven ways in which information technology
can leverage student and faculty effort.[8]

1) Technology promotes active learning and fully engages students in
   their education. The new tools enable students to be masters of an
   interactive universe of ideas rather than passive receptacles of knowledge. Aided by powerful computers, students can tackle complex real-
   world applications and sophisticated simulations instead of watered-
   down textbook problem sets unrelated to life after college.

2) Technology can bring a much-needed elasticity to academe's historically rigid structures: for example, by transforming the university's
   vertical organization—with its "silos" of isolated departments—into a
   horizontal networked structure that promotes group problem-solving
   and cooperative knowledge exchange among disciplines, professors,
   and courses.

3) Technology's greatest impact on instruction will fall in the area of so-
   called codified knowledge—the transmission of facts, theories, and
   the development of cognitive skills. Some participants felt that technology could well play a primary educating role in this regard,
   enabling students to learn certain concepts independently of place
   and time. One participant reported a research finding that at least

two-thirds of existing instructional material could be effectively presented on CD-ROM for this purpose.

4) Technology means that students are no longer intellectually limited to the confines of their campus. Given a robust campus infrastructure that provides quick and convenient access to a rich diversity of network resources, students can seek out knowledge at the frontiers in addition to (or in place of) "canned" wisdom they receive from instructors in lecture form.

5) Technology promotes cooperative learning. The group thought that the computer's usefulness as a communications facilitator might in fact exceed its value as an instructional device. (Email, course web pages, and instructional management software have in fact dominated educational applications so far.)

6) Technology can tailor instruction to an individual's preferred pace and learning style. The customization of broad-based higher education is no longer economically infeasible. One can design technology that allows students to learn at a natural and appropriate level for their ability rather than being artificially constrained by the level of other learners in the classroom or even by the nominal level of their institution. In other words, technology opens the door to "mass customization."

7) Technology will shift the faculty's prime role from delivering theory and facts to modeling competence. A professor's comparative advantage will lie in his or her ability to motivate and to convey noncodified knowledge: describing context and relevance, helping students interpret what they are learning, and demonstrating from personal experience how practitioners approach the challenges in their disciplines—in short, acting in the role of master to apprentice.

Other commentators have reached similar conclusions. For example, technology will shift learning "from reception to engagement, from the classroom to the real world, from coverage to mastery, and from isolation to interconnection."[9] Multimedia provides new ways to represent material, and simulations enable students to get beyond the mechanics of laboratory experiments and thus gain new understanding. Technology also focuses attention on education as a process, not just as the product of academic work. This conclusion offers an important lesson for educational competency.

Some authors go substantially further by predicting a "shift from a campus-centric to a consumer-centric model" of higher education.[10] The campus-centric model assumes students will take courses on a conventional campus whenever they can. This leaves curricular content in the hands of the provider and holds students hostage to the provider's admissions, financial aid, and administrative functions. The consumer-centric model shifts higher education from the campus "to the workplace, the home, the library, and even the network," where students can learn independently of time and place. According to this view, conventional campuses would have little role except as places for socializing traditional-age students who can afford, or be aided in affording, that "luxury." Most consumers would bypass conventional campuses and get their education directly, just as many mortgage seekers now bypass local banks and get their money from national providers—a process called "disintermediation." Conventional campuses would be disintermediated. Virtual universities would dominate the industry.

Disintermediation?

Most Stanford roundtable members were reluctant to endorse disintermediation as the dominant force in higher education's future. For one thing, they argued that socialization is more than a luxury. Four years on a college campus represents:

> ... a valuable rite of passage that molds comportment and smoothes the transition into adult life. Beyond developing intellectual skills, a well-structured undergraduate experience can enhance a person's "emotional intelligence"—the set of skills that some researchers have deemed as significant as conventional intelligence for future success.[11]

Most observers also believe that face-to-face interaction will retain its comparative advantage for many educational purposes—especially those that involve non-codified knowledge.

> The dynamic characteristics of a dynamic classroom cannot be digitally duplicated. Classroom students capture rich contextual cues and learn appropriate behavior by observing

instructors and classmates. They enjoy the spontaneity of real-time interactions. Electronic instruction lacks the "electricity" that an enthusiastic professor sends through an audience. The praises and prods of a respected live instructor compel students more than the synthetic "sticks" and "carrots" of a computer.[12]

Advocates of the consumer-centric model argue that these advantages are not so important or that they will be overcome by technology. Therefore, they believe the campus-centered institutions eventually will become marginalized. Only time will tell whether this view is correct.

One thing does seem clear, however. Campus-based and virtual universities will coexist for a long time to come. Indeed, the line between them may blur to the point where the distinction between campus-centric and consumer-centric becomes meaningless. Already, research on e-learning at the University of Pennsylvania shows that potential distance applications are being used more frequently in on-campus than distance settings.[13] We'll see shortly how education quality work makes instruction consumer-centric, whether it is on campus or via the web. Similar forces are driving convergence on the technology side.

Asynchronous Learning

Asynchronous and multimode learning provide the key bridging concepts. Unlike synchronous learning in classroom and office settings, asynchronous learning frees students and faculty from the need to convene at the same time and place. Multimode learning uses both face-to-face and distance methods, each where its comparative advantage is greatest.

Asynchronous learning networks make it possible for students to interact with each other and with professors while working in their own space and time. Email, chat rooms, and web sites provide excellent examples of such "asynchronous interactivity." Students can query the web site or interact with each other anytime. They can ask questions while the professor is sleeping and have answers when they wake up late the next morning. Research shows that, in many settings, asynchronous learning networks can produce learning gains comparable to those from traditional synchronous methods.[14]

Asynchronous learning also occurs when students use electronic information resources. Online course materials and web searches fall into this category. So do simulations and expert systems designed to introduce material and test students' ability to use it. Professors or teaching assistants should be available to help students operate the learning system and to answer substantive question, but most of the "instruction" is computer-mediated.

Today's technology permits both synchronous and asynchronous methods to operate synergistically in both on-campus and distance settings. Television and virtual contact can be either synchronous or asynchronous, for example, and asynchronous networks and computer-mediated instruction can operate on a single campus or across vast distances.

Multimode learning takes advantage of the virtual environment but brings students together when face-to-face contact confers significant advantages. Such contact may take place at traditional or satellite campuses, and the latter may be linked electronically to the central campus. Increasingly, these days, distance education providers contract with local colleges or individual professionals to supplement the online materials with face-to-face contact. Traditional institutions that cater to nontraditional students can minimize commuting burdens by providing most of the education online, but they also can ask students to come to campus when that is important for learning. Students on residential campuses can combine online and face-to-face learning in almost limitless combinations.

Information technology does not need to be an "impersonal" alternative to "intimate" face-to-face contact. It offers a twofold continuum of alternatives: from synchronous to asynchronous and from local to distant. Asynchronous email communication can be more intimate than synchronous, but one-way, communication in a large lecture hall. Distant students can interact intensively with teachers online and through periodic visits to local learning centers. On-campus students have the most options. Professors ought to be able to design educational experiences that are superior to those available in distance settings, but full-time on-campus education will cost more than virtual education. Some students will find it worthwhile to pay the extra cost or will be assisted in so doing, but attending college is no longer an all-or-nothing affair. Information technology provides a variety of viable alternatives for all kinds of students.

Effects on Faculty
Many professors fear that information technology will change their lives, and not for the better. Indeed, few will be unaffected. Many will have to

learn new skills, and some will prove better at this than others. Some institutions that operate comfortably in the present environment will fare less well in the new one. The increased competition made possible by technology guarantees there will be losers as well as gainers, and professors will share in the discomfort. However, one also can project that technology will confer important benefits on faculty.

Teaching and learning processes that have been reengineered to take full advantage of information technology will permit faculty to focus on their highest and best uses. By shifting some of the routine and repetitive aspects of teaching and student evaluation to the technology, faculty will be able to concentrate in areas where they have a comparative advantage. Technology lends itself to systems thinking, and thus to a more effective division of labor among faculty and staff. Finally, the technology may allow professors' to concentrate their discretionary time—for example, through asynchronous processes that get away from the lockstep "n-times-per-week" routine of conventional courses and office hours—and thus improve their research.

Developing new technology applications will stimulate the scholarship of teaching, and such work will be more interesting that revising a dusty lecture yet again. The work also may generate reviewable outputs that compete with conventional publications in faculty portfolios. Finally, the ability to leverage student as well as faculty time will enable professors to engage with more prepared and motivated students. This will boost the intrinsic rewards obtainable from teaching—which, after all, provide the dedicated teacher's most basic impetus.

THE DYNAMICS OF TECHNOLOGY ADOPTION

Achieving information technology's potential won't be easy. The barriers are as much organizational and sociological as technical. The mantra at the Stanford roundtable was "the culture has got to change." Participants felt that change would more likely come from crisis than opportunity. There is no urgency without emergency, and institutional leaders "are generally loath to suggest substantial policy changes that might give rise to unpleasant politics and campus commotion unless the institution faces an immediate threat to its well-being."[15] Market pressure may well produce the necessary sense of urgency. The market won't let new technologies languish simply because they are disruptive.

Full acceptance of information technology won't take place overnight. Even under optimal conditions, it takes years to refine the concepts and methods, build expertise, and change the academic culture. People who seek an immediate transformation will be disappointed. The adoption of innovations usually starts slowly and then accelerates once a critical mass of successful experience has been achieved. We should not expect the adoption of information technology to behave differently.

Figure 5.1 presents the so-called s-curve of adoption—the classic diffusion curve for innovations.[16] The five labels reflect the category names often associated with the successive adopter groups.

Innovators, who represent the first few percent of the population of eventual adopters, are more likely to seek out and experiment with new ideas than people who adopt later. They also participate in informal information networks that include other innovators. The early adopters, the next 15% or so, may be moved to adopt once the innovators have perfected the innovation and demonstrated its benefits. They generally are tightly connected to others in the field, and they often are viewed as opinion leaders. Members of the early majority, roughly the next third of the population, display less leadership than the early adopters but they are open to new ideas and tend to be well respected by their peers. The so-called late majority, the next 33%, are people who adopt after half the population has

Figure 5.1

The Stages of Technology Adoption

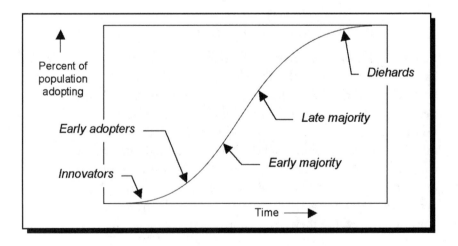

already done so. They are followers, either through conservatism or because their attention was focused elsewhere during the earlier adoption stages. The last 15% or so, the diehards, resist adopting the innovation despite its advantages and the risk of becoming isolated from the population mainstream. In the end, of course, the diehards die or retire from the field.

Saturation occurs when the ranks of potential adopters have been depleted. Further growth may be limited to population increases, or the stage may be set for a new breakthrough and a new adoption cycle. The breakthrough may introduce the innovation to new populations, or it may represent new applications for current users. Either way, it superimposes a new s-curve on the earlier one. Sometimes the new innovation overtakes the old one at an early stage of its adoption cycle. This produces a complex situation that is hard to analyze and predict even though the underlying processes are straightforward.

Today's applications of technology in education present this kind of complexity. The five adoption cycles shown in Figure 5.2 appear to be operating simultaneously. The five represent different levels of innovation.

Figure 5.2

Levels of Technology Adoption

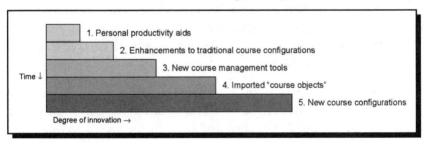

Each new level builds on the previous one, is more difficult technically, and requires a bigger paradigm change.

1) **Personal productivity aids** allow teachers and learners to perform familiar tasks faster and more effectively. Examples include word processors, spreadsheets, graphing programs, and routine email communication.

2) **Enhancements to traditional course configurations** inject new materials into teaching and learning processes without changing the basic mode of instruction. Examples include course web pages, organized email communication about course materials, student access to information via the Internet, and the use of video, multimedia, and simulation to enhance classroom presentations and homework assignments.

3) **New course management tools** enable professors and students to interact more efficiently. They provide integrated tools for communicating with students, providing access to course materials, managing online interactions, and administering and grading examinations. Commercial vendors like Web-CT and Blackboard now offer such course management tools.

4) **Imported "course objects"** enable professors to embed a much richer variety of materials in their courses than is possible with traditional do-it-yourself learning devices. Examples range from compressed video presentations to complex interactive simulations. Online entities are springing up to collect, refine, distribute, and support electronic course objects.[17]

5) **New course configurations** result when faculty and their institutions reengineer teaching and learning activities to take full and optimal advantage of the new technology. The new configurations require professors and students to accept new roles, with each contributing what they can do best.

The five levels stand at different stages of their adoption cycles. Personal productivity aids have become ubiquitous to the point where non-adopters can reasonably be called diehard. Enhancements to traditional configurations have reached the early majority stage, and late-majority status cannot be far away. Course management tools are moving rapidly through early adoption and the importation of course objects may be entering early adoption. Development of new course configurations in on-campus instruction remains at the innovation stage, however.

Limited and uneven access to equipment, software, and support services represent major impediments to the adoption of paradigm-changing course configurations.[18] So do ineffective institutional planning, lack of information about emergent best practices, and the mistaken idea that plans should focus on technology for its own sake rather than on teaching and learning. In the end, though, it is cultural factors that represent the biggest barriers to adoption. Most professors don't invest time in paradigm change, and given today's rewards and incentives they have little incentive to do so.

The education competency gap inhibits the needed change. For example, better assessment of student learning would make bolder experiments possible. Without assessment, professors can be reluctant to change too much lest they hurt the students without knowing it. With good and timely assessments, one can make mid-course corrections as soon as difficulties become apparent and thus mitigate the consequences of error.

Academic and institutional norms also stand in the way of change. These include faculty autonomy and notions of productivity, and also teaching methods and timetables, teaching loads, class sizes, and student-teacher ratios. Paradigm change requires faculty to address what they might prefer to leave untouched. We'll see that the new technologies also may challenge the faculty's traditional definition of autonomy—that professors can decide individually what, when, how, and how well to teach.

Professors aren't the only ones with norms. An acquaintance once described how he tried to get the registrar's office to change the timetable for his course so he could try a paradigm-changing technology application. "Too much trouble," came the reply. "And the change might inconvenience colleagues and confuse students." Being busy, he abandoned the experiment instead of fighting a bureaucratic battle.

The last norm relates to money. History teaches that technology substitutes capital for labor and changes the kinds of labor used for particular tasks. Yet given the choice of spending extra money to support information technology or on another faculty line, most professors would choose the additional colleague. Few would advocate spending on information technology if the result would be a smaller faculty. Most institutions treat information technology investment as an add-on to current spending. In the long run, however, there will have to be substitution.

A NEW WAY OF THINKING ABOUT COURSES

Innovative new course configurations represent the ultimate in paradigm change—the fifth innovation level depicted in Figure 5.2. Such configurations usually balance technology-mediated course objects, applied asynchronously, with hands-on faculty involvement. Getting the balance right requires careful analysis of what's needed at each stage of the educational process. First, though, we need a better understanding of course objects.

Course objects perform the following functions.[19]

1) They encapsulate knowledge in software by storing information in the form of text, formulas, pictures, data, etc.

2) They provide methods to help students access the information and process it effectively.

3) They generate events that stimulate student activity and ascertain learning progress or lack thereof.

Imagine, for example, a "cannon object" for teaching Newton's laws. The object encapsulates the effects of force, inertia, friction, and gravity (knowledge elements) in a simulation (method) that allows the student to play cannoneer. The software invites the student to test his or her knowledge by aiming the cannon in a particular circumstance (event), and then evaluates readiness to move on to the next learning event. Notice that the software does more than simply make information accessible. It engages the student in active learning, allows repetitive trials, and signals mastery. It leverages student and teacher time, and lets them participate in the learning process asynchronously.

Course objects "embody ideas into software," an idea that has become very important in computer science.[20] They represent "intelligent agents" that help teachers teach and students learn. Learning how to use such agents effectively at each stage of the education process should be high on the faculty's list of priorities—an indispensable element of education competency.

Barbara Walvoord, director of the Kaned Center for Teaching and Learning at the University of Notre Dame, suggests a useful scheme for analyzing an educational process.[21] Her "assignment-centered course design" organizes educational tasks according to phase of learning and type of space involved, not just by of units of content.

Phase of learning

- First exposure: when students first encounter new information, concepts, or procedures

- Process: when students analyze the material, synthesize it, use it to solve problems, apply it to actual situations, and so on

- Response: when the teacher or peers respond to the student's attempts at synthesis, analysis, problem solving, or application[22]

Space variables

- Synchronous space: simultaneous effort by students and teachers, either face-to-face as in a conventional class or through telecommunications

- Student space: activities like studying and paper writing, done alone or in groups but without real-time input from the teacher

- Teacher space: preparation, grading, and other activities performed by professors and course assistants while not in direct contact with students

Walvoord advises professors to organize their courses so each assignment can be handled in its own uniquely effective way. Some assignments would cover first exposure, others would stimulate and facilitate process activities, and still others would provide the responses students need to solidify their learning. Each assignment should use the space that is most cost-effective for that phase of learning.

Traditional lectures rely on professors to handle first exposure in synchronous space, because most students either don't read the textbook before class or don't get what they need from it. Then students are sent home to perform the all-important process activities in student space: for example, to synthesize their notes, write papers, solve homework problems, and read or reread the course materials. Responses usually are prepared in teacher space, at home, one student at a time.

The traditional system is inefficient for these reasons:

> It uses the time of the most highly paid and experienced person—the faculty member—for *first-exposure* lecture and leaves the more difficult *process* part of learning to students alone or to students in recitation sections with less experienced teaching assistants. Second, it requires the faculty member or teaching assistant to mark and comment on one

paper at a time to one student alone, in an exchange that takes place without the benefit of face-to-face contact ...

Because teachers and teaching assistants are so pressed by sheer numbers of student papers, responses may be "hasty, unreadable, truncated, or hostile." Because response must be made one on one on the teacher's own time, any increase in class size or number of assignments exerts a heavy price in teacher or teaching assistant time.[23]

Student time commitments to first exposure and processing often are skimpy (less than six hours a week for all classes according to one study[24]) and centered around deadlines. Class time often can't be used for interactive processing or for response to student work because students are poorly prepared or the teacher feels she must lecture on new material.

Consider, now, the hypothetical teaching/learning configuration depicted in Figure 5.3. To set ideas, suppose the course is introductory economics and that the figure represents the first course module—say the principles of supply and demand. It begins with the department's most articulate and charismatic professor delivering a short sequence of motivating lectures: for example, on how economic knowledge contributes to society and why one should study it. The lectures are prepared very carefully and are enhanced with multimedia. (Being asked to give these lectures is considered to be an honor.) After the initial orientation and motivation, each module addresses one of Walvoord's three learning phases.[25]

Figure 5.3

An Alternative Teaching/Learning Configuration

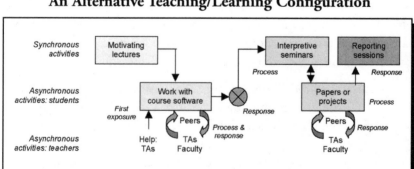

First exposure: Students work their way through a series of interactive course software objects (e.g., tutorials and simulations) that introduce them to supply-demand theory. The software operates asynchronously in student space, but TAs stand ready to help with procedures and to clarify specific points where needed. Students correspond with each other and their teachers online via email, chat rooms, threaded conversations, and other features of modern course management systems. Professors monitor the traffic and intervene directly in the conversations or through the TAs when they deem necessary.[26]

Process: Students advance to interpretive seminars once they have mastered the principles of supply-demand theory. The seminars provide opportunities to explore the theory's implications and apply it to practical situations. Tenure-line professors teach the seminars and the students are guaranteed to be well prepared. (Mastery can be determined directly from the first-exposure course objects, for example.) Students also work asynchronously on projects or papers, which are discussed extensively in the seminars, and they communicate online with each other and with their teachers. Professors don't lecture on first-exposure material although they do offer enhancements and interpretations at teachable moments. (Where necessary, they will refer students back to the course objects rather than using class time to reiterate material for the few who need remediation.)

Response: Response to student papers and project work takes place mostly in a group setting, either in class or online. The seminars provide venues for individual reports, and larger groups may be convened to discuss team reports. Papers are submitted for peer review either in class or online, and students learn by criticizing each other as well as getting feedback from professors and TAs. Group feedback improves learning and mitigates the drudgery of repeating the same comment again and again. Professors and TAs monitor the online communications to assure the quality of feedback and inform themselves about the progress of learning.

Content knowledge examinations can be given under the new system as well as the old, but there may be less need for them given the mastery tests after first exposure. Teacher-student interaction during the process and response phases permits teachers to get to know students and to evaluate more learning dimensions than does the traditional model. Grades can of course be given anywhere in the system and discussed with students individually as appropriate.

The new configuration redefines the roles of students and faculty by making students more actively responsible for their own learning, but under close supervision by teachers. Active learning improves retention and understanding and it leverages professorial and TA time. The new configuration also provides competency-based learning by advancing students from first-exposure to processing activities as soon as they are ready rather than holding back the best until the majority has mastered the material. Finally, it can exploit technology through course management and course object software.

Professors retain their critical role in the new configuration. They set learning goals, design the sequence of activities, and select course objects and other technology vehicles. They monitor student progress and the performance of course assistants and technology vehicles. They facilitate student processing and respond to learning efforts. They offer their own knowledge and insights to students at the time most conducive to learning, not in batch-processed, first-exposure doses.

Both students and faculty will benefit from the new configuration. Students will learn more actively and receive better feedback on their learning. Professors will see less dull and repetitive work, and they will be able to interact with students in more satisfying ways. Finally, the new kind of course configuration can produce cost savings once professors have climbed the learning curve and development costs have been amortized.

TECHNOLOGY'S IMPACT ON COST

While the main impetus for embracing information technology will be to improve education quality, technology also affects cost. The experience so far seems to say that technology adds cost without commensurate savings, but this most likely is transitory. Technology moves education away from handicraft, which should make savings possible over the long run.

The shift from handicraft means putting more educational value in course objects. Instead of repeating one-off lectures to each new group of students, for example, professors can record their lectures on video. The videos can have high production values and include on-scene descriptions of events, demonstrations, and animations. Producers can work with professors to update the material as needed, and revisions can be brought out on a regular basis.

Course objects raise the distinction between "product" and "service" in education. Course objects are products. They have an independent and durable existence, and they represent intellectual property that can be bought and sold. Services are perishable as in the case of teacher-student contact. Providing information to students as a service can be less efficient than providing it through a product because the same material must be reiterated for each new group. However, helping students use product-based information effectively may best be done in a service mode.

While textbooks and similar products have been important for a long time, the course object adds a dramatic new dimension. The intelligence contained in the course object reduces the level of needed services and also may enable one to use service providers with less expertise. The example depicted in Figure 5.3 shows how faculty and TA time can be leveraged, for example. Help should be available during students' courseware usage, but the software agent embodies the main knowledge base needed at this stage. The interpretative sessions require faculty expertise, but for a more limited duration than is needed in conventional configurations. In distance education settings, moreover, the embodiment of content knowledge in course objects may enable one to use local faculty with less expertise to handle the interpretive sessions.

What are the new configuration's cost implications? First, substantial up-front investments are required—investments that must be amortized over large numbers of students. On the other side of the ledger, variable costs are lower than for the conventional lecture. Professors don't have to mouth the same words for each class section. Furthermore, they don't have to prepare the lecture anew each semester—even dusting off the yellowed notes requires some time if the lecture is to be delivered well. This doesn't mean that variable cost goes to zero, however. In addition to the cost of electronic transmission, quality and intimacy may dictate direct interaction between teacher and student. Interpretive sessions require faculty time, in class and for preparation, but not as much as delivering the lecture *and* allowing for discussion. In effect, technology capitalizes educational content into course objects so that human inputs can be leveraged.

Capitalizing educational content produces three kinds of benefits: economies of scale and scope, processes with more exploitable learning curves, and improved cost trajectories. We'll examine these benefits and then address the bottom-line question: "Will technology reduce the cost of education?"

Economies of Scale and Scope

Handicraft processes are not very scalable. That is, production of the nth unit costs nearly as much as production of the first unit. In conventional higher education, the cost of planning and organizing a course usually is small relative to the cost associated with contact hours, office hours, and student evaluation. Variable cost dominates. Even when students are added to a section with empty seats (in which case the marginal contact cost is zero), the requirements for office hours and evaluation grow proportionately. While individual faculty can achieve preparation economies by teaching multiple sections of the same course, teaching-load norms and intellectual fatigue limit the benefits.

Information technology can shift higher education away from the handicraft tradition, but only if it significantly alters course configurations. In the example given earlier, more than the traditional amount of faculty time would be allocated to plan the course, select or create the course objects, train the TAs and help staff, prepare the introductory lectures, and manage the overall process. These costs don't depend on student numbers. Because direct faculty-student contact is focused mainly on process and response is done in group settings, the variable cost per enrollment is lower than with traditional methods. Most of the first-impression burden is carried by the technology and by course assistants who are paid less than faculty.

Suppose a technology-intensive course costs no more than the conventional one it replaces. Spending more on technology while holding total cost constant increases the fraction of cost represented by technology. (The fraction may increase even if total cost grows.) This generally means that fixed cost goes up and variable cost goes down. It follows, then, that the new configuration will enjoy better economies of scale than the conventional one. Additional students can be enrolled with less-than-proportionate cost increases and undiminished quality, thus breaking the iron linkage between faculty size and student numbers.

The technology-based reconfiguration also offers economies of scope. Because faculty put more time into course planning and less into the routine aspects of pedagogical delivery, they may be able to adapt educational content and methods to nontraditional groups and settings more easily than is common with conventional teaching and learning methods. Student self-pacing plus closer and more interactive contact with faculty in small-group sessions also should help. By freeing professors from the routine of first-impression teaching, the technology allows them to put more time and energy into customizing process and response tasks to meet particular student needs.

Learning Curves

Technology also improves one's ability to build cumulatively and institutionally on pedagogical experience: in other words, to exploit the process's learning curve. By "learning curve" I mean the well-documented tendency for quality to improve and unit cost to decline with the cumulative number of units produced by a given organization. This phenomenon has become well known in areas ranging from manufacturing to consulting, but it is seldom recognized in higher education.

Traditional teaching methods limit learning curve improvements for at least two reasons.

1) Because most faculty spend relatively little time thinking about the process of teaching and learning, they tend to replicate the traditional approaches again and again. Individuals get better with experience (they become better lecturers or discussion leaders, for example), but the scope of improvement is bounded by individual limitations and by the tendency to devote most discretionary time to research.

2) Because faculty don't work together on teaching to any great extent, the experience gained by individuals rarely gets propagated across their department, let alone across the school or institution. Often technology-based enhancements, on which one professor may have labored mightily, get dropped or diluted when a new professor takes over the course.

Technology-intensive education, and the reconfiguration process itself, should mitigate some of these difficulties. More conscious effort in the course planning stage offers an opportunity to observe the work of others and see how it might be applied to current tasks. Perhaps even more important, the up-front commitment to use technology requires a course team to make conscious choices. Should they use materials developed elsewhere as opposed to developing them in-house, for example? Debating the choices and then reaching a mutual commitment enhances organizational learning.

Learning curves also affect the development of course objects. Objects must incorporate both subject-matter content and pedagogical strategy, and getting the right design places heavy demands on developers. Because objects must be updated from time to time, successful developers will move up the learning curve. They will learn to produce better objects at lower cost than amateur developers. Professors will develop local material to fill in coverage gaps and experiment with novel pedagogies, but the comparative advantage will lie increasingly with imported objects. Learning-curve effects will combine with economies of scale and scope to drive quality up and costs down on a continuous basis.

It is not uncommon to see concentration in product development even as the associated service delivery remains decentralized. This is a direct consequence of the product's status as a durable artifact that can be reviewed and replicated for wide adoption. Even if many course objects can perform approximately the same function at similar prices, one or a few may embody deeper content, incorporate better methods and higher production values, and enjoy "five-star" ratings by well-respected professors. Demand will gravitate toward "best of breed," which in turn will allow those producers to ascend the learning curve and do even better. One can hope that sufficient numbers of developers remain to spur continued improvement and price competition, but the also-rans will surely fall by the wayside.

Business school professors have used materials from the Harvard Case Clearing House for more than 50 years. Cases represent a kind of course object, and because new materials are shared widely, quality-enhancing innovations flow naturally into courses as a consequence of local faculty choice. The Case Clearing House foreshadowed the networks that now distribute electronic course objects. Case writing is expensive and requires specialized skills, so it is not surprising that the development of these "products" has become highly concentrated—as it turns out, at Harvard. Nevertheless, the *use* of cases, the service side of the product-service duality, remains highly decentralized. Business education enjoys the benefits of efficient and effective case production while presenting a local and human face to students.

Improved Cost Trajectories

Technology-intensive processes increase the ratio of capital cost to labor cost in education. Even if total cost remains constant, for example, spending more on technology means that a smaller fraction of spending goes for salaries and fringe benefits. This mitigates future cost-rise pressures even if current expenditures are not reduced.

Economist William Baumol and his colleagues argue that colleges and universities suffer from the "cost disease" associated with high labor content and limited opportunities for productivity improvement, that is, with handicraft production.[27] Consider the economics of the string quartet playing to live audiences, for example.

> A thirty-minute piece requires two labor hours, the same is it did centuries ago. Trying to boost productivity by playing faster or dropping the "extra" violin would diminish quality. Yet the musicians' real wages escalate year after year because of productivity growth elsewhere in the economy. If they do not share in the fruits of such growth (to which they have contributed by improving the quality of life), the supply of musicians would dry up. Therefore, the large fraction of the quartet's cost that is represented by salaries will grow inexorably in real terms. The quartet will get steadily more expensive relative to the average of other goods and services.

Like traditional higher education, the classic string quartet reflects what Baumol calls a "stagnant industry." It seems doomed to become ever more expensive in real terms, all the more so as the economy gets more productive. Or is it? Technology changed everything for the quartet, and everything did turn out to cover a lot. Now string quartets can "capitalize" their best work on CDs and their members can collect royalties while they sleep. Of course the best quartets will continue to perform to live audiences, and people will pay to come because such performances provide extra value. But quartet economics have been fundamentally altered. The best quartets sell CDs and make lots of money, some of which can be used to subsidize live concerts, whereas mediocre ones lose demand and eventually disappear.

But that's not all. The cost trajectory for the best quartets has been altered as well. Recording, packaging, distribution, and similar costs now make up a large part of what people pay for CDs. Add in the cost of playback equipment, and the musicians' salary becomes insignificant. The other cost elements benefit regularly from productivity gains, especially

those associated with electronics. Therefore, quartets should not be classified as economically stagnant—they no longer suffer from the cost disease.

Baumol believes that higher education, though a stagnant industry by
his definition, can prosper even as it becomes more expensive—by virtue
of its value and because a more productive economy makes the cost
increases affordable. I agree, but becoming more expensive should be a last
resort. Technology-intensive education reduces labor as a proportion of
total cost, thus mitigating the cost disease. While labor will always be a significant part of higher education's cost structure, there appear to be
enough technological opportunities to improve cost trajectories for a long
time to come.[28]

Will Technology Reduce the Cost of Education?

Suppose it turns out that information technology *can* reduce higher education's costs once startup inefficiencies have been overcome. But would
it? Would technology in fact reduce costs or will it end up increasing
them? The answer depends on what the public wants to pay for. The nonprofit economic model shows that efficiency gains don't fall to the bottom
line as in for-profit enterprises. Instead, universities recycle them into
improved quality or larger cross subsidies. Often the substitution occurs at
the grassroots level, so higher authorities never recognize the gain. In
other words, efficiency improvements don't automatically bring down
expenditures. Cost cutting occurs only when revenue shortfalls force the
issue.

Whether markets, donors, and government appropriators drive
resource levels down depends, in principle at least, on whether they value
the extra education quality and research more than the savings from cost
cutting. If they value the output more they will leave resource levels alone.
Indeed, technology-based productivity gains might induce payers to provide more money to obtain even more quality. On the other hand, payers
may prefer to extract the productivity gains from the institution so they
can spend the money elsewhere. Or they may choose less expensive virtual
alternatives, where quality has also been boosted by technology, to traditional on-campus alternatives.

What actually happens will depend on the dynamics of competition
and the visibility of the productivity gains as well as on payers' value systems. One can expect for-profit educational suppliers to pass at least some
cost savings on to customers, and this will pressure traditional providers to

do so as well. Traditional institutions will be able to resist the pressure if and only if customers value the extra quality of a traditional experience more than the savings attainable in the nontraditional sector. Donors and appropriators may applaud visible productivity gains and encourage institutions to produce more by leaving their funding in place or even increasing it. Or they may send the money elsewhere.

The only credible prediction holds that information technology will provide new alternatives and thus increase uncertainty. Productivity gains can be forthcoming if institutions and professors work hard enough to get them, but barriers to implementation make this less than certain. Such gains may be recycled or squeezed out by market pressure or funding cuts, but failing to boost productivity won't protect institutions from these forces. Institutions should promote productivity in order to protect themselves competitively if for no other reason. Certainly public policy should encourage this. All parties will be better off if productivity can be improved, regardless of whether the cost of education goes up or down.

Appendix

TWO CASE STUDIES

While paradigm-changing technology adoptions have yet to become the norm, there are a growing number of good examples. Space permits the description of just two: those at Northwest Missouri State University and Rensselaer Polytechnic Institute.[29] Northwest's program is noteworthy because it has been concentrating on education core competency for years because it was one of the nation's first wired campuses. Rensselaer's program is noteworthy because its studio courses improved quality and reduced cost simultaneously.

Northwest Missouri State University

In 1987, Northwest Missouri State University launched the first comprehensive electronic campus at a public institution by linking every residence hall room and faculty and administrative office via a network of terminals and PCs. Users could access a variety of sources both on- and off-campus including the library, software and instructional videos, administrative applications such as course registration, the Internet, and the World Wide Web. Northwest upgraded classroom facilities to take advantage of portable computers and high-capacity computer networks to improve the quality of student learning. Wired classrooms include a computerized chemistry lab and electronic classrooms where each student station is connected to the Internet as well as to on-campus information sources.

In fall 1995, Northwest piloted a program to evaluate the effect of each student having a portable computer connected to a high capacity computer network. The computers were used in a specially designed classroom where each student station is connected to the Internet as well as the campus network. Dubbed "Electronic Campus Plus," this approach moved computing to the center of the teaching and learning process. Results from the pilot reveal, among other things, the potential of computers to make learning more active, the importance of teaching students how to best make use of the potential of the web, and the importance of providing real-time feedback.

Most recently, Northwest has expanded its mission to extend the Electronic Campus to use information technology to enhance and facilitate learning on and off campus. Northwest now serves as the state's center for seeking out and evaluating software packages as well as for developing new applications where the need exists. Labeled the Center for the Application of Information Technology to Learning, the center's work will be made available to institutions throughout the state. As part of the expanded mission, Northwest is preparing to pilot modularized learning which will allow learners to enter the curriculum where and when they need to, navigate through at their own pace, and decide when and where to devote time to their studies.

Technology affects teaching and learning in several ways. Professors consider presentation graphics programs to be the norm for classroom presentations; standard overheads are nearly obsolete. Northwest's wired classrooms make it easy for faculty to plug in their portable computers and use such programs. Professors rely heavily on email and to a lesser extent course listservs to communicate asynchronously with their students. Email extends student-faculty interaction and has largely replaced traditional office hours. Online discussions put students at the center of the discussion, whereas a typical in-class discussion usually focuses heavily on the teacher.

Professors make heavy use of discipline-specific programs that enhance student learning and have ample opportunity to use such programs because of the number of wired classrooms on campus. Such applications replace traditional laboratories, augment course books, and allow students to develop computer skills while they are mastering course material. Wired classrooms allow teachers to guide students through Internet sites, assisting them in successfully locating and analyzing information. Students are taught how to ask focused questions, which is a vital skill given that the amount of information available via computer is expanding rapidly. Dedicated home pages free faculty from having to copy and hand out syllabus, course notes, tests, and quizzes.

Professors overwhelmingly cite the importance of the institutional context in their decision to integrate technology into their teaching. Though professors are never forced to utilize technology, many interviewees spoke of the assumption that pervades the institution: faculty will utilize technology to improve every aspect of their job. Several noted that Northwest's mission defines it as a "learner-centered" university and said that using technology in the classroom, teaching students to become familiar with technology, is the best thing a faculty member can do to prepare students for the kinds of challenges they will face upon leaving college. The university president has championed the use of technology on and off campus and has managed to secure state and other funding to pay for hardware, building reconfiguration, and ample support staff. Administrators have rewarded faculty early adopters by continuously upgrading their hardware, and they remove bureaucratic and other roadblocks so that faculty can develop their ideas.

Professors believe they have a strong voice in decisions regarding technology on campus. This has been especially apparent in the reconfiguration and rewiring of classrooms. The faculty who teach in the classrooms, not administrators or outside consultants, are the ones who make decisions about room design. They cite the school's "Culture of Quality" as perhaps the most significant institutional factor supporting the adoption of technology in teaching and learning. Core concepts include continuous improvement and an enriched learning environment. Professors spoke of the "symbiotic relationship" between the Culture of Quality and the adoption of technology and believe that they are mutually supportive concepts.

Northwest's Electronic Campus has put the institution at the forefront of the application of technology to teaching and learning. Though generally pleased with the progress of the technology on campus, interviewees made mention of a few critical issues. Assessment of the use of technology at Northwest has been slow; a comprehensive assessment plan is only now being developed. Professors have little free time to develop new ways to integrate technology into the classroom. Faculty cited course relief as their single biggest desire. And while most faculty are using computers in some way, a small but noticeable minority have refused to do so.

Rensselaer Polytechnic Institute

Rensselaer represents the best available example of what can be done to fully integrate technology to increase educational productivity. From 1988 to 1993, the university shifted its educational paradigm by introducing studio courses in physics, chemistry, calculus, engineering, computer science, and biology. These courses systematically incorporate the use of technology in a cooperative learning environment, using simulation software to reduce or eliminate conventional laboratory sections and consolidating lectures, "labs," and discussion sections.

Rensselaer began by reexamining the conventional wisdom that the traditional course is the most cost effective way to educate hundreds or thousands of students per semester. They found that the traditional large lecture/small recitation and lab model left them with 57 to 72 events to be staffed each week in each of these courses. Under the new model, the approximately 700 students enrolled in each large course are divided into 12 to 15 sections of 48 to 64 persons. A team of one faculty member, one graduate student, and one or two undergraduates staff the resulting 12 to 15 weekly events.

In such studio courses, students' previous six weekly hours (two lecture, two recitation, and two lab) in the classroom have been reduced to four (taught in two or three one to two hour blocks). Instead of getting information from lectures, students are expected, and helped, to use print sources and computer technology to prepare more fully on their own. Class time then becomes highly interactive, as students are asked to use what they have learned for problem solving and projects. The physics studio contains short (20 to 40 minutes) hands-on laboratories in greater number than in the traditional course, tightly integrated with both the homework and class discussion, and often combined with a computational activity. Other lab activities include microcomputer-based laboratories, video laboratories, and model simulation projects.

The studio classroom itself is designed to facilitate the integration of laboratories, discussion, lecture, problem solving, and computer use. Each pair of students is seated at a two-meter table equipped with swivel chairs and a computer workstation. Often the tables also contain the equipment for the day's hands-on laboratory. The tables are arranged in three concentric half-circles, with an opening in the front of the room for the teacher's workstation and for projection. The arrangement is such that when the teacher wishes to lecture or conduct a class discussion, the students turn away from their small group workspace and toward the center of the room. When the students are working on their own, with their backs to the teacher, the teacher can see all workstation screens and can thereby monitor student progress.

Rensselaer's 33% reduction of class contact time through the introduction of studio physics saved between $10,000 and $20,000 per semester. In spite of the one-third reduction in class time, more topics were covered, and students performed as well or better than students in the traditional courses. Student response was enthusiastic. Faculty evaluations in the studio format were far higher than in the traditional mode, a significant issue in an institution where faculty rewards are increasingly tied to teaching performance. Successes also were achieved with other studio courses. Rensselaer reduced academic budgets over roughly the same period in order to cope with revenue shortfalls. They would have done this without the studio courses, but the new technology allowed them to increase educational quality concurrently—literally, "to do more with less."

Rensselaer reports the following performance statistics for the first five years of studio physics compared to the previous eight years.[30]

- Attendance: 75 to 80% from 50 to 75%

- Pre-test and post-test: 10 to 13% increase from 2%

- Retention: 80% from 70%

When asked whether the course should be taught in the studio format versus some other way, 91% of the students voted for the studio format.

Endnotes

1. Hughes (2000).

2. Both quotations are from Hughes (2000), p. 1.

3. MIT's Richard Larsen, in a presentation to the conference on "Technology and the Future of the Research University," Government-Industry-University Research Roundtable, National Academy of Sciences. (Washington, DC, January 22, 2001.)

4. Adapted from Massy (1997a), p. 197.

5. Menchen (2000), p. 91. On page 182 he sums up the confusion by quoting a passenger arriving in Ogden, Utah, not long before the changeover: "At Ogden trains running West are ruled by San Francisco time, which is 3 hr. 2 min. slower than Washington time, 3 hr. 26 min. than Boston, 3 hr. 14 min. than New York, 2 hr. 20 min. than Chicago, 2 hr. 9 min. than St. Louis, 1 hr. 46 min. than Omaha, and 42 min. slower than Ogden time."

6. Stanford Forum for Higher Education Futures (1995). (The Stanford Forum was the predecessor organization of the Forum for the Future of Higher Education, resident at Yale from 1996 to 2000 and now resident at MIT) The author facilitated the roundtable and Sally Vaughn wrote the report.

7. Stanford Forum for Higher Education Futures (1995), p. 15, description of Suppes's keynote talk.

8. Stanford Forum for Higher Education Futures (1995), pp. 7–9, with minor editorial changes.

9. Green and Gilbert (1995), p. 13. They cite Kozma and Johnston (1991).

10. Twigg and Oblinger (1996), p. 9.

11. Stanford Forum for Higher Education Futures (1995), p. 8.

12. Stanford Forum for Higher Education Futures (1995), p. 8.

13. Robert Zemsky, Susan Shaman, and the author, work in progress at the Institute for Research in Higher Education.

14. See, for example, Mayadas (1997).

15. Stanford Forum for Higher Education Futures (1995), p. 14.

16. Adapted from Rogers (1964), p. 61.

17. One such entity, called "Merlot," was recently written up in *University Business* (Making Quality Work, July/August, 2001).

18. Discussion of these and other impediments can be found in Gilbert (1996), p. 11.

19. Technically sophisticated readers will note the similarity between the functions of course objects and the "objects" used in computer languages like Visual Basic and C++. Such objects have properties (i.e., stored data), methods, and events. The similarity cannot be accidental, which almost surely accounts for the name "course object."

20. Stu Feldman (director, IBM Institute for Advanced Commerce, and head, computer science, IBM Research) at the conference on "Technology and the Future of the Research University," Government-Industry-University Research Roundtable, National Academy of Sciences. (Washington, DC, January 22, 2001.)

21. Walvoord and Pool (1998) and personal communications.

22. Walvoord and Pool (1998), p. 38, slightly edited.

23. Walvoord and Pool (1998), p. 39. They cite Sommers (1982) in saying that responses may be hasty, unreadable, truncated, or hostile.

24. Warren (1997), p. 16; cited in Walvoord and Pool (1998), p. 39.

25. Walvoord and Pool (1998) describe their own new system for teaching Shakespeare. While the system is less advanced than the one suggested in the text, it uses the three categories to achieve better quality at lower cost (12.5 hours of faculty time versus 15.6 hours) than the conventional system.

26. Although the assignments are designed for first exposure to supply-demand theory, the online communication also provides elements of processing and response. Still, the time of professors and TAs is used efficiently because their responses go to all students simultaneously. Because most responses are online, the TAs could be located at a distant campus or help center if that were to prove less costly.

27. See for example, Baumol, et al. (1989).

28. Baumol and Batey Blackman (1983) argue that the cost of technology may fall so much that it becomes a negligible part of the university's expenditure mix, at which time the industry would once again be stagnant. While this could happen in any industry, it will take a long time and in any case the university would have achieved major productivity gains during the interim.

29. The two case studies were published in Massy and Wilger (1998), pp. 55–58. Andrea Wilger wrote the Northwest case based on fieldwork at the university. The Rensselaer case is based on personal contact and the published literature, especially Wilson (1997).

30. Statistics provided to Northwest Missouri State during its benchmarking visit, circa 2000.

PART TWO:
IMPROVING PRACTICE

6
Education Quality Processes

The excitement of the young man's voice jerked me from my musings about the price of his Abercrombie and Fitch T-shirt. He described a terrific course. Offered by the college of agriculture, it consisted of realistic problems tackled by student teams exploring and using the resources of a research university.

"I have never learned so much in a class," he said. "I didn't even know I could learn like that."

"That professor must be a wonderful teacher," I responded.

The student laughed. "We did all the work; he just assigned the problems and helped us out. He doesn't know how to teach."[1]

This humorous vignette from Larry Spence's "The Case Against Teaching," which appeared in a recent issue of *Change* magazine, illustrates the difference between the traditional view that teachers should "talk and test" and the broader view of education espoused in this book. It also underscores the confusion that surrounds the whole educational quality issue.

The casual observer can be forgiven a sense of bewilderment about educational quality at American colleges and universities. On the one hand, upbeat images of record numbers of students crowding college campuses and America's continued leadership in higher education and science reinforce the view that US institutions are the best in the world.

HOW PROFESSORS VIEW QUALITY

Professors are the guardians of educational quality, but what does this responsibility mean to them? To get the answer, interviewers from the National Center for Postsecondary Improvement asked faculty respondents what educational quality means to them. (The study was introduced in Chapter 4.) About 100 offered opinions about whether education quality issues were significant for themselves or their departments.

Slightly more than half of the respondents, located disproportionately in the more prestigious colleges and universities, reported that deep discussions about education quality are infrequent or nonexistent. The following quotations illustrate the prevailing view.

> Educational quality does not come up as an issue in the department because it is closely aligned with course content and we generally don't discuss course content. Everyone here is doing a good job. (Professor, English, research university)

> Educational quality is not something that we discuss explicitly. We assume that each person is trying to keep up with the materials in all of the various areas that they teach in. Our faculty work reasonably hard and want to stay current, so we don't really have a concern about quality. (Professor, economics, liberal arts college)

> We [the department] have not had any discussion about that [educational quality]. We've not dealt with that at all. I've not felt it to be a major problem here. (Professor, history, research university)

> I would say that these things [educational quality issues] haven't been addressed in any focused way. They do come up from time to time, but I think they never have been a forefront issue for us. There is an assumption that it is not a problem. (Associate professor, English, comprehensive university)

Two patterns can be observed. First, professors tend to believe that quality is synonymous with course content and that faculty who keep up with their field will get the right content into their courses. Second, discussions about quality rarely occur without evidence that there is a problem. In other words, professors tend to assume that quality is all right unless there is some reason to believe the contrary.

The remaining respondents did indicate that quality is a concern, but their answers do not provide much reassurance. For example, some indicated that consideration of quality is informal rather than systematic, or even that it "creeps into" the department's thinking.

> Well, I mean, people are very concerned about educational quality. People complain about quality informally. And so, sure, I do think people talk a lot about it. (Professor, psychology, doctoral granting university)

> At both the graduate and undergraduate level, educational quality creeps in a lot. (Associate professor, English, doctoral granting university)

Such comments suggest that education quality is a secondary rather than a primary concern, and that it's something to complain about rather than to take full responsibility for.

Most respondents offered at least a partial definition of education quality. The major pattern reinforced the view that education quality is synonymous with course content—the stronger the content, the better the educational quality. Furthermore, professors tend to equate good course content with a strong research program. These beliefs are well represented by the following.

> Well, I think it [research] has the effect of exposing them [undergraduates] to a much higher quality version of sociology, without any question whatsoever. (Professor, sociology, research university)

> Our undergraduates do very well, and we give them an excellent education. I don't think it would be as good if most of us weren't active researchers. Without research, a certain piece of the education is missing. (Professor, physics, research university)

> I used to think it didn't matter about having good researchers as professors. I think that's wrong. I realized how my research keeps informing my work and I think that link has to stay there. (Assistant professor, economics, research university)

Our goal is to have a high-quality program that involves a reasonable amount of effort by each faculty member. We realize
that strength in research really complements strength in
teaching. There's a delicate balance there, and we need to be
careful not to balance it too far in one or the other direction.
But quite a number of courses really benefit from the fact that
faculty are more active in research than might be typical of a
somewhat smaller college. (Assistant professor, biology, liberal
arts college)

Their quotations illustrated not only professors' strong convictions
about the contributions of research to course content, but also the difficulty they have in describing how these contributions occur. They asserted
that good research produces exciting, groundbreaking courses, and that
such courses represent the necessary and sufficient condition for quality.
Unfortunately, the "sufficiency" assertion generally remains untested.

QUALITY AS VIEWED FROM OUTSIDE THE ACADEMY

American businesses have learned a lot about quality during the last two
decades. Whereas quality issues might once have been taken for granted,
or dismissed with the aphorism "you know it when you see it," successful
firms now understand that well-thought-out processes and concentrated
effort are necessary for producing quality. For example, quality pioneer W.
Edwards Deming stressed that meeting user needs represents the defining
criterion for quality and that all organization members should participate
actively in "constant and continuous" quality improvement.[2]

Quality experts also learned that any dimension of quality that cannot
be assessed, even judgmentally, cannot be systematically improved. Assessment provides the feedback producers need to monitor their performance
and make mid-course corrections. It provides data for diagnosing difficulties and pinpointing opportunities for improvement. Arraying the measurements in time series can mark improvements or identify trends that
need reversing. Comparing the time series across similar enterprises or
operating units allows producers to benchmark their progress and gauge
what might be accomplished with different approaches.

US companies awoke to quality issues in the 1980s. Companies that
lost market share to Japanese and European competitors realized that

having a well-engineered product, good production facilities, and a competent workforce wasn't enough. The product had to satisfy user wants and needs and the production facility had to be designed with an eye to quality processes. Most important, the company's *people* had to understand quality, be motivated and empowered to produce it, be trained in quality improvement processes, and be supported with the right tools and infrastructure. They had to commit themselves to the idea that quality can always be improved—that "good enough isn't."

The Malcolm Baldrige National Quality Award, established by Congress and first presented in 1988, raised the country's consciousness by recognizing exemplary quality performance. "The Baldrige," as the award came to be called, embodied a set of criteria and a process for evaluating companies' performance against the criteria. The seven original Baldrige criteria illustrate the questions one can use to assess an entity's quality prowess. They are listed below, each followed with observations about how the typical college or university would measure up.[3] These observations illustrate why external stakeholders don't accept the academy's quality claims at face value.

1) **Leadership.** Have senior leaders clearly defined the enterprise's quality values, goals, and ways to achieve the goals? Are senior executives personally involved? Does this involvement include communicating quality excellence to groups outside the company?[4]

   Few college or university leaders have clearly defined their institution's "quality values, goals, and ways to achieve them." Personal involvement with quality usually involves seeking the best professors and creating the best infrastructure possible, and then letting faculty initiative and governance take its course. External communication consists mainly of reiterating the traditional views about faculty qualifications and the importance of research.

2) **Information and analysis.** Is the information used to guide the enterprise's quality management system reliable, timely, and accessible?

   Few institutions maintain effective education quality information systems. While some institutions track gross indicators like graduation rates, class size distributions, and overall grade-point averages, detailed information about student outcomes and the value added by courses and majors is conspicuous by its absence. Student course evaluations are collected routinely, but professors discount their worth and their use in quality improvement is spotty.[5] Peer evaluation of teaching is rare.

3) **Strategic quality planning.** How does the enterprise plan to achieve or retain quality leadership? How are these plans integrated into its overall business planning?

Most institutions plan strategically for faculty quality, and some departments and schools plan curricular content.[6] Indeed, faculty and program planning join enrollment and financial planning at the core of the academy's strategic planning competency. However, other aspects of quality like educational processes and student assessment receive little attention. This is consistent with the faculty's views about quality, described earlier.

4) **Human resource development and management.** How does the enterprise develop the full potential of its workforce?

Faculty development and "management" (in the sense of policy, not day-to-day direction) are strong suits in successful colleges and universities. This includes mentoring young faculty on research and professional development and, at the other end of the spectrum, counseling on retirement. Without evidence of weak performance, however, most institutions don't press faculty to improve their teaching skills. Hardly any schools help faculty develop the skills required for quality assurance and continuous improvement of educational processes.

5) **Management of process quality.** How does the enterprise assure the quality of its goods and services?

Quality assurance should be one of the academy's strong points, but in fact it receives relatively little attention beyond debates about grading standards and number of credit units required for graduation. (Note that these measures refer to student performance, not faculty or institutional performance.) Taking a broader view, "management of process quality" focuses attention on the *processes* of production and the methods used to assure that they're working right and being continuously improved. Most institutions have educational development units, but they tend to address personal teaching skills rather than systemic improvement. Except for distance education, colleges and universities seldom think strategically about the processes of teaching and learning, and they do little to systematically improve performance in this area.

6) **Quality and operational results.** What are the enterprise's quality and operational performance results and trends?

Few institutions know their "quality and operational performance results and trends," either in terms of how well teaching and learning processes are working or the resulting student outcomes. Among other things, the shortfall stems from inadequate knowledge about what is important and how to collect the data. Gaining the knowledge needed to apply this standard will require improvements in process design and student assessment.

7) **Customer focus and satisfaction.** What is the enterprise's relationship with its customers? How does the enterprise satisfy current and future customer needs?

Most colleges and universities possess little data about how well they are satisfying current student needs, let alone future ones. (Whether students should be viewed as "customers" will be taken up later.) To do better would require more detailed information about what one's students really need—for example, the needs of actual or potential enrollees rather than some hypothetical "good" student. The main exception applies to students who seek prestigious degrees as opposed to educational value added. Elite institutions focus strongly on such students, and cater carefully to their desires.

Many within the academy dismiss the Baldrige criteria as irrelevant to higher education. They say the true worth of a course or degree can't be measured, that faculty expertise is the only important quality variable, and that universities exist to create, preserve, and extend knowledge rather than to "serve customers." Such beliefs stand in the way of education quality improvement—of the "core competency" addressed in this book. Why, for example, should professors not concern themselves with *all* the important dimensions of educational quality? Why should the academy not tune its teaching and learning processes to satisfy the wants and needs of their students? Why should professors not develop the assessment measures needed to ascertain their success in so doing?

The answer, of course, is that they should. To this end, the new "Baldrige for Education" adapts the original Baldrige criteria for use in primary, secondary, and post-secondary education. Changes include language adjustments to eliminate words like "customer" that tend to be resisted by the academy. ("Students and other stakeholders" is used instead.) They also broaden the focus beyond education quality to include all aspects of university operations.

But while the Baldrige for Education has proven helpful, it has not received broad-based support within colleges and universities. One reason, of course, is that academics resist anything associated with business. But my analysis suggests something more: Colleges and universities lag in their understanding of what it takes to produce education quality, and that the Baldrige doesn't go far enough in providing the needed insight.

Dean Hubbard, president of Northwest Missouri State University and a longtime Baldrige examiner, has identified the main barrier to quality as making the transition from people issues to process issues. Figure 6.1 shows that the first four Baldrige criteria concern themselves with organizational and people issues. The organization should do a better job of leading and planning. It should get better information and analyze it more effectively. It should upgrade the skills of its people and if necessary hire more high-powered individuals. Such actions will improve quality, but after a while they will suffer from decreasing returns. Getting over the wall

Figure 6.1

The Quality Barrier

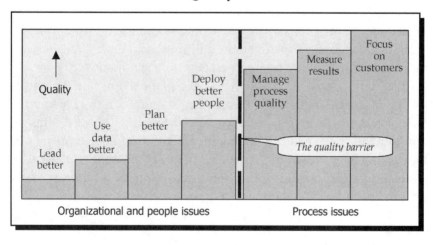

requires one to manage process quality, measure results and use the measurements to provide feedback, and focus on customers.

While colleges and universities offer content expertise, most don't know how to get over the quality barrier. Faculty and staff responsible for quality view shortfalls as people issues, and then become frustrated when academic autonomy and tenure limit their ability to effect improvement. Viewing the shortfalls as process issues opens many more degrees of freedom. Modest behavior changes by the people already in place can produce significant education quality gains. But few academics have been trained to think in process terms. They don't know how to apply the last three Baldrige criteria, so it's not surprising that they tend toward skepticism. The answer is to develop a process-based approach to education quality improvement.

PROCESSES FOR QUALITY IMPROVEMENT

"Education quality processes" ("quality processes," for short) play a key but usually underappreciated role in the improvement of undergraduate education. Such processes can be defined as organized activities dedicated to improving and assuring educational quality. They systematize a department's approach to quality rather than leaving it largely to unmonitored individual initiative. They provide what higher education quality pioneers David Dill and Frans van Vught call "...a *framework* for quality management in higher education...drawn from insights in Deming's approach [and that of the Baldrige], but grounded in the context of academic operations."[7] That few colleges and universities can demonstrate quality process excellence represents the gap in education core competency that needs to be closed.

Quality processes should not be confused with teaching itself. They are "meta" activities that define planning and provide the feedback and control system needed to guide teaching and learning.[8] For example, finding the most appropriate curricular content and inventing new teaching methods are education quality processes, but content delivery falls under teaching. Designing better assessment methods is a quality process, but the assessment of individual students is part of teaching. Peer evaluation of teaching is a quality process, but the act of teaching is not.

Nor should quality processes be equated with quality assurance, for example, with student course evaluations or a faculty senate's approval of proposed course content. Quality processes include these things, but they span a greater range of activities. Indeed, good quality processes focus more on quality improvement than quality assurance.

University Business recently interviewed me about education quality processes. They began by asking why such processes are so important. Not surprising in view of Chapter 4, our conversation began with the teaching-research balance. Here is what emerged.[9]

> UB: The issue is not just the pressure on faculty to focus on research rather than teaching, it's that there's no real focus on improving education quality—whether it takes more time or less time, more resources or fewer.
>
> WM: Right. The real focus is not so much on the effect of research on teaching loads nor even the specific preparation for class. I think most faculty try to do a decent job of preparing for class, but the fact is, research keeps blocking this third area of work [i.e., work on education quality processes]. They are not—or at least not in an organized way—carefully thinking through what we're trying to accomplish: writing it down, debating it, talking about it, thinking about measures we can use after the fact to determine how well we're doing, and then working on better designs for the teaching and learning process. I think it's the pressure to conduct research that inhibits [this kind of] faculty intellectual activity; otherwise it would probably be occurring spontaneously. Work on quality processes is intellectually interesting and challenging, but schools don't reward professors for doing it. Research gets rewarded and faculty put their efforts where the rewards are.
>
> I think the saddest thing to me is that the system reinforces itself. All the forces tend to perpetuate the status quo, and I think we have to find a way to break through and inject enough energy to change the system.
>
> UB: What happens if we remain at the status quo?
>
> WM: I think a couple of things will happen. First, there will be a big opportunity cost: students could be getting a better education than they now get. But also, my sense now is that

institutions abroad are getting ahead of us. I will describe Hong Kong's program. The U.K. is working very hard on quality issues, though they've had their problems. Sweden, Denmark, and New Zealand are working on it. Australia has just announced a new approach. Singapore is in the process of developing a new approach. I think that with another generation of our standing pat, people won't be calling the U.S. system the best in the world anymore. We may still be the best in graduate education, but in terms of undergraduate education, more and more people will be raising serious questions.

Subsequent questions addressed the importance of collaborative work on the systematic design, disciplined implementation, and continuous improvement of teaching and learning processes (topics we address throughout this chapter). This led to the following exchange about the academy's reaction to quality process ideas.

UB: I would expect many professors to have one of two reactions to what you're saying: either, "You're reducing teaching to delivery," or "What about academic freedom?"

WM: Let's take them in order. Teaching is delivery? It's perhaps a natural reaction, but it's not so. No design is going to be so tight that you're just doing it by rote. A professor still needs to have spontaneity in interacting with students. But you teach better when you're working within a framework that's been thought out in advance. And because it's thought out and documented, it's subject to improvement, discussion with colleagues, and so on. But the actual act of teaching can and should be spontaneous.

As for academic freedom, professors never had the freedom to do a bad job. They have the freedom to set intellectual priorities, to speak what they believe to be the truth intellectually, and not be inhibited by some political line or policy from the institution. Quality processes do not inhibit academic freedom at all. Furthermore, there's a collegial argument: Suppose you're teaching an introductory course with other faculty members. Academic freedom never intended that you be able to depart from the syllabus or not teach things that are going to be required later in the program. That's a caricature of academic freedom.

I trust the foregoing provides a convincing argument for serious consideration of education quality processes. We'll begin that consideration by describing the relevant domains of activity. Then we'll address the principles by which a department can improve its education quality processes and an approach for gauging its progress up the maturity curve.

QUALITY PROCESS DOMAINS

Education quality processes' five domains of activity cover both design quality and implementation quality.[10] Design quality refers to the specifications for the product or service, whereas implementation quality refers to how well production actually meets the specifications. A car's design quality is high if its specifications meet certain standards such as performance, safety, and durability. However, anyone who has purchased a "lemon" knows that even a well-designed car can be produced poorly. High implementation quality requires that all cars be produced to specification, even when production occurs on Monday morning (when the workforce may lack focus) or when production levels strain capacity. In higher education, the best course content and educational designs will produce poor outcomes if the professor isn't prepared for class or doesn't respond to students on a regular basis.

Design quality considers the purpose to which the product or service will be put and the price that will be charged. While the design of a luxury sedan can be viewed as embodying more "absolute quality" (e.g., high performance) than a subcompact, the latter may be well designed given its purpose (basic transportation) and target price (low). Quality gurus call this "fitness for purpose" or "fitness for use."[11] Spending more usually improves absolute design quality, but the fitness-for-purpose principle says that more is not always better. In fact, the best designs are those that produce outstanding value for money instead of pouring on cost to achieve quality by brute force.

Education quality processes span five domains of activity. The first domain addresses the educational effort's underlying purpose.

1) **Determination of desired learning outcomes.** What should a student who successfully completes the course or program know and be able to do? How will the course or program build on the student's prior knowledge and capability? How will it contribute to the student's future employment opportunities, capacity to make social contributions, and quality of life?

The second and third domains deal with design quality.

2) **Design of curricula.** What will be taught, in what order, and from what perspective? How will the above contribute to the desired learning outcomes? What course materials will be used? How will these materials relate to other parts of the student's program?

3) **Design of teaching and learning processes.** How will teaching and learning be organized? What methods will be used for first exposure to material, for answering questions and providing interpretation, for stimulating involvement, and for providing feedback on student work? What roles and responsibilities will the faculty need to assume? What other resources will be required and how will they be used?

Most professors think education quality revolves around getting the right course content, they focus mainly on domain two. Getting the right content certainly is necessary, but it is far from sufficient. The design of teaching and learning processes requires just as much effort, or perhaps even more effort now that information technology offers so many alternatives.

The fourth domain deals with student assessment.

4) **Student learning assessment.** What measures and indicators will be used to assess student learning? Will they compare performance at the beginning and end of the term, or simply look at the end result? How will the long-term outcomes of the educational experience be determined? Will baseline and trend information be available? Who will be responsible for assessment? How will the assessment results be used?

The Accrediting Commission for Senior Colleges and Universities of the Western Association of Schools and Colleges (WASC) offers this good advice about the kinds of evidence that should be collected to assess student learning. The evidence should 1) cover knowledge and skills taught throughout the program's curriculum, 2) involve multiple judgments of student performance, 3) provide information on multiple dimensions of student performance, and 4) involve more than surveys or self-reports of competency and growth by students.[12] An assessment program that covers only one or a few courses, uses a single type of judgment, taps only knowledge retention or any other single dimension of performance, or involves only course evaluation surveys would fall short of the WASC standards.

The fifth domain addresses implementation quality.

5) **Implementation quality assurance.** How will faculty assure themselves and others that content is delivered as intended, that teaching and learning processes are being implemented consistently, and that assessments are performed as planned and their results used effectively?

Effective implementation of curricular, process, and assessment designs requires planning, diligence, and reinforcement. Most of all, professors should fend off competing demands on their time and the dulling effects of routine. Implementation quality depends first on self-discipline, then on close interaction with colleagues in the work team and department, and finally on organized quality processes. Assuming that implementation quality is good absent evidence to the contrary simply isn't sufficient.

Maintaining implementation quality requires frequent reminders and performance reviews. For example, some schools convene weekly meetings of all faculty teaching in a given course or programs where participants share experiences with particular assignments and collaborate to solve problems as they arise. Teachers consider feedback from students. Sometimes they visit each other's classes and offer constructive evaluations, which are discussed by the group as a whole. The weekly meetings provide regular reminders about the importance of implementation quality, spurs improvement, and provides practical information about how to do better. Moreover, participants find it hard to hide lapses from the group. Although important, student course evaluations at the end of the semester and queries into teaching performance at tenure or promotion time cannot substitute for day-to-day reinforcement.

Effective quality processes address many of the same issues as total quality management (TQM), but making the association is dangerous. The greatest resistance to quality process improvement comes from professors who think it's just another business-oriented fad. The language of some TQM advocates contributes to this view. Consider this statement by Professors George Bateman and Harry Roberts, pioneers in the application of TQM to teaching at the University of Chicago.

> [TQM adherents] continually serve customers better and more economically, using the scientific method and teamwork, and concentrating on the removal of all forms of waste.[13]

"Customer," "scientific method," and "removal of all forms of waste" are sure to raise the hackles of academics.

My quality process definition avoids the hard edge of TQM. It represents nothing more nor less than common sense. While it does rely on certain principles to be discussed in the next chapter, there is no faddish formula. Indeed, some quality process activities have been around for a long time. Curriculum committees are familiar parts of the academic landscape, for example, and professors regularly develop courses, design teaching processes, and assess students. Student course evaluations now represent the centerpiece for many institutions' quality assurance programs.

People who study quality say that "good people working according to good processes accomplish more than good people working with poor ones." Processes reflect the way people organize their work and the kinds of data they use to inform decisions. Good processes represent a necessary condition for high quality. It's true, of course, that good processes are not sufficient. Sufficiency also requires the right resources. Quality processes help the department use its available resources effectively, but the quality and sufficiency of resources lie outside their scope.

Endnotes

1. Spence (2001), p. 11. He advocates the kinds of change espoused in this book.

2. Deming (1986) as interpreted by Dill (1992).

3. The Baldrige has recently been extended to cover nonprofit entities including colleges and universities, but the original criteria provide the better platform for my purposes here. The questions were taken from the 1993 Baldrige documentation. The current version can be obtained from the Office of Quality Programs, National Institute for Standards and Technology (NIST). See also

Baldrige for the Baffled, A Friendly Guide to the Malcolm Baldrige National Quality Award (Minneapolis: Honeywell Inc., 1996).

4. Office of Quality Programs, National Institute for Standards and Technology (NIST) web site (circa 1993). "Enterprise" has been substituted for "company" to fit better in the present context.

5. See for example, Williams and Cici (1997).

6. Many departments, particularly in the humanities and social sciences, fail to plan strategically for curricular content (David Dill, personal communication.)

7. van Vught (1994), p. 13; also Dill (1992). Emphasis added.

8. I hope the dual use of "process" won't prove confusing. I have not been able to find an alternative.

9. "Making Quality Work" (2001), pp. 46–47, with minor changes to fit the present context.

10. The terminology comes from David H. Maister, "Professional Service Firm Management" (personal communication, February 1985).

11. See Ball (1995) for an early application of the "fitness for purpose" concept to higher education.

12. Western Association of Schools and Colleges (WASC) (2002), p. 8. Prepared with the assistance of Peter Ewell of NCHEMS, this "Evidence Guide" contains much additional advice useful for the development of education quality processes.

13. Bateman and Roberts (1993), p. 3.

7

Core Quality Principles

How can an institution improve its education quality processes and how can one gauge its performance? At the simplest level, putting more emphasis on desired learning outcomes, curricula, educational processes, student assessment, and implementation quality will produce improvement. However, applying certain principles will make the effort more effective. The principles represent "tricks of the trade" for quality improvement and assurance. They also provide criteria for gauging quality process competency.

Working from the American Productivity and Quality Center's library of materials on quality, NCPI colleague Andrea Wilger and I distilled seven core quality principles that we then translated to the vernacular of higher education.[1]

- Define education quality in terms of student outcomes

- Focus on the processes of teaching, learning, and student assessment

- Strive for coherence in curricula, educational processes, and assessment

- Work collaboratively to achieve mutual involvement and support

- Base decisions on facts wherever possible

- Identify and learn from best practice

- Make continuous quality improvement a top priority

The principles encapsulate two decades of quality experience in business, government, and nonprofit entities outside academe, but they may well seem unfamiliar to academics. I ask my colleagues for a willing suspension of disbelief as we address their application to higher education. I hope to convince you that the core principles, and education quality processes generally, reflect practicality and are consistent with academic values. Perhaps the common-sense explanations in Figure 7.1, adapted from the *University Business* interview cited in Chapter 6, "Making Quality Work," will pave the way for the more detailed discussion that follows.

Figure 7.1

The Seven Education Quality Principles

Define Education Quality in Terms of Outcomes.
This is the fitness-for-use criterion, which really asks: "What outcomes are we trying to get for these students and why?" It makes sure we're providing outcomes appropriate for their needs.

Focus on the Process of Teaching, Learning, and Student Assessment.
Typically, faculty believe that once they have expressed the content in some form, their job is mostly done. Of course, that simply is not true. Learning is a process, and so faculty have got to design a process that will engage the student and produce the outcomes they want. Simply exposing to student to the content isn't sufficient.

Strive for Coherence in Curriculum, Educational Process, and Assessment.
Much of the work our students do is fragmented: they take individual courses, which aren't consistent across the curriculum. There is a conflict with the ability to take electives and diversity, and in my opinion we've gone too far in allowing choice. There need to be better worked out criteria for coherence in curriculum.

Process coherence means that these various kinds of assignments you make should articulate with other processes. You should use that lesson in a later part of the process to solve some kind of problem. The student should be able to see that the various things he or she is doing in the process of education fit together, that there's an overall rhyme and reason for it.

Work Collaboratively to Achieve Mutual Involvement and Support.
Faculty tend to be lone wolves, particularly in their teaching, where after a minimal amount of coordination in a faculty meeting, they go off and do their own thing. There are several problems with that. One is it's hard to get process and curricular coherence when you are not working collaboratively, and two, it's hard to hone your own thinking. If you want to innovate and improve, you need people who care about the same things, with whom you can share experiences and work collaboratively.

Base Decisions on Facts Wherever Possible.

We're talking about a network of judgments, and the question is what's going to inform the judgments. The typical academic approach is to rely on disciplinary training, conversations, and contacts. That's very important, but you really have to talk with colleagues in other disciplines who rely on what you're doing for their teaching and also to people who know what the students are going through and what happens to them afterwards—employers, former students, and so forth. You should turn some of the chairs outward some of the time so you can be stimulated by external information.

Identify and Learn From Best Practice

There's no reason to reinvent the wheel. Look around, both within and outside your institution, to see how others are doing the job. Then adapt the best approaches for your use. You wouldn't ignore best practice in research, so why do it in teaching?

Suppose now that you're a dean or chair. If you've got a performer that you judge to be doing a good job, and you've got a unit that is not, you automatically have some dimensions on which you can suggest improvements in the low-performing unit. You should use this informa-tion. You should take it as a responsibility to bring the low end of the tail, whatever it is, toward the higher end. Believe it or not, when you point out that department or professor x is doing a better job than y, some deans or chairs will say, "Oh my gosh, I didn't know that."

Make Continuous Improvement a Top Priority

This is the "quality is job one" idea. To really enhance and maximize quality, you've got to be constantly on the alert for ways to do the job better, to do the teaching better, to design better curricula and processes. There's a tension here with the other dimensions of faculty life. In an ideal world, you would say that whenever a significant opportunity to improve teaching and learning comes along, you ought to spend the time and effort and resources needed to take advantage of it. But when you've got an environment where there are other objectives, such as research and scholarship, that's harder to accomplish.

Research and scholarship tend to dull the instinct to improve teaching and learning. The principle says that if you really want to be practical about the quality of your teaching, you ought to—on a significant number of occasions—set other things aside and work hard for improvement.

DEFINE EDUCATION QUALITY
IN TERMS OF STUDENT OUTCOMES

Defining quality in terms of outcomes brings the fitness-for-purpose principle to life in higher education. "Outcomes" means student learning and its consequences. Therefore, "education quality" means the extent of learning and its relevance to what is or will become important for the student. Put more provocatively, education quality should be defined as meeting "customer" needs and wants."[2]

In the business quality literature, a customer is anyone who receives the benefits of the output from another individual or organization. The definition includes both external customers and internal customers. Surely students qualify as customers by this criterion. Delivering what customers want and need provides purpose and direction for the organization. Delivering what customers want and need also improves competitiveness and goodwill, and thus contributes to long-term organizational success.

Quality champions believe that making customer focus the defining aspect of all jobs can play an important role in shaping and changing organizational culture. Customer focus provides an external purpose for an activity. It encourages people to move from being inwardly directed to being externally directed. Customer focus also helps instill values of cooperation and service, both of which improve products and services and improves operational efficiency. The notion of customer focus has taken hold not only in business but also in government and other non-profit organizations such as health care.[3] Quality-disciplined enterprises satisfy customers by exceeding their needs and expectations, or even providing products and services they did not know they needed but truly appreciate once they have them.[4] Such enterprises call this "customer delight."

In education, customer focus doesn't imply that "the customer is always right." Anyone who has graded an exam or paper knows that "the student is not always right." Most academics resist use of the word "customer" for exactly this reason.

I prefer to describe students as "clients" rather than "customers." The clients of lawyers, accountants, and consultants are not always right. In fact, such clients usually know relatively little about the subject in question. It is the professional's job to research the client's problem and apply his or her knowledge and skills to provide the best possible solution. Is it any different with professors? The fitness-for-purpose principle holds that professors should ascertain the needs of their students and then apply their expertise to benefit the students.

Unfortunately, academics usually give "education quality" a more inward-focused definition such as "mastering an academic discipline." One of our NCPI interview respondents put it this way:[5]

> We're interested in theory and we think that students need the theory. It's different from what they desire, and . . . I'm not interested in that. If the students don't like it, they can take something else. They can't know their true desires because they're not educated yet. That's what they're here for. (Professor, political science, liberal arts college)

Readers may recall Henry Ford's dictum about the Model T: "They can have any color they want, as long as it's black." The dictum went out the window when Ford lost its monopoly over low-priced cars—the subsequent Model A was available in a variety of colors. Professors' belief in the primacy of traditional academic standards has not been seriously challenged—at least not yet.

To be fair, some professors express a broader view of the applicability of disciplinary knowledge to the undergraduate curriculum. For example:

> I have thought very carefully about that [educational quality]. I guess it's if students are coming away from the program with a good set of basic knowledge, but probably more importantly, knowing how to think about biological problems and think about experimental biology, and biological processes. So we have some emphasis on problem solving and to some extent, some of us de-emphasize rote learning of facts. A good quality education, I think, involves really encouraging students to think about scientific problems, perhaps even to think as scientists . . . so if they wanted to, they could move into a research area in biology. (Assistant professor, biology, liberal arts college)

Yet even here there's a bias toward the would-be scientist and only some emphasis on problem solving and de-emphasis of rote learning. No departmental standards or peer pressures to adopt a fitness-for-purpose approach are evident.

Achieving a discipline-oriented academic standard is consistent with another popular idea among faculty: teaching one's specialty. Kenneth T. Jackson, professor at Columbia University, put the problem this way in his first message as president of the Organization of American Historians:

> We don't take our teaching seriously enough. We may be too free to teach our specialties, rather than what students need to know.... Sometimes the only course that's open may be a history of 19th century railroads in Tennessee.[6]

I encountered a similar situation when reviewing quality work at an overseas science and engineering university that relied heavily on faculty recruited from the United States. A course billed as addressing power relations in American society provided an option for meeting the general education requirement. Sounds interesting, but imagine the students' surprise when the syllabus dealt disproportionately with the potlatch ceremony of the Northwest American Indians—the thesis topic of the newly minted PhD teaching the course. Imagine the dismay when this proved to be the only general education course with open seats. While studying the potlatch ceremony would be fine in some circumstances, it hardly fit the general education needs of science and engineering students with few ties to the United States. Worse, the dean met student complaints by saying that to challenge the course would infringe the professor's academic freedom. So much for putting student needs first.

Professors like to teach specialized courses for several reasons. Such courses are more interesting, partly because the material is academically challenging and partly because they attract students with compatible interests. Specialized courses require less preparation because the professor knows the material well and often is working with it currently. Such courses also tend to have small enrollments (few students have the requisite interests and preparation), which minimizes the professor's workload. Perhaps most important, specialized courses reflect the traditional definition of quality: mastering an academic discipline.

Achieving the traditional academic standard is essential for the few students who wish to get a doctorate, but it is at best a means to an end for the vast majority of students. To define quality in terms of student outcomes means that the case for mastering a discipline should be made explicitly, not simply assumed because the student has chosen a particular major. One should ask how the disciplinary material will help students in later life and craft educational programs accordingly.

Until recently, most universities could avoid thinking about fitness for purpose. Because they controlled the certification of degree-worthiness, universities could maintain the traditional academic disciplinary criteria. Now, however, competitive forces make serving student needs "job one" in many segments of the higher education marketplace. Institutions that get this right will have a comparative advantage. The traditional academic disciplines will continue to play an important role, but the exact role will be shaped to achieve particular purposes. The first step on the journey toward effective quality work is to ask, answer, and keep asking and answering the following question: "What is the education's purpose and how can the faculty's expertise and other university resources be deployed to serve the students?"

The following précis of exemplary practice describes the first quality principle, "Define education quality in terms of student outcomes."

> Professors systematically research the needs of their students—the ones actually enrolled in the institution and major, not some hypothetical "good student." Among other things, the research addresses student preparation, learning styles, and probable requirements for employment. Professors regularly seek data from outside academe—e.g., from past students and employers—as well as considering the standards of their discipline. They analyze the data carefully in light of their own professional knowledge, then incorporate the findings in the design of curricula, learning processes, and assessment methods. They understand that it is the quality of student learning, not faculty teaching, that ultimately matters, and they spare no effort to ensure that the learning outcomes meet student needs.

FOCUS ON THE PROCESSES OF TEACHING, LEARNING, AND STUDENT ASSESSMENT

All activity is process and teaching, learning, and assessment are activities. Yet professors view education quality mostly in terms of content, not activity.[7] They take process more or less for granted: "Content is the responsibility of professors and learning is the responsibility of students." But even if this view was valid historically, the massification of higher education has made it obsolete. Today's average undergraduate has neither the preparation nor the inclination to "sit at the feet of scholars," as academic tradition would have it. The second quality principle, then, is to stop taking process for granted, to give it equal status with content.

In the business literature, a "process" is any activity or group of activities that takes inputs, transforms and adds value to them, and delivers an output to an internal or external customer. Processes have specific purposes that produce value for customers or stakeholders. Effective processes have distinct start and end points, and they consist of actions that are definable, repeatable, predictable, and measurable. One begins thinking about quality improvement by studying how processes work and how their elements interact. Then one identifies the causes of quality defects and figures out how to mitigate them. As Einstein said about physics, "God is in the details" of the process when it comes to quality.[8]

Process design refers to the specifics of determining how various resources—people, materials, and machines—can be brought together to produce the desired outcomes with minimal defects. Process design also refers to the redesign or reengineering of an existing set of activities.

Process design tends to involve certain identifiable steps. First, one uses flowcharting and other analytical techniques to develop a clear understanding of the current process and what might be wrong with it. Second, one develops ideas for design or redesign in response to clearly defined requirements for the new process. Such requirements might include improved effectiveness or accuracy, reduced cycle time (the elapsed time between key process steps), fewer failures, or the use of technology to leverage people's time. Once a new process is up and running, one can benchmark its performance against similar processes in other enterprises.[9]

In the production of services, tight process design does not imply the loss of humanity or spontaneity. Key process elements are controlled, but people can be encouraged to act independently within these limits when such independence benefits the user. For example, Nordstrom employees are trained to interact with customers in a spontaneous and friendly way even as they maintain the rigorous standards needed for process integrity. In education, professors can interact spontaneously and proactively with students even as they maintain design standards for content coverage and timing, provision of planned student experiences, and assessment. Without process design standards, on the other hand, providers can do whatever they wish whenever they wish. This makes it hard to refine the process design by performing systematic analysis, comparing results with expectations, and building cumulatively on successful experience.

There are several reasons why professors don't focus sufficiently on educational processes. First, they are not trained to do so. Doctoral training emphasizes the content of the discipline and the process of research. Candidates learn teaching by doing. They learn existing processes, but not the analytical techniques needed for process analysis and improvement. Second, until recently the range of process options was seen to be limited—certainly more limited than the range of content options. One could lecture, lead a Socratic dialog, or facilitate student-initiated discussion as in the traditional seminar. One could jiggle class sizes and breakout arrangements, and assign homework and individual or group projects, but beyond this most professors' thinking ran dry. Finally, there was little incentive to think "outside the box" with respect to teaching methods. Colleagues and institutions rewarded research and, to some extent, innovative course content, but until recently they showed little interest in teaching and learning processes.

Interactive learning enhances students' critical thinking far more than the traditional lecture-based approach.[10] As a first step, one may ask students to write more and discuss what they are learning. Barbara Walvoord's "assignment-centered" course planning methodology, described briefly in Chapter 5, goes further. She uses "problems, questions, or issues—not merely content coverage—as points of entry into the subject and as sources of motivation for sustained inquiry."[11] To apply the methodology, professors ask what activities they want their students to engage in and what assignments will elicit participation in these activities. Walvoord reports that her workshops have been well received by faculty across the country.

We have seen that information technology creates new options for educational process design. Some of the new approaches will be better than the best of the traditional ones and some will be worse. Professors will have to design and test many alternatives in order to identify the most promising innovations. Getting good results requires that the designs and tests be systematic and build cumulatively on prior work. In other words, professors should learn educational design and measurement skills appropriate to their disciplines, just as they now learn research skills. Then they should commit the time needed to exercise these skills.

The following précis reflects focus on the processes of teaching, learning, and student assessment.

> Professors carefully analyze the processes by which they teach and by which students learn. They consult the literature, in their field and more generally, on what works and what doesn't, and they collect their own data where possible. They experiment with new process designs on a regular basis: for example, to enhance active learning and make more effective use of information technology for both learning and assessment. Colleagues quickly adopt successful design innovations, which become part of the department's modus operandi and form the baseline for future experimentation and improvement.

STRIVE FOR COHERENCE IN CURRICULA, EDUCATIONAL PROCESSES, AND ASSESSMENT

Coherence has been a hot topic in academe at least since the curricular destructuring that took place in the 1960s.[12] Although student demands for choice triggered the initial destructuring movement, they were not the only cause. In 1985, for example, the Association of American Colleges stated that lack of a clear sense of mission in many colleges and universities has led to a "marketplace philosophy . . . a supermarket where students are shoppers and professors are merchants of learning." The report placed much of the blame on faculty in departments who have become "protectors and advocates" of their interests (including the desire to protect jobs and teach their specialties) at the expense of institutional responsibilities and curricular coherence.[13] While there has been some increase in coherence in recent years, many commentators believe that today's curricula are still too fragmented.

Discussed less is what one might call "process coherence"—the juxtaposition of learning process steps and materials within a student's program. For example, having students learn a statistical tool in one course and then immediately apply it in another reduces cycle time and boosts learning. Situations like these do occur, but high levels of student choice and the rigid structure of semester-long courses make it hard to coordinate assignments. However, the problem also stems from faculty inattention to process coherence issues.

Once again the United Kingdom has moved further in the definition of good practice than the United States. For example, the Quality Assurance Agency's code of practice includes the following reference to "coherence":

> [Faculty should consider] the overall coherence and intellectual integrity of the programme, . . . which should be designed in a way that will ensure the student's experience has a logic and integrity that are clearly linked to the programme's purpose.

The code extends the idea of coherence to the progression of student experience during the program or course:

> The curriculum should promote an organized progression so that the demands on the learner in intellectual challenge, skills, knowledge, conceptualization, and learning autonomy increase.[14]

Taken together, these two statements sum up what is missing from the curricula in many US colleges and universities.

W. Edwards Deming's "theory of profound knowledge," of which the "organizations as systems" idea was one of the cornerstones, underpinned his entire view of quality. Two of the requirements for a system, he explained, are that it must have an aim or purpose and that it must be managed. The secret to that management, he said, is "cooperation between components toward the aim of the organization."[15] The systems concept builds on the process orientation discussed in the previous section. In conceptualizing processes as systems, designers concentrate less on what the separate parts are doing and focus instead on how the interactions among them affect overall system performance. They modify the interaction patterns to enhance synergies among elements, reduce redundancies and complexity, and mitigate negative interactions that impede performance.

Peter Senge, author of *The Fifth Discipline: The Art and Science of the Learning Organization,* also puts the systems view at the heart of his thinking. Senge developed a series of "archetypes that characterize critical behavior patterns in organizations." For example, certain feedback loops and choice points can enhance or undermine efforts to produce quality. By focusing on these archetypes, one can more effectively diagnose organizational problems and discover what changes will have the greatest leverage for improvement.[16]

The following account of quality control in the production of color television picture tubes illustrates the importance of feedback loops and choice points. Education is far different from manufacturing, but the need to analyze processes in systemic terms applies to both. Interestingly, I heard the story on a university campus—from an alumnus who had been invited to share his firsthand knowledge about quality.[17]

TV tube production involves many sequential steps. Each step is held within tight tolerances, but the accumulation of small errors can produce a blurred picture. Traditional quality assurance inspected the tubes as they came off the production line. Tubes with blurred pictures, counted in double-digit percentages, were scrapped. Viewing the process as a system rather than as a series of discreet steps showed that the cumulative effects of small errors could be mitigated in later production steps—provided the errors could be identified in time. When no adjustment could do the job, the prior steps sometimes could be reworked at a fraction of the cost of scrapping the whole tube. Timely knowledge also alerted workers when the process was going out of control so they could correct problems before extensive mitigations or rework became necessary. Systems thinking reduced the cost of achieving high performance, which in turn allowed the standard for outgoing quality to be increased. Conceiving the process as a coherent system, complete with multiple feedback loops and choice points for remediation, increased output quality and saved the company a great deal of money.

This example illustrates the primitive view of coherence in higher education. Administrators at a California state university were shocked to discover, years after the fact, that standard curricula had been applied to part-time students without any consideration of how their status would affect coherence. Instead of taking science and engineering courses concurrent with or soon after preparatory math courses, for example, part-time students experienced gaps of a year or more between learning the mathematical tools and having an opportunity to apply them in major-field courses. That students forgot much of the math before being asked to apply it could have been predicted by even a rudimentary analysis or discerned by measurement soon after implementation. Yet the problem was baked into the curriculum and continued for years before discovery.

Educational process coherence also means viewing class sizes and skill development opportunities through the lens of the student's whole educational experience. For example, a mix of large lectures and small seminars often produces more learning for a given resource commitment than a succession of medium sized "lecture-discussion" classes. Adding students makes little difference once a lecture exceeds a certain size (communication is one-way anyhow), yet the larger lectures make room for small seminars. Medium-sized classes are inferior to the combination of seminars and lectures, yet they are the option of choice if classes are viewed in isolation rather than as part of a student portfolio.

Rensselaer's studio physics course, described in the appendix to Chapter 5, provides another example of education process coherence. The virtual rather than hands-on laboratories provided by these introductory courses might be questionable if viewed in isolation, but it makes sense as part of the students' portfolio of experiences. The needed hands-on experience will be provided in a variety of follow-on engineering courses.

This précis illustrates good practice in the area of educational process coherence.

> Professors think carefully about how each part of the educational process affects the other parts and the student's learning overall. They assess teaching and learning performance deeply and frequently enough to cover all desired outcomes and execute timely midcourse corrections rather than concentrating measurements at the end of the course. They provide regular feedback to colleagues about individual students' learning shortfalls, so problems don't persist or worsen over time. They consider class sizes and opportunities for skill development in the context of the student's whole educational experience rather than as isolated activities. In summary, professors view education as an end-to-end process where interactions among the parts can be as important as the parts themselves.

WORK COLLABORATIVELY TO ACHIEVE MUTUAL INVOLVEMENT AND SUPPORT

Strange as it may seem in light of the academy's stated emphasis on collegiality, professors rarely work together on the design, implementation, and quality assurance of teaching and learning. This is consistent with the so-called organized anarchy that many authors associate with academic processes.[18] One experienced commentator puts it this way: "Academic specialists retreat into the forts of their specialized knowledge-fields and they are no longer concerned with the relationships of their work to that of colleagues."[19] Another goes even further:

> ...although the ideology of the professorate posits a collective and continuing concern for their institutional homes and workplaces, the reality is that collectivity is increasingly rare and faculty concerns are seldom for the well-being of the entire college or university or for the integrity of the academic affairs of their universities, their schools, or even their departments.[20]

The resulting isolation and fragmentation inhibits efforts to improve quality work and the delivered quality of undergraduate education.

My article with Andrea Wilger and Carol Colbeck, "Hollowed Collegiality," describes the high degree of atomization on teaching issues that emerged from the NCPI faculty interviews.[21] As one professor stated, "This place is full of people who don't talk to each other." We found that the isolation and fragmentation stem from specialization, efforts to maintain civility, generational splits, and personal politics.

> **Specialization:** Even within the department...we're all in such different areas, we're all so specialized that it's hard for us to even talk.

> Specialization pervades the academy, both in teaching and research. Disciplinary sub-fields are so narrowly defined that many faculty find it virtually impossible to discuss their work with one another. While most professors realize that specialization reduces community and hinders communication, they also understand that it represents the key to success:

e.g., specialization is the route to publication, which, in turn, determines tenure, promotion, and salary increases.

Efforts to maintain civility: We have avoided fighting and discourtesy. We have kept up a façade of good manners at the cost of not accomplishing much.

Respondents reported a veneer of civility that pervades faculty interactions and undermines discussion of issues that may be divisive or provoke debate. Unfortunately, this often means that the most crucial issues facing the department are never discussed. One faculty member, explaining why the department had not made changes to the curriculum in 20 years, said, "I think we're afraid to look at it [the curriculum] because of the big fights over what should be required." Another professor noted, "By not discussing departmental policy we don't disagree too much—on the surface." Relations may seem calm, but this calm is achieved at the expense of common purpose and community.

Generational splits: Unfortunately, there is a strong junior/senior faculty division here.

Junior faculty complained that senior colleagues don't work as hard as they do, that they "don't recognize as valuable" much of what junior members do, and that they refuse to recognize disciplinary changes. For their part, senior faculty members believe administrators treat junior colleagues with greater "privilege," that tenure-seeking junior faculty "have little perspective beyond themselves," and that senior professors too often are viewed as "teaching fodder."

Personal politics: What has happened now is the politicization of all departmental issues such that everything passes through an appropriate ideological filter.

Not without irony, several faculty noted how much more intense political polarization is in the academy today than in the late 1960s and early 1970s. The polarization is so intense, in fact, that some professors "perceive each other as good or wicked depending upon their ideological stance." In several disciplines, personal politics, as much as any other factor, sharpens conflict among individual faculty members and makes communication virtually impossible.

While these causes of fragmentation are powerful and deep-seated, collaboration on education quality processes can, under the right circumstances, cause faculty to pull together more effectively than they typically do in curricular debate and individual teaching. Teamwork provides the key to such collaboration.

"Teamwork" refers to groups of associates who work together to achieve a common objective. Teams provide mutual involvement and support, aid communication, and minimize duplication of effort. Whether addressing the problems of single departments or working across functions, teamwork helps eliminate destructive internal competition and contributes to a culture where everyone works together to benefit stakeholders. Effective teamwork requires training in a variety of skills such as interpersonal communication, meeting organization, group decision-making, the use of improvement tools, and the handling of difficult people. Substantial benefits can be achieved when teams are empowered and interpersonal difficulties can be overcome.[22] To quote Bill Creech in *The Five Pillars of TQM,* "Organizational change is imperative, and the team approach is the most effective way to reorganize."[23]

Some may argue that universities already have too many teams—except that we call them "committees." Most schools do have too may committees, but there is fundamental difference between a team and a committee. A committee usually is charged with policymaking or advice giving: In other words, it addresses the activities of others. In the case of a team, members already are charged with achieving some important outcome. The team's purpose is to help the members do a better job or do the job in less time. This changes the dynamics dramatically. It's hard to hold a committee accountable for results, but team members already have accepted responsibility.

Collaboration breaks down the isolation and fragmentation that stand in the way of effective quality work. It forces individuals to confront quality questions in the course of day-to-day problem solving. Frequent practice-oriented conversations are more effective in breaking down barriers than are the loftier policy-oriented debates of committee and faculty meetings. Team members contribute a variety of problem-solving skills and perspectives. Such variety is particularly important during the early days of organized quality work, when all participants are feeling their way. Team members also can legitimize quality work for each other, thus blunting the criticism that most academic change processes seem to generate.

Collaboration also improves accountability. It's hard for a chair or other academic officer to track a professor's effort and progress toward better education performance, but it is relatively easy for fellow team members to do so. A quiet word from the team leader or other respected colleagues usually is sufficient to spur a laggard to pull his or her own weight. Most professors will take such communications seriously, and in any case there is nowhere to hide. Professors know what their colleagues are doing and not doing. Failures of collaboration break the chain of mutual support. They betray a trust and are resisted rather than ignored by colleagues.

Ironically, professors often work in teams when doing research projects, but they don't carry the experience over into undergraduate education. Better collaboration in education will bring more resources to bear, improve communication, and help solve the accountability problem. Most importantly, the process of working together to achieve shared goals will help faculty develop a culture of quality in undergraduate education.

This précis illustrates the benefits of collaboration.

> The department encourages collaboration in education quality work. By working together, colleagues break down the isolation now associated with teaching. They overcome issues of specialization, generational splits, and personal politics. They bring more resources to bear on quality work and provide the mutual involvement and support needed to change departmental routines. They hold each other accountable for performance in all activities relating to education. Visitors to the department see not only a high degree of teamwork, they see a shared culture of quality in undergraduate education.

BASE DECISIONS ON FACTS WHEREVER POSSIBLE

Basing decisions on facts would seem to be a matter of common sense, yet surprisingly few decisions relating to education quality meet this standard. The following observation by the Pew Higher Education Program applies to quality as well as to its original context, strategic positioning and program planning: "All too often, higher education institutions seem willing to accept on faith that a decision is the right one, simply because it is consistent with their mission and has been reached through collegial discussion. Many institutions today are facing financial crises stemming from earlier decisions made with little or no consultation of strategic data."[24]

I once saw a play entitled *The Downstairs Dragon,* which dramatized the problem.[25] The characters were very concerned about whether a dragon had moved into the basement. They debated at length about whether dragons exist or can exist and about the philosophical implications of actually finding one. The conversation went on and on without resolution as they cited learned sources and spun elaborate arguments. When a bold soul suggested that "maybe we should take a look," he was overruled—not because of danger but because looking would be uninteresting work! Dare I suggest that, like the characters in the play, professors rely too much on received wisdom and too little on data when making education quality decisions? The received wisdom is important and using it is easy, but it is no substitute for information about what's actually happening on the ground.

The business quality movement holds that information should drive decision-making. Information serves a number of important purposes. It provides knowledge about external circumstances that may affect performance. It provides feedback on the results of process changes, without which processes cannot be controlled. Information also focuses discussion and helps team members enact a common view of reality. For example, it may call out discrepancies between the team's current view of reality and the external environment—discrepancies that invite constructive reinterpretation and problem solving. Finally, data in the form of trends can help a team assess progress toward goals, identify areas that need greater attention, confer a sense of challenge or closure, and provide a basis for extrinsic rewards.

Visit a quality-oriented manufacturing facility and you will see evidence of "fact-based management." Production teams routinely track output levels, machine performance, defect rates, attendance, time lost due to accidents, and other measures they deem important in their circumstances. They may collect the data themselves or they may track data collected or processed by others, but in every case the team members "own" the data and believe it to be essential for their day-to-day effectiveness.

They continuously improve the data sources and displays as part of their overall responsibility for quality. If fact-based management can work on the shop floor, and it does, one can expect even greater success with highly trained professionals.[26]

Higher education offers many opportunities to improve fact-based decision making, but four come most strongly to mind. First, curricular design teams could consult more closely with employers, former students, and other experienced nonacademics through surveys, focus group interviews, external advisory committees, and joint projects. "Turning some of the chairs to face outward," as this behavior can be characterized, gets around the problem of talking mostly to fellow academics. This would go a long way toward mitigating what one of our faculty respondents called his "lack of feel" about educational fitness for purpose:

> I don't think we [professors] can be judged in terms of what our graduates do or the grades our people get. That was always one of my frustrations. I felt if I had gone into construction, I could point to a building and say, "I did that." I have no way of measuring it: no feel for it. (Assistant professor, biology, liberal arts college)[27]

Professors also could collect better data on the day-to-day performance of educational processes. Student course evaluation surveys represent a start, but more information can be obtained, for example, through periodic classroom visits by colleagues and from student-faculty consultative committees that meet regularly during the semester. Unfortunately, most departments don't countenance classroom visits:

> Faculty don't visit classrooms. We don't walk into each other's classrooms and do stuff like that. We don't have a visitation procedure. (Professor, biology, comprehensive university)

Likewise, most professors don't think students can provide much useful feedback. There's some truth to this when it comes to curricular content, but it definitely is not true for teaching and learning processes. Students know when the material is clear, for example, when assignments are challenging, and when learning is active. In fact, the experience with student-faculty consultative committees has been overwhelmingly favorable—-all the more so when data are obtained in time to make mid-course corrections.

Third, faculty could pay more attention to scientific findings about the learning process. The 1990s spawned a considerable body of research on the neurological processes within the brain that produce learning, as well as research by social psychologists on the dynamics of situated learning as it occurs in different contexts. Doubtless such work will continue within the relevant disciplines, yet few faculty outside these disciplines are applying the discoveries about learning to improve their teaching.

The assessment of student learning and student outcomes provides a fourth big opportunity. The best assessments measure the value added by a course or program. Some focus on knowledge gained and others focus on general and specific skills, including the search for new knowledge, reasoning ability, individual and group problem solving, and oral and written communication. Assessments may be based on formal tests, on faculty judgment or on student behavior. Whatever the approach, good assessment adds to the stock of knowledge available for decision making.

Besides the intrinsic value of the information obtained by consultation and assessment, basing decisions on facts helps break down the isolation and fragmentation that hollows collegiality. It's harder for personal differences and ideology to dominate when team members must confront facts than when discussion remains at the level of lofty principle. ("There *is* a dragon in the basement! What should we do?" versus "My philosophy doesn't allow for dragons!") Illuminating education quality discussions with facts can help faculty pull together in the improvement of undergraduate education.

This précis illustrates the fact-based decision-making principle.

> Professors actively seek data from employers, former students, and other relevant parties to inform decisions about educational purpose and curricula. They seek and use data from students and colleagues about the design and performance of educational processes. They seek out and apply other disciplines' research findings about learning. They find ways to assess student performance relative to agreed educational goals, and then use the data as feedback to improve teaching and learning processes. While received disciplinary knowledge remains important, faculty cannot imagine making educational decisions without a firm base of current facts.

IDENTIFY AND LEARN FROM BEST PRACTICE

Searching out best practice and adapting its lessons to the local situation should become a key education quality process. "Benchmarking," as this process is called, compares the local process with another believed to be of comparable or greater effectiveness. Benchmarkers identify best practices and then adopt or adapt those that can improve their own performance. They do not, as some skeptics would have it, force fit others' work into their own.

Identifying the best practices in a particular area sets up a goal and provides insights about how achieve the goal. Outstanding performers of a particular process do not have to be in the same type of institution. For example, provision of students with certain skills may be invariant across types of universities. One should consider the process itself, not necessarily the entity in which it is undertaken.

When properly done, benchmarking follows a highly structured set of steps. These steps include 1) identifying precisely what the organization will benchmark, 2) creating a list of benchmarking candidates, 3) comparing data that highlights differences between the organization's activity and the benchmark, and 4) establishing goals and action plans for improvement based on what the organization has learned from the benchmarking project. Without such discipline, benchmarking can degenerate into "industrial tourism."

Benchmarking dates from the dawn of the quality movement in the 1970s. It proved effective for identifying areas for improvement, learning how much improvement may be possible, and gaining insight about how to go about the improvement process. Originally benchmarking was used in engineering, manufacturing, and scientific research, but it is being applied to service functions with similarly good results.[28] Entities like APQC have honed the benchmarking methodology to a fine art.[29] Universities like Northwest Missouri State, whose culture of quality initiatives are described in the appendix to this chapter, will not launch a significant quality improvement initiative without systematic benchmarking.

Performance variations within a given department, school, or institution provide a natural opportunity for benchmarking. The idea is simple: Find the best-performing unit and work to equal or exceed its achievements. Professors or departments can initiate the search as part of their own education quality processes, or the impetus can come from chairs (with respect to professors), deans (with respect to departments), provosts (with respect to schools), or system-wide administrations (with respect to campuses). When leaders initiate internal benchmarking and then act on the results, they are said to be "minimizing internal quality variation." This illustrates another important quality principle: Performance variations often present opportunities for improvement.

Quality experts understand that there always will be variations among actions within a system and that these variations will affect the system's outputs. The variations will be large or small depending on how effectively the system is operating and their magnitude will tend to increase if left unchecked. Deming believed that failure to understand the information available in variation represents a fundamental failure of quality management. When a system is in control, one can determine the amount of variation to be expected from natural causes; these expectations determine the upper and lower control limits of the process. The only way to decrease variation with an in-control system is to change the system in some way. However, when a measurement falls outside control limits, it should be possible to identify and correct its causes without changing the system's basic design. Reinforcing the causes of positive variation and mitigating the negative ones will cause average performance to move upward. This should be a central goal of quality improvement work.[30]

The idea that performance variations present opportunities seems foreign to academics. The NCPI interviews show that most believe variations in learning performance stem from differences in student ability or motivation, for example, and that they are seldom controllable by the teacher. But one can challenge this assertion. Professors control teaching processes and they influence learning processes. Might another approach to teaching have tapped a different dimension of student ability or been more effective at spurring interest and motivation? Teachers should attribute learning problems to students only as a last resort, not as the prevailing assumption.

The information value in quality variation came home to me when, in 1996 and 1997, I chaired Hong Kong's first-ever teaching and learning quality process review (TLQPR). The review included meetings with department chairs, faculty, students, deans, and senior officers at each of the territory's seven (now eight) colleges and universities. Hong Kong adopted education quality work earlier than the United States, in part due to the stimulus of the TLQPR. Nevertheless, there was much variation in the rate of adoption. Some departments were well up the learning curve at the time we visited them, whereas others didn't have a clue.

Asking deans about quality-process variations observed within their schools produced some interesting results. Some were aware of the differences and were helping laggard departments improve their performance. Others were blissfully ignorant of the variations, but expressed concern when laggards were identified. Still others were aware of the variations but were doing nothing to reduce them. Members of the latter group would say "yes" when asked whether they thought departments with effective quality processes were delivering better value to students, and some answered affirmatively when asked whether decanal action could spur improvement. Yet the idea that the performance variations within their school represented a call for action hadn't sunk in. We encountered similar views among chairs and professors. That some departments were doing better than others either was viewed as providing no information about what could be accomplished, or the dean felt no responsibility for moving the low-end performers toward the exemplars.

Such opportunities exist at the level of the individual professor as well as at the oversight level. For example, one can ask, "what was my worst performance last week and how can I improve it?" Keeping a personal performance diary can help stimulate one's thinking, memorialize actions taken, and track results. In other words, minimizing personal performance variation provides another engine for quality improvement.

This précis illustrates how departments can identify and learn from best practice.

> Faculty search out and evaluate best practice in curricular design, learning processes, assessment methods, and quality assurance. They recognize that best practices may be found inside or outside their field or institution, that something always can be learned from others, and that such learning is as important for their educational duties as it is for research. Deans and chairs carefully monitor the quality-process performance of departments and individual professors and spur the laggards to emulate the exemplars. In other words, they view performance variations as opportunities for improvement.

MAKE CONTINUOUS QUALITY IMPROVEMENT
A TOP PRIORITY

Continuous quality improvement (CQI) has become a cornerstone of the business quality movement, but the idea has yet to pervade higher education. Known as *kaizen* in Japan, it endorses the notion that organizations can continuously improve all processes and activities through the application of systematic techniques. This requires a disciplined process that includes first, a commitment to excellence and second, ongoing efforts to identify and eliminate all defects, inefficiencies, and nonconformance to stakeholder needs and legitimate expectations.

Quality experts believe that all processes, including those that currently are "in control," present opportunities for incremental improvement. Continuous incremental improvement contrasts with process reengineering, in which the current approach is replaced with a new and improved design. While reengineering can pay dividends in some situations—as when radically different technology options are being introduced, for example—it is not the only way to effect change. Incremental improvements almost always can be made, and doing so is vital to the organization's success.

Continuous improvement offers yet another advantage. Whenever a product or service is launched, stakeholders, competitors, and producers learn two things: how well it works and the ways in which it doesn't work. Any organization that sits still and does not continuously improve the quality and utility of its offerings will become a target for competing organizations that do embrace continuous improvement. Competitors may add benefits or find new ways to deliver the benefits. Or they may reduce costs and lower prices, which boosts value for money.

Despite these obvious advantages, many professors regard "continuous quality improvement" as irrelevant or offensive jargon. They feel that education quality is fine as it is, and resent assertions that it can and should be made better. The root problem, however, is that continuous improvement takes time—time that most faculty, and their departments and institutions, would rather spend on research. Continuous educational improvement is threatening because it exposes a contradiction in the work lives of many professors.

Most professors care deeply about their teaching and their students.[31] Even at institutions where teaching is less important than research, the

NCPI interviews show that teaching is not unimportant. Indeed, teaching may well place the first call on faculty time up to the point where "good" or at least "acceptable" teaching performance has been achieved. Calls for continuous improvement escalate job stress because they ratchet up the definitions of "good" and "acceptable," usually without diminishing the expectations for research.

Many professors feel caught between wanting to do a better job in the classroom and in mentoring students, and what it takes to further their own careers. Responding to outside pressures, many institutions have pushed harder on teaching quality—yet the NCPI respondents report that the need to publish and get grants is stronger than ever. Unable to compensate by cutting back on teaching effort, some professors—especially junior faculty—feel overwhelmed and frustrated. Others reach an accommodation that avoids the necessity to maximize two contradictory goals simultaneously. They put enough effort into teaching to achieve acceptable performance and then turn their attention to research.

Economists call this "satisficing": doing enough to reach a performance threshold, then turning one's attention elsewhere once the threshold has been achieved.[32] Rather than trying to do the best job possible, a satisficer commits only enough effort to attain what he or she perceives to be an acceptable result. Satisficing is a fancy way of saying, "good enough is okay." This contradicts the quality mantra, "good enough isn't." Continuous quality improvement requires substantial effort over and above what it takes to achieve acceptable quality. It is very hard to sustain continuous improvement when most or all of the responsible people are satisficing.

The NCPI interviews provide strong evidence for satisficing. For example, professors do seek to reach an acceptable teaching standard.

> There is an [assumption] that you'll get to at least a reasonable level of academic competency in the classroom, and everybody, I think, is pretty invested in it. (Associate professor, biology, research university)

Yet they are eager to return to their research once the accepted standard has been attained.

> The [faculty's] values—I'm not saying anyone has them in such naked fashion—are to put as little as possible into your undergraduate teaching so you can devote most of your time

to writing and research and your graduate students. So the undergraduate teaching becomes simply a means to an end, to meeting your obligations here. (Professor, English, research university)

Because I value autonomy a lot, I enjoy teaching less than I enjoy research. Teaching is one of the few things I do that demands that I be in a particular place at a particular time prepared to do a particular thing. But I guess that teaching is what I do in order to enable me to do research. (Professor, psychology, research university)

Autonomy means discretionary time—time that can be invested in research. Professors will "earn" their discretionary time by teaching, and they will try to do a good job of it, but the real definition of productive behavior lies in research. Faculty care about educational quality, but with research always waiting to be done, the amount of time they will spend pursuing it is distinctly limited. A few respondents even complained about their department's "pinball mentality" with respect to teaching: "If you do a exceptionally good job you may be asked do more." (In pinball, winning means you get to play again.)

While the satisficing concept describes the attitudes of a large segment of the NCPI faculty respondents, the phenomenon is not universally dominant. Liberal arts college professors appear to balance their teaching and research efforts more often than colleagues in other institutional types. We also observed a tendency to balance teaching and research in a few research-university departments. (Physics comes particularly to mind.) Research is critical for promotion and tenure in these departments, but there also seems to be a greater emphasis on teaching than is common generally. Such nonsatisficing departments may be among the first to embrace continuous educational improvement, and indeed quality processes generally.

This last précis illustrates the continuous improvement philosophy in action.

The department features continuous educational improvement in its vision statement, strategic plan, and criteria for departmental rewards. Professors deliberate regularly about the quality agenda, then assign responsibility for particular tasks and follow up rigorously. While satisficing remains a problem, certain mitigations have proven effective. Newly tenured professors may be relieved of research obligations for periods of time during which they are expected to lead the department's educational improvement efforts, for example, and then encouraged to spend "catch-up" time on research. Senior professors who have not achieved research stardom are encouraged to lead educational improvement efforts for longer periods, perhaps spanning the remainder of their careers. While educational improvement may not replace research as the prime element in career development, chairs assiduously reward good performance with salary increases and departmental perquisites.

DEMONSTRATING A "CULTURE OF QUALITY" IN EDUCATION

Departments demonstrate a "culture of quality" in education when they spontaneously and regularly apply the seven quality principles to all five domains described in the aforementioned quality framework. Faculty who operate within such a culture don't have to be told what to do or how to do it. Quality work comes naturally for them, and to fail at it implies a shortfall in professionalism. Chairs, deans, and others understand and support these activities, and work hard to improve them whenever and wherever necessary. Institutions that meet the Baldrige criteria demonstrate a culture of quality across all departments and programs—a culture that is exemplified by effective education quality processes.

One knows a quality culture when one sees it, but it helps to know what to look for. The best way is to ask how the seven quality principles are being applied in the department. In the beginning of the chapter, Figure 7.1 summarizes them in ways that may help determine whether a department exhibits a culture of quality.

Figure 7.2 presents some additional indicators. They came from reviews of quality work at Hong Kong's seven colleges and universities, but they apply to institutions everywhere.[33] Indicators like these allow departments to perform a quick self-assessment of their quality culture. They also provide visibility to deans, provosts, and external observers.

Figure 7.2

Indicators of a Departmental "Culture of Quality"

Positive indicators	*Negative indicators*
• The department exudes strong sense of educational mission; quality processes are viewed as controllable by the department and essential to furthering the mission.	• The department exudes a sense of complacency coupled with a fuzzy view of the educational mission and a low sense of empowerment to improve education quality.
• Professors constantly look for ways to enhance their quality processes and adapt others' processes to local circumstances.	• Professors tend to view quality processes as pro-forma and paper oriented, and they don't believe they can learn from others.
• Professors value and act upon student feedback and they are proactive in efforts to consult with students and other stakeholders.	• Professors don't seek or act energetically on stakeholder feedback, and they tend to blame the students for being passive.
• The department's educational programs and quality processes have a strong and coherent intellectual core.	• The department's educational programs and quality processes have a weak intellectual core.
• The department has strong leadership.	• The department has weak leadership.
• Responsibility for quality is maintained at the departmental level	• Quality responsibility is relegated to the course or individual-professor level.

Adapted from Massy & French (1997), p. 11.

The Hong Kong reviews identified many examples of exemplary quality work, and also many situations where a quality culture in undergraduate education had yet to take hold. Here is what Nigel French (then secretary general of the Hong Kong University Grants Committee) and I had to say about the indicators in a 1997 presentation to the International Network of Quality Assurance Agencies in Higher Education.

> At institution after institution, the [review] panel found itself evaluating whether educational quality assurance and improvement processes have been embedded in core values or

whether they are seen simply as activities needed to satisfy bureaucratic requirements. In other words, does the institution exhibit a strong "culture of quality" and does this extend all the way to the operating unit level—to the individual academic departments and programs? . . . For example, we were more likely to find the quality culture in departments with a strong sense of mission, strong leadership, and a strong and coherent intellectual core. These departments feel empowered, and they operate energetically at the unit level. In contrast, ineffective departments are likely to have a fuzzy sense of mission, weak leadership, and abdicate responsibility to individual professors rather than taking collective responsibility.[34]

Additional indicators will be provided in later chapters.

The appendix illustrates how one institution developed a comprehensive program for deploying the quality principles and achieving a culture of quality in education. Other approaches are of course possible. The important thing is for departments to systematize their education quality processes and then follow through diligently.

Appendix

NORTHWEST'S CULTURE OF QUALITY

Northwest Missouri State University provides a good example of how the "culture of quality" idea has been applied in American higher education. Northwest pioneered the Baldrige principles in higher education, and these principles now permeate the whole organization. The university won the Missouri Quality Award in 1998. (The Missouri Quality Award clones the Baldrige for Education at the state level.) Most important, though, Northwest's quality culture and associated education quality work has demonstrably improved student learning and outcomes.

Northwest's quality journey began on August 22, 1984, when newly appointed President Dean Hubbard announced the university's commitment to quality and proposed an explicit quality strategy at his first official meeting with faculty and staff.[35] The statements about mission, vision, core values, academic key quality indicators, and service key quality indicators presented in Table 7A summarize the resulting strategy. The importance of these statements lies not only in their individual content, but also in the way they work together to form a coherent whole. The "mission" calls out the university's purposes and the broad means by which they will be achieved. The "vision," which defines Northwest's culture of quality, adds an element of specificity to the mission statement. The "core values" provide a conceptual framework for thinking about quality—a screen for choosing among competing policy and course design options and criteria for judging the quality of educational processes. Finally, the key quality indicators (KQIs) list the kinds of performance outcomes that Northwest seeks for its educational programs. (Additional KQIs apply to administrative and support services.) Perhaps most important, all four statements were developed by a highly collaborative process that helped establish Northwest's core commitment to quality.

Table 7A
Northwest's Key University-Level Quality Statements

Mission

Northwest Missouri State University is a moderately selective, learner-centered regional university offering a focused range of undergraduate and graduate programs. Historically, the University serves 19 northwest Missouri counties, emphasizing programs relating to agriculture, business, and education.

In its underlying programs, Northwest is committed to providing students with a strong general education core preparing them for a world of constant change. The University is a national leader in applying information technology to improve learning processes and in promoting continuous quality improvement to enhance performance in all of its activities. As a leader and initiator of cooperative efforts within its region, Northwest seeks to expand and improve access to learning and to promote applied research designed to address regional and state issues.

Vision

Northwest will have a student-centered "culture of quality" dedicated to the continual development of all individuals associated with the University. Interactive resources—human and technological—will be utilized to provide seamless learning opportunities to diverse populations in a variety of settings.

Core Values
• High expectations are the starting point for quality.
• Quality education is talent development.

- Learning is an active, not a passive, process.
- Assessment must link process improvement to individual achievement.
- Instruction should be learner-centered and holistic, challenging students to utilize all levels of cognition and to develop physically, socially, and ethically.
- The living/learning environment must be aligned with the academic goals of the University.
- An effective curriculum promotes sustained interaction and teamwork among students, faculty, and staff.
- The nurturing, development, and empowerment of employees at all levels are critical to a quality living/learning environment.
- Ethical behavior will be modeled and promoted by the University.

Educational Key Quality Indicators
- Competence in a discipline
- Communications competencies
- Problem solving competencies
- Critical/creative thinking competencies
- Computer competencies
- Self-directed learning competencies
- Personal/social development
- Team work/team leading competencies
- Multicultural competencies
- Cultural enrichment

The educational KQIs are based on fitness for use principles. They guide Northwest's quality processes in two critically important ways. First, they help professors improve curricular and educational process designs, for example, by reminding them to include competency development as well as mastery of a discipline. Second, they define broad performance assessment criteria that department- and program-level teams can translate into operational tests and indicators.

Northwest's annual planning cycle begins with a Strategic Planning Council review of the institution's mission, vision, and values in light of an environmental scan that identifies demographic, competitive, economic, technological, social, and political/legal trends that might impact the university and its students.[36] The council also reviews progress relative to operational plans in each major unit of the university and strategic initiatives adopted in prior years. This essential yet easily overlooked first step, called a "pre-plan review" in some planning systems, provides a baseline for new decisions and initiatives.

Operational planning centers on the school's "Seven-Step Planning Process," which is summarized in Table 7B. Designed as a "universal" operational planning tool, the process is unusual in that it applies equally well to university-level planning and to departments in both the academic and service areas. (The term "program," used throughout the process description, refers variously to central initiatives, academic areas like general education or a departmental major, and service units.) According to its *Guidelines for Implementation,* "The Seven-Step Process brings a common, more rigorous planning process to all units of the University and enhances interdepartmental communication and understanding about programs. Ultimately it should lead a University that is more market driven, coherent and efficient in its overall design and operations."[37]

Table 7B
Northwest's Seven-Step Planning Process

Step 1: Define departmental Key Quality Indicators (KQIs).

- *Identify your customers:* (a) define "customer" segments (e.g., current students, alumni, professional programs, graduate schools, employment organizations, and other departments within the University); (b) identify potential contacts to represent each segment; (c) select specific contacts and establish means of communicating with them.

- *Generate customer-defined attributes for describing your program:* (a) ask the contacts what attributes your students should possess when they complete the program; (b) generate a list of customer responses; (c) combine like items while maintaining the language of the customer as much as possible.

Step 2: Validate the KQIs.

- *Confirm the draft KQIs with customers:* (a) verify that the list reflects customer intent and language; (b) invite customers to add items; (c) ask customers to identify 2–6 items as being the most important.

- *Link each KQI to relevant external KQIs:* for each KQI, indicate linkages to (a) the University KQIs; (b) other organizations' KQIs where possible.

Step 3: Establish goals and develop a deployment strategy.

- *Establish goals:* for each KQI (a) lay out one or more goals based on your interpretation of what the customer wants; (b) goals may be short-term (one to three years) or long-term (three to five years), and they must be clearly stated.

- *Develop a deployment strategy:* for each goal (a) define critical success factors, things that must occur before you can conclude that success has been achieved; (b) determine where in your program you can influence the critical success factors; and (c) assign an individual or team the primary responsibility monitoring success and improvement.

Step 4: Formulate an assessment strategy to track performance.

- *Specify:* (a) formative and summative measures and/or indicators that can be tracked and used to identify trends; (b) the assessment method, frequency, audience, and usage for each measure and indicator.

Step 5: Establish baselines, track trends, and do competitive comparisons.

- *For each indicator and measure, identify:* (a) a baseline consisting of one or more data points; (b) a method for tracking trends; (c) which internal or external organizations you want to compare against and how you will obtain the data.

Step 6: Benchmark "competitive" organizations.

- *Where "competitors" identified in Step 5 have better performance than you:* (a) learn to understand how their processes differ from yours; (b) adapt your processes to the best aspects of theirs where applicable.

Step 7: Set performance targets and stretch goals.

- *For each KQI:* (a) set a performance target that represents where you would like to go from here; (b) identify how your existing resources can be used to meet the target and what additional resources, if any, will be required; (c) set "stretch goals" to enhance motivation where possible.

Steps 1 and 2 bring the institution-level KQIs down to the program level. Departmental teams create operational KQIs, in part by interacting with "customers." The KQIs are couched in the customer's language rather than that of the academic discipline. For example, communication and problem-solving competencies are defined in terms of job-related needs rather than writing academic papers and solving homework exercises. Professors bring their disciplinary values to the table when setting KQIs, but they don't permit these values to dominate. Using the customer's language reminds team members that their ultimate goal is to achieve fitness for purpose.

Step 3 presents the crux of the Seven-Step Process. It consists of two parts: (a) setting specific operating goals for each KQI, and (b) developing a strategy for achieving the goals. Goal setting translates the customer's language into language that is operationally meaningful for team members, for example, a well-defined and testable level of writing or problem-solving ability.

What critical success factors influence goal achievement becomes the natural next question (Step 4 of the process). The university's list of success factors includes "a focus on embedded continuous improvement" as well as matters related to the campus environment, financial flexibility, and relations with the local community. Program-level success factors usually include continuous improvement plus items that operationalize the local KQIs. If good writing depends on learning grammatical rules, for example, then knowing the rules becomes a critical success factor. Issues like these get team members thinking about how curricula and teaching methods might be changed to improve goal achievement. Then, having agreed on goals and tasks, it then becomes natural to assign specific responsibility for overseeing implementation and tracking results.

Steps 4 and 5 establish the particular measures, indicators, and datasets that will be used to track results. Northwest defines a "measure" as a precise quantifier that *demonstrates* the achievement or nonachievement of a critical success factor. They use "indicator" to denote an indirect quantifier that *suggests* achievement or nonachievement.[38] A single "measure" calls out success or failure, whereas multiple "indicators" may be needed if definitive measures are lacking. The ability to quantify performance is necessary for something to be a measure, but it is not sufficient. For example, a precise test that doesn't fully reflect the target critical success factor would be an indicator, not a measure. Definitive measures are rare in programs like general education, for example, but multiple indicators usually can be found. If the available indicators can't provide the needed insight, the success factor lacks operational meaning and the team should replace it.

Having determined what measures and indicators will be used, team members decide in Step 5 what data will be compiled and displayed. The dataset for each measure or indicator begins with baseline information. Ideally one should use at least three planning cycles to establish a baseline, but one or two data points are enough to start. Establishing baselines and tracking trends usually involve graphical displays because pictures carry more meaning than words or figures. The level of aggregation also matters. For example, it can be important to track student attainment by ethnicity, gender, family background, or other descriptors.

"Benchmarking" (Step 6) seeks comparisons with other organizations. Teams start by identifying benchmarking partners, either other Northwest departments or departments at other institutions. The university advises teams to consider the following factors when choosing units for comparison:

• Select an organization/unit that does essentially the same thing you do for essentially the same reasons you do it.

• Obtain data on [applicable] measures/indicators and compare their results with those of your program. You should look for [an entity] that performs significantly better than you do in this comparison.

• If you find an [entity] that you would like to compare against, but they do not use the same assessment measures/indicators that you do, you may want to negotiate with that organization/unit to establish common measures/indicators to allow for future comparisons.[39]

The last step in operational planning at Northwest calls for commitment to specific performance targets for each KQI and, where departments feel they can, to "stretch goals." Team members debate vigorously about how much improvement should be embodied in the performance targets, and the debates do much to energize the department around quality issues. Once the targets are agreed, faculty teams address the quality variation, coherence, and process issues that stand in the improvement. Because the targets should reflect attainable expectations, faculty must exercise their knowledge about teaching and learning processes at both the goal setting and implementation stages.

How has Northwest's culture of quality actually worked? The performance indicators developed for general education provide a good answer. Of the ten institution-wide KQIs listed earlier, the eight shown in Table 7C apply to general education. (The data for team development were not available and disciplinary mastery is addressed in the colleges' individual majors.) The table's data came from the College and Alumni Outcomes Surveys, various normed tests, and locally developed assessment instruments. The data were provided to President Hubbard in late 1999 as part of Northwest's regular reporting process.

Honoring the Trust

Table 7C

Performance Trends for General Education at Northwest Missouri State University

Key quality indicator	Number of critical success factors identified	Number of indicators defined	Number of indicators				
			Rising or stable	Falling	No clear trend	*State* equal or above norm	*Nat'l* equal or above norm
Communication	15	2	2	0	0	-	-
Problem solving	19	9	5	2	2	4	5
Critical/creative thinking	63	53	12	37	4	38	39
Computer	8	0	-	-	-	-	-
Self-directed learning	4	4	4	0	0	3	2
Personal/social development	6	6	3	2	1	5	5
Multicultural	7	7	2	1	4	5	5
Cultural enrichment	11	11	9	0	2	10	10

The first column shows how many critical success factors the general education team associates with each KQI. For example, the communication competencies category has 15, problem solving has 19, and critical/creative thinking has 63. Column 2 reports the number of success factors that are being measured currently. For example, the team has defined indicators for two of the communication factors and 53 of the critical/creative thinking factors.

The next three columns show the numbers of indicators that are rising, falling, or fluctuating over time. Both communication indicators are rising, for example. Five of the problem-solving indicators are rising, two are falling, and two show no clear trend. The last two columns compare the measures' current values to average scores for the state and nation. Of the problem-solving measures, four exceed the Missouri norms and five exceed the national norms. Norms aren't available for all the measures, which explains the lack of entries for communication.

Table 7C conveys two lessons. First, quality can be assessed if the work is done at the local level. For example, Northwest's general education faculty routinely uses 92 performance indicators and more are on the way. Second, quality processes pay off in terms of performance. Most observers would agree that Northwest's report card is very good. A substantial number of critical success factors are being measured regularly, many are trending upward, and a majority exceeds the state and national norms. Areas that need improvement, like critical/creative thinking for example, can be readily identified. Similar tables have been constructed for the majors in each of Northwest's three colleges, with roughly similar results. In time, the report will be extended to the departmental level.

Endnotes

1. Thanks to C. Jackson Grayson and Carla O'Dell, chairman and president of the American Productivity and Quality Center (APQC) of Houston, Texas, for providing access to the library. APQC works with business and nonprofit institutions on quality improvement and benchmarking, and was a cofounder of the Baldrige.

2. Bogue and Saunders (1992, p. 270) put the matter this way: "There can be little doubt that there are many 'customers' of higher education ... At the origin of the views of quality there is ... a student: a researcher being prepared for science and industry, a new teacher being prepared for ... our schools, a city manager completing a master's program in public administration, an attorney returning to learn about computers, or a farmer or plant manager being served by an agricultural or manufacturing extension service."

3. See Rosenbluth & Peters (1992), Whiteley (1991), Zeithaml, Parasuraman, & Berry (1990), Zemke & Schaaf (1989). This and the subsequent footnotes collect the authors whose work informed the preceding one or two paragraphs in the text.

4. See Joiner (1994), Berry (1991), Whiteley (1991), Senge (1990), Deming (1986), Juran (1989).

5. First published in Massy and Wilger (1995), p. 19.

6. Quoted by David S. Broder in "Neglecting History" (Washington Post op ed, July 2, 2000).

7. Stark and Lattuca (1997) as well as the NCPI interview findings reported in Chapter 4.

8. See Joiner (1994), Davenport (1993), Melan (1993), Harrington (1991), Lareau (1991), Scholtes (1988), Deming (1986).

9. See Davenport (1993), Hammer & Champy (1993), Juran & Gryna (1993), Scholtes (1988).

10. Laurillard (1993).

11. Walvoord and Breihan (1997).

12. See, for example, Zemsky (1989); also Bok (1886), p. 41, and Sykes (1987), pp. 79–82.

13. Association of American Colleges (1985), pp. 2, 4.

14. This and the previous statement come with minor editing from the Quality Assurance Agency for Higher Education (UK), "Code of good practice: programme approval, monitoring, and review": www.qaa.ac.uk.

15. Deming (1986), p. 54.

16. Senge (1990).

17. The campus was Northwest Missouri State University, whose quality processes are described in the appendix to this chapter. The executive had been with the Corning Glass Company.

18. Cohen, March, and Olson (1972).

19. van Vught (1995), p. 10.

20. Keller (1983), p. 37.

21. Massy, Wilger, and Colbeck (1994). The quotations are from pp. 11–13.

22. See Manz & Sims, Jr. (1993), Orsburn et al. (1990), Scholtes (1988).

23. Creech, 1994, p. 12.

24. Pew Higher Education Program (March 2000); quoted in *University Business* (June 2000, p. 67).

25. I have not been able to find the citation, but I'm sure the play was performed at Yale between 1952 and 1956.

26. See Joiner (1994), Pitt (1994), Sonnenberg (1994), Miller & Krumm (1992), Harrington (1991), Senge (1990), Juran (1989), Deming (1986).

27. First published in Massy and Wilger (1995), p. 19.

28. See Bogan & English (1994), Boxwell, Jr. (1994), Watson (1993), Spendolini (1992), Camp (1989).

29. The American Productivity and Quality Center brings together groups of clients to achieve economies of scale in benchmarking. Their process is highly disciplined and it produces actionable results. The author served as content expert for APQC's first foray into higher education, a study of resource allocation processes.

30. See Joiner (1994), Deming (1993), Miller & Krumm (1992).

31. The quotations and certain text passages in the remainder of this section were first published in Massy and Wilger (1995), pp. 16–19.

32. The term "satisficing" was first used by Cyert and March (1963).

33. I describe Hong Kong's "Teaching and Learning Quality Process Reviews" in Chapter 8.

34. Massy and French (1997), p. 11. The terminology in the quotation and table has been changed slightly to conform to American usage.

35. As part of its commitment, the university developed and attracted a cadre of administrative and faculty leaders noted in the state and nation for their expertise in quality. For example, President Hubbard attended the Jureen Quality Institute and served four years as a national Baldrige examiner (for industry generally), the provost and president were founding members of the national Academic Quality Consortium, and all three academic deans have written about and presented on some aspect of continuous quality improvement in higher education. The resultant networking opportunities provide important input and reinforcement, and the outside activity demonstrates commitment to quality to on-campus constituencies.

36. The Strategic Planning Council consists of representatives from every major area of the university community including the faculty, the Student Senate and Student Graduate Council, and the administration; oversees the University's strategic planning process.

37. Northwest Missouri State University (1996), p. 1.

38. ibid., p. 6.

39. ibid., p. 9.

8

Education Quality Oversight

Oversight has become a fact of life in higher education. Without oversight, it is impossible for external stakeholders to know whether colleges and universities are performing their missions effectively. External oversight also provides a needed stimulus for internal reform. The issue, therefore, is not whether there will be oversight, but what form it will take.

The evaluation of education quality by external agencies is a key element of oversight. Evaluation already has become a global phenomenon. US accreditation represents the oldest example, although it is by no means the only one. In 1998, for example, the Danish Centre for Quality Assurance and Evaluation of Higher Education and the French Comité National d'Evaluation reported that 11 European Union countries had established systematic national evaluation procedures and three others were in the process of doing so. Only Greece, Luxembourg, and the French-speaking community of Belgium had not introduced such procedures.[1] South Africa, Chile, and Argentina operate formal evaluation programs and Australia, New Zealand, Hong Kong, and India have done so for some years. The International Network of Quality Assurance Agencies in Higher Education (INQAAHE), founded in 1991, attracted 300 participants from some 46 countries to its 6th biennial conference in Bangalore, India, in 2001.

Oversight agencies now recognize that education quality evaluation serves several purposes. First, it helps colleges and universities improve the quality of teaching and learning. Second, it helps hold institutions accountable for quality and assures taxpayers that the money they invest in higher education is being spent wisely and is producing good results—outcomes that may stimulate further investment. Third, it provides information that helps students choose among competing institutions and programs—information that improves efficiency in the marketplace. Finally, evaluation, and the standards upon which it is based, supports the globalization of higher education. Only by making explicit the assumptions, goals, standards, and performance of particular degree programs can one compare credentials internationally and enhance the mobility of students across national boundaries.

THE HIGHER EDUCATION QUALITY SYSTEM

Quality evaluation is part of the larger higher education quality system depicted in Figure 8.1. The system encompasses teaching and learning, quality processes, and quality oversight. Traditional academic thinking concentrates on teaching and learning. Education quality processes, the subject of Chapter 6, get some attention but not nearly enough to achieve optimal results. Quality oversight is the province of trustees and regents, and external agencies like accreditors and state higher education coordinating boards. This chapter describes the various approaches to external quality evaluation and recommends one, academic audit, that is becoming recognized as particularly effective.

Figure 8.1

The Higher Education Quality System

Responsibility	Activity
Faculty and students	Teaching and learning
Faculty and chairs	Departmental quality processes
Deans	School quality processes
President, Provost	Institutional quality processes
Trustees and regents	Institutional quality oversight
State coordinating boards	External quality oversight
Accreditation agencies	

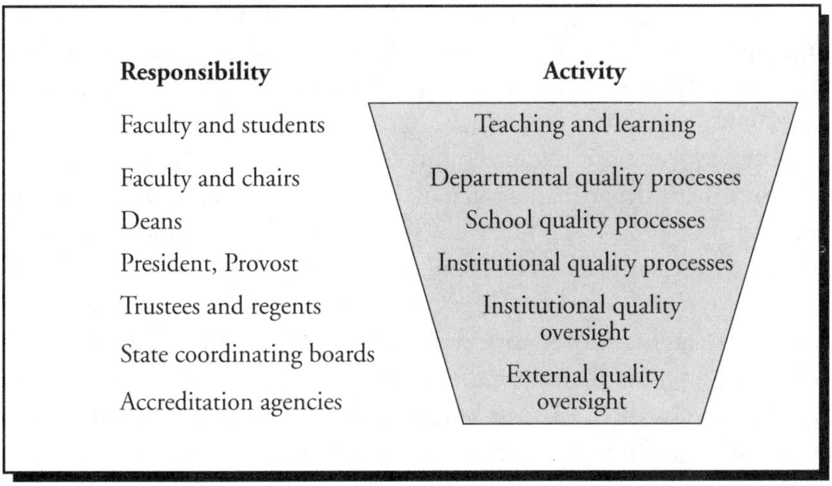

Education quality processes begin at the departmental level with the kinds of activities described in Chapter 5. Professors are the only ones close enough to teaching and learning issues to perform these first-level quality process activities effectively. Department chairs also play a key role, since they are the only officers close enough to professors to ensure that the requisite tasks are being performed.

School and institution-level education quality processes stimulate, support, and assure the departmental processes. The responsible parties provide leadership, resources, rewards and incentives, information and skill development workshops, interdepartmental venues for discourse on quality and quality processes, as well as periodic evaluations of departmental work. Among other things, deans, presidents, and provosts can convene quality councils, encourage departments to benchmark best practice within and outside the institution, and encourage professors to attend workshops on quality processes and participate in networks of like-minded colleagues. They also can hold departments accountable for quality processes by using the audit methodology to be described presently, and then acting energetically on the results.

Deans, presidents, and provosts should be proactive when it comes to quality, but they should not disempower those directly responsible for producing it. Leaders should manage *for* quality, which is different in philosophy and practice from the direct management (some would say micromanagement) *of* quality.[2] Professors rightly ridicule the idea that a "teaching police" can assure quality. "Managing for quality" involves a lighter touch, one that does not disempower professors or impinge upon academic freedom.

Quality oversight energizes and assures the effectiveness of quality processes at the departmental, school, and institutional levels. Contrary to most current practice, education quality oversight should begin with trustees and regents. By establishing the quality process agenda and monitoring progress, boards can spur improvement without micromanagement. State higher education coordinating boards and accreditation agencies can and should do the same.

Effective quality oversight holds people accountable for performance at the same time that it stimulates improvement. (This also applies to the quality process activities of department chairs, deans, provosts, and presidents.) Oversight bodies typically collect data and then engage institutions in discourse about their education quality processes and the delivered quality of education. The discourse will be supportive as long as an institution is working in good faith, embracing the issues energetically, and showing signs of progress. Lack of commitment should trigger sanctions, and demonstrated progress should produce rewards. There is nothing unusual about such behavior: Effective leaders in other walks of life practice it all the time when delegating responsibility to associates.

ACCOUNTABILITY FOR EDUCATIONAL QUALITY

All universities are subject to the accountability of the marketplace and political processes, that is, the power of external constituencies to make individual choices that supply or withhold vital elements of institutional support. Students, parents, donors, employers, politicians, public servants, and members of the media believe they have a legitimate interest in the performance of colleges and universities. They want to know about educational outcomes and why costs are rising. They devour institutional rankings like those published by *U.S. News & World Report, Asiaweek*, and the *Good Universities Guide* (*London Times* in association with PricewaterhouseCoopers). Many express concern about the quality and cost of undergraduate education, even as they reaffirm the importance of access for qualified students. They assert that such education has become too important, and too expensive, to exempt institutions and professors from informed and effective accountability.

Accountability epitomizes a major difference between traditional nonprofit colleges and universities and their for-profit counterparts. For-profit universities accept accountability from top to bottom—from senior management to individual teachers—as a matter of principle. Traditional universities, on the other hand, may well assert that market forces and oversight initiatives by external agencies impinge on institutional autonomy and academic freedom. Professors feel very strongly about this, to the point where most presidents, provosts, and deans try to shield faculty from the impact of markets and oversight initiatives.

Traditional universities and their professors cite inconsistencies between the calls for accountability, particularly those of oversight agencies, and the heavy demand for college degrees. "Why," in the words of the Spencer Foundation's 1995 study report on accountability, "is American higher education the subject of such high regard and consumer demand and at the same time the subject of escalating, sometimes vitriolic, criticism and calls for greater accountability?"[3] Why don't the pundits and politicians just leave colleges and universities alone? Why use scarce resources to fend off or respond to endless queries about what we're doing and why we're doing it?

NCPI interview respondents echoed these sentiments as they lamented the political process's loss of trust and lack of understanding of academic values and academic work. In print, former Harvard President Derek Bok wryly noted, "To be so admired in other parts of the world while being so roundly criticized at home [has been] a singular achievement of our institutions of higher learning."[4]

Chapter 1 described how colleges and universities have entered what one European commentator called "the age of disenchantment... Society is no longer prepared to accept that higher education is self-justifying... [It] wishes to expose the activities of the secret garden."[5] Closer to home, the National Governors' Association's (NGA) 1991 report on education minced no words in making the case for accountability.

> The public has the right to know what it is getting for its expenditure of tax resources; the public has a right to know and understand the quality of undergraduate education that young people receive from publicly funded colleges and universities. They have the right to know that their resources are being wisely invested and committed.[6]

The NGA recently announced plans for a three-year study of college costs, curricula, and university research. According to John Thomasian, director of best practices at the association, "The way courses are now laid out is not flexible enough... Governors are looking at universities and asking, 'Are we turning out the type of graduates to continue growing the economy?'"[7]

At the national level, Senators Fred Thompson and Joseph Lieberman of the Committee on Governmental Affairs continue to question the cost and quality of higher education.[8] Members of the public and their representatives in government want evidence about value for money—what they are getting for the massive sums now being plowed into colleges and universities. Similar questions have been raised overseas by the United Kingdom's Dearing Report, Australia's West Report, and Hong Kong's Education Commission. In the words of the Dearing Report:

Students need to be clear about the requirements of the pro-
grammes to which they are committed, and about the levels
of achievement expected from them. Employers want higher
education to be more explicit about what they can expect
from candidates for jobs.[9]

In other words, the demands for accountability and education quality
evaluation will not go away. Nor will resources flow freely enough to
finance all of higher education's perceived needs.

Governments have for years used regulation and education quality
evaluation to hold public universities accountable for performance, and
accreditation agencies have performed the evaluation role for private as
well as public institutions. Regulatory approaches include minimum faculty teaching loads and mandated student assessment programs. Quality
evaluations can inform funding decisions and provide information that
makes the market more efficient.

Regulatory efforts always are intrusive and often they prove ineffective
as well. They disempower the very people (the faculty) who make the myr-
iad of day-to-day decisions needed to produce educational quality. They
produce a culture of compliance rather than a culture of quality. And
because regulations can be circumvented, the culture of compliance
becomes a culture of apparent compliance. For example, creative definitions of "teaching load" and the faculty population used to calculate load
statistics can blunt the force of regulation and permit professors to pursue
academic business as usual. Furthermore, technological innovation soon
will make even the most rigorous definitions obsolete: What is the meaning of "class contact hours" when professors are responsible for large numbers of students who spend much of their time working independently?

The evaluation of education quality by oversight agencies has more
potential than regulation, but two problems have complicated its development. First comes academic skepticism about the need for evaluation and
the technical means by which it is accomplished. Second comes the difficulty and cost of the evaluation process itself. I'll return to external quality
evaluation shortly.

The market's evaluation of higher education quality also remains in a
fairly primitive state. Market information revolves mostly around prestige,
which is more closely related to institutional wealth than to the value
added by education. We have seen that generous resources don't guarantee

quality. Without the ability to monitor quality, moreover, expenditure reductions caused by market forces or governmental cost containment efforts may come disproportionately from undergraduate education as faculty strive to protect their discretionary research time.

The country's experience with health care illustrates what can happen when quality objectives collide with cost constraints.[10] Concerns about cost-rise, fueled largely by the growth of technology and the open-ended character of what medical science can do, led government and business to develop health maintenance organizations (HMOs) and managed care systems. The ideas were simple: Costs could be contained by managing the "total quality" of medical interventions—before one gets sick as well as after—and then placing strict limits on expenditures. The program has delivered some successes, but many doctors, patients, and commentators believe it has diminished the quality of health care. The resulting cost-quality crunch has spawned lawsuits against HMOs and Congressional efforts to pass a patients' bill of rights.

The medical experience becomes all the more telling when we remember that quality assurance in health care benefits from four factors not present in higher education:

- Many outcomes are relatively unambiguous in that the patient recovers fully or with identifiable side effects, or dies.

- Doctors pledge themselves to provide high-quality patient care, and most do in fact dedicate themselves to that goal.

- Governments, hospitals, and medical associations maintain elaborate quality assurance procedures, including but not limited to licensure requirements and reviews of questionable outcomes.

- The threat of malpractice litigation and the cost of malpractice insurance loom large for institutions and practitioners.

It is easier to sacrifice quality to achieve cost reductions in higher education. Educational outcomes are more ambiguous than those in health care. Many faculty care more about research than teaching. University quality assurance processes are primitive compared to those in health care, there are no licensure requirements, and there is no provision for review of individual learning outcomes. And fortunately for the nation's colleges and universities, "education malpractice" lawsuits are virtually unknown.

Good students usually succeed in later life no matter what, but they could do even better if their education added more value. The differential is probably greater for average students, and greater yet for those who are educationally challenged. The key to accountability, then, lies in the development of effective quality oversight methodologies.

APPROACHES TO QUALITY OVERSIGHT

Quality assurance agencies around the world have developed three approaches to quality oversight. US state agencies and accreditors have sought reports on the assessment of student learning by institutions and departments. Evaluation of education quality at the subject level by teams of outside experts has been the mainstay in the UK and a number of other European countries. Audit of education quality processes, originally developed as part of the United Kingdom's quality oversight program, is a central feature of quality evaluation in Hong Kong, Sweden, and New Zealand, and Australia recently announced its adoption of audit and has created a new quality assurance agency to do the job.

Readers may wonder why accreditation isn't included in the list. This is because accreditation cuts across all three approaches to oversight. US regional accreditation usually includes the assessment of student learning, for example, and professional accreditation can take the form of external quality evaluation. Audit offers great potential for both types of accreditation, and at least one regional accreditor is developing an audit program.[11] In other words, accreditation provides an institutional structure for oversight, whereas assessment, evaluation, and audit represent alternative oversight methodologies.

Until recently, America's accreditation agencies focused mostly on binary questions such as whether credits from one institution should be accepted at another and whether an institution's students should be eligible for federal financial aid programs. Traditional accreditation asked whether an institution has the resources needed to provide threshold levels of education—on inputs like the quantity and quality of faculty, libraries, physical plant—and whether it complies with standards on diversity, academic freedom, and the like. Accreditors offered recommendations for improving practice, but until recently their public reports focused mainly on resources and compliance.

Quality oversight goes deeper: It seeks to evaluate the quality of educational provision at all levels, up to and including the so-called high-quality institutions. For example, how much value do selective institutions add to their gifted and well-prepared matriculants? Are the offerings of institutions up and down the prestige spectrum "fit for purpose," or do they simply emulate those of traditional universities? In other words, quality oversight presses institutions to make the best use of the resources they have— to be the best they can be.

Happily, US accreditors now are redesigning their processes to evaluate and improve quality at all levels as well as to certify threshold standards. For example, the Senior College Commission of the Western Association of Schools and Colleges (WASC) now defines itself as a "capacity building organization with regulatory functions," where "capacity" includes the ability to improve and assure education quality.[12]

Assessment of Student Learning

Working from the idea that measurement holds the key to quality assurance and improvement, many states now hold universities accountable for measuring student learning. Specific requirements vary, but schools must demonstrate that they have organized assessment programs and be able to report results. New Jersey and Tennessee led the way in the late 1970s, and by 1990 a majority of states had such programs. As of 1997, only four states (Delaware, Michigan, Pennsylvania, and Vermont) had no assessment initiatives at the state or system level.

All six regional accreditation associations began focusing on assessment during the 1990s. The new emphasis on evaluating learning outcomes, as opposed to mainly inputs like faculty numbers and quality and the size of the library, represented a much-needed reform in the United States' quality oversight system. Because regional accreditation is necessary for institutions to be eligible for federal student aid programs, reforming the process offers considerable leverage in the private as well as the public sector.

The updated accreditation requirements provide a quick snapshot of what is meant by assessment. Institutions must document their identification of important student outcomes, their analysis of the outcomes, and their ability to act on the outcomes. For example:

- The North Central Association's 1996 guidelines required measures of student "proficiency in skills and competencies essential for all college-educated adults; completion of an identifiable and coherent undergraduate level general education component, and mastery of the level of knowledge appropriate to the degree attained."

- The Western Association suggested including "effective communication, quantitative reasoning, critical thinking, and other competencies judged essential by the institutions."

- The Middle States Association listed "cognitive abilities, content literacy, competence in information management skills, and value awareness" as measures of student achievement.

The accreditation associations believed that the distinct and diverse purposes and goals of their member institutions demanded equally diverse assessment approaches. Hence they did not require specific processes or measurement instruments.[13] The standards can be viewed as precursors of the UK's Benchmarking Statements but the UK statements are more detailed and comprehensive.

The state assessment initiatives reflect more variation and thus are harder to characterize. NCPI researchers from the University of Michigan report that in 1997, of the 46 states with assessment initiatives, 17 used common performance indicators for all colleges and universities and eight of these used common measurement instruments. (Twenty-nine states allowed the institutions themselves to define the indicators and instruments.) Some tests measure student performance during the college experience rather than at exit: For example, Florida's program seeks to "ensure that college students . . . entering the upper division at a state university possess basic or essential skills deemed necessary for success." Other programs measure proficiency at graduation: For example, Tennessee and South Dakota use the ACT-COMP standardized test to evaluate student achievement in general education and Kentucky uses the multiple choice component of the Praxis II test to measure the preparation of K–12 teachers. Other indicators include performance on professional licensure exams and student satisfaction surveys. There appeared to be a slight trend toward the use of standardized indicators to provide comparability among institutions, but the issue remains controversial with most schools opposing commonality.

Have state-level assessment programs improved the quality of undergraduate education? To answer this question, the aforementioned NCPI researchers queried 1,393 chief academic officers about how their institutions "support, promote, and use student-assessment data to improve student learning and institutional performance."[14] The results were not encouraging. For example, public-sector respondents felt that:

> Resistances at the institutional and/or faculty levels hinder the effectiveness of states' assessment policies. Faculty who are unwilling to consider how students learn in new and perhaps unconventional ways [represent an] an obstacle, as is the "limited sophistication of personnel," primarily at smaller institutions. . . .

> Academic officers, as well as many scholars in the assessment field, [believe] that many assessment policies are problematic because of the difficulties associated with developing, much less perfecting, meaningful and valid measures of teaching and learning. The absence of a common understanding of adequate measures—across disciplines and across institutions—remains a barrier to the improvement of teaching and learning.[15]

The same can be said of the private sector. Institutions have learned to meet accreditation requirements, but efforts to embed assessment in faculty quality regimens have not been very successful. Charles Cook, director of the New England Association of Schools and Colleges' Commission on Institutions of Higher Education (a regional accreditation association), summed things up this way: "Millions have been spent by thousands going to hundreds of assessment workshops, and you need a microscope to find the stuff."[16]

The problems stem partly from a mistrust of available assessment measures, but they also have more fundamental causes. To quote the NCPI researchers once again:

> On many campuses, the use of assessment data to guide academic planning is undermined by a lack of corresponding commitment to faculty accountability for student performance.[17]

Few institutions link the results of assessment to budget decisions or faculty rewards. For example, only 4% of the surveyed institutions use assessment results to inform resource allocation among departments—which is the best way to get the chairs', and hence the faculty's, attention. While no data are available, the percentage using assessment results to inform routine salary and promotion decisions is probably low as well. According to the NCPI researchers:

> Assessment is oriented toward improving academic outcomes, but there remain relatively few links between measures of student assessment, on the one hand, and the faculty's classroom responsibilities on the other.

A second problem stems from the fact that the United States' mandated assessment programs were developed in isolation from grassroots academic work. Because assessment was injected by administrative fiat into an inhospitable departmental culture, professors don't see its benefits and resent the time it takes. Indeed, most presidents, provosts, and deans try to shield professors from assessment-related tasks by assigning as much of the work as possible to nonacademic staff. This produces a vicious circle: Little effort goes into developing and perfecting assessment measures, which limits growth in the state of the art, which constrains credibility, which further limits effort. The emphasis most programs place on institution-wide indicators and inter-institutional comparability exacerbates these problems. Such measures often are too broad to provide useful information for departments, let alone professors. In other words, the problem isn't faculty resistance per se, but rather how the mandated assessment programs were designed and promulgated.

Evaluation of Education Quality
In contrast to the US focus on the assessment of student learning, European oversight agencies have tended to rely on direct evaluations of education quality by outside experts. Britain calls its evaluations "subject-level assessments" to emphasize that the focus of attention is the department rather than the institution. The program began with the polytechnic universities in the late 1980s, and was extended to all of the country's 150 or so institutions a few years later. The Netherlands started its program at about the same time. Denmark created its evaluation agency in

1992, and a number of other countries have implemented or are considering similar programs.

Education quality evaluation requires that a team of experts in the discipline visit the department and gauge the quality of education as actually seen by students. Departmental self-studies help focus the visit, but team members also review syllabi and examination papers, interview faculty and students, and visit classrooms. The teams form their own conclusions about education quality rather than using institutional or departmental evaluations.

The teams must compare the quality of education as observed in a given department and institution with some kind of standard. But because each institution has its own mission, the standard must reflect local circumstances. For example, it is not appropriate to use the same standards for a highly selective school from which most students go on to graduate work and a school that trains for entry-level jobs. To solve this problem, the UK Quality Assurance Agency defined two kinds of standards:

1) **Benchmark Standards.** Following recommendations in the Dearing Report on the future of British higher education, the agency convened "small expert teams to provide benchmark information on standards..." The teams produced "broad statements that represent the general expectations about standards for the award of an undergraduate degree in a particular subject area."[18] The benchmark statements include options that make them applicable to all kinds of institutions. Excerpts from several statements can be found in Figure 4.1 of Chapter 4.

2) **Program Specifications.** Prepared by departmental faculty, the specifications describe the program's goals, the methods to be used to achieve them, and how the resulting outcomes will be assessed. Making these things explicit represents an important education quality process and provides the standard needed for external evaluation.

First the evaluators ask whether the program specification is consistent with the benchmark standards and the institution's mission. Then they ask whether the teaching and learning methods called for in the specification can be expected to achieve the program's goals, and whether the assessment methods tap the information needed to gauge goal achievement. Last but definitely not least, the site visit allows evaluators to determine whether the specifications are being carried out and whether the results meet expectations.

Because quality evaluation requires disciplinary expertise, the assessments must address particular disciplines rather than institutions as whole entities. A given evaluation cycle compares all the institutions that teach a particular discipline, for example, all the programs in history or electrical engineering. The nature of direct evaluation dictates a discipline-by-discipline approach: Only experts in the field can make judgments about the delivered quality of education. While the evaluators may consider input measures like the size and quality of the faculty and the adequacy of library resources, they focus mainly on teaching and learning. Detailed examinations of curricula are standard and classroom visits by the site visitors are not uncommon. Students are interviewed to get their reactions to the teaching and learning process. The Danish Centre for Quality Assurance and Evaluation even commissions consulting firms to survey employers about how well graduates do on the job and what changes they might recommend in curricula and educational processes.[19] The evaluation reports always are made public, and although most agencies resist the idea of rankings, some kind of comparisons usually emerge.

Many US institutions conduct "program reviews," where teams of outside experts evaluate a department or program. Program review bears a superficial resemblance to subject-level assessment, but the differences are substantial. Program reviews are commissioned by the institutions themselves rather than by external oversight agencies and the reports usually are kept confidential. Such reviews rarely assess educational quality against predetermined standards. Usually they focus of faculty and student quality, resource adequacy, and departmental governance. While program reviews can be valuable, their critics say the results are all too predictable, for example, "the department needs more money to realize its potential." Few program reviews contain the hard-edged education quality evaluations associated with external subject-level assessment.

External education quality evaluation provides significant incentives for improvement. For example, student learning assessments become matters of institutional self-interest when schools know that external evaluators eventually will show up on their doorsteps. It's better to identify and fix problems early than to be surprised with negative external evaluations that are widely disseminated. The shortcomings of US-style assessment programs show up clearly against this background: In the United States, the reported assessment indicators usually are too crude and the consequences of performance shortfalls too small to make assessment an institutional priority.

Despite its advantages, external education quality evaluation has some serious downsides. It is expensive in large systems where the number of site visits (equal to the number of institutions times the number of disciplines) can reach well into the hundreds for each evaluation cycle. The UK, which until recently ran the largest assessment system in the world, spent many millions on its program every year.

External quality evaluation also tends to be intrusive. One cannot evaluate education quality without "getting inside" the department. Once inside, the experts may trigger defensiveness and resentment by second-guessing local professors on what are essentially matters of judgment. This problem is particularly severe when the outside experts have less research prestige than the local faculty. Research prowess doesn't necessarily confer good pedagogical judgment, but experience in the UK, particularly, demonstrates how the lack of a strong research record can undermine an outside expert's credibility.[20]

Defensiveness makes it hard to use the evaluation results to improve educational performance. Faculty disclose as little as possible, and site visits of a few days or less limit the outside experts' ability to identify and interpret key quality indicators. They focus on what they think are the rules of good practice rather than on making the best judgments possible in the circumstances. This triggers a culture of compliance, which can inhibit rather than stimulate quality improvement.

Opinions differ about whether the advantages of external education quality evaluation outweigh its disadvantages. On the positive side, the external evaluations provide credible information to further the sponsoring agency's accountability, public reassurance, and market information goals. On the negative side, the intrusiveness of subject-level assessment tends to undermine evaluation's improvement agenda. Direct evaluations also are very expensive, and many commentators question whether site visit teams can produce meaningful evaluations in the time available to them.

Audit of Education Quality Processes

"Academic audit," as this approach to oversight is usually called, positions itself between US-style assessment programs and European-style external quality evaluations. Audit encompasses student learning assessments, but it embeds them in a broader framework that includes site visits to institutions. In contrast to external evaluation, however, audit teams do not make *de novo* judgments about education quality. They ask whether the institution and its constituent parts are performing the activities necessary to produce quality, whether they obtain and act on student assessment and other quality data, and whether the judgments they make are well thought out and appear consistent with stated objectives. In other words, academic audit evaluates an institution's education quality processes rather than education quality itself.

The approach is simple: Find out whether institutions and professors take education quality processes seriously and whether they are performing them effectively. For example, auditors might ask how many departments consciously apply the quality principles discussed in Chapter 7. If the incidence is sparse, they will ask what the institution is doing to correct the problem. If exemplary practice is plentiful, the auditors will ask what the institution is doing to sustain and build on its success. Audit usually addresses the institution, with departments and schools being covered on a sampling basis. The process begins with a self-study that focuses faculty and staff on quality process issues. It culminates with a site visit by people trained to evaluate quality processes—not disciplinary experts as in the case of direct external evaluation. We shall see that audit avoids the intrusiveness, second-guessing, and expense of external evaluation while retaining the advantages of oversight.

Academic audit zeros in on the institution's core competency in education. Quality expert David Dill puts the idea this way:

> In contrast to accreditation, program review, or student assessment initiatives, audits look deeply into the heart of the academic enterprise. They test whether institutions and their faculties in fact honor their public responsibility to monitor academic standards and improve student learning.[21]

In other words, academic audit asks whether a college or university is honoring the trust placed in it as the primary custodian of educational quality.

The International Standards Organization (ISO) defines a "quality audit" this way:

> Quality Audit: A systematic and independent examination to determine whether quality activities and related results

comply with planned arrangements and whether these
arrangements are implemented effectively and are suitable to
achieve the stated objectives.[22]

In the language of education quality processes, one asks whether educational goals have been considered carefully in light of the institution's mission and the needs of its students. Then one asks how well curricula, teaching and learning processes, and student assessment methods support the goals. Finally, one asks whether these planned arrangements are being implemented effectively.

Proponents of alternative oversight methodologies sometimes complain that audit ignores data about education quality. In fact, audit can make very effective use of such data. American-style assessment programs task institutions with assessing student learning, but they don't ensure that the data are reliable and fit for use. Direct evaluation tasks external reviewers with collecting and interpreting quality data, but this produces its own problems. In audit, the responsibility for collecting and interpreting the data remains with the institution, but these tasks are subject to review as part of the school's overall program of quality process work. Among other things, auditors ask whether the available data are sufficient to inform judgments about the delivered quality of education and whether faculty respond to the data in ways that are consistent with the facts.

Failure to collect sufficient student assessment and other quality data constitutes a black mark in the audit. Failure to interpret and act on the data in reasonable ways also constitutes a black mark. For example, an institution that rationalizes high dropout rates or adverse student assessment trends by blaming the students or external forces instead of examining its own performance would fail the reasonableness test. Such explanations may be defensible, but only after the controllable possibilities for improvement have been exhausted.

The judgments made by auditors are like the determinations of an appellate court: were appropriate processes followed and do the trial court's findings fall within the envelope of reasonable judgments based on the facts? Failure of either test will send the case back to the trial court. Like an appellate judge, academic auditors will press the institution to do a better job of evaluating quality but will not take the job out of its hands. They recognize that no outsider can do as good a job as faculty on the ground, and that disempowering local faculty will do more harm than good. At the same time, they feel responsible for certifying to external stakeholders that quality data provided by the institution are meaningful and are being acted on appropriately.

Similar principles apply to financial reporting and auditing. Management bears the full responsibility for preparing accurate financial reports, but their judgments must follow generally accepted accounting principles. Independent auditors test for compliance with the principles, but they do not take on management's responsibility to provide accurate data and make effective interpretations. The board and other stakeholders use the audited reports to hold management accountable for performance. Preparation of reports by outside experts becomes necessary only in extreme cases, as in bankruptcy proceedings or when fraud is suspected.

Because academic audit does not disempower institutions and faculty, the process can be used to spur improvement as well as maintain accountability. I'll discuss this in more detail presently. For now it is enough to say that audit's improvement dimension stems from its ability to elicit structured conversations about education quality processes: first within the institution and then with the site visit team. (Indeed, to jump-start such conversations is one of audit's prime objectives.) Conversations are important because that is how actions get launched in academe. Structure is important because it focuses the conversations on performance in all five quality-process dimensions and on generally accepted quality principles.

The conversations should explicitly address each of the five quality domains described in Chapter 6: 1) determination of desired learning outcomes, 2) curricular design, 3) teaching and learning process design, 4) student assessment design and utilization, and 5) implementation of quality assurance.

The seven quality principles provide standards by which an institution and its constituent departments can evaluate performance in each domain. The principles are repeated here in the form of questions a department might ask itself, a dean might ask a department, or a provost might ask a dean—and which an auditor might ask any of the above.

1) Does the department define education quality in terms of student outcomes? Does it apply fitness-for-use criteria?

2) Do professors focus on the processes of teaching, learning, and assessment?

3) Do they strive for coherence and progression in curricula and educational process?

4) Do they work collaboratively rather than as isolated individuals?

5) Do they base educational decisions on facts wherever possible?

6) Do professors identify and learn from best practice? Do they view quality variations as opportunities for improvement?

7) Does the department make continuous quality improvement a top priority?

The appendix to Chapter 11 describes how each principle can be applied to each of the domains.[23] However, trying to fill all the cells in the resulting matrix would cause the process to collapse under its own weight. The questions are intended simply to get the conversation going—participants should feel free to engage their own sense of priorities and to identify additional questions if they desire.

Figure 8.2 illustrates one way to get the conversations going at the department level. Rather than beginning with a full-scale self-assessment of the department's education quality processes, one identifies the areas where these processes are most developed. This breaks the ice on what otherwise would appear as an abstract and daunting exercise—abstract because quality processes are presented as concepts rather than realities and daunting because such processes are unfamiliar. Once successful instances are identified, it is natural to ask why they are successful and how they can be improved further. From there it is only a short jump to ask what other processes could benefit from the same analysis and to make commitments for so doing.

The steps are straightforward. Perhaps most important, they do not require large commitments of time from rank-and-file faculty. As discussed in Chapter 11, a quality-process champion or small team consults with colleagues, writes up the results, and circulates the draft for comments at each step of the way. The final version can be discussed at a departmental meeting and then submitted to the institution or directly to the audit team as the department's self-study.

Auditors can ask the individuals and committees responsible for institution-level quality processes whether they press departments to engage in the aforementioned structured conversations. If the answer is "yes," they

Figure 8.2

Jump-Starting Quality Process Conversations at the Department or Program Level

- Address each of the quality process domains, one at a time.

- For each domain, identify one or a few exemplary accomplishments. For example, the department may take pride in a well-informed statement of purpose for its major, the coherence of its curriculum, its innovative use of technology, or its ability to assess student learning.

- For each such accomplishment, ask how the quality principles contributed to the success.

- For each accomplishment, ask how the application of other principles could further improve performance.

- For each domain, ask what activities are most in need of improvement and how the quality principles could help.

- Select a manageable number of activities and develop goals, timetables, and commitments of responsibility for improvement. If at all possible, the areas of commitment should span all five quality process domains.

might examine a sample of departmental self-studies to verify that all the quality process domains are being considered and that relevant quality principles are being taken into account. The auditors also might verify that the president, provost, and deans have made quality-process excellence a key results area. Are departments expected to attain quality-process excellence? Are they expected to extend their competence by attending workshops? Does the incentive and reward system recognize quality-process activities? Are academic leaders aware of performance differences, and do they work with less mature departments to effect improvement? The audit team also may interview students to gain their perspectives on the institution's quality processes—in particular, whether students are consulted about quality and whether their inputs are taken seriously.

Face-to-face dialog at the departmental and school level provides the audit team with another important input. Did the sampled departments take the self-assessment exercise seriously? Do they embrace all the quality domains and try to apply quality principles? Do they understand and follow institutional quality-process policies and priorities? Do faculty attend workshops and actively participate in quality-process networks? Can students see evidence of the quality processes in action? In short, does the academic unit demonstrate a culture of quality?

I noted earlier that US accreditation agencies are beginning to experiment with audit. The Teacher Accreditation and Evaluation Council (TEAC) adopted audit for its subject-level professional accreditation and the Western Association of Schools and Colleges (WASC) has been pilot testing audit as an element of institutional accreditation. The North Central Association uses a cousin of the audit methodology in its application of Baldrige principles to accreditation, and the Middle States Association's new accreditation standards also contain elements of audit. Pilot projects in the application of audit by state systems are under discussion and may be operational by the time this book sees print.

Quality Process Maturity

The so-called capability maturity model provides a useful language for gauging performance on education quality processes. Developed by engineers to track the capacity of development teams to manage complex systems, the model applies equally well to quality processes at the departmental and institutional levels. Low maturity levels imply a lack of attention to quality processes, while high ones indicate high levels of systematic attention that include self-correction mechanisms. Academic auditors can use the criteria as benchmarks for evaluating progress up the quality process maturity curve.

Figure 8.3 depicts the model as applied to departmental processes.

- *No effort* means there are no organized quality processes.

- *Firefighting* means that departments respond to problems, but mostly with ad hoc methods. The seven quality principles receive little attention.

- With *emergent effort,* one sees individual initiatives and experimentation with the seven principles in one or more quality process domains.

- With *organized effort,* quality process initiatives begin to be planned and tracked, work methods are systematically rooted in the principles, and the department has begun to develop performance metrics and norms.

- With *mature effort,* quality processes have been embedded in departmental culture, continuous improvement is a way of life, and organizational learning about quality process is fully established.

Figure 8.3

Departmental Quality-Process Maturity Levels

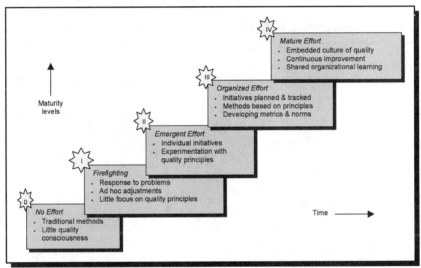

One hopes that few if any departments fall into the first category, even before the initiation of an academic audit program. Most probably apply informal effort to the education quality process. Once the program has been announced, departments should use the audit preparation period to organize their quality process efforts. Some will approach the third level in as little as six months or a year. Others will take longer, but all should be expected to operate at a fully mature level within five years.

Figure 8.4 adapts the model for use at the school, campus, or system-wide level. Auditors ask whether institution-level behavior reflects commitment to education quality process improvement and whether departments are in fact moving up the maturity curve. Mature organizations will routinely apply the seven Baldrige criteria discussed in Chapter 7 at the institutional level. They will provide strong leadership, use information and analysis effectively, engage in strategic quality planning, and include quality processes in their human resource programs. They will insist that operating units manage process quality, link quality to operational results, and focus on students as well as other stakeholders. As we discussed in Chapter 6, the first four criteria refer to people while the last three refer to systems. Institutions with mature quality process programs will use central initiatives to solve the people problems and maintain systems to ensure that departments address the systems issues effectively.

Figure 8.4

Institutional Quality-Process Maturity Levels

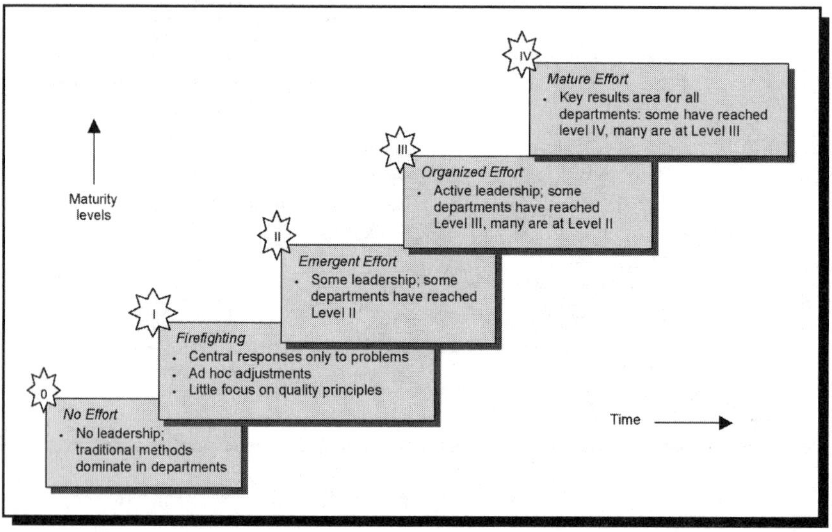

ACCOUNTABILITY VERSUS IMPROVEMENT

Oversight programs cost both the institutions and the oversight agency time and money, so they should provide improvement along with accountability. The idea is not unfamiliar—boards and managers frequently combine improvement and accountability when they assign responsibility to subordinates or agents. "Let me help you be the best you can be," they say, "and I will reward you for good performance or apply sanctions if you fail." But while this may seem like common sense to people outside the academy, many academics believe that any element of accountability poisons an evaluation's developmental goals.

Researcher Martin Trow's fourfold typology for quality evaluation, shown on the left side of Figure 8.5, emphasizes the alleged incompatibility between improvement and accountability.[24] The rows differentiate between internal reviews (e.g., by deans or provosts as part of institutional quality processes) and external reviews (e.g., by governing boards and oversight agencies as part of quality oversight). The columns distinguish between reviews oriented toward improvement (supportive) and those oriented toward accountability (evaluative). Trow argues that no review can be both supportive and evaluative, and that supportive internal reviews (Type I) tap intrinsic motivation and produce the greatest improvements in teaching and learning. Conversely, he claims, externally driven evaluative reviews (Type IV) trigger evasive strategies and produce little improvement.

Figure 8.5

Quality Evaluation and Accountability

Origin of the review	Function of the review		Origin of the review	Function of the review
	Supportive	Evaluative		Supportive & Evaluative
Internal	I (most effective)	II	Internal	**Quality processes**
External	III	IV (least effective)	External	**Quality oversight**
	Incompatibility Model			Compatibility Model

Trow's arguments offer comfort to those wishing to resist accountability, but they frustrate would-be change agents. Oversight boards and system-wide administrations want to help universities improve education quality, and many are prepared to fund initiatives that support this end. But what happens if improvements are not forthcoming? Should one be proactive or is it necessary to wait patiently until people who share the change agent's agenda become ascendant within the university? Many responsible public stewards choose the proactive route, which means they must find levers to stimulate change.

Intrinsic motivations are especially powerful in academe, but that doesn't mean rewards and sanctions are irrelevant. Research in psychology and sociology shows that people are rational actors who make conscious decisions based on anticipated consequences. For example, expectancy theory holds that relevant consequences can include rewards or sanctions as well as good or bad feelings based on altruism.[25] Chapter 4 described how a combination of intrinsic and extrinsic factors drives faculty attention toward research. Banning the accountability dimension from education quality oversight means the bias toward research will continue unabated, but this is not in the public interest. We proved in Hong Kong that quality-process audits *can* successfully combine improvement with accountability by applying a "light touch of accountability" and an evasion-resistant review methodology to what is mainly a developmental agenda.

Peter Ewell of the National Center for Higher Education Management Systems (NCHEMS) offers a useful model for external quality evaluation. Processes with the following characteristics "add value to institutional-level management and quality-improvement efforts" as well as fulfill their accountability function.[26]

1) The processes are consciously informed by "theories of institutional development."

2) They consciously distinguish compliance from the "deep engagement" functions associated with self-study.

3) They focus review criteria on broadly defined institutional functions and results, not on the specific structures or activities used to achieve them.

4) They emphasize existing evidence and documentation, and their use by the people concerned, not extensive one-off reports.

5) They allow institutions to raise and address their own problems within the context of evaluation.

Academic audit scores well on all points. Audits are informed by quality-process principles. They ask deep questions about engagement with quality processes, defined broadly rather than in terms of specific rules or procedures.[27] They test the sufficiency and use of evidence and documentation, and they provide ample opportunity for institutions to raise and address their own issues.

The right side of Figure 8.5 recasts Trow's model into the world of coexistence. Because expectancy theory indicates that the absence of an evaluative edge undermines the impetus for improvement, both internal and external reviews should be simultaneously supportive and evaluative. Experience indicates that internal reviews tend to be more supportive and external ones more evaluative, but the difference need only be a matter of degree. External reviews conducted at the early stages of a quality oversight program should be more supportive than evaluative, with the accountability dimension receiving more emphasis later when institutions have had time to become familiar with the education-quality concepts and processes.

Transparency presents another area of controversy. The traditional view in the United States holds that accreditation reports should be private except for the "bottom line"—whether the institution is accredited, put on probation, or denied accreditation. Making the reports public, it is said, would inhibit institutions' willingness to disclose problems and undermine the improvement agenda.

The worldwide trend flows the other way. Transparency provides better information to the public and furthers accountability. It also furthers improvement, since the prospect of a negative private report provides less incentive for change than the prospect of a public one. The main action in quality improvement occurs within departments. Hence departmental faculty need to receive the reports, compare their performance with that of other departments, and commit themselves to corrective measures. Yet to disseminate a report widely within the institution almost surely means it will become public. Institutional leaders may not want to embarrass themselves or their institutions, so they hold the reports closely. Unfortunately, this limits their ability to effect improvement.

To have maximum impact, evaluation reports should be published either by the agency or the institutions themselves.[28] At least two regional accreditation agencies, the Western Association and the Middle States Commission on Higher Education, have recognized this fact. They now require institutions to disseminate the final accreditation report widely within the institution.[29] While this is not the same as publication, it does safeguard effectiveness for internal purposes and makes it likely that newsworthy reports eventually will become public.

Advantages of Academic Audit

I noted earlier that audit elicits structured conversations about education quality processes: first within the audited unit and then between faculty members and the site visit team. Conversations get people focused on education quality issues and inform the self-study and audit reports. Yet conversations without structure lack the focus needed for effective audit. Chapters 6 and 7 provided the needed structure. The five quality process domains delineate the audit's scope—conversations that don't cover all the domains can't be regarded as sufficient. The seven quality principles focus the conversations on good practice, on questions that spur improvement. Finally, the capability maturity categories described earlier in this chapter provide a language for self-evaluations of progress up the quality process learning curve.

The United Kingdom, New Zealand, Hong Kong, and Sweden have completed their first cycle of academic audits, and each experience has been formally evaluated.[30] Thus we now are in a position to assess the methodology's advantages and disadvantages. The reviewers generally agree that academic audits have:

- "Made improving teaching and learning an institutional priority."

- "Facilitated active discussion and cooperation within academic units on means for improving teaching and learning."

- "Helped clarify responsibility for improving teaching and learning at the academic unit, faculty [i.e., school], and institutional level."

- "Provided information on best practices within and across institutions."[31]

The advantages stem from fundamental characteristics of the audit approach, not just its novelty or the happenstance of favorable conditions for implementation. The benefits stem from these factors.

1) Academic audit focuses on education quality processes, which represent a necessary (though not sufficient) condition for educational quality. These processes involve matters that are of direct consequence to faculty, not lofty abstractions or requirements sent down by some remote oversight body. Improving quality processes will almost surely improve the delivered quality of education. Moreover, such improvements will surely include more meaningful student assessment measures that will in time document the improvement.

2) External agencies can evaluate education quality processes more easily than education quality itself. Quality standards may well differ across institutions, but the standards for judging quality processes are much less variable. Core principles like customer focus, regular performance feedback, and continuous improvement are universally desirable. Furthermore, because the audit data are easy to interpret and difficult to fake, it is not hard for site visitors to determine whether institutions

and departments have embraced the quality process principles. For example, even a short dialog with departmental faculty enables auditors to discern whether the self-study documents are "for real" or not. If they are, the faculty will be able to describe their thinking in detail. If not, they will soon lapse into generalities.

3) The focus on quality process principles allows easier selection and better training of auditors than is possible for external education-quality evaluators. External evaluators must have subject-matter expertise and their training must take into account both subject and institutional differences. Auditors should be familiar with (or be willing to learn) academic quality processes, but they need no particular knowledge of the subject or institution. Training can focus on the quality-process domains and principles and on how to evaluate quality-process maturity, matters that do not vary greatly across subjects or institutional types. Over time, the standards for auditor training and effectiveness can become more refined than is likely to prove possible for external evaluators.

4) Audit cycle times can be significantly less than those for external evaluation. (Frequency of reinforcement matters when one is trying to change behavior.) Because universities tend to cover a broad range of fields, the typical subject-level evaluations in large systems must cover a great many schools. If there are n institutions and m subjects, the number of assessment visits may approach $n \times m$, whereas there would never be more than n audits. The smaller number of audits means that the evaluation agency can maintain shorter cycle times without unduly burdening itself or the universities.

5) Audit respects institutional diversity to a greater extent than is practical with external evaluation. External evaluators must define what is meant by "quality education" in each university and subject area. There are two choices: the evaluating body either must set its own standards or it must rely on standards established by the universities themselves. Centrally determined standards are not consistent with diversity. On the other hand, reliance on local quality definitions requires one to ask how the standards were developed, how they are being used, and whether they are being continually improved—in other words, on the kinds of things looked at in academic audit.

6) Finally, audit provides a better basis for steering an educational system toward improved quality than does external evaluation. Audit introduces and reinforces the kinds of behaviors needed to improve quality—behaviors that institutions otherwise would have to invent for themselves. Audit provides more logical linkages to funding than does assessment, so the budget process can be harnessed to provide needed incentives. In other words, audit provides the light but firm touch needed to steer the system without regulation or micromanagement.

I predict that effective education quality processes, verified by academic audit, eventually will eliminate the need for external quality evaluation. Suppose a program passes all the quality-process tests: a well-qualified faculty works collegially to make fact-based design decisions in light of well-elaborated standards, they assure that the designs are carried out effectively, and they continually evaluate learning outcomes and refine curricula and teaching methods in light of this feedback. What external evaluator would substitute his or her opinions for such careful, hands-on, and well-informed judgments? Would second-guessing add value, or would it disempower professors and thus undermine their efforts to improve quality? Even if second-guessing could be avoided, would external subject-level assessment be worth its cost?

I should acknowledge that many adherents of external quality evaluation do not accept these arguments.[32] They believe that accountability requires external evaluations of educational provision, not just audits of education quality processes. Time will tell whether academic audit will prove sufficient. One thing is certain, however: Failure to establish effective education quality processes will buttress the case for external quality evaluation.

Because student learning assessments are integral to education quality processes, academic audit also could supplant the current US-style student assessment initiatives. Any institution that does not maintain and continuously improve a program of learning assessment for every major and for general education should fail its academic audit. There will be no need for freestanding programs to spur assessment, although targeted programs and funding to facilitate improvement will remain important.

Let me conclude the case for academic audit by again quoting David Dill.

Academic audit offers a working model of external accountability that provides incentives and support for cooperative faculty behavior that improves teaching and learning. In response to academic audits, universities have changed their internal norms and policies for academic quality assurance. As they adapt to these audits, universities more closely approximate academic "learning organizations," building their capacity for developing and transferring knowledge for the improvement of their core academic processes.[33]

Appendix

ACADEMIC AUDIT IN HONG KONG, SWEDEN, AND NEW ZEALAND

Hong Kong, Sweden, and New Zealand provide good examples of how audit's introduction can change the academic environment. I'll illustrate the approach using Hong Kong's experience[34] and add material from Sweden and New Zealand where it provides extra insight.[35] None of these early adopters of audit implemented the methodology exactly as recommended in this book. Hong Kong's second round of audits launched in 2002 will come fairly close, however, and I believe that other applications will follow in due course.

Hong Kong's University Grants Committee (UGC) began its comprehensive quality evaluation program in the early 1990s. The UGC is a quasi-governmental body that funds and oversees the territory's eight higher education institutions.[36] Hong Kong's universities are self-accrediting in the sense that they can determine their own curricula, but the UGC is responsible for quality overall. In US parlance, the committee functions as a "strong" higher education coordinating board because of its influence on funding. Antony Leong, then chair of the UGC and now the territory's financial secretary, recognized soon after taking office that public accountability required performance measurement and that accountability would become even more important once Hong Kong became part of China in 1997.

The committee's first foray into quality evaluation took the form of a Research Assessment Exercise (RAE), patterned after a similar exercise in the UK.[37] Putting the RAE first made sense because improving Hong

Kong's research performance was a major priority at the time, and also because research is easier to evaluate than education quality. Institutions submitted the best three publications or equivalent output items for all faculty believed to be active in research. Discipline-specific expert panels rated each professor as research active or not. The UGC used the aggregate scores to allocate about 25% of the government subsidy—money intended to provide the basic faculty, library, equipment, and infrastructure resources needed for each school's research program. (The remaining funds were allocated mostly on the basis of enrollment.[38]) Few observers doubt that the RAE contributed strongly to the growth of research in Hong Kong.

The RAE's success triggered a massive shift of attention from teaching to research, a quintessential example of the academic ratchet discussed in Chapter 4. Better research spurred improvements in faculty and infrastructure that benefited education quality. However, the UGC was concerned that the shift would move past the point of diminishing returns. Something had to be done to arrest the ratchet before it could undermine the quality of education. That something was the Teaching and Learning Quality Process Review, or TLQPR for short.[39]

The committee had known for several years that some type of education quality evaluation would be necessary, but members had balked at implementing direct subject-level assessment for the reasons described earlier. The UK had introduced academic audit a few years before, and although the program stressed quality assurance over improvement and seemed to overemphasize formalities like documentation and committee structures, the approach seemed promising. Fortunately, Hong Kong's need coincided with the emergence of ideas like those expressed in Chapters 6 and 7. By broadening audit to include all the education quality process domains, while at the same time reducing its formalities, we hoped to institutionalize education quality processes and balance the incentives favoring research. Dubbing the exercise a "review" called out the distinction from the UK's quality assurance audits.

Sweden's academic audit program emerged from events in the late 1980s, when the country concluded that centralized regulation could not spur quality improvement and efficiency. As institutions became more autonomous, professors were asked to take full responsibility for their work and its results and institutional self-regulation came to be viewed as necessary for continual development: "Universities [were] expected continuously to follow up and evaluate their own activities and take action on the basis of the results."[40] That, of course, left accountability issues up in the air.

The dominant university viewpoint held that an "invisible hand" would produce educational quality as long as research quality could be maintained. Starting in 1993, however, Minister of Education Per Unckel and newly appointed University Chancellor Stig Hagström challenged this view.[41] Staffan Wahlén, coordinator of the Quality Audit Programme for the University Chancellor, describes their agenda:

> Each institution was responsible for maintaining and improving the quality of its own activities, and was accountable to the Government and society for this. [One can say] that universities and colleges have always been quality-driven. What has now been added... is that they must have (and demonstrate that they have) systematic improvement processes regarding undergraduate education, graduate education, research, and administration. They are required to develop routines for reflecting on their activities, and make corrections wherever necessary for the sound improvement of the institution."[42]

The academic audit program, which began in 1996, sought to verify that institutions were carrying out the education portion of this agenda.

In New Zealand, comprehensive academic quality audits of all universities were carried out over the period 1995–1998 by the country's Academic Audit Unit (AAU) under the leadership of David Woodhouse.[43] The audits sought to enhance education quality processes, strengthen institutional quality units, increase benchmarking activities, encourage thorough program-level reviews, and stimulate more discriminating use of performance indicators. To keep the process fresh and relevant, the second cycle of audits focused on a smaller number of factors: one selected (system-wide) by the AAU, and a second factor in each individual institution selected by the institution. The nature of the third cycle is currently (early 2001) under discussion.

Audits use the familiar sequence of a written submission followed by site visit to elaborate and check on the written material. In Hong Kong, the written submission was expected to cover four of the aforementioned five education quality domains: curricular design, educational process design, student assessment, and implementation quality assurance.[44] (Determination of desired learning outcomes was included under curricular design at this early stage.) The Swedish audits covered similar ideas but in more general terms.

We provided Hong Kong's universities with briefing documents describing the quality domains and examples of good practice several months before the site visit, then met with faculty and staff to discuss the concepts and materials. The goal was to stimulate discussions about quality processes at all institutional levels, and to a large extent this was achieved. More detailed descriptions of quality processes and principles would have sharpened the discussions, but the information provided did prove sufficient to achieve the goal.

The written submissions were not "self-studies" as that term is used in US accreditation, but rather descriptions of the institutions' quality processes. Traditional self-studies assume broad faculty familiarity with the issues being addressed, but this assumption is problematic during the first round of audit.[45] The descriptions enhanced self-awareness and provided a basis for discussion with the audit team. Institutions did identify shortfalls in their quality processes, some of which were fixed before the site visit, but we viewed this as a bonus rather than a requirement. Later audit rounds can place more reliance on the faculty's ability to judge itself, as in traditional self-studies.

We used a single 18-member panel for all institutions, but limitations imposed by the use of overseas panelists limited each visit to only one to two days. Large panels allow one to sample more departments and get more people involved in the process, but the logistics become unwieldy. Sweden's panels were much smaller, and Hong Kong's will be smaller in its second round. Our panel consisted of eight UGC members (about half were from overseas), two foreign experts on quality evaluation, and eight members from the institutions themselves.[46] The institutional members participated fully, even when their own institution was being evaluated.

The panel interviewed institutional and academic leaders, faculty, and students. The interviews were informal, with the emphasis being on what really was being done and how the respondents felt about it rather than the formalities of committee structure and record keeping. Samples of relevant records were available in the interview rooms, and respondents and panel members consulted them from time to time. By breaking itself into three-person subgroups for the school- and department-level interviews and allowing two rounds of subgroup interviews, the panel was able to sample 12 such units at each institution. This proved sufficient to get a good feel for what was happening on the ground. A wrap-up session near the end of the site visit afforded the subgroups an opportunity to compare notes while the material was fresh in everyone's mind.

Panel members used the emergent quality principles to help structure their thinking and communicate ideas to the audit respondents. It proved fairly easy to determine whether respondent behavior was consistent with the principles. Chairs and faculty who had embraced the principles would talk authoritatively about their activities, whereas nonadopters would lapse into platitudes after only a few minutes. The difficulty of faking these conversations made the TLQPR strongly evasion-resistant. We became more comfortable with the principles as the sequence of site visits progressed, and by the end were treating them as nascent audit standards.

The eight institutional panel members provided insider descriptions of institutional thinking about quality processes and examples of good and bad practice. A consultative committee consisting of multiple representatives from each institution also helped facilitate communication throughout the process. Each institution published its report (in print and on the web[47]), so the last institutions in the visit sequence had the benefit of the early institutions' experience. We felt that broad communication was desirable because the main purpose of the first TLQPR round was developmental, to establish education quality processes as an ongoing routine in every institution. A territory-wide convocation, convened by the consultative committee after all the reports had been published, also facilitated communication and benchmarked good practice across the institutions.

While accountability was of secondary importance, it remained a significant goal. The UGC stated publicly that the review would "inform funding." That is, over the long run, institutions that took education quality processes seriously would fare better than those that didn't. The committee refused to answer questions about how funding would be informed—partly to retain flexibility and partly because specificity might have undermined the review's developmental goals. We did reiterate that no formula would be used. Eventually the criterion became the degree to which each institution demonstrated seriousness about its quality-process agenda, not actual performance at the time of evaluation. Future rounds can be expected to weight actual performance more heavily.

As things worked out, funding for only one institution was directly and immediately affected. That institution had received the poorest audit evaluation. Worse, it dragged its heels about making commitments for improvement. Concluding that the school didn't take quality processes seriously, we removed some doctoral student funding. Improvement was apparent within months, and the funding was restored after a favorable progress report the following year. The sum withheld was not large, but it was enough to demonstrate that the committee meant business. Education quality advocates within the university applauded the action because it strengthened their hands. By limiting the cut to doctoral enrollments (which in effect squeezed discretionary research funding), we forestalled any criticism that undergraduates were paying the price for the university's dilatoriness.

The most immediate impact of Hong Kong's Teaching and Learning Quality Process Reviews was to engage universities and faculty in a dialog about education quality processes. The dialog involved people that otherwise would have been unaware of quality work and its possibilities. By and large the response was favorable—"these things makes sense, they are worth doing." All eight institutions have developed initiatives for keeping the dialog going. These include education quality councils, quality process support units for internal consultation and skill development, and in at least one case an "internal academic audit unit." Education quality processes also are finding their way into departmental evaluation protocols and individual faculty work plans.

Following good quality protocols, the UGC commissioned its own external evaluation of the TLQPR. A team from the Center for Higher Education Policy Studies at the University of Twente, the Netherlands (a global authority on higher education quality and quality assurance), concluded that the review was "the right process at the right time" and that it should be continued and made more rigorous.[48] The committee is continuing to "keep up the beat" by monitoring quality processes in the context of triennial funding, sponsoring benchmarking projects, and planning a second round of reviews to begin in 2002.

Sweden's experience was similar to Hong Kong's, and for the same reasons. Discourse about quality processes empowered quality advocates within the universities and helped embed such processes in institutional routines. When I conducted interviews at Swedish institutions, respondent after respondent said the program's "light touch" and thoughtful demeanor made it easier to engage professors in substantive quality discussions.[49] Reacting to a failed proposal in which subject-level assessment results would have driven funding according to a formula, the chancellor had assured the institutions that the quality process audits would not inform funding. In retrospect, however, allowing for a small judgmental linkage could have further spurred the diffusion of quality processes without undermining the program's developmental goals.

Endnotes

1. Kirstein (1999), Section 4.

2. Barnett (1992), p. 80; also van Vught (1994), p. 12.

3. Graham, Lyman, and Trow (1995), p. 3.

4. Quoted in Graham, Lyman, and Trow (1995), p. 3.

5. Barnett (1992), p. 216. Quoted in van Vught (1995), p. 8.

6. National Governors Association (1991); quoted in Nettles, Cole, and Sharp (1997), p. 6. The report was written by John Ashcroft, then governor of Missouri.

7. *The Chronicle of Higher Education,* "Governors Announce 3-Year Focus on Higher Education" (Today's News [web], July 13, 2000).

8. *Congressional Record,* Senate Committee on Governmental Affairs, February 9, 2000.

9. Dearing (1997). The document can be accessed through: www.leeds.ac .uk/educol/ncihe/nr_142.htm.

10. For further discussion see Massy (1996), Chapter 8.

11. The Western Association of Schools and Colleges (WASC) is experimenting with academic audit.

12. Ralph Wolff, executive director, Senior College Commission of the Western Association of Schools and Colleges." Personal communication.

13. The materials in this and the next paragraph come from Nettles, Cole, and Sharp (1997), pp. 37–45.

14. The Institute for Research on Higher Education (1999), p. 53.

15. Nettles and Cole (1999), pp. 11–12.

16. *The Chronicle of Higher Education,* "Accreditors Revamp Policies to Assess Student Learning" (July 7, 2000, p. A31).

17. This and the quotation on the next page are from The Institute for Research on Higher Education (1999), p. 55.

18. Presentation by John Randall, then executive director of the QAA, the 6th biennial conference of the International Network of Quality Assurance Agencies in Higher Education (INQAAHE), Bangalore, India, March 19–22, 2001.

19. Massy (2000). The so-called stakeholder surveys produce findings for the discipline as a whole, not for the graduates of the individual institutions.

20. Personal communications. The UK experienced serious problems assessing education quality at its top research institutions. On the one hand, the best researchers were not necessarily the best assessors, and in any case they were seldom available for this time-consuming task. On the other hand, faculty at the top research universities would not recognize any but top researchers as peers qualified to do the assessments.

21. Dill (2000), p. 35.

22. Based on ISO 9001 (1987).

23. Chapter 11 introduces a sixth domain and an eighth principle to take into account cost consciousness. It includes technology in the question set.

24. Trow (1994), p. 21.

25. See Vroom (1964), Lawler (1981), Nadler and Lawler (1977) for descriptions of expectancy theory. The theory has been applied in nonuniversity settings by Mitchell (1974) with varying degrees of success. Staw (1983) argues that expectancy theory may be helpful for understanding the motivation and choice behavior of higher education faculty members.

26. Ewell (1999), pp. 7–9, modified slightly to fit the present context.

27. The original UK academic audit procedures were criticized for focusing too much on the formalities of quality assurances, but that has been corrected in the Hong Kong, Swedish, and New Zealand approach.

28. See for example, Swan (2001).

29. Presentation by Jean Avnet Morse, executive director of the Middle States Commission, to the 6th biennial conference of the International Network of Quality Assurance Agencies in Higher Education (INQAAHE), Bangalore, India, March 19–22, 2001.

30. Coopers & Lybrand (1993) for the UK; Meade and Woodhouse (2000) for New Zealand; Brennan, et al. (1999) for Hong Kong; Stensaker (1999a, 1999b) and Nilsson and Whalen (2000) for Sweden. Working for NCPI, Massy (2000) evaluates the Swedish program and contrasts it with Denmark's assessment-based approach.

31. Dill (2000), p. 36.

32. Christian Thune, director of the Danish Centre for Educational Evaluation, is a particularly articulate spokesman for assessment (Massy, 1999 and personal communications). The UK's Quality Assurance Agency persisted in its use of subject-level assessment until the spring of 2002, when it adopted audit as its primary method. The issue is debated regularly at the biannual meetings of the International Network for Quality Assurance Agencies in Higher Education.

33. Dill (2000), p. 37.

34. See Massy (1997b), Massy and French (1997, 1999).

35. Massy (2000).

36. Hong Kong has three research universities, two comprehensive universities (formerly polytechnic universities), two liberal arts universities, and one teacher-training institute. The Hong Kong government subsidizes about 80% of the institutions' operating costs. The UGC has between 20 and 22 members, of which about half are overseas academics. The author served on the UGC since 1990. Further information about the Hong Kong higher education system and the UGC can be obtained from the UGC's web site: www.ugc.edu.hk. The site contains links to the UGC related papers cited herein and to the TLQPR reports for each institution.

37. French, et al. (1999); French, Massy, and Young (2000). See also El-Khawas and Massy (1996) for a description of the British system.

38. Massy (1996), Chapter 10.

39. The disappearance of the so-called binary line, wherein Hong Kong's polytechnics and liberal arts colleges became self-accrediting universities, also contributed to the need for a TLQPR. (A similar circumstance occurred in Britain.) More systematic quality assurance processes were needed to handle the larger and more heterogeneous group of institutions under the UGC's purview.

40. Wahlén (1998), p. 28.

41. Per Unckel, conservative MP, drove an agenda of decentralization with accountability. He recruited Stig Hagström, a physics professor at Stanford University and former Xerox executive, to the newly strengthened post of chancellor. Hagström was familiar with quality processes from his work at Xerox, and he also believed strongly in the "light touch" needed to balance executive action with academic freedom. For a detailed account of the Swedish experience see Massy (2000) and the references cited therein.

42. Wahlén (1998), p. 35.

43. Meade and Woodhouse (2000).

44. A fifth domain, adequacy of resources, also was used, but this did not elicit much useful information because the UGG itself is responsible for resource provision.

45. Dill (2000), p. 39, points out that traditional self-studies may prove to be misdirected exercises, generate frustration, and produce documents of limited value to the audit team.

46. Christian Thune, head of the Danish Centre for Quality Assurance and Evaluation of Higher Education, and John Stoddard, chair of Britain's Quality Council (the entity that performed the UK academic audits) served as foreign experts. The author, a member of the UGC, chaired the panel. One of the so-called institutional members, the representative from the newly formed Institute of Education, served as an observer.

47. Go to www.ugc.edu.hk for links to the institutional reports.

48. TLQPR Review Team (1999). *A Campaign for Quality: Hong Kong Teaching and Learning Quality Process Review.* Hong Kong: University Grants Committee of Hong Kong. A summary is available online at www.ugc.edu.hk/english/documents/speeches/s_0804_d.html.

49. Massy (2000).

9

Balancing Cost and Quality

Education quality processes help institutions and faculty improve the quality of undergraduate education and achieve a better balance between teaching and research. However, nothing discussed so far addresses the cost side of the value-for-money equation. In other words, quality processes by themselves do not address the cost-effectiveness of educational delivery.

This chapter fills the gap by marrying education quality processes with cost containment. Activity-Based Costing (ABC) turns out to be the method of choice. One applies it at the level of a course or educational module in a union called Q/ABC.[1] I'll start by defining Q/ABC in broad terms and then go on to more detailed descriptions of conventional and activity-based costing principles. Subsequent sections describe how to apply activity-based costing to educational processes, how to deal with the knotty question of faculty time, and how one institution has systematically linked its quality work to ABC. The chapter's appendix describes how computer-aided course design software might help departments apply Q/ABC and share their experiences across departmental and institutional boundaries.

QUALITY, ACTIVITIES, AND COST

Figure 9.1 sums up higher education's traditional view of cost and quality. The first graph shows the perceived relation between the two if enrollment is held constant. Institutions that spend more produce better quality as indicated by the upward trend of hypothetical data points. The points are tightly clustered, which suggests that faculty and administrators can do little to improve efficiency. According to the conventional view, most programs already operate at or near the "efficient frontier" (the upper limit of

Figure 9.1

Cost and Quality: The Conventional Wisdom

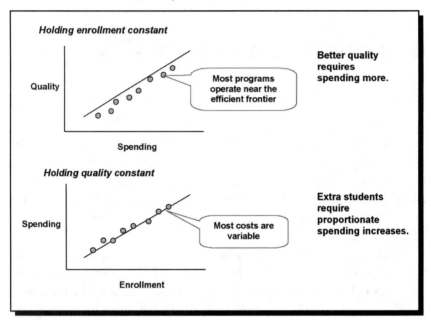

quality achievable at a given spending level). One must spend more in order to improve quality.

The second graph suggests that spending must rise with enrollment if quality is to remain constant. The data points are tightly clustered around a rising trend line. Notice that the line seems to emanate from the origin—which means that most costs are variable and extra students require proportionate spending increases. According to this view, the university cannot take advantage of scale economies.

The marriage of education quality processes with activity-based costing challenges the conventional wisdom. Viewed broadly, Q/ABC refers to the "activities of faculty, academic leaders, and oversight bodies that are aimed at improving and assuring education quality *and balancing the cost of educational improvements with their impact on quality.*" The first part of the definition is identical to the one presented in Chapter 6 for basic education quality processes. The second part, shown in italics, adds the cost dimension. Like basic education quality processes, Q/ABC is fully consistent with faculty values and academic freedom and it also fits comfortably into the overall higher education quality system.

Most importantly, Q/ABC provides new opportunities for improving quality at the same or lower cost as traditional education methods. Curricular design might focus more carefully on student needs, for example, and this would not necessarily add cost. Assignment-based active learning processes can improve quality without adding cost, and so can paradigm-changing technology innovation. Only by analyzing the cost of individual teaching and learning activities can one balance the cost of a given process with its quality and figure out how to do better. That's what Q/ABC is all about.

Rensselaer Polytechnic Institute's experience with studio courses illustrates the power of Q/ABC. As described in the appendix to Chapter 5, Rensselaer applied quality-process principles to redesign its introductory offerings in physics, chemistry, and calculus. The new designs relieved many of the quality problems inherent in its conventional course offerings such as student passivity that led to class cutting and high dropout rates. But that was not all. Cost analysis revealed that the new courses would save money as well as improve quality. Studio physics requires about one-third less in-class time by faculty, which produced a saving of between $10,000 and $20,000 per semester including the cost of technology.[2] The savings strengthened the case for technology investment and thus helped pave the way for implementing the new course designs.

Marrying quality work with activity-based costing allows departments to break the perceived proportionality between cost and quality. The new methodology begins by guiding users through the process of cost estimation. With the estimates in hand, users can compare the projected cost of alternative course designs with judgments about quality. Designs that improve quality with the same or less cost, or maintain quality while reducing cost, present a strong case for implementation. Designs that greatly improve quality at modest extra cost also may prove attractive. Once a design has been implemented, follow-up Q/ABC permits one to check the predications against actual results so the organization can learn from experience.

Figure 9.2 presents the realistic view of cost and quality—one that becomes apparent once a department embraces costing and quality work. Departments recognize that many programs don't operate near the efficient frontier, that quality often *can* be improved without spending more.

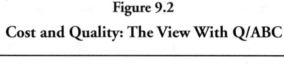

Figure 9.2

Cost and Quality: The View With Q/ABC

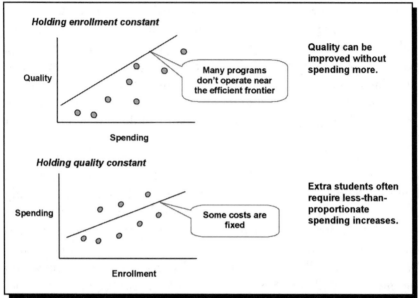

They understand that some instructional costs are fixed (the trend line intersects the spending axis well above the origin), which means that extra students can be accommodated with less-than-proportionate cost increases and no diminution of quality. Q/ABC contributes to such thinking in three ways: 1) by identifying opportunities to improve cost effectiveness, 2) by spurring paradigm-changing technology applications that reduce variable cost, and 3) by identifying each program's real cost drivers as described below.

Q/ABC is neutral on the question of whether an institution's costs should go up or down. However, the heightened cost consciousness triggered by such work should help contain the cost of education over the long run. Just as important, colleges and universities will have evidence to demonstrate their ability to analyze and manage cost. Such evidence may allow them to reverse stakeholder skepticism about higher education's stewardship of resources.

APPROACHES TO COST ANALYSIS

There are two ways to think about costing: what something costs and why it costs what it does. Higher education's approach has typically focused on the overall cost of teaching and research, not on the costs of individual teaching and research activities. Yet it is the individual activities that answer the "why" question. Without knowledge of what activities are being performed and what they cost, one cannot gauge efficiency, compensate for changes in the prices of inputs, or work intelligently on process improvement.

When asked why costs are high, administrators and faculty say that universities are labor-intensive enterprises, that governments are regulating more, that investments are being made in technology, and simply that "quality costs." They tend to respond in generalities rather than describing alternative teaching and learning processes, the cost effectiveness of each, and why one mix has been chosen over another. Nor do they describe programs, like Q/ABC, that can help departments continuously review and improve their cost effectiveness.

The conventional approach to costing in colleges and universities begins with cost as defined by their accounting systems. Accounting provides answers to the penny about how much is spent on each line item of expense, such as on salaries, library books, travel, and equipment.[3] It also tracks spending by "function"—for example, on instruction and departmental research (note the commingling described in Chapter 3), organized (mostly sponsored) research, public service, libraries, student services, administration, and physical plant—and by organizational unit. However, the system doesn't associate costs with grassroots activities like lecturing, course preparation, and out-of-class contact with students in the office and over the Internet.

Working from accounting records, cost analysts estimate the full cost and unit cost of education and research. To get full cost they allocate overhead expenses across functions and organizational units. For example, the full cost of organized research includes not only the expenses accumulated under that functional heading in the accounting system (direct cost), but also a "fair share" of expenditures for libraries, administration, physical plant, and other support activities. The definition of "fair share" has spawned countless hours of debate by accounting professionals within institutions and government agencies, and intense (though often uninformed) resistance by professors when they think the overhead charged on research projects is too high.

To estimate unit cost one divides full cost by an appropriate measure of output, for example, the number of full-time-equivalent students. Despite their importance for students, parents, and funding agencies, unit cost estimates often rely on remarkably simple rules of thumb. "Cost per student," for example, usually means total "educational and general" expense divided by enrollment. ("Educational and general" means current expenditures other than sponsored research, student room and board, patient care in medical schools, and a few similar items.) The standard definition ignores the cost of capital while erroneously including departmental research and the portion of infrastructure that supports sponsored research. These distortions make the standard definition of per-student cost highly problematic for comparing institutions and programs and for identifying ways to improve efficiency.

"Cost per student" can be determined down to the level of the individual course. However, the tradition of tying cost estimates to the accounting system (and the faculty's lack of interest in the subject of costing) has caused analysts to allocate previously determined estimates of full cost to courses instead of building up from the costs of activities required for teaching and learning. As Robert Zemsky and I put the matter few years ago, this wrongly assumes that cost precedes activity rather than the other way around.

> The faculty cost associated with teaching a specific course is determined by dividing the total faculty salaries paid on the department's instructional budget by the total number of courses that group of faculty teaches... The premise is... that the department's basic costs are essentially fixed and therefore must be allocated over the department's total set of activities. *With cost preceding rather than following activity, departmental [production] functions become fixed rather than variable and the activity itself is assumed to be beyond analysis.*[4]

The premise that the "department's basic costs are essentially fixed and therefore must be allocated over its total set of activities" is acceptable if one wants to distribute the department's current spending among multiple payers. However, it won't help identify potential cost savings. To do that one must start with the activities and their individual contributions to quality, then build up to the cost estimates. Failure to associate costs with specific activities also makes higher education's production processes "sticky" (hard to change) and thus unresponsive to shifts in technology and the price and availability of inputs.[5]

The disconnect between cost and activity produces a vicious circle. Data on the costs of individual activities aren't very useful if the redesign of educational processes isn't put in play. As long as processes remain frozen, the low demand for cost data inhibits efforts to improve analysis methods and perpetuates the myth that good data can't be obtained. In turn, poor data stymies efforts to redesign educational processes and reinforces the attitude that cost-effectiveness isn't worth pursuing. Good activity-based costing data, on the other hand, suggests ways to make educational processes more efficient and provides incentives for further improvement of costing methods. In other words, getting better data on the cost of individual teaching and learning activities—a key tenet of Q/ABC—will help solve the "sticky production" problem.

ACTIVITY-BASED COSTING PRINCIPLES

Texas Instruments developed activity-based costing in the late 1970s as a practical solution for problems associated with traditional costing systems,[6] but its antecedents can be traced back to accountants in England in the 1890s.[7] Instead of listing expense by line item and then allocating the total to products or services using assumed rules like those described above, ABC analyzes the process used to produce a product or service and then estimates the cost of each process activity. Then the activity-level costs are aggregated to provide an estimate of total process cost.

Figure 9.3 illustrates the difference between ABC and the kind of accounting reports typically provided to management. It helps explain Dartmouth Professor Jack K. Shank's assertion that, "Traditional management accounting is at best useless, and at worst dysfunctional and misleading."[8]

The traditional accounting display compares a hypothetical insurance company claims department's actual outlays for each line item of expense with its planned expense for that line item. Such information may seem natural to accountants, but it fails to inform those responsible for the process about two crucial facts: why the department is running over or under plan and how changes to its processes might improve performance. For example, the extra salary expense might arise from overtime needed to process an unexpected influx of claims (a "high-class problem") rather than from any fault of management. Nor does the display provide insight about whether, for example, expenditures on equipment might save salary cost by automating certain high-volume activities.

ABC breaks cost down by activity instead of by line item. For example, it costs $31,500 to scan claim forms into the computer and another $121,000 to analyze them. The far right-hand column shows the main "cost driver" for scanning and analyzing claim forms—not surprisingly,

Figure 9.3

Comparison of Traditional Accounting and ABC for a Hypothetical Insurance Company Claims Processing Department

Traditional View

Line item	Actual	Plan	Variance
Salaries	$621,400	$600,000	$21,400
Equipment	161,200	150,000	11,200
Travel	58,000	60,000	(2,000)
Supplies	43,900	40,000	3,900
Facilities	30,000	30,000	0
Total	$914,500	$880,000	$34,500

Activity-Based Costing View

Activity	Actual	Driver
Scan claim forms	$31,500	# cases
Analyze claims	121,000	# cases
Suspend claims	32,500	# cases
Receive inquiries	101,500	# inquiries
Resolve inquiries	80,400	# inquiries
Process batches	45,000	# batches
Determine eligibility	119,000	# cases
Make copies	145,000	# cases
Write correspondence	77,100	# cases
Attend training	158,000	# workers
Total	$914,500	

Source: Cokins (1994)

this is the number of forms received. While not shown in the figure, a typical ABC report would include the planned number of forms and planned cost for each activity, and the two variances from plan. This shows at a glance whether expense deviations stem from variations in the cost drivers or from factors controllable by management. Moreover, managers can see which activities generate the largest costs and thus may be candidates for efficiency improvement. Another typical refinement in the ABC methodology breaks out the line items of expense for each activity so managers can determine the amount of each input being used for that particular job. While such displays don't tell one how to improve efficiency, they do provide useful hints. We'll see later how activity-based costing can direct faculty attention toward areas of potential improvement in course design, for example.

Activity-based costing is catching on in higher education, particularly for online courses where process receives more than the usual amount of attention and cost is acknowledged to be a significant problem. For example, it underpins the Pew Charitable Trust's Grant Program in Course Redesign and the TLT Group's so-called Flashlight Program: Shining Light on Teaching and Learning with Technology.[9] (The TLT Group is the Teaching, Learning, and Technology Affiliate of the American Association for Higher Education.) The "BRIDGE" cost simulation model developed by the California State University System's Frank Jewett and the Technology Costing Methodology Handbook being developed by the National Center for Higher Education Management Systems and the Western Cooperative for Educational Telecommunications[10] also incorporate activity-based costing elements. In Britain, the Costing Study Steering Group of the higher education funding councils of England, Scotland, and Wales has developed guidelines for including institutional costing programs.[11] In 1995, Robert Zemsky and I wrote a paper on activity-based costing and facilitated an EDUCOM-sponsored roundtable that pioneered the use of course-level ABC in the United States.[12]

Activity-based costing comes in two flavors, only one of which currently appears practical for broad application in colleges and universities. "Analytic ABC" addresses the activities and costs of individual processes (e.g., the cost of processing claims or teaching a course). It's not necessary to analyze all the organization's processes, just the ones that need attention immediately. In other words, analytic ABC takes a decision support rather than an accounting orientation. It requires just enough data to model the target process, not data for the enterprise as a whole. Enterprise ABC, on the other hand, looks at all the organization's activities. It extends the accounting system to include activities as fundamental elements along with line items of expense, functions, and organizational units.

Enterprise ABC provides a comprehensive and seamless view of an entity's cost structure, but at the price of centralization and complexity. For example, enterprise ABC in colleges and universities would require faculty to report to central authorities on all their activities, not just to collect data on particular courses for self-use or use by colleagues. Professors would rightly question the practicality of such a centralized and all-inclusive program, not to mention its long-term effects on professional autonomy if applied in a heavy-handed way. Chapter 3 advocates the use of sampling to provide data on the distribution of activities. This represents an alternative to enterprise ABC for purposes of obtaining aggregate data.

One shouldn't rule out some variant of enterprise ABC for higher education's long-run future, but for most institutions it isn't worth the expense and controversy that would arise from implementation anytime soon. Higher education's experience with comprehensive workload modeling, a distant cousin of enterprise ABC in that it covered all aspects of faculty work, is not reassuring.[13] Launched with enthusiasm during the1960s, the program petered out a decade or so later because the results proved controversial and weren't worth the effort. Analytic ABC, on the other hand, is neither centralizing nor particularly complex. It can be used at the departmental level to model teaching and learning processes in a highly cost effective way. Analytic, not enterprise, ABC is what's needed for the marriage of quality and activity-based costing.

COURSE-LEVEL COSTING

Analytic ABC involves four common-sense steps that apply to teaching courses (or parts of courses) just as much as to claims processing in an insurance company.

1) Identify the activities needed to produce the product or service according to the current or proposed process.

2) Describe the resources consumed by each activity.

3) Find out how much the resources cost.

4) Cost out the resources consumed by each activity and add the results to get the total cost of the process.

I'll illustrate the steps by applying them to a conventional lecture-discussion course of the kind found in many college and university departments. The references to higher education cited in the previous section contain more comprehensive examples.

Figure 9.4 identifies the activities associated with teaching the course, as required by step one. The shaded boxes depict the weekly cycle during the semester: two lectures followed by a breakout discussion section, plus office hours. (Quizzes, papers, and midterm exams are ignored for the sake of simplicity, but they could easily be added.) Each activity is shown separately. Arrows indicate chronological order where that is important: The two lectures must occur before the breakout session, but the office hours can occur anytime during the week. The weekly activity sequence is replicated over the 15 weeks of the semester. Other activities, including syllabus preparation and the selection of teaching assistants (TAs), take place before the start of the semester. Still others, including exam preparation and grading and the finalization of course grades, occur after the semester is over. Taken together, the activities comprise the course's "activity configuration."

Figure 9.4

**Activity Configuration for a Conventional
Lecture-Discussion Course**

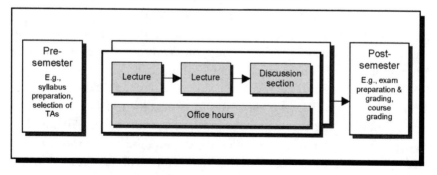

Figure 9.5 fulfills step two by describing the resources needed for each activity. Let's assume that each class is one hour long, and that tenure-line professors teach the lectures and TAs the discussion sections. Professors

estimate that they spend three preparation hours on average for each lecture (six for the whole week) and they provide three office hours a week for each section they teach. Economies in preparation accrue if a given professor teaches two sections. Similar assumptions apply to TAs and to pre- and post-semester activities, but the latter are not included in the table.

Figure 9.5

Weekly Resource Requirements for a Conventional Lecture-Discussion Course

A. Assumptions Gross hours/section:	Lecture	Discussion	Office hours	Preparation	Max. sections per teacher
Professor	2	0	2	6	2
Teaching assistant	0	1	4	2	3
Normal class size	110	20	Total enrollment		500

B. Results	Lecture	Discussion		Professors	TAs
Number of sections	5	30	Max.hours	50	210
Facilities hours	10	30	Min. hours	38	170

Next comes the question of how many professors and TAs will be required to teach the course. This depends on the number of students enrolled (the so-called driver variables called out in Figure 9.3), which we assume equals 500. Suppose the lecture room assigned to the course holds 110 students, and that this number is judged by the faculty to be acceptable from a quality point of view. Suppose, also, that the faculty wants no more than 20 students per discussion group and that all the students in a given group must come from the same lecture section.

Doing the math shows that five lecture sections and 30 discussion sections will be required. This translates to 38 faculty and 170 TA hours a week if maximum preparation economies are achieved and 50 and 210 hours if there are no such economies. In addition, the lecture room will be tied up for 10 hours a week and breakout rooms will be occupied for 30 hours a week.

Step 3 addresses the unit cost of the resources: in this case the cost of faculty time, TA time, and facilities utilization. Figure 9.6 provides representative unit cost data. Faculty cost includes salary and fringe benefits, plus an average pro-rata cost for a desktop or laptop computer, secretarial support, and travel. These costs vary directly with the number of professors. Overheads might also be included, but many analysts prefer to deal only with costs that are directly variable. Analysts also debate whether to use the average salary for all applicable faculty ranks (in this case assistant, associate, and full professors), or try to determine who actually will teach the course and use their salaries. I prefer the simpler approach, since one is looking for ballpark estimates of what the course will cost on average over time. Another question concerns the faculty's workweek and number of working weeks per academic year. Again, ballpark estimates suffice. Then the bottom line of the unit cost calculation provides a cost per faculty hour that can be multiplied by the number of hours used in the process.

Figure 9.6

Unit Costs for a Conventional Lecture-Discussion Course

(Based on academic year totals)

	Faculty	TAs		Lecture	Breakout
Salary and benefits	$80,000	$15,000	O&M expense	$20,000	$4,000
Support	$16,000	$375	Cost of capital	$33,000	$6,600
Total	$96,000	$15,375	Total	$53,000	$10,600
Hours worked	1,440	640	Hours available	1,440	1,440
Cost per hour	$67	$24	Cost per hour	$37	$7

TA and facility costs are determined in a similar manner. In the case of facilities, for example, one may limit unit cost to outlays for operations and maintenance or include the cost of capital. One may calculate availability based on normal workweek hours or include evenings and weekends. These are questions for professional cost accountants working in conjunction with university planners. They will supply departments with agreed-upon unit cost data for use in Q/ABC. The costs should reflect the department's particular circumstances and they should be updated every year, but they need not be accurate to the penny.

Figure 9.7 shows the total cost for our hypothetical course (step 4), together with some simple "what-if" analyses. The base case shows a total cost of $144,507 and a per-enrollment cost of $289. (Pre- and post-semester costs aren't included but they would be built up from their own activity analysis if this had been a real case.) Interestingly, the largest element of cost is not faculty, but rather teaching assistants. Some of this cost might be attributed to graduate student financial aid, but such a result would indicate that, like faculty time, TA time is a scarce and costly resource.

Figure 9.7

Total Cost and What-if Analysis for a Conventional Lecture-Discussion Course

Base case
(Based on maximum preparation hours)

	Hours	Total
Faculty cost	750	$50,000
TA cost	3,150	$75,674
Lecture hall cost	150	$5,521
Breakout room cost	450	$3,313
Pre and post cost		$10,000
Total cost		$144,507
Cost per enrollment		$289

Variations from the base case
(Alternatives for reducing cost per enrollment)

	Total cost	Cost/enr.
Minimum prep. hours	$118,093	$236
Incr. lecture size by 25%	$128,137	$256
Incr. breakout size by 25%	$131,343	$263
Cut office hours by 25%	$131,197	$262
Incr. enrollment by 25%	$171,409	$274

The what-if analyses examine potential cost-reducing variations from the base case. Preparation economies provide the most leverage among the alternatives considered: They cut per-enrollment cost by about 18%, from $289 to $236. Increasing class sizes, cutting office hours, and boosting enrollments by 25% produce smaller benefits. Of course these results are illustrative only: An empirically grounded analysis would produce different figures. Still, the example is sufficient to show that course-level costing can produce interesting and sometimes counterintuitive results even when the situation under study is as simple as a conventional lecture-discussion course.

The aforementioned analysis of Rensselaer's studio courses proceeded along similar lines. Its conventional courses used smaller class sizes, all of which were taught by professors, plus laboratories where applicable. By merging the labs and lectures into larger computer-aided sections, faculty teaching hours were cut by a third and quality was improved. Because the course software was content-rich and provided many cues for steering the class, professors' weekly preparation time was reduced as well. (Pre-semester preparation and the cost of facilities and equipment increased, but not enough to offset the term-time labor savings.) Once completed, the results of the analysis seemed obvious. Without course-level costing, however, the savings might never have been identified. The potential for savings could be even greater for more complex configurations of the kind illustrated in Chapter 5.

ABC is not an arcane exercise motivated by cost accountants. Cost accounting does enter the picture in the form of unit cost estimates, but once these have been agreed it's up to professors to identify activity configurations, estimate resource utilization and, in Q/ABC, to judge how changes in configurations and resources will affect quality. No one but professors can implement promising changes, and it's professors who should measure actual resource utilization and learning achievement and decide if they meet expectations. While not traditionally part of the academic job description, improvements in cost-effectiveness should become a professorial responsibility. If not, who is to do it? Q/ABC provides the needed visibility about resource utilization, cost, and educational performance.

FACULTY TIME

Rensselaer's experience illustrates the importance of including faculty time when doing course-level ABC—recall that it was the one-third reduction of in-class contact time that produced the cost saving. Including faculty time raises two important questions. First, how can one estimate the time required for particular teaching and learning processes? Second, what happens to any time "saved" by adopting a more cost-effective approach?

Time estimation should be viewed as a judgmental exercise, not as something that requires detailed measurement. Professors can log their time while teaching a course if the categories are meaningful, and they can reconstruct their activities after the events took place if not too much time has elapsed. Averages over courses usually suffice, for example, "How much time, on average, did you spend preparing for Econ 101 lectures this semester?" Indeed, when Robert Zemsky and I asked professors to provide "on-average" time estimates at about the midpoint of a semester, they provided stable and consistent data and felt that the exercise was meaningful.[14]

Whether judgmental estimates will prove meaningful depends on the purpose of the exercise and whether the participants buy into it. In course-level costing, professors should be motivated to provide the best reconstructions possible—after all, they are the ones who will use the results. The data may be noisy, but they're likely to be better than no data at all. One can expect the estimates to get better as the categories are refined and the estimators gain experience. Keeping a simple diary can dramatically improve one's time consciousness, for example.

Estimating the time requirements for newly conceived activities is more difficult. For example, how can one predict the time needed for student email correspondence when face-to-face contact during prescribed office hours represents the only applicable experience? While the initial estimates are bound to be rough, they will improve in subsequent iterations. Moreover, the estimates shouldn't be viewed as definitive but simply as targets to be modified based on subsequent experience. In any case, the estimation process will boost one's ability to understand the cost of new course designs.

What to do with time "saved" presents a thornier set of issues. People often view faculty resources as fixed because tenure and other contractual commitments prevent time saved during a given semester from being turned into cash. However, it's the scarcity of faculty time rather than its financial fungibility that makes course-level costing so important.

Most professors are, or at least feel, overworked. I pointed out in Chapter 4 that faculty time is the university's scarcest resource, and that most try to make the best possible use of it. Educational processes that require less faculty time are better than those that require more, other things being equal. It doesn't matter that the savings can't be cashed out—most professors will redeploy their effort to worthwhile alternative uses.

Such uses include other education-related tasks, education quality processes, and of course research. To ignore the faculty time input to educational processes is to miss the most important opportunity for breaking the proportionality of cost to quality. It also ignores opportunities for mitigating the workload pressures associated with the improvement of education quality processes.

Our NCPI interview respondents complained that while many people can add to the faculty's workload, few can safely offload current responsibilities and their associated time commitments. For example, professors shortchange research at their peril despite assurances from presidents, provosts, and deans that good teaching will be rewarded. Course-level costing gives individual professors and departmental workgroups the chance to do for themselves what others cannot do: shift their time obligations in ways that risk no penalties.

Course-level costing differs from so-called faculty activity analysis, which for decades has been a subject of research in higher education.[15] Faculty activity analysis seeks to determine the total professorial workweek and how work time is distributed among the whole range of things faculty do. This is a difficult task. First, many activities can't be pigeonholed into neat categories. Should sitting at home reading an interesting journal article be viewed as work, personal development, or recreation? Is talking with doctoral students about their theses "teaching" or "research"? Second, the complexity of judgments about the faculty's whole range of activities makes accurate reporting difficult. Respondents must decide which of the many elements of their work lives are worth mentioning, and then determine how to characterize them and how much time to report for each. Many activities occur sporadically with individual occurrences that may last only a few hours or even minutes, which exacerbates the difficulty. These problems also arise in connection with course-related activities, but they are far less severe than when one is looking at the whole range of faculty work.

The perceived purpose of faculty activity analysis also inhibits accurate reporting. Jonathon Fife, professor of higher education at George Washington University and director of the well-known ERIC Clearinghouse on Higher Education, puts the problem this way.

> ...faculty workload studies are funded by state legislatures or boards of trustees because of a deeply held suspicion that faculty are not working very hard.[16]

Many professors mistrust administrators' motives in collecting activity data, and of course they mistrust the motives of external stakeholders who may accuse them of shirking. Therefore, professors tend to shun centralized workload surveys and one may suspect that answers to such surveys are heavily biased. Course-level costing is different because the activity analysis of is of limited scope and done by and for the professors themselves.

Course-level costing should never be linked to downsizing. Such linkages undermine incentives and kill participation. Participants need assurances that, for the foreseeable future, most time saved will go to improve their own productivity and relieve their workload burdens. In other words, the lion's share of short-term benefits should go to those who devise and implement the new methods and not be siphoned off for other institutional objectives. Without such gain-sharing, the more efficient methods will be implemented half-heartedly or never identified in the first place.

Efficiency gains need to produce some beneficial financial consequences, however. Better time utilization opens degrees of freedom for decision makers at all levels from professors and department chairs to deans, provosts, and funding agencies. While decisions about the redeployment of time saved usually should be left to professors in consultation with chairs, circumstances may dictate that some decision-making migrate upward. For example, a provost or dean may note that efficiency has improved and decide that additional student numbers can be accommodated with less-than-proportional increases in faculty. And should downsizing become necessary, it can be accomplished with less damage to education quality than if faculty time were being used less efficiently.

Farsighted academic leaders will let efficiency gains stay in the department as long as possible, but never guarantee that all the gains will remain there forever. Neither faculty nor administrators want to damage educational programs unnecessarily when budget cuts become necessary or enrollments rise faster than income. Therefore, it's sensible to make adjustments in areas where past efficiency gains allow one to do so with the least damage to education quality. Thoughtful faculty members will understand this, especially if some of the gains do remain even after the budget adjustments.

A PILOT TEST OF Q/ABC

Quality/Activity-Based Costing combines work on education quality processes with the cost analysis power of course-based ABC. We have seen how each works separately. Now it's time to look at the whole. Northwest Missouri State University, whose seven-step quality program I described in the appendix to Chapter 7, provides a pioneering example.[17]

Working under a grant from the Alfred P. Sloan Foundation, Northwest integrated course-level ABC with its award-winning process for assuring and improving educational quality. Viewed broadly, the university's strategy was to use Q/ABC in two ways: to analyze existing teaching and learning processes, and to use the resulting insights to design new ones. (Northwest also applied Q/ABC to a number of administrative and support processes during the pilot program.) More specifically, the strategy involved the following five tasks:

1) Identify key quality indicators (KQIs) and value added assessment measures for a test set of course modules.

2) Teach each module as currently configured, describe the required activities, analyze them using the ABC methodology, and establish baseline assessment and cost data.

3) Review the baseline data and benchmark the current process against similar ones elsewhere to see where cost and quality improvements appear possible.

4) Design a reconfigured module in light of this analysis and estimate the resulting changes in cost and quality.

5) Teach the reconfigured module and measure the resulting cost and quality. Compare the results against expectations and adjust the cost and quality models as needed, then go back to step three.

Course modules are sequenced sets of activities designed to produce a common KQI, in this case competency in the material being taught as measured by the difference between pre- and post-module test scores. The decision to use modules stemmed from a desire to test Q/ABC in a manageable environment before extending it to complete courses.

The five tasks map closely to Northwest's existing seven-step quality program.[18] For example, task one (identifying and validating KQIs) corresponds to quality steps 1 and 2 shown in Figure 7B of Chapter 7. The mapping was no accident, since the university wanted to build on its successful history of continuous quality improvement. Indeed, the participating professors felt so strongly about the seven-step process that they urged the project team to leave it unchanged while the costing part of Q/ABC was being elaborated and assimilated.

Fourteen volunteer professors pilot tested tasks one through three during the spring semester of 2000 by collecting baseline data for six different course modules: classroom configurations in accounting, educational leadership, and theater communication; and online and classroom configurations in finance, management, and philosophy. (Some online students lived on campus or close to campus.) The participating professors were offered thousand-dollar stipends to try out the new methods. They received training in the fundamentals of course-based ABC before proceeding, and they implemented steps 4 and 5 during the 2000–2001 academic year. Accounting professor Rahnl Wood, who served as project coordinator, provided the focal point for the data collection, analysis, and reporting. It is interesting and encouraging that, when departments and faculty were asked about participating in the project, the list was oversubscribed.

Several findings emerged from the first-stage pilot. First, the faculty participants had no trouble identifying the key quality indicators and designing the value added assessment measures called for in task one. (This was not surprising given the faculty's familiarity with the seven-step quality process.) In task two, the flowcharts for all the classroom courses "showed a marked similarity in their basic structure. This suggests that the elements of teaching, although not universal, bear a marked similarity irrespective of topical area when delivered through conventional means."[19] The flowcharts for the online courses were similar to the classroom flowcharts in overall structure, but they differed in the activities "used to develop the topical area and the more frequent feedback in the assessment loop."[20]

Also in task two, the participants had little difficulty completing the time logs needed to describe their activities. Participants recorded the time they spent on module-related activities in 15-minute intervals throughout the duration of the module. While the total amount of time varied by professor and discipline, the percentages were fairly stable. Perhaps most important, no one reported a problem in using the time logs. Indeed, the majority said that using the logs increased their awareness and stimulated ideas about how to improve time-use efficiency.

Figure 9.8 shows the average weekly time percentages by activity for the two sets of classroom configurations and the online configuration, based on a standard reporting format developed by Northwest for purposes

Figure 9.8

Faculty Time Breakdown for Current Module Configurations Northwest Missouri State University Q/ABC Pilot Test

	Accounting, Educ., & Theater Classroom (%)	Finance, Management, and Philosophy Classroom (%)	Online (%)
Teaching and learning activities			
Group activities	3.5	3.1	
Review	2.0	2.4	
Lecture	8.3	11.0	
Discussion	5.9	4.8	
Seminar			
Active learning	8.9	5.4	
Technology assisted	2.7	1.5	
Telephone/student visit	1.0	4.8	4.9
Chat rooms	25.7		
Threaded discussions	19.5		
Email	1.3	4.0	
Formative responses to tests	4.0	4.3	2.5
Other	3.8		
Subtotal	*41.4*	*41.3*	*52.5*
Preparation			
Brushing up on content	12.7	11.4	7.1
Preparing presentations	11.1	4.7	
Preparing assignments	4.9	5.9	3.9
Electronic presentation	0.8	0.2	
Other	5.4		
Subtotal	*34.9*	*22.0*	*11.2*
Assessment			
Test administration	4.0	4.7	
Preparing tests, quizzes	3.8	4.0	19.8
Grading	10.5	20.4	13.4
Other	3.3	0.8	
Subtotal	*21.7*	*30.0*	*33.1*
Maintenance tasks			
Clerical tasks	2.7	6.7	0.8
Supervision of students			
Web page maintenance	2.5		
Subtotal	*2.7*	*6.7*	*3.3*
Total percent	100.0	100.0	100.0
Total hours	*na*	*255*	*282*

Source: Wood (2001, Figure 2) and Wood and Wilson (2001, Figures 1 and 2)

Figure 9.9
Recommendations for Changes in Activities

- Shift from lecture-dry erase board format to more electronic-assisted presentations accompanied by handouts. This would free time to review and cover new material. The result: improvement in exam performance and greater knowledge.

- Shift from instructor presentation to student presentation of assigned homework. This may require more faculty time but will result in improved understanding and retention of knowledge by the student. The result: improvement in student performance.

- Delegate grading to lower-cost student labor. The result: freed time for higher cost faculty to engage in other productive activities and contribute to outcomes (brushing up on content, development of new material and methods, etc.).

- Delegate some PowerPoint preparation to lower-cost student labor. There would be the additional time requirements of interaction and monitoring of student labor, but there would be a net time saving for faculty. The result: freed time for faculty to engage in other productive activities.

- Shift the cost of some consumable supplies to students (or eliminate the cost) by creating a web site that has handouts, review sheets, and other normally printed materials. The student can view materials on the monitor or print them out at his or her option. Creating the web site will require time, but after the initial development it will require only routine maintenance. The result: a net cost saving for the module while maintaining outcomes (perhaps improving outcomes since the material is more accessible).

- Reduce office and telephone time with students by creating a web site with answers to frequently ask questions, reviews, and answers to problems. Result: after the initial development of the site, a net time saving to faculty that can be redeployed to other productive uses.

- Substitute in-class discussion for discussion in chat rooms and email. Although initially believed to be more efficient and effective, we found that using electronic discussion was more time-consuming and less effective because of the need to monitor student effort. Given the verbal and nonverbal clues in class, students enjoyed the discussion much more and feedback was more immediate for both the instructor and the student. The result: using less technology will produce time savings and improvements in outcomes.

- Provide more training and in-service experience on online features that reduce clerical work and maintenance tasks. The result: substitution of technology for faculty effort.

- Provide more training on exam features and grading features available online. The result: substitution of technology for faculty effort.

- Develop a mentor system to provide faculty with a better understanding of online course features and possibilities.

Source: Wood (2001, Figure 3) and Wood and Wilson (2001, Figure 3).

of the exercise. The first category, "teaching and learning," covers synchronous activities like classroom instruction and office or telephone conversations, and asynchronous ones like email, online chat rooms, and threaded discussions.[21] The other categories reflect the faculty's preparation, assessment, and maintenance tasks. Experience will show whether these categories represent the best way to reflect faculty activity. For example, separating "teaching and learning" into subcategories like those illustrated in Figure 5.3 of Chapter 5 may prove better in the long run.

The data suggest relationships that will prove interesting if repeated in other settings. For example, only 41% of faculty time in classroom courses goes into direct teaching and learning activities, whereas the direct-contact figure jumps to more than half in online courses. The rest goes into "overhead": the preparation, assessment, and maintenance tasks. Improving the efficiency of these tasks would reduce cost without diminishing faculty-student contact. The pilots in finance, management, and philosophy were designed to compare online with classroom delivery under conditions where the two versions were taught by the same professor. This made it possible to compare the total hours spent, as shown at the bottom of the table. The online courses took about 10% more time than their classroom counterparts, for roughly the same number of students. Economies in preparation of presentations and assignments, grading, and clerical tasks appear in the online courses, but these are offset by more time spent on test preparation and web page maintenance. (The economy observed in the "brushing up on content" line may reflect each professor's teaching of two sections.) Within the teaching category, the majority of faculty time in online courses goes to chat rooms and threaded discussions.

To implement task three of the pilot, participants were asked to prepare a post-semester narrative report describing what they had learned and identifying opportunities for improvement. Figure 9.9 illustrates the kinds of improvements suggested. Because of Q/ABC's dual focus, the improvements reflect both quality improvement and cost reduction. Some suggestions mitigated large time requirements that had emerged from the ABC analysis: they included the substitution of student labor for faculty labor in grading and PowerPoint preparation, and posting answers to frequently-asked questions on web sites. Others would boost faculty time budgets in order to improve learning. One interesting suggestion, to reduce the reliance on technology in certain modules, would conserve faculty time and improve learning simultaneously.

No fundamental paradigm changes were expected given the exercise's short duration, and none emerged. However, the application of Q/ABC did produced meaningful results that will be implemented in subsequent semesters. That these results represent common sense rather than rocket science should be viewed as one of the process's strengths—commonsensical results are more likely to be implemented and their effects can snowball. As in the RPI, Flashlight, and Pew course redesign programs, Q/ABC has focused faculty attention on the relation between cost and quality. It has jump-started continuous improvement and may also lead to paradigm changes. If Q/ABC can become as firmly embedded in Northwest's academic culture as the seven-step quality process, the university will enjoy continuing improvements in cost-effectiveness.

Appendix

COMPUTER-AIDED COURSE DESIGN

Few professors know how to do course-based costing, let alone Q/ABC. For example, Barbara Walvoord reports that her seminars to a national cross section of interested professors go well until the participants are asked to design a new course configuration that makes better use of faculty time.[22]

So far most course-level costing has relied on spreadsheets. But while spreadsheets can perform the "what-ifs" needed to identify a good solution, participants in the Pew and Flashlight programs also report that such analyses can be difficult and labor-intensive. Part of the problem stems from unfamiliarity with activity-based costing concepts, but a lack of good tools exacerbates the problem. Spreadsheets work up to a point, but they are difficult to use and they fail to unlock the full potential of the course-based costing methodology. Spreadsheet structures can't handle complex configurations of activities or multiple linkages among activities and resources, for example, and they don't guide users through the activity specification, configuration building, and data input processes. Nor do spreadsheets support the databases and simulation models needed to fully implement Q/ABC and provide the kinds of reports that users truly need.

These shortfalls suggest the need for computer-aided course design (CACD) software that would help professors do a better job of course-level costing. Like computer-aided design (CAD) in architecture and industry, CACD could provide professors and planners with a user-friendly and powerful tool for analyzing existing course configurations and designing new ones that can be used in on-campus, distance, and hybrid settings. If and when implemented, CACD will be a major advance over the spreadsheet models that represent the current state of the art. I suppose such a tool will be adopted first in online education, but it applies equally well to technology-enhanced or even conventional on-campus courses.

Figure 9A presents the model in graphical form. Activities are organized into configurations, which specify the activities' durations, intensities,

Figure 9A
CACD Architecture

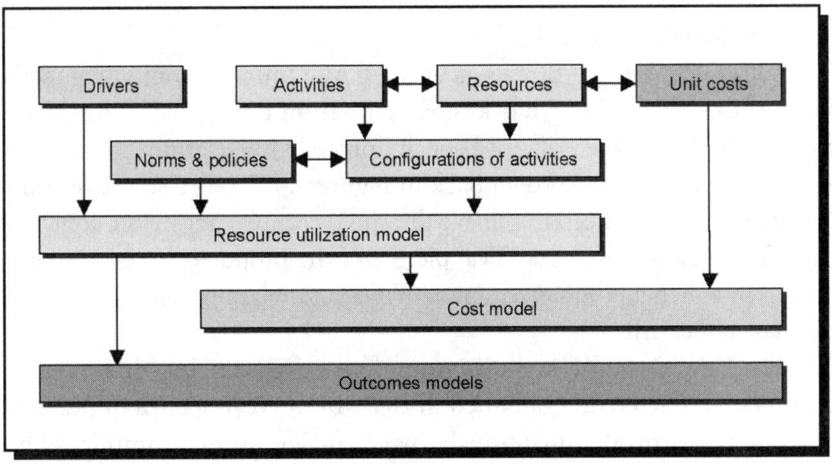

precedence relations, and number of replications during the course of a module or semester. Each activity requires resources, and resources have unit costs. Cost drivers, or simply drivers, represent the system's throughput. (Enrollment is a typical driver.) Norms and policies determine the effects of driver changes on activity levels, and resource utilization determines quality. For example, larger enrollments will require increases in office hour availability or the amount of time a professor spends in email correspondence if learning is to remain constant. The norms and policies inform the costing model about the faculty's intentions with respect to these matters.

The activity configurations, drivers, and norms come together in a resource utilization model that lies at the core of course-based costing. It determines how activity levels will vary with the drivers, for example, how many class sections and office hours will be required for each enrollment level. Then it determines the amount of each resource that will be needed to sustain the activities. Finally, a cost model applies the unit costs to the resource requirements to obtain the cost of each resource and the total cost of the system. (Despite the name "ABC," costing is the easy part of the analysis because it can be automated. The hard part is estimating activity levels, their associated resource requirements, and how these vary with the drivers—not determining the cost of the resources.)

Moving from costing to the broader aspects of Q/ABC, the outcomes models shown at the bottom of the diagram predict the effects of the activity configurations and resource utilization on student learning. So far such relationships must be intuited on the basis of judgment or guesswork. In time, however, it may be possible to systemize some aspects of the outcomes models as discussed below.

To implement Q/ABC, users of the CACD model would drag icons representing the building blocks of activity from predefined pallets, drop them onto a timeline grid, and specify precedence relations in a design workspace like the one shown back in Figure 9.4. Users also might indicate where students need to achieve threshold competency before continuing. The result will be a graphical picture of the proposed course configuration, in which all the significant activities and relations among activities are depicted clearly.

The CACD would be built around an initial database of activities and their characteristics obtained initially by surveying current practice and then improved continuously by an online user community. The database would include traditional seminars, lectures, labs, and discussion sections, plus "noncontact" activities like group projects and office hours. It also might include a suite of web-based and asynchronous learning activities like those described in the previous section. (Activities would be linked to online course object databases where possible.[23]) Each activity could be characterized by, for example, its purpose (e.g., first exposure, process, or response), the kinds of resources required to sustain it, and the norms and policy variables needed to link resource utilization to applicable drivers.

Users would be asked for judgments about needed data elements and given the opportunity to override stored data if desired. They would input the number of students who are expected to take the course and, in advanced CACD versions, certain characteristics that might mediate learning capacity and resource consumption. Once all the data have been entered, the model would use a sophisticated resource utilization model to estimate the activity volume and resource consumption.[24] Then unit cost estimates, supplied to the CACD database by the university's accounting department, would be applied to the resource requirements to produce cost estimates.

Advanced versions of CACD might include the student contact or learning goals that faculty associate with modules, courses, and programs. As in the Northwest Missouri State's Q/ABC project, users might specify key quality indicators and make judgments about the likely performance of individual modules or courses, the effects on learning of replicating different kinds of learning experiences, and similar factors.

In addition to its decision support role, CACD would store and display data on actual cost and quality outcomes, on actual resource utilization and learning as measured by the quality indicators. Thus CACD could become an instrument for organizational learning and for spurring the adoption of Q/ABC. In time, moreover, it might stimulate research on the efficacy of alternative activity definitions and course design configurations. The model might also play a useful standard-setting role. Without some degree of standardization for definitions and data structure, it will be difficult to share information and benchmark the costs and benefits of alternative teaching and learning processes. Institutions and faculty would still be able to design their own processes to meet local needs, but at least they would be speaking the same language.

Endnotes

1. The term "Q/ABC" was invented at Northwest Missouri State University, by President Dean Hubbard and Professor Rahnl Wood, in the course of a pilot project on marrying the two methodologies. They used it in the context of Northwest's "Seven-Step Quality Process" (described in Chapter 3), but I'll use it generically to reflect the merger of any EQW process with activity-based costing at the course level.

2. Wilson (1997), p. 115.

3. The line items also are known as "objects of expense" and "chart-of-accounts categories."

4. Zemsky and Massy (1995), p. 47. Emphasis added.

5. Ibid. The article describes the "sticky production" phenomenon in some detail.

6. Weisman and Mitchell (1986).

7. Hearth, Kaplan, and Waldron (1991).

8. Quoted in Cokins (1994), p. 1. See Cokins (1996) for a useful overview of ABC.

9. See, for example, Ehrmann and Milam (1999) and Milam (2000).

10. National Center for Higher Education Management Systems (NCHEMS) (2000). The handbook is being prepared by Dennis Jones, director of NCHEMS.

11. Westbury (1997).

12. Massy and Zemsky (1995). EDUCOM stood for the "Interuniversity Communications Council," a predecessor to today's EDUCAUSE.

13. Faculty activity analysis was embodied in the so-called CAMPUS and Resource Requirements Prediction Model (RRPM), not ABC. See for example, Hussain (1971). For a general discussion of such models and a criticism of CAMPUS and RRPM in particular, see Hopkins and Massy (1981).

14. Zemsky, et al. (1999).

15. See for example, Yuker (1984).

16. Meyer (1998), p. ix.

17. The project was conceived and led by Dean L. Hubbard, Northwest's president. The author served as primary consultant on the project.

18. Wood and Hubbard (2001), Figure 6, provides a description of the mapping.

19. Wood (2001), p. 49.

20. Wood and Wilson (2001), p. 61.

21. Northwest labeled this category "classroom instruction" but I changed the name to more accurately reflect its content. I also moved "formative responses to tests" from the assessment category to "teaching and learning." Finally, I removed the education faculty's special field trip, described on page 52 of Wood (2001), from the column-1 "preparation: other" category because it was anomalous and significantly distorted the comparisons.

22. Personal communication.

23. For example, the "Merlot" database or its successors. Merlot is described in "Swap Shop: The Future of online learning lies in course objects, and the place to find them is an organization Merlot" (*University Business*, 3(6), July/August 2000, pp. 35–40).

24. In addition to calculating the interactions among norms, policies, and drivers, the model might use stochastic cueing theory to simulate student movement through mastery thresholds, so that the time pattern of resource demands at subsequent stages of the educational processes can be projected.

10
Performance-Based Resource Allocation

Universities aren't about money, but money enables them to pursue value-producing activities. The activities also may generate revenue that, together with philanthropic and investment income, allows institutions to do good work and maintain financial viability. We have seen how universities behave as economic enterprises, how education quality processes can improve learning, how university leaders and external agencies can monitor and stimulate such processes, and how information technology and improved cost analysis can boost productivity. This chapter extends these ideas to include resource allocation. It asks how, as a practical matter, universities and higher education oversight bodies can get the most value from the money they spend.

The nonprofit enterprise model says that resource allocators should maximize value as defined by the institution and its stakeholders, subject to the limits imposed by markets, finances, and production possibilities. The model's "practical decision rule" states that universities should arrange their allocations so the relative financial contributions from their various programs are consistent with its values. However, the rule provides no guidance about how a university should organize the process of resource allocation. Understanding of the requisite methodologies is beginning to emerge but we shall see that, as in many other processes in higher education, the devil is in the details.

Resource allocation should further the university's strategic vision. For example, provosts should invest in academic areas they believe are or will be important and where their institution has a chance to excel. They may stress certain educational programs or attempt to achieve world-class research in one area or another. Such decisions become more difficult as resource constraints prevent schools from covering all fields equally.

274

Rather than trying to be all things to all people, successful universities now practice "selective excellence" by concentrating resources where they can achieve the most.

An institution's strategic vision should include markets and production processes as well as academic coverage. For example, schools may invest in enrollment management or institutional advancement in order to expand their markets and boost margins. Success may not add intrinsic value directly, but it furthers academic goals by augmenting revenue. Likewise, schools may improve teaching and learning or education quality processes—actions that add value by improving production. Many schools ignored the market until fairly recently, and most still pay little attention to academic production processes. (Administrative processes do receive intense scrutiny, however.) Correcting this shortfall should be a high priority for university leaders.

This chapter focuses mainly on resource allocation within universities—particularly on the academic side of the enterprise. For example, how should provosts allocate money to schools and how should deans allocate it to departments? However, the same principles apply to higher-level resource allocation, that is, how state governments should allocate money to their universities and how system-wide administrators should allocate money to campuses. Certain methodologies, particularly those involving performance funding, have been deployed mainly at these higher levels.

PERSPECTIVES ON RESOURCE ALLOCATION

Talk to academics at different levels within institutions and you will get a variety of views about the principles that should govern resource allocation. Many professors believe that "property rights" should govern. Provosts and deans, on the other hand, are more apt to espouse the "objective and task" philosophy. A hardy few, now joined by an increasing number of nonacademic stakeholders, are adopting "performance-based" principles.

Property Rights

The property rights perspective holds that once an academic program has been put in place, it should continue as long as performance remains acceptable and there are no overriding financial exigencies. For example, most academics believe the following message from a dean to a program head would represent a betrayal of trust:

> I've got good news and bad news for you. The good news is that you're doing a fine job and your program is well regarded by your peers and students. The bad news is that we're cutting your budget to make room for a new initiative that I believe is more important.

The program's faculty won't recognize the worth of the alternative initiative. They'll see only the need to make do with less, which would feel unfair if in fact they have been performing well.

Claims of property rights may seem a bit strong, but many professors do behave as if they and their departments own the resources that have been placed at their disposal.[1] They will wage political warfare to defend their resource base unless compelling reasons for change are presented. Such warfare may include appeals to the provost, the president, the trustees, or even the state legislature in public institutions. (To cite an extreme example that occurred during the 1980s, the University of Minnesota's decision to close a small and outdated program in mortuary science on a small branch campus was appealed all the way to the state legislature.) Making room for new initiatives rarely represents a sufficient reason for change in the eyes of those whose budgets are under the ax, and professors not personally at risk often rise to defend their colleagues.

Justifications for property rights transcend the narrow self-interest of professors. The most powerful argument concerns equity. Professors' reputations depend on academic accomplishment, which requires resource availability as well as individual effort and creativity. To spend years developing a program only to see it closed or decimated by budget cuts does more than erode one's self esteem—professional recognition, rewards, and in some cases whole careers may be threatened as well. To impose such penalties simply because the university sees brighter prospects elsewhere may well seem unfair to academics. Businesses and similar organizations make such moves all the time, but the affected individuals suffer less damage because their careers depend more on general ability and performance and less on the continuation of specific programs. Professors, on the other hand, tend to be personally invested in and closely associated with their programs. Abrupt changes induce trauma even when the person's job is protected by tenure. Why, one may ask, should the university inflict such trauma when it agreed to support the program in the first place and the professor fulfilled his or her part of the bargain by doing high-quality work?

Students and alumni also assert property rights. When Stanford eliminated its architecture program, for example, current students and graduates felt the value of their degree had been reduced. By its action, the university implied that the program lacked quality, importance, or both, and no new graduates or faculty publications would enhance its future reputation. Current students were allowed to finish, but they felt cheated nonetheless. So did alumni. Although Stanford's decision could not be reversed, the political fight and resulting sense of malaise made it more difficult to eliminate programs in the future.

The observance of property rights confers stability and predictability as well as protecting individual careers. This is consistent with the financial commitments of tenure, and also with the intrinsic demands of academic work. Markets turn on a dime, but intellectual prowess can take years to develop. By observing property rights wherever possible, universities foster the conditions needed for long-term academic development within established fields and programs.

But what about new fields and programs? Protecting property rights means that investments in such programs must be made mostly with new money. This accounts for the so-called growth force in university budgeting. The growth force reflects the inexorable expansion of knowledge and academic opportunity. New disciplines and subdisciplines are constantly being formed, yet old fields remain important even as new ideas demand attention.

Most external stakeholders now believe the need for investment in new fields and programs in an era of constrained resources trumps the property rights argument. Universities should be sensitive to property rights for the reasons described earlier, but they cannot allow such rights to preempt new investment. I'll describe some strategies for finding the right balance and dealing with the resulting difficulties later in this chapter.

Objective and Task Method

The objective and task perspective addresses the amount of resources to be invested in a given program, once one has committed to the program in the first place. It is grounded in the view that education, especially, requires a fixed amount of money per student to attain a given level of quality and access. Patrick Callan of the California Higher Education Policy Center calls this the "black box" theory of resource allocation.

> Higher education can be described as a "black box" that moves forward in serving students when money is inserted. When money is withdrawn, the box moves in reverse, reducing educational opportunity.[2]

In other words, achieving a given educational objective requires that certain tasks be performed, and these tasks require a certain level of expenditure. Failure to spend at the requisite rate undermines performance. According to this view, budget makers identify the tasks associated with each institutional objective, determine their cost, and allocate the money needed to perform them. Few look inside the black box to see if the objectives can be attained with less money. This book challenges the black box theory, but the fact remains that many higher education policymakers believe in it wholeheartedly.

The objective and task philosophy drives the higher education funding models used by many states and foreign countries.[3] While details vary, the basic idea is that funding should equal student FTEs, credit hours, or degrees, multiplied by a "unit of resource" appropriate for the type of institution, student level, and field. Suppose, for example, that an institution enrolls 20 upper-division physics majors and 50 upper-division English majors, and that the standard unit of resource is $12,000 for physics and $8,000 for English. These enrollments would generate a funding requirement of $12,000 x 20 + $8,000 x 50 = $640,000. Other enrollments would generate additional needs. A funding agency might add up these requirements, and then deduct expected tuition revenue and supply the difference by direct appropriation. In fact, this is very close to the methodology used in places like the UK, Hong Kong, and some US states.

Governments usually determine the unit of resource in two steps. First they benchmark the relative expenditures for different fields and student levels for each type of institution under their purview. In the above example, cost allocation studies might have shown that universities average 50% more spending on physics than on English. The benchmarking studies need not be performed frequently, since the ratios of teaching cost among disciplines seldom change dramatically over short periods of time.

The second stage, which must be performed each funding cycle, determines the total amount of resources to be distributed among the disciplines. This decision depends on politics because higher education must compete for funding with other societal needs. Funding agencies benchmark other jurisdictions' spending levels and try to sell the larger figures to governors and legislators, but in the end they take what they can get. Often this is a small increment over the prior year's appropriation.

Taking Account of Performance

Whether the unit of resource should be adjusted for institutional performance represents a lively topic of debate. Performance is hard to measure, but the situation would remain clouded even if perfect assessments were available. Black-box theory holds that subpar quality stems from resource shortfalls, not performance shortfalls, and that the antidote is to spend more. However, failure to spend wisely or in accordance with objectives can undermine quality as fast or faster than failure to spend enough. The cross-subsidy of research by education provides a case in point. Departments can spend large sums on research without improving the quality of education. Applying the black box theory in this case would boost appropriations to departments where education quality lags, thus increasing the research subsidy without benefiting education. Performance-based principles, on the other hand, might lead one to freeze or even cut funding in departments where education quality lags while simultaneously taking steps to improve these departments' quality processes.

Emotions run high when performance-based funding is brought up for consideration. Advocates argue that agencies and institutions should invest where they get the best payoff, for example, where quality processes are good and additional spending would go directly to education. Conversely, they should reduce spending where people are performing poorly or diverting funds into activities that contribute only marginally to education. Black-box advocates vigorously dispute these presumptions. They claim that most if not all academics do a good job and deny that funds are being diverted from mission-critical tasks. According to this view, cutting the budgets of poor-performing departments or schools will reduce quality even further and thus unjustly penalize students. Because many academic leaders and professors don't believe education quality varies independently of funding, they won't accept performance-based resource allocation. I have seen heads of institutions become intensely hostile when the subject is even mentioned, after which the discussion quickly leads to impasse.

As in many cases of impasse, the problem is that both sides can claim elements of truth but neither can prove its case. This book shows that education quality and cost-consciousness *can* be improved if faculty and institutions try hard enough. Yet one cannot prove there is potential for improvement without testing the needed changes. Absent such improvements, the black-box theory may well turn out to be correct: Reducing budgets *will* penalize both students and faculty in this case. The objective and task methodology avoids these risks, but it perpetuates the status quo by taking performance out of the resource allocation equation.

Rather than insulating professors and their departments from the need for change, performance-based funding puts them at risk, if not for penalties, then at least for missing out on rewards. The risk provides an incentive for improvement, without which change is far less likely. The essential premise of this chapter is that resource allocation is too important a tool for stimulating reform to be left on the sidelines. For me, the issue is not whether performance should be brought into the equation, but how. The risks to students and faculty need to be managed, but not by eliminating incentives. The remainder of the chapter describes how one can accomplish this goal.

GROWTH BY SUBSTITUTION

To sum up the discussion so far, resource allocation processes should be designed with two purposes in mind: to maintain the institution's ability to invest in new initiatives and to provide incentives for improvement. The two purposes are self-reinforcing. Unfortunately, though, most institutions' budget processes do not take full advantage of the potential.

Financial equilibrium requires that an institution's current budget be balanced, that its growth rates of income and expense be sustainable, and that there be no hidden liabilities.[4] Maintaining these conditions limits a school's ability to fund initiatives with new money. Failure to impose such limits can trigger financial problems. For example, programs started on soft money represent hidden liabilities that will come due if the funding runs out and property rights need to be honored. Likewise, spending too much from endowments or deferring building maintenance limits future flexibility. The penalties for violating the equilibrium principles can be harsh, so well run universities take financial management seriously. Usually this means growth must occur by substitution rather than by adding large annual funding increments. In other words, current activities must be scaled back on a regular basis in order to make room for new initiatives.

Figure 10.1 shows how universities typically achieve growth by substitution. The initial approach usually involves periodic episodes of across-the board budget cutting. The central administration can initiate such cuts by top-down action. The cuts seem equitable because they spread the pain: everyone's property rights are violated a little. The amounts aren't large enough to be problematic, but across-the-board reductions as small as fractions of 1% can generate sizeable reallocation pools. Sometimes the reduction scheme is less than overt, as when Stanford decided not to fund inflationary increases in supplies, travel, and the like.[5] Departments suffered real budget cuts even when their nominal budgets increased by small amounts. People knew what was going on, but somehow the cuts seemed less painful when presented this way.

Figure 10.1

Approaches to Growth by Substitution

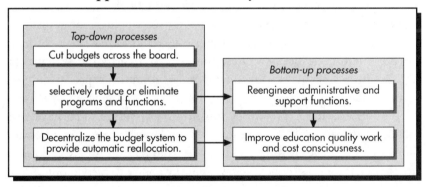

Across the board cuts can work for a while, but sooner or later they will leach the flexibility out of the university's financial system. I have seen departments eliminate most travel and equipment money, for example, as they try to defend faculty positions against a succession of small budget reductions. An accumulation of small cuts can produce misallocations that would not be tolerated if the adjustment occurred as a single episode. Moreover, successive small cuts preclude the strategic choices associated with selective budget adjustments.

Selective adjustments allow the university to exercise its strategic priorities and take advantage of reallocation opportunities. For example, experienced deans maintain lists of departments where faculty who depart will not be replaced. Such positions become available for reallocation to other departments where the need is greater. Even with tenure, the aggregate number of departures can be substantial. Suppose, for example, the average tenured professor stays at an institution for 30 years. This means that, on average, 3 1/3% of faculty slots become available for reallocation every year. The problem, of course, is that the openings don't necessarily occur when and where the dean most needs the flexibility. Moreover, perceived departmental property rights may make it difficult for deans to achieve their reallocation goals. The problem is even more difficult at the institutional level, since deans can marshal substantial constituencies to help defend their faculty rosters against provostial reallocation.

Decentralizing budget decisions can mitigate the political difficulties. So-called responsibility center systems devolve tuition and other enrollment-driven revenue to the deans, who allocate the funds within their schools after payment of "taxes" for central support services and administration. (I'll describe these systems presently.) Enrollment fluctuations force immediate reallocation of money among schools—reallocation that occurs automatically without the need for provostial judgment or justification. Pure responsibility center systems may emphasize market forces to the detriment of academic values, but we'll see that hybrid systems can mitigate these difficulties while maintaining substantial capacity for automatic reallocation.

The approaches to growth by substitution discussed so far have been top-down in nature. Top-down schemes are easier to implement because they can be handled by directive. One needs to consult widely and calculate the consequences of the directive, but the ability to carry it out usually is not an issue. Unfortunately, though, top-down schemes can take the institution only so far. They allow one to move money around, but they cannot generate the productivity gains needed to offset the negative consequences of reallocation. That takes bottom-up initiatives of the kind discussed in earlier chapters. While such initiatives may be suggested and facilitated by university leaders, implementation depends on rank and file professors and managers.

Bottom-up initiatives almost always start with the reengineering of administrative and support services. Hundreds of institutions have mounted formal reengineering projects and many hundreds more have achieved a measure of gain using informal methods. Reengineering can boost service, reduce cost, or both. It enables growth by substitution at the micro level. Streamlining and automating travel reimbursement eliminates the cost of handwork and unnecessary process steps, for example, while at the same time getting travelers their money faster. Mid-level managers will deploy the savings elsewhere without any need for top-down reallocation schemes.

Improving education processes is harder than administrative process reengineering, but the results can be more far-reaching. Such programs are just now getting off the ground, but earlier chapters have indicated what can be accomplished. The challenge for resource allocation, then, is to stimulate academic process improvement and thus produce the capacity for reallocation. Chapter 9's discussion of faculty time indicated that savings should initially accrue to the department or other local unit, but that makes them no less valuable. We now turn to the question of how such stimulation can be achieved.

RESOURCE ALLOCATION PROCESSES

Traditional university budgeting takes the form of incremental line-item allocation. Deans, chairs, and other managers make requests for specific items during the annual budget exercise, for example, another assistant professor of engineering to cope with new enrollment or a secretary in the English department to relieve paperwork burdens. The central authority sorts these requests according to priority and funds as many as the institution's financial situation will allow. The process works in reverse if budgets need to be cut. Managers propose items for elimination and the central administration chooses among them in ways they hope will minimize adverse consequences. People focus on the individual line items proposed for allocation or reallocation. They pay little attention to the rest of the budget.

Incremental line-item allocation allows the central administration to exert tight control. Proposed items are vetted for conformance with institutional priorities, and while managers have some flexibility to move money around during the year they are expected to follow the spirit of their budget allocations. (For example, the secretarial money allocated to English shouldn't go for teaching assistants without prior approval.) In theory, the provost or university resource allocation committee knows all parts of the institution well enough to exercise informed judgments about each line item, not only on its individual merits but also relative to other institutional needs. Unfortunately, however, such omniscience can exist only in smaller and simpler institutions.

Stanford's experience illustrates the problem. We operated an incremental line-item system until the early 1980s, at which point the process became so complex that even tight-control advocates agreed that something should be done.[6] First came the aforementioned problem of bounded knowledge. A year's budget exercise involved hundreds of line items, and despite hard work only a small number could be understood and placed in context. We found that budgeting had degenerated from reasoned priority setting to an exercise rich in rhetoric, posturing, and power brokering. We read purple prose describing "ineluctable needs" and tried vainly to compare apples and oranges to achieve a rational, or at least defendable, final allocation. In the end, we realized that information overload and the inability to verify assertions precluded the overall optimization expected from line-item systems.

Years when budgets required cutting presented particular difficulties. Stanford's deans and managers are no more competitive than most, but they weren't above using the "Washington Monument" gambit when asked for budget-cutting proposals. (In what may be an apocryphal story, the Interior Department is said to have proposed closing the Washington Monument when asked for budget-cutting alternatives—a strategy calculated to produce the greatest possible public outcry relative to achievable savings.) The game became one of finding reasonable-sounding proposals that, in the end, would prove sufficiently unpalatable that someone else's budget would get cut. I tried zero-based budgeting (ZBB) in my own division in an effort to get everything on the table, but soon drowned in a sea of paper.[7] In short, the advantage of central priority setting evaporates as an institution becomes complex, especially when budgets must be reduced from time to time.

Line item budgeting depends on the objective and task perspective, so it would suffer the shortcomings of that genre even if its informational problems could be overcome. Evaluators view each funding request on the basis of need in relation to mission, not in terms of performance. Incentives don't enter the picture—indeed, deans and chairs learn to beg for funds, not work more efficiently to make extra funds unnecessary. They do try to get the most for their money, but tend to do so in spite of the university's budgeting system rather than as a result of it. For example, deans and chairs take full responsibility for the effective use of gift funds even as they disclaim responsibility for tasks that are proposed for university support but turned down. They cling to the property rights notion in defending their university budget allocation even as they reallocate the uses of other funds. Line item systems disempower deans and chairs with respect to their core budgets, and they provide no incentives for improving education quality processes or cost consciousness. No wonder, then, that people began searching for alternatives.

Economic agency theory has helped guide the search. Agents carry out the work of principals—work the principals cannot easily accomplish on their own. Agents are supposed to represent their principals faithfully, but sometimes they divert the principal's resources for their own purposes. Schools and departments can be viewed as agents in the university context. They are expected to pursue university and stakeholder objectives, but the potential for resource diversion is omnipresent. In large public systems, where the university or campus plays the role of agent with state government or the system-wide administration being the principal, the likelihood of resource diversion is even greater.

Agency theory identifies three ways by which principals can guard against resource diversion.[8]

- **Regulatory.** The principal may restrict the agent's freedom of action, for example, by requiring prior approval for decisions that involve resources. Tight control prevents resource diversion, but at the cost of efficiency. The costs of regulation ("transaction costs" in the language of economists) become greater as tasks get more complex and the organizational distance between principal and agent lengthens.

- **Formulaic.** The principal may devise payment formulas that align the agent's objectives with those of the principal, so that, in pursuing his or her self-interest, the agent automatically furthers the principal's interest. Commission systems, where payments depend on sales, fall under this rubric. Unfortunately, such formulas become less effective as tasks become more complex, as when agents offer discounts and garner fat commissions based on gross sales while the principal pays the penalty of reduced profits, for example. Devising good formulas and fine-tuning them as conditions change can be a daunting task.

- **Judgmental.** The principal may use persuasion, the prospect of discretionary rewards, and the threat of punishment to align incentives and motivate the agent to diligently pursue the principal's goals. Persuasion may convince the agent that his long-term goals coincide with those of the principal, that while resource diversion might be attractive in the short run it would eventually prove dysfunctional. Discretionary rewards and punishments can reinforce the message and make the effects seem more tangible. While less predictable than well-functioning formulas, judgment-based systems are easier to design and manage and thus may be more effective overall.

Line-item systems are grounded in the regulatory principle and they suffer from the high transaction costs associated with centralized systems. Hence the search for alternatives focused on formulaic and judgment-based decentralization.

Responsibility center management (RCM) exemplifies formulaic decentralization.[9] Known colloquially as "every tub on its own bottom" or "ETOB,"[10] such systems decentralize both the income and expense side of the budget. First they assign revenue to academic units on the basis of activity. For example, a school that teaches 20% of the university's credit units might get 20% of the tuition dollars. Each "tub" is expected to make due with the revenue so assigned, but it is free to allocate expenditures as it wishes.

Early users recognized that pure ETOB systems tended to limit the institution's ability to cross-subsidize. What if a university wants to have a divinity school, for example, but divinity cannot generate enough enrollments to pay its way? To mitigate this problem, responsibility center systems tax revenues and redistribute the proceeds in the form of subventions. (These "income taxes" may be called "participation fees" to emphasize the university's holistic nature.) The subventions give effect to the university's values. In the example, the value of divinity is positive at the margin and so, according to the ideas of Chapter 3, it should receive a positive cross subsidy.

Responsibility center systems also include mechanisms for recovering the cost of administrative and support services. Such mechanisms become necessary when most or all revenue is devolved to academic units, which leaves the central administration with too little money to meet its needs.[11] Good practice requires that services be direct charged where practical so that schools and departments will use the resources as efficiently as possible. Costly services that departments get for free will invariably be overused, whereas paying for services keeps usage in line with the their true value. Limits to direct charging include the cost of transaction processing and negative incentive effects. For example, charging students for each book borrowed from the library would require costly record keeping and deter library usage.

The remaining service and central administrative costs are charged indirectly by applying an overhead rate to expenditures. Refined systems base the overhead rate on the variable cost of supplying services and administration, that is, the extra cost incurred when a program expands or the cost saved when it contracts. Variable costs, which typically run in the range of one-third to two-thirds of total indirect cost, cover the services and transaction processing associated with departmental expenditures. The remaining fixed costs cover outlays for general administration, policy determination, systems management, and other factors that don't vary significantly with departmental expenditures. Systems based on variable cost result in better resource allocations than ones based on average cost, even when variable cost is roughly approximated. Suppose a university's variable overhead rate is 25% and its average rate is 55%, for example. The 25 cents paid by departments represents a real cost of program expansion, and thus does not distort decision-making. Paying 55 cents on every dollar would deter worthwhile expansions, however, because the extra 30 cents bears no relation to the expansion. Universities that use marginal cost systems pay fixed indirect costs from unrestricted revenue or, if necessary, from participation fees.

Responsibility center management puts budgeting "on automatic" in the sense that, once the system is set up, allocation proceeds by formula with no academic judgments required except those involving subventions. If enrollments shift from social science to engineering, for example, the latter automatically gains funds at the former's expense. Schools and departments have maximum incentive to generate enrollment. Furthermore, administrators can fend off protests over property rights by saying, "It was the market that did it."

Responsibility center management empowers deans to the maximum possible extent. They describe the empowerment as "emancipating." Deans may worry about the increased managerial burden associated with decentralization before it is put into effect, but they usually applaud the idea afterwards.

Unfortunately, the advantages of formulaic budgeting also represent its greatest weakness. While avoiding the stultifying effect of regulation, such systems remain vulnerable to problems of formulaic design. Consider the tuition paid by engineering students taking mathematics courses, for example. Should these revenues go to the engineering school, which is responsible for program design, advising, and sometimes for student recruitment? Or should they go to the mathematics department, where the instruction actually takes place? If the latter, what is the appropriate transfer price? Paying mathematics the average revenue received per credit hour ignores engineering's program development and management costs. Worse, because the variable cost of instruction usually is less than revenue per credit hour, paying that sum to mathematics would allow it to make a profit at engineering's expense. Engineering would want to teach math in order to keep the profit for itself, but allowing it to do so would duplicate instructional effort. Aside from the merits in the particular situation, the example illustrates the complexity of formulaic revenue allocation. Some formulas come easily, but others bog one down in endless debates and complexities.

Decentralizing the revenue side of the budget also weakens the central administration's ability to further the university's overall mission. Once the revenue is assigned to the schools it is hard to get it back. Deans object when large sums are taxed away to cross-subsidize weaker programs, and they resist spending "their" money to further the university's goals at the expense of their own. Presidents and provosts can impose such actions on schools, but such actions incur political costs. It may be better not to give the revenue away in the first place, but still decentralize the expenditure side of the budget. Such systems go by the name of "block budgeting," and this is what Stanford tried in the mid-1980s.

Block budgeting retains central control of revenue but allocates funds to schools (or in the case of schools, to departments) as a lump sum rather than line item by line item. Deans and chairs can spend the resulting "one-line budget" in whatever way makes the most sense to them, so long as they observe general guidelines for salary levels, tenure rates, and the like. Provosts appreciate the freedom from information overload, the requests for small funding increments, and the battles over specific budget reductions. They will say, "You have a problem? Solve it within your block—that's what it's for. You have an opportunity? Reallocate from something you currently fund or improve your productivity—I won't lay claim to the saving." Block budgeting is similar to responsibility center management in this respect, but the central administration retains the ability to further the university's mission and reward or penalize performance variations with judgmental adjustments to the block sizes.

Unfortunately, block budgeting works better in theory than it does in practice. Determining block size presents a big practical problem. Sometimes block size decisions are informed by a funding formula, but many just add or subtract a small amount from the prior year. In principle, the decisions can take performance into account but in practice they tend not to do so. Adding the performance dimension requires one to develop explicit indicators and criteria in advance of the funding exercise, and then follow up systematically to document what actually happens. Most block budgeting systems fail to do so. Fuzzy or nonexistent performance criteria make it hard to justify the reallocation of funds. Such problems erode incentives and reinforce the property rights perspective. They tend to freeze the distribution of funds.

Combining the block budgeting and responsibility center approaches offers significant advantages that are just now being seriously explored.[12] For example, Provost John Geiger at the University of Dayton developed a hybrid called "Mission-Market Budgeting." Graduate and summer school tuition, and most special fees, were distributed to schools by formula whereas undergraduate tuition went to the provost for distribution in block form. This avoided the worst problems of transfer pricing, which arise disproportionately in regular undergraduate courses, while emphasizing the holistic nature of the university's undergraduate program. Such systems allow the provost to use enrollment trends as performance indicators, but they filter the market effect judgmentally in light of the schools' performance in relation to the university's mission. Putting as many revenue elements "on automatic" as possible allows one to focus judgment where it can be most effective, without loosing the beneficial effects of market forces elsewhere.

PERFORMANCE FUNDING

Public agencies have applied multi-campus performance funding methodologies for many years. Tennessee embraced the idea in 1974, for example, and South Carolina, Virginia, and Missouri, among other states, now have well-articulated systems.[13] In 1997, US Commissioner of Educational Statistics Pat Forgione noted that 34 states used some kind of performance funding, and that 15 states "mandated submissions of performance measures as part of the state budgetary process."[14] Performance funding has, if anything, been used more extensively overseas. For example, the Netherlands and Sweden use such systems for a substantial portion of institutional funding, and the UK and Hong Kong allocate institutional research funding on the basis of measured performance. Additional countries, including Australia, Denmark, and the People's Republic of China, regularly publish performance indicators as part of higher education oversight. The World Bank advocates the use of performance indicators and the Organization for Economic Cooperation and Development (OECD) has created a set of multinational indicators.[15]

The design of performance indicators has proved more difficult than one might think.[16] For example, indicators may measure inputs, processes, or outputs; if inputs or outputs, they may or may not be adjusted for quality. Indicators vary in terms of accuracy and relevance, and they don't always meet the minimum requirement of identifying directions of movement as unambiguously favorable or unfavorable. Some indicators can be manipulated, for example, by reducing grading standards to improve pass rates. Some can be calculated from readily available data while others require costly collection efforts. Some indicators cannot readily be aggregated (e.g., from departmental to institutional level), which makes comparisons difficult. Finally, several indicators may measure the same thing and thus distort the weighting scheme used to summarize results. In short, difficulties in the design of robust performance indicators make the process an art rather than a science.

Most universities remain skeptical of performance funding despite its adoption by public agencies. The following account, reported in *The Chronicle of Higher Education*, illustrates the frustration that performance funding sometimes elicits.

> Austin R. Gilbert had heard enough. A scowl underscored his thick, graying mustache, and his glare hushed the audience.
>
> The state-college presidents in the crowd had misjudged Mr. Gilbert, chairman of South Carolina's Commission on Higher Education, if they thought he would be receptive to the litany of excuses and complaints they had aired... Instead, he rose to

his feet and, sounding like an exasperated basketball coach, told them to shape up and deal with the task at hand: finding a way to hold their public colleges financially accountable for how they perform...

Figure 10.2
South Carolina's Performance Indicators

1) **Mission:** An acceptable mission statement and a strategic plan based on it; the amount spent on achieving the mission; a curriculum in place to achieve it; success in achieving the strategic plan's goals.

2) **Quality of faculty:** Credentials of professors and instructors; faculty reviews that include student and peer evaluations; post-tenure review for tenured professors; the level of faculty compensation; professors' availability to students outside the classroom; unpaid public service performed by professors.

3) **Instructional quality:** Class sizes and student-teacher ratios; number of credit hours taught by faculty members; ratio of full-time faculty members to other full-time employees; whether degree-granting programs are accredited; institutional emphasis on teaching quality and reform.

4) **Institutional cooperation and collaboration:** sharing of equipment, technology, and other resources within the college and with other institutions and businesses; collaboration with private industry.

5) **Administrative efficiency:** Amount spent on administration versus academic programs; use of best management practices; elimination of unjustified duplication and waste; amount of general overhead costs.

6) **Entrance requirements:** Credentials of students, including standardized-test scores, high school standing, grade-point averages, and activities; applicants' achievement, before enrollment, in nonacademic areas; priority given to enrolling in-state students.

7) **Graduates' achievements:** Graduation rate; graduates' rate of employment and scores on professional, graduate, employment, and certification tests; employer feedback on graduates; number of graduates who continue their education; credit hours earned by graduates.

8) **User-friendliness of institution:** Ease of transferring credits to and from the college; continuing-education programs offered; accessibility to the state's citizens.

9) **Research spending:** Spending on reforms in teacher education; value of public and private grants received.

"We are faced with a crisis of accountability," he warned. If South Carolina's 33 public colleges want more state money, he said, they must submit to high-stakes performance evaluations and demonstrate that they have improved.[17]

South Carolina's legislature had decided that public funds should be allocated among institutions based on 37 performance indicators. The indicators mandated in the 1996 law, which are broadly representative of the genre, fell into the nine categories shown in Figure 10.2. Many such indicators are straightforward, such as class sizes and student-teacher ratios, equipment sharing, and value of research grants and contracts. Some address areas covered in this book, including whether faculty reviews include student and peer evaluations and whether departments get feedback on graduates from employers. Some require a certain amount of judgment, such as whether the institution has an acceptable mission statement and strategic plan and whether it is carrying them out effectively. Such judgments may prove controversial, but it's hard to argue that oversight bodies have no right to make them.

Universities fear being disadvantaged by factors not under their control or penalized for making educationally sound decisions that affect certain measures negatively. For example, the South Carolina presidents felt that legislators did not "appreciate how difficult it is to define, much less measure, what a 'good' public institution does." Furthermore, they said, "Some of the indicators contradict other indicators... On the one hand, you are evaluated on access. On the other hand, you are evaluated on SAT scores [which tend to decline as the institution broadens its admission criteria] ... [Furthermore,] you could take any of those indicators and argue that high is better or low is better."[18]

I don't want to take sides in the South Carolina debate, which in any case has receded into history. My purpose is to illustrate the tension that performance funding so often engenders. On the one side are funds providers who have become frustrated with what they perceive as a lack of accountability by universities to the public—a problem to which I have alluded many times in this book. On the other side are academics, who find it easy to poke holes in any selection of indicators that can be devised. The resulting impasse can't be resolved by finding a flawless indicator system because no such system exists. Nor can governments abandon their concerns about accountability—the sums spent on higher education are too large and the potential for performance shortfalls too great to make this acceptable. What, then, can be done?

Several strategies can be used to break the impasse. The first limits the amount of money put at risk in any given performance funding exercise. In South Carolina, the legislature's initial proposal called for *all* the state's higher education money to be allocated by performance funding. Raising the stakes to this level guarantees strong resistance. Most states and countries limit performance funding to small percentages of the total allocation. Such figures recognize the inexact nature of performance indicators and honor the academy's need for funding stability. Experience shows such percentages are large enough to matter, especially when the exercise's results are made public. The so-called trim-tab effect allows one to steer performance by using small amounts of energy, appropriately leveraged. Disclosing the allocations encourages competition among institutions, which allows agencies to affect behavior without putting large amounts of money at risk.

A second strategy limits the number of performance indicators, defines them carefully, and relates them directly to well-understood priorities. For example, Missouri's Funding for Results program addresses only a small number of indicators. The Higher Education Department designates a specific sum of money for distribution according to each indicator. The program dates from 1994, which is longer than most programs. Although the sums are small, conversations on campuses in Missouri support aforementioned trim-tab effect.

Such strategies are consistent with the idea that "simpler is best even if it initially seems less attractive on technical grounds."[19] They recognize and accept the fact that the performance indicator system can't be comprehensive. Instead, the system highlights a small number of factors to which the agency wants to give priority attention. This contrasts to the system of 60 indicators once recommended by the National Center for Higher Education Management Systems (NCHEMS), the 41 indicators and 284 subindicators used in the UK, and the 359 indicators listed by the Australian government.[20]

The third strategy adds a qualitative element to the evaluation. I'll illustrate it by describing the performance funding system now used by the Hong Kong University Grants Committee. The committee's block grants cover about 80% of funding for the region's eight higher education institutions. It determines the education component, which accounts for about three-quarters of the total, by a model that takes account of each institution's mix of fields, student levels, and modes of attendance. The remainder depends mostly on a Research Assessment Exercise (RAE) conducted by the committee before the start of each funding triennium. The RAE, discussed briefly in Chapter 8, applies peer evaluation to the scholarly output of every active researcher in the region.[21] It produces numerical scores for each subject area, which when aggregated to the institutional level drive the distribution of research funds. Needless to say, driving almost a quarter of higher education funding with the RAE produced a powerful incentive for research.

Until recently, education received no performance funding except as might be applied through ad hoc adjustments of the funding model results. (Chapter 8 described how academic audit informed one such adjustment.) During 1999, discussions with the SAR government's secretary for education and manpower led the UGC to consider systematic performance funding for the nonresearch aspects of university operations. While accountability provided the initial impetus, we soon realized that performance funding provided an important lever for steering higher education in Hong Kong.

The committee began by commissioning a comprehensive review of performance indicator schemes as are they are practiced around the world.[22] The review reinforced our conviction that formulaic reliance on performance indicators for a large fraction of nonresearch funding would be a mistake. Yet some kind of scheme was needed. Our answer was to adopt the strategy described below. In doing so, we emulated the processes being developed by well-managed universities for internal resource allocation.

The exercise was implemented for the first time, in April 2001, with meetings between a panel of UGC members and the president or vice-chancellor of each institution.[23] The institutions received the following seven questions in advance of the meeting. Each question reflected an announced policy or priority where the UGC wanted to focus attention. For example, mission statements had been agreed upon some years before but the committee perceived a drift in mission from teaching toward research. We told the institutions that the relative emphasis on the seven questions would vary depending on the school's mission and stage of development.

1) What does the institution see as the community's needs and the HKSAR's priorities, and how is the institution's academic programme mix responsive to such needs and priorities?

2) Has the institution balanced teaching and research, and what specific kinds of research and scholarship does the institution carry out to achieve relevance to mission statement?

3) Apart from knowledge of subject matter, what values and attributes does the institution consider as important to instill in its students, and how are the students trained on such values and attributes?

4) Has the institution demonstrated diligence in promoting quality in teaching and learning, and in following up on the outcome of the first-round TLQPRs [the academic audits described in Chapter 8]?

5) What does the institution perceive as the most important collaborative projects with other institutions, and how have these projects benefited or will benefit Hong Kong?

6) What does the institution perceive as its most important collaborative projects with industry, and in what ways do these projects support the institution's mission?

7) What does the institution consider as its most significant improvement in recent years?[24]

A packet of performance statistics compiled from the UGC's database accompanied the questions. The statistics included funding and expenditure patterns, faculty and student characteristics and attainment, and the performance of graduates. Comparisons among institutions were provided where meaningful. The presidents and vice-chancellors were asked to ground their responses in the performance statistics wherever possible and provide additional data if they wished. The meetings went smoothly and all parties judged the discussion to be substantive and useful. The panel had no difficulty distinguishing between good and less-good performance or justifying the resulting allocations. Feedback after the event indicated that the process had improved communication and reinforced incentives, and that it should be continued.

By asking the institutions to interpret the performance measures and introduce new measures where they could be helpful, the UGC avoided the misunderstandings described earlier. By focusing on well-understood priorities, we avoided diffusing attention with large numbers of indicators. Most importantly, the committee opened a dialog with the institutions about their performance in relation to the HKSAR's priorities. The money at risk was modest (about US$90 million for the triennium, less that 1% of the block grants), but it was enough to get the institutions' attention. Not only did it provide the institutions with valuable discretionary funding, the public nature of the exercise and the interest of government and the media raised the nonfinancial stakes to a significant level.

The UGC based its performance-funding scheme on the third principle of economic agency theory: "One may use persuasion, the prospect of discretionary rewards, and the threat of punishment to align incentives and motivate the agent to pursue the principal's goals with high priority." Formulaic performance-funding schemes rely on the second principle, which is much more difficult to implement. The remainder of this chapter describes how the third principle can be applied to resource allocation within institutions.

BUILDING A BALANCED SCORECARD

The nonprofit model says that resources should go to programs and activities that produce the most value for money. If they go elsewhere, results can be improved by shifting money from activities that produce low returns to those that produce higher ones. Performance funding helps in two ways: 1) good performance enhances value more than poor performance does, other things being equal, and 2) the system provides incentives for people to do the best job possible. The problem, of course, is to find ways to evaluate performance.

Organizational behaviorists Jeffrey Pfeffer and Robert Sutton believe action-oriented performance measures should[25] be relatively global in scope, focusing less on trying to assess individual performance and more on factors critical to organizational success; focus more on processes and means to ends, and less on end-of-process or final outcomes; be tied to and reflect the business model, culture, and philosophy of the firm; result from a mindful, ongoing process of learning from experience and experimentation; use comparatively few metrics; and close the decision-making loop by auditing and assessing what the firm is doing, thereby ensuring that the firm "knows what it knows."

Action-oriented measures spur organizational learning on relatively few critical issues and processes. Measurement should be tailored to the local environment, and the complexity that comes with comprehensiveness should be avoided. Such measures help organizations develop knowledge and turn that knowledge into action.

The "balanced scorecard" concept invented by Harvard Business School Professors Robert Kaplan and David Norton provides a template for performance evaluation.[26] The scorecard expresses all the organization's important long- and short-term goals, not just the financial ones. It depends on criteria that are widely understood and accepted. The concept has been widely adopted in business, and it applies as well to nonprofit enterprises. Its application to colleges and universities is straightforward.

In addition to financial information, the balanced scorecard includes data on customers, internal business processes, and organizational learning and growth. It considers the results obtained from operations and progress on initiatives designed to improve future performance. It expresses criteria of interest to internal as well as external stakeholders, and it includes measures that require judgment as well as ones that are easily quantifiable. Kaplan and Norton stress that the scorecard's "financial and nonfinancial measures must be part of the information system for all employees at all levels of the organization."[27] They should provide grassroots guidance as well as evaluations for use by people up the line.

In higher education, internal stakeholders include faculty, students, staff, and trustees—people whose views are reflected in the nonprofit model's "value" element. External stakeholders include funding agencies, research sponsors, donors, and the general public. External stakeholders represent the "market" element of the nonprofit model, although many also buy into the academy's value system. (Students might be considered external rather than internal stakeholders because of their status as customers, but the distinction doesn't matter.) Business processes include teaching and learning, research and scholarship, public service, education quality processes, libraries and information resources, student services, and administrative and support functions. Measures associated with these processes refer to the nonprofit model's "production function."

Figure 10.3 illustrates the balanced scorecard as it might be applied in a college or university. It follows the business scorecard except for semantics and one structural change dictated by the nonprofit enterprise model: the separation of output valuation from financial performance. Many outputs are valued for their own sake in nonprofits, not for the money they bring in. Separating finance from outputs emphasizes that money is a means to an end, that surpluses cannot be distributed to stakeholders, and that the budget is supposed to be balanced over the long run. Turning to semantics, the term "market position" couches the business scorecard's "customer" perspective in more academically acceptable terms and "internal process" restates "business process."

Figure 10.3
A Balanced Scorecard for a College or University

1) Outputs in relation to mission
- Enrollments and degrees by field, student level, and mode of attendance
- Student persistence and attainment
- value added student assessments
- Research, scholarship, and intellectual property
- Public service and athletics
- Collaborations with industry, government, and other universities

2) Market position in relation to mission
- Application and yield rates for target market segments
- Quality and preparation of applicants, admittees, and matriculants
- Diversity of applicants, admittees, and matriculants
- Prospective applicants' awareness of and attitudes about the institution
- Employer and graduate school evaluations of degree holders
- Penetration of relevant fundraising segments
- Penetration of relevant sponsored research segments
- Performance in hiring faculty of the type, quality, and diversity desired

3) Internal processes
- Demonstrated performance in education quality work
- Demonstrated cost consciousness in academic programs
- Faculty quality, retention rates, and attitudes toward the institution
- Teaching method and class size mix; faculty teaching loads; technology utilization
- Documented continuous improvement of teaching and learning
- Documented continuous improvement and periodic reengineering of administrative and support services (e.g., research administration;

> intellectual property management; public services management; administrative and support service management; and financial management)
>
> **4) Finance**
> - Surplus/deficit: whether the budget is balanced and in control
> - Revenue profile: e.g., degree of reliance on tuition; tuition growth rate
> - Expenditure profile: e.g., instruction cost as a percentage of total expenditures
> - Long-run financial equilibrium: balanced growth rates of revenue and expense; provision of appropriate reserves; absence of hidden liabilities
>
> **5) Organizational learning and growth**
> - A well-articulated and meaningful statement of mission and values
> - A strategic plan that considers strengths, weaknesses, opportunities, and threats
> - Documented linkages between strategic plans, operational plans, and budgets
> - Training and support for initiatives like reengineering, quality work, and technology
> - Evidence of a quality culture, continuous improvement, and organizational learning

References to "outputs" and "market position" include the caveat "in relation to mission" to emphasize that scorecards should reflect institutional uniqueness. For example, not all institutions should stress research accomplishments or the penetration of sponsored research markets. Not all institutions should define student quality in terms of SAT and ACT scores, and not all should aspire to admit from the blue chip market segments. The words "demonstrated" and "documented" appear frequently to emphasize the importance of evidence. Many scorecard elements must be assessed qualitatively, but the assessments should be based on evidence rather than assertion or wishful thinking.

The scorecard's organizational learning and growth component addresses the institution's ability to change and improve. Colleges and universities pride themselves on being learning organizations, but they often shortchange information, training, and improvement functions.

This element of a university's scorecard should include operating and strategic information functions, training (including faculty training in education quality processes), and the institution's record on continuous improvement.

Kaplan and Norton recommend that objectives, targets, and initiatives be included on the balanced scorecard along with performance measures. Objectives provide context for the measures and set the direction of desired change. Targets provide the standards needed to gauge results. Descriptions of initiatives provide guidance about how the targets will be achieved. Indeed, the descriptions themselves become de facto standards—whether the initiatives are being carried out represents an important performance measure in its own right.

Quantitative data should be expressed relative to benchmarks wherever possible. Figure 10.4 illustrates an innovative chart format developed by higher education consultant John Minter. The chart displays instruction expenditures as a percentage of the educational and general budget (one of the items in Figure 10.3), for Northwest Missouri State

Figure 10.4

**Instruction as a Percentage of Total Budget: 1990 v. 1999
Northwest Missouri State University and
Two Benchmark Cohorts**

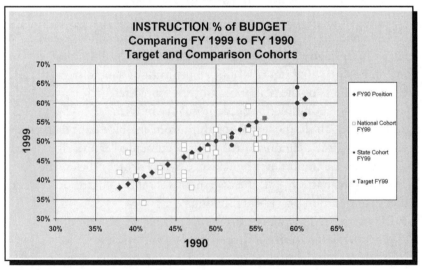

John Minter Associates: reproduced with permission.

University and two benchmark institutional cohorts. The national cohort consists of comprehensive institutions similar to Northwest, whereas the state cohort includes all schools in Missouri. Showing cohort data for 1990 and 1999 allows one to track trends and compare them with Northwest's own target, depicted by the shaded square, which happens to be unchanged since 1990. (The black diamonds depict the chart's diagonal.) The data show that Northwest's 55% of expenditures spent on instruction exceeds that of all but four institutions in the two cohorts. The university uses these and similar data to help drive its budget process.

An effective scorecard will become part of the university's strategic management system. Taken together, the objectives, measures, targets, and initiatives should help leaders achieve the following.[28]

1) Clarify vision and strategy and translate them to operational terms.

2) Plan, set targets, and align strategic initiatives with one another.

3) Communicate objectives and link them to performance measures.

4) Boost feedback and organizational learning.

The scorecard provides a framework for structuring dialog up, down, and across the organization. Measuring results within the framework of the organization's strategic objectives, targets, and initiatives grounds performance in reality and points the way toward improvement.

Every institution should decide for itself what elements to include in its scorecard and what standards will be acceptable. The choices should reflect the university's value system and its perceived threats, weaknesses, opportunities, and threats. This makes the scorecard meaningful up and down the organization. Instead of being bureaucratic, the process stimulates good operating performance, and also organizational learning and growth.

BUDGETING AS AN INSTRUMENT OF CHANGE

We have seen that colleges and universities should be market smart and mission focused. The budget process can be a powerful instrument for improvement, but most institutions fail to exploit its full potential.

Assume for purposes of discussion that an institution's leaders are committed to change, but that schools, departments, and faculty have yet to be convinced. They want to protect the status quo and they view resource allocation from the property rights and objective and task perspectives. The president and provost have described the need for improvement and laid out a program for accomplishing it, but few within the campus community seem to be listening. What can be done?

The first requirement is for initiatives from the top of the organization to break through the noise level and permeate peoples' agendas. Cogent arguments can be helpful, but departments and professors may not see the changes as being in their best interest even if they help the institution in the long run. Harnessing resource allocation as a driver of change can overcome these difficulties.

The following two-pronged approach builds on the Mission-Market system described earlier. By combining responsibility center management with performance funding based on a balanced scorecard, it drives strategic change without undermining academic values. Responsibility center systems make the deans responsible for revenue. This ups the financial dimension of accountability, but it also elevates school missions and priorities relative to those of the institution. Problems also arise when actions that produce revenues in the short run don't reposition the school or institution to compete effectively in the future.

The second element, performance funding based on a balanced scorecard, mitigates these difficulties. The scorecard should include the institution's change agenda as well as the operating results for which the schools are held accountable. Improving education quality processes might represent a central change agendum, for example, while maintaining desired class size distributions and the number of faculty who advise undergraduates could be operational scorecard measures. Put the two elements together and one has a Mission-Market-Performance (MMP) budgeting system.

To set up an MMP system, one first divides the institution's revenue into three categories: assignable revenue, attributable revenue, and central revenue.[29]

1) Assignable revenue can be linked to schools without ambiguity. Graduate, summer, and special-program tuition often fall into this category, as does income from restricted funds. Assignable revenue will be devolved by formula using responsibility center principles.

2) Attributable revenue can be linked to schools, but the association is ambiguous. Tuition from traditional undergraduates, where more than

one school may have a legitimate claim, often falls into this category. Instead of being devolved by formula as in a pure responsibility center system, these revenues will be allocated by the central administration. Claims to attribution are included in the schools' scorecards, where they inform funding judgments instead of dictating formulaic allocations.

3) Central revenues, such as from totally unrestricted endowments, cannot be linked to schools. They are not candidates for devolvement and do not enter the schools' scorecards.

The assignable and central revenues provide funds to be allocated judgmentally by the central administration, based on mission and the balanced scorecards, and to cover the fixed cost of administrative and support services. If necessary, they can be topped up by assessing participation fees on assigned revenues. Variable support costs are recovered by charging overhead on all department and school expenditures, regardless of funds source. A simple spreadsheet simulation can quantify the financial flows before the university finalizes the new system.

The judgmental allocations include scorecard-based elements as well as the cross subsidies used in classic RCM. The scorecard elements need not be large, and they can be based on qualitative as well as quantitative indicators. However, the scorecard and associated evaluation methods need to be worked out in advance, documented carefully, and implemented consistently across units and over time. I recently designed such a system for the National University of Singapore. The system was accepted enthusiastically and is being implemented as this book goes to press.

Linking resource allocation to performance is good policy at all levels, from the agencies that oversee public institutions, to system-wide administrations, to campus administrations, all the way down to schools' allocations to departments. Most higher education decision makers want to do the right thing, but many conflicting demands compete for their attention. Building a visible linkage between funding and performance accomplishes two things. First, it launches a dialog about what is desired, why, and how the changes can be accomplished. Second, it raises the stakes to where the desired changes can compete effectively with the unit's other priorities. This two-step program satisfies the dictum, "To move a stone in sand, one must dig in front as well as push behind." The dialog "digs in front" and the financial stakes "push behind." The next chapter embeds this idea in higher education's overall reform program.

Endnotes

1. The property rights idea comes from former Stanford colleague Henry Levin, now a professor at Columbia Teachers College.

2. Callan (1993), p. 1. He goes on to say that "perhaps it is time to open the box, examine the components and see if they can be arranged in a way that will induce more efficient and effective operations than in the past—for example, through more streamlined curriculum, administrative organization, greater use of technology, more relevant priorities."

3. See Chapter 10 of Massy (1996) for a discussion of funding models.

4. Massy (1996), Chapter 4.

5. This occurred in the mid-1990s, well after my tenure as chief financial officer.

6. See Massy (1996), Chapters 1 and 2.

7. The business and finance division employed about 1,500 people and was responsible for nearly all nonacademic support operations. We employed the best consultants available and made ZBB work for a few years, but in the end the process proved to be more trouble than it was worth.

8. Massy (1996); Hoenack (1983).

9. See Whalen (1991).

10. Harvard, the grandfather of decentralized systems, coined the "ETOB" description.

11. Harvard's ETOB system has no need for cost recovery mechanisms because its large unrestricted endowment provides more than enough money to fund administrative and support services.

12. Massy (1996), Chapter 12. Recently I have assisted the University of Dayton, Mercer University, the National University of Singapore, and a group of Hong Kong universities on the optimization and deployment of decentralized budgeting systems.

13. See for example, Burke and Serban (1998).

14. Forgione, Pat, "A vision of information-based decision making" (speech made to the Association for Institutional Research in Orlando, FL, 1997); quoted in Zhang (1999), p. 2.

15. Center for Education Research and Innovation, OECD (1992).

16. The list of issues is based on criteria developed by Cave, et al. (1997), p. 209.

17. "Rancor and Confusion Greet Change in South Carolina Budgeting" (*The Chronicle of Higher Education*, April 4, 1997, p. A26).

18. Ibid.

19. Gaither, Nedwek, & Neal (1994); quoted in Zhang (1999), p. 17.

20. Zhang (1999), p. 18.

21. French, Massy, and Young (2001); see El Khawas and Massy (1996) for a discussion of the UK system. The UGC provides research project funding through its Research Grants Council in addition to the research component of the block grants.

22. Zhang (1999). I described some of the results of that review earlier.

23. The panel consisted of overseas UGC members and local members not affiliated with any institution. It was chaired by the author. Some institutions follow the British system and call their head a "vice-chancellor," while others use the US terminology of "president."

24. UGC letter to heads of institutions (February 2001), with slight editing.

25. Pfeffer and Sutton (2000), pp. 173–174.

26. Kaplan and Norton (1996).

27. Ibid., p. 8.

28. Adapted from p. 10,. ibid.

29. More detailed descriptions, including the financial system design details and numerical examples, can be found in Massy (1996), Chapter 12. There I call the system "Value Responsibility Budgeting." The treatment here expands on the system's performance-based elements.

11

Higher Education's Action Agenda

That colleges and universities cannot continue on their traditional path represents the central thesis of this book. New opportunities, driven by information technology and the new emphasis on markets, challenge their traditional modes of operation. New competition, often enabled by technology, challenges their local monopolies and erodes financial margins. New ways of looking at quality and cost open the way for improvement, but require a reshaping of traditional academic values. Schools that learn to meet these challenges will find exciting new opportunities. Those that don't will fail to be the best they can be. They will find themselves increasingly marginalized.

Suppose you are convinced that change is needed. Suppose further that you are in a position to influence institutional policy and behavior, for example, an academic officer, influential professor, board member, or someone involved in higher education oversight. Conscious of academe's tremendous inertia, you wonder what steps, if any, you can take to effect change. How can you and like-minded colleagues spur reform without undermining the academy's core values? It is to this action agenda that we turn in this chapter. First, however, we will review the case for change.

THE CASE FOR CHANGE

Chapter 1 described the academy's journey from ivory tower to economic mainstream and the stresses associated with life in the mainstream. The stresses have spawned some serious contradictions between the public posture of higher education and what actually happens within institutions. The academy's continued assertion that improving educational quality requires spending more, that there is nothing faculty can do to improve value for money in education, represents one such contradiction. The

306

pursuit of prestige at the expense of demonstrable education quality represents another. Such contradictions, coupled with the steady advance of tuition rates and costs, have eroded trust in universities at the same time that higher education itself enjoys strong popular support.

We began exploring these contradictions by looking at universities as economic enterprises. Chapter 2 described how nonprofit enterprises balance values and market forces. They view success in the marketplace as a means of mission fulfillment, not as a way to maximize profits. Yet the incentives for meeting "customer" needs and maximizing the productivity of individual programs should remain strong, just as it is for businesses. The difference between nonprofit and for-profit enterprises lies in "Bowen's Law": Universities will raise all the money they can and they will spend all the money they raise. Corporations seek revenue but they try to minimize expenditures. This difference helps explain the seemingly inexorable advance of cost in higher education. Market power explains much of the rest. Market power enables universities to raise prices and produce financial margins that can cross-subsidize other programs.

Chapter 3 showed that cross subsidies are ubiquitous in higher education. They represent the defining feature of nonprofit as opposed to for-profit enterprises, for it is through cross subsidies that the nonprofits superimpose their values upon those of the market. Cross subsidies provide incentives for operating efficiency: A dollar saved in one area can be redeployed to produce value elsewhere. They also fuel the academic ratchet: Margins earned from popular educational programs can be used to fund faculty research, even though the cross subsidies never show up in the university's accounting system.

Accounting ambiguities conceal important cost trends and make benchmarking across institutions very difficult. They prevent institutions from understanding their cost structures and engender mistrust among stakeholders. Chapter 3 advocated better disclosure of costs and cross subsidies, especially those between education and research. Such disclosure would honor the trust placed in higher education institutions. They would improve the performance of markets and raise the quality of dialog between institutions and their stakeholders.

Institutionally funded faculty research is an important recipient of cross subsidies. Professors value research because it's intrinsically interesting and because it enhances their careers. For institutions, it confers prestige and funding. Both believe that research enhances education, but we saw in Chapter 4 that this view represents an oversimplification. While research does make teaching more lively and up-to-date, it also takes time away from educational tasks. We found that while research complements teaching up to a certain point, it hurts education quality if carried too far. No built-in regulatory mechanism halts research at the point of diminishing returns for education. Instead, the academic incentive system drives research inexorably forward through a process called the academic ratchet.

Such cross subsidies would not pose much of a problem if buyers could evaluate education quality before committing themselves to an institution or program. But because education quality is notoriously difficult to measure, it tends to be equated with prestige and its correlate, research. This produces a vicious circle: cross subsidies from education to research boost prestige and thus market power, which allows higher prices to be charged for the same education quality, which enables larger cross subsidies. Buyers pay more for the same quality, or perhaps they pay more for less as research consumes increasing amounts of faculty time.

Information technology was the last stop on our tour of the higher education landscape. Today's technology provides unprecedented opportunities to reshape teaching and learning processes, but doing so requires out-of-the box thinking and the willingness of faculty to invest substantial amounts of time and energy. Today's strong emphasis on research makes such investment difficult. Therefore, much of what passes for innovation represents nothing more than the bolting of technology on to existing educational methods. This may improve quality at the margin, but it fails to realize technology's full potential.

WHAT NEEDS FIXING?

Higher education's strategic agendum can be stated in one sentence: Colleges and universities need to improve their core competency in education. This sounds strange, since they are, first and foremost, educational institutions. Yet close examination reveals that the traditional university's core competency lies in creating and disseminating knowledge, not in education. I asserted in Chapter 1 that while professors do research and scholarship and make knowledge available to students that take their courses, most spend little time on the processes of teaching and learning. They don't focus on the backgrounds, needs, and learning styles presented by their students. They don't think deeply about the assessment of learning outcomes, or about quality assurance. They don't concern themselves sufficiently about costs, and they don't exploit the full potential of technology. I trust the ensuing chapters have presented convincing arguments in support of this assertion.

In today's world, core competency in education requires more attention to all of these. Traditional universities possess some elements of competency, but they fall short on others. The shortfalls may not have mattered in past decades, before the advent of technology and competition, but they matter now. This book argues that colleges and universities should 1) improve education quality processes, 2) adopt paradigm-changing technology, and 3) become more cost conscious, in order to 4) rebuild their core competency in education. The action steps described later in this chapter are designed to achieve these objectives.

Education Quality Processes

Chapter 6 defined "education quality processes" as organized activities dedicated to improving and assuring educational quality. Such processes should not be confused with teaching itself. They are "meta" activities that define planning and provide the feedback and control system needed to guide teaching and learning. Quality processes enable faculty to organize their work and improve the data they use to make decisions. They are no substitute for adequate human and financial resources, but they help get the most from whatever resources are available. Those who work to improve the quality of academic programs often report that "good people working with good processes accomplish more than good people working with poor ones."

Unfortunately, quality process excellence does not come naturally for most faculty. Most professors view teaching as an individual endeavor not susceptible to systematic improvement. Many believe that "good teachers are born, not made." While most faculty want to do a good job in teaching, many are eager to discharge these obligations and turn their attention to research. Improving education quality processes will itself require systematic effort. Faculty contributions in this arena will have to be recognized in the institution's incentive and reward structure. Finally, measures of education quality process maturity need to be put in place so that individuals and departments, and deans and provosts, can track progress up the learning curve.

Paradigm-Changing Technology

Paradigm-changing technology removes education from the realm of handicraft, where individual professors reinvent the wheel with each new cohort of students. Chapter 5 described how educational process options can be expanded with technology, and how economies of scale and scope, learning curve exploitation, and cost trajectory improvement can change education's economic parameters. Whether technology will inflate or reduce cost is not the issue. That depends on the availability of funding— on how stakeholders trade off cost and quality. One thing is sure, however: If technology is used wisely, it will offer opportunities to produce today's quality at lower cost as well as opportunities to produce better quality at higher cost.

Successful innovation also may lead the institution to new markets and new partnerships. Distance education provides many good examples of market entry, but new segments can be served on campus as well. Partnerships can be forged among peer institutions—for example, to effect a division of labor in new technology applications. Other partnerships can involve institutions higher or lower in the pecking order, as when one institution acts as a local outlet for a more prestigious provider, for example. Still others bring together traditional and for-profit entities. Institutions already are jockeying for position. They fear they'll miss out on the good markets and partners if they don't act aggressively now. However, most schools must change faculty attitudes and create new incentive and reward structures in order to be successful.

To change the educational paradigm, professors must learn to exploit the technology to the fullest extent possible, not just use it to enhance conventional teaching. They must learn to import course objects and assessment instruments as a routine matter, rather than usually trying to build their own. They also need assurance that time spent on the new approaches will be supported by their colleagues and the institution. The department and institution must leverage individual faculty efforts and reward good work with promotion, tenure, and compensation.

Cost Consciousness

Universities don't know what it costs to educate students or do research and scholarship. Bundling the costs of education, educational development, departmental research, and scholarship denies university leaders and faculty key information they need to manage effectively. Bundling makes it impossible to analyze cost tradeoffs and prevents comparisons among institutions and programs. Without such data, one cannot benchmark programs or hold people accountable for the effective use of resources.

Most colleges and universities would claim they already are cost conscious. And so they are if this is defined as cost control, that is, establishing budgets, holding people to them, and recording costs accurately as they are incurred. Schools quickly run into trouble if they fail to exercise cost control. Just as for educational core competency, however, the traditional costing methodologies represent only part of what entities outside higher education mean by cost consciousness. Educational competency requires more attention to cost, and this must include the academic side of the enterprise.

Cost consciousness means an understanding of the relations among cost, enrollment, and quality. Viewing quality as proportional to per-student cost, such as manifested in class sizes, rules out paradigm-changing innovation. This perpetuates cost growth and places unnecessary burdens on students, parents, and the public. In a resource-constrained world, such myopia also adds to the faculty's burdens and saps institutional vitality. Cost-conscious institutions work constantly to make learning more efficient. They know that competitiveness and vitality depend on spending no more than necessary to achieve objectives. They know rather than assume that the financial burdens placed on their constituents are truly necessary.

As a practical matter, academic cost consciousness means analyzing cost at the activity level. Activities produce outcomes and consume resources, and resource consumption generates cost. Even when a resource commitment is fixed in the short run—as in the case of a tenured professor—using the resource for a particular purpose precludes its use for another purpose. The resulting "opportunity loss" can be used in activity-based costing calculations, just as if the commitment itself was variable. And even tenured faculty commitments get transformed to variable cost if one considers a sufficiently long planning period.

Like quality process improvement and technology deployment, cost consciousness must begin with individual faculty members and be consolidated at the departmental level. Activity-based costing is not something professors can leave to others. Because they control the activities of teaching and learning, their job description should include the design of cost-effective processes. There are built-in incentives to the extent this means the effective use of professors' own time. However, a good cost analysis also may provide the justification for using other kinds of resources, including technology, to leverage faculty time. Departments should be receptive to such justifications and maintain sufficient budget flexibility to fund worthwhile proposals.

Deans, provosts, presidents, and boards also need to become more cost conscious. First, they should ensure the institution embraces activity-based costing at the grassroots level and that professors have the skill development and technical support they need to do it well. But that is not all. Academic leaders also need to understand the cross subsidies within their institution and be prepared to justify them in terms of mission and values. This means unbundling the costs, and also the revenues, of education and research. The data need not be precise, but they should be made public in reports to stakeholders and notes to the institution's financial statements. This is the only way to resolve the longstanding controversies about the direction and level of cross subsidies—especially the cross subsidy between teaching and research.

Core Competency in Education

Rebuilding an institution's core competency in education will require better education quality processes, paradigm-changing technology, and cost consciousness. We've looked at them separately. Now it's time to weave them into an integrated program. To do that, I'll expand the "domains, principles, maturity" structure introduced in Chapters 6, 7, and 8 for quality processes.

Figure 11.1 presents the domains in which competency needs to be rebuilt. The set has been relabeled "Educational Competency Domains" to distinguish it from the quality process domains of Chapter 6. A new domain that addresses resource conservation has been built into the structure, and explicit references to technology have been added throughout. "Resource conservation" focuses on cost analysis, which is like student learning assessment in that it provides essential feedback for improvement and continuing efforts to produce better quality at the same or lower cost. Technology provides a key input to the design of teaching, learning, and assessment processes. Moreover, curricular materials should be selected with an eye to potential technology utilization and students in virtually all disciplines should understand how technology impinges on their specialty and on life in general.

Figure 11.1
Educational Competency Domains

1) **Determination of desired learning outcomes.** What should a student who successfully completes the course or departmental major know and be able to do? How does the course or major program build on the student's prior knowledge and abilities? How does it contribute to the student's future employment opportunities, capacity to make social contributions, and quality of life? Does it include technology as a major factor in today's world?

2) **Design of curricula.** What should be taught, in what order, and from what perspective? How does the content contribute to the student's overall knowledge and learning? What course materials are used? How do materials relate to other parts of the student's program? Do they exploit the benefits of technology?

3) **Design of teaching and learning processes.** How are teaching and learning activities organized? What methods are used to expose students to the material for the first time, stimulate engagement, interpret material and answer questions, and provide feedback on student work? To what extent does technology facilitate active learning and leverage faculty and student time?

4) **Student learning assessment.** What measures and indicators are used to assess student learning? Do they provide performance comparisons between the beginning and end of term, or simply report the end result? Do they measure long-term outcomes of the students' experience? Are baseline and trend information available? Who is responsible for assessment? To what extent is technology exploited in the assessment process? How are the assessment results used?

5) **Resource conservation.** Do departments consider cost in their pedagogical designs? Do they perform activity-based cost analyses? What tasks do professors perform and what do they outsource or delegate to others? Is technology used to help contain costs or as an add-on?

6) **Implementation quality assurance.** How do professors assure themselves and others that content is delivered as intended, that teaching and learning processes are implemented consistently, that assessments are performed as planned and their results used effectively, and that costs are properly balanced with quality?

Expanding the quality principles is just as easy. Technology enters the existing set in obvious ways. For example, consideration of teaching and learning processes should include technology, and the use of technology should be continuously improved. Only one new principle is needed: Substitute low-cost for high-cost resources where possible without hurting quality. This is fundamental to resource conservation. It can produce big gains in cost effectiveness if practiced consistently, but most institutions pay little attention to such possibilities. The expanded set of principles follows.

- Define education quality in terms of student outcomes

- Focus on the process of teaching, learning, and student assessment

- Substitute low-cost for high-cost resources where possible without hurting quality

- Strive for coherence in curricula and educational process

- Work collaboratively to achieve mutual involvement and support

- Base decisions on facts wherever possible

- Identify and learn from best practice

- Make continuous quality improvement a top priority

The appendix to this chapter provides examples of how the eight educational competency principles can be applied to the six domains. These questions provide a starting point for structured conversations about improving core competency in education.

IMPLEMENTATION STEPS

Suppose an institution's leaders have decided to improve its core educational competency. What should they do to implement their strategy? How can they overcome organizational inertia and resistance to change? Do they have to wait for clear and present danger, or can they achieve change while the institution still has discretionary resources and market power?

The following seven-step program, based on extensive on-campus experience, provides a roadmap for would-be change agents.

1) Build awareness and commitment.

2) Commission pilot projects.

3) Create venues for ongoing discussion and development.

4) Organize skill development and consultation services.

5) Broaden the rewards, recognition, and incentives environment.

6) Adopt performance-based resource allocation.

7) Develop an internal oversight and review capacity.

I'll describe things in the language of presidents, provosts, and deans. However, others ranging from department chairs to trustees can adapt the ideas for their own use. So can system-wide administrations and higher education oversight boards. Chairs can adopt parts of the program on their own, without approval from higher-ups. Oversight bodies can suggest strategies, apply persuasion, ask questions about progress, and hold their agents accountable. As I have said repeatedly throughout the book, improvement should be approached in a sprit of partnership. However, the need for change has become so great that people involved in oversight should not hesitate to instill a sense of urgency.

The seven steps do not guarantee success, but skipping any of them will sharply reduce one's prospects. The journey toward improvement will be contentious, even though neither the goals nor the program challenge essential academic values. The successful leader will proceed carefully, with due regard for the sensitivities of faculty and staff. He or she must be persuasive, patient, and above all persistent. As a successful presidential change agent once told me:

> The faculty has learned two things about my reform efforts. First, I won't quit—they can turn me down, but I'll be back again and again. Second, I'll listen carefully, work in partnership with them, and be quick to abandon changes that aren't paying off. So what's the risk? Mostly they decide to skip the haggling and get on with the program . . .

Step 1. Build Awareness and Commitment
Building awareness and commitment is the first step on the road to improvement, and in some ways it is the most important one. Readers will

be familiar with the need to get buy-in from the people who will implement a reform program, but "getting buy-in" seems too shallow relative to the depth of change represented by the improvement agenda. The late organizational consultant Joe Engle offered the following good advice as my Stanford team was about to embark on a major reengineering project. "You are asking people to change their lives," he said. "They deserve to know why this will be important and what they can expect. They will need a decent period of time to process the information, suggest changes and gauge your reactions, and reach a decision about commitment."

Roundtable discussions provide a good vehicle for initiating awareness building and commitment. Robert Zemsky has organized such roundtables on more than a hundred campuses over the past decade as part of the Pew Higher Education Program and the Knight Collaborative.[1] While their agenda varies from campus to campus, the general theme is to build awareness about markets and the need for change, the same themes that drive the improvement program proposed here. The experience has been good: Most participants emerge from the roundtables with a better sense of how the world is changing and what they and their colleagues need to do in order to respond. Hence the process is worth describing in some detail.

Roundtable participation always includes the institution's leadership, faculty, senior staff, and students. Presidential and provostial participation is very important, and one or two deans and trustees usually are included as well. Most important are faculty members, who represent the roundtable's target constituency. Every faculty has a group of "wise heads," people who are regarded by their colleagues as opinion leaders. They may not be the political leaders of the faculty, senate chairs and the like, but most professors know who they are. Bringing these leaders together in a roundtable setting represents the exercise's *sine qua non.* Senior staff members contribute both as resources and general participants. So do students, who sometimes provide key insights and perspectives that might be missed otherwise. Roundtable size should not exceed 25 or so people, so pruning the participants' list usually turns out to be more difficult than coming up with the original names.

The roundtable consists of two sessions, spaced a month or so apart. Each session begins with a dinner meeting and continues through most of the next day. The first deals mainly with higher education's changing environment and its implications for the institution. The second reprises these themes and moves toward an action agenda—how each of the participants and his or her colleagues can help meet the new challenges. Ideally, the discussion ends up legitimizing initiatives identified by the roundtable for follow up by the institution's leadership.

This format has proved effective for two reasons. First, participants need enough time to become familiar with each other and with the issues. They need to get past the speech-making phase, where each person describes his or her perceptions and philosophy, so they can begin grappling with the issues in a free and open manner. For example, the opening dinner meetings are designed to achieve familiarization and set the stage for a more intense discussion the next day. Second, there needs to be gestation time: the overnights and the month or so between sessions. The issues are important and complex, and one's first impressions may not prove durable. Since the roundtables are intended to produce lasting change, it is important to get second thoughts onto the table so they can be addressed as part of the process.

Skilled facilitation represents the second *sine qua non*. The facilitators come from outside the institution in order to provide an aura of objectivity. Even more important, they know how to draw the participants into serious discussion and in the end to achieve closure and, if possible, consensus. Without a skilled facilitator, the discussion can degenerate into unstructured "talkie-talk." With it, participants depart with a feeling of accomplishment and an agenda for future work.

Three ground rules are worth mentioning. First, participants are asked to agree that while the discussion is "on the record" in that it is intended to shape institutional behavior, there should be no attribution to individuals. People should be free to explore ideas without fear of being quoted outside the room or challenged later about ideas in their formative stage. Second, participants are asked to dedicate their time to the roundtable while it is in session—no stepping out to take phone calls or handle other business. (This is especially important for senior people.) Finally, a scribe takes notes during the meetings and prepares a report summarizing the discussion and, especially, the emergent consensus and follow-up items. Without such a report, the roundtable's accomplishments may well be lost as the discussion fades in people's memories.

The Pew/Knight roundtables provide a model that can be applied intact by institutions that wish to embrace the reforms recommended in this book. The model is based on free and open discussion—the partnership approach to problem solving. While the overarching objectives of quality process maturity, technology innovation, and cost consciousness may represent institutional imperatives, how to go about achieving them is eminently negotiable. My experience in discussing such objectives with faculty indicates that most will accept the arguments if given enough time, provided they feel empowered as to approach and confident they will be supported rather than penalized if they invest time in the endeavor. Skilled facilitation and an atmosphere of openness offer the best chance for achieving this result. If consensus has not been achieved by the roundtable's end, the facilitator should leave the issues open so they can be revisited later in other venues.

Care and planning constitute the approach's second lesson. Participants are selected carefully and briefed on the purpose of the exercise. The format provides the right configuration and sufficient time to dig deeply into the issues. Skilled facilitation and dedicated resources for report writing are provided. Most important, the institution's leaders set a good example by dedicating their time to the exercise. They also trust the facilitator by participating actively without trying to dominate the discussion.

Once a roundtable or similar exercise has legitimized the program's objectives and broad approach, the institution's leaders should use the amplifiers of office to spread the word across the institution. Articulate repetition is a must: One should never assume that once the message has been propagated in a speech or memo it has been received and digested by the recipients. Leaders should develop an outreach plan that includes all campus media and exploits all available opportunities for face-to-face dialog, such as academic senate briefings, retreats, and visits to departments and student residences. The plan also may include workshops to explore particular aspects of the program, activities that merge into permanent venue creation as discussed in step 3.

Step 2. Commission Pilot Projects

Talk is important but actions speak louder than words. The sooner faculty begin actual work on education quality processes and cost containment, the sooner they will realize that the goal is worthwhile and the solutions are rooted in common sense. Endless talking, while a proclivity of the academic establishment, can raise concerns and barriers as well as pave the way for action. Even when such barriers don't arise, there is a substantial gap between knowing what should be done and actually doing it.[2]

Pilot projects should be commissioned as soon as possible. They offer two specific benefits. First, the projects remove some of the mystery from the change agenda. The devil you know often is less daunting than the one that can only be imagined. For example, professors who work on education quality processes report that they are neither difficult nor unsatisfying—they turn out to involve common-sense academic tasks rather than jumping through bureaucratic hoops. Second, pilot projects provide opportunities for learning and removing bugs. Individuals climb the learning curve, and in the process they identify areas for improvement. If the project is successful, the participants become advocates and an important resource for helping those who come later.

Ensuring pilot project success is crucial, since early failures can have disproportionate consequences. One should choose areas where the circumstances favor success—as the saying goes, "to pick the low-hanging fruit." The tasks required for the projects should not be too complex, and those who will perform them should be enthusiastic about the prospect. The tasks should not be so simple as to trivialize the experiment, however, nor should the application lie outside the mainstream of institutional activity. It does little good to prove the program can work in a marginal program whose faculty are not well respected by their colleagues.

Most readers are familiar with piloting the application of technology. The same principles apply to developing quality processes and cost consciousness. Take quality processes, for example. At Göteborg University, in Sweden, the political science department decided to embrace quality work in a self-initiated pilot project for the university.[3] Political science is a mainstream department, although not one with complicated laboratory courses or external professional bodies with power over curricula. Most important, its chair, Bengt-Ove Boström, was an important advocate for quality process improvement. He rallied his colleagues to the cause and implemented many of the principles described in Chapter 6. He was assisted by the university's central quality unit, and by the attention generated by the quality process audits that had been recently announced by the National Agency for Higher Education.

Northwest Missouri State University provides another example, this time in the area of cost analysis. Working under a Sloan Foundation grant, the university requested proposals for pilot projects to merge its education quality processes with activity-based costing.[4] Participation was voluntary, and the proposals were screened for feasibility before being accepted. The grant provided a modest financial incentive for faculty, but the university relied mainly on intrinsic enthusiasm to get the work accomplished. Extensive skill development and consultation services were provided during the course of the project, which ended up providing valuable experience and a number of success stories.

The examples illustrate several additional considerations in the commissioning of pilot projects. Such projects may arise spontaneously, and when they do they should be supported wholeheartedly unless there are overwhelming reasons to the contrary. (Pilots are not experiments in the classic sense, so getting a representative sample isn't important—what matters is enthusiasm and feasibility.) One need not wait for projects to arise spontaneously, however. Institutional leaders can solicit project proposals for funding by a gift or grant, as at Northwest, or with the university's own resources. Program planning may include fundraising, and potential donors may well be interested in the kinds of improvements discussed in this book. However, the improvement program is so important that the institution should budget its own funds for pilot projects if external support does not materialize. In the end, of course, the rollout and continuation of successful projects will have to be covered by institutional funds.

In addition to funding, skill development and consultation services need to be provided in order to make pilots successful. Institutions should organize for this before the projects are commissioned, and be prepared to augment support levels quickly if the work appears to be faltering. I'll return to the support question when discussing step 4. For now, it is enough to say that support is never more important than at the pilot project stage and that failure to meet this need can easily prove catastrophic.

Step 3. Create Venues for Ongoing Discussion and Development

Good work may produce its own rewards, but it helps to be able to tell someone about it. That's one reason why venues for ongoing discussion and development are so important. The others are to maintain focus and disseminate ideas for improvement.

While Stanford's vice president for business and finance, I launched a program called "Quality, Service, and Productivity" ("QSC" for short). It included a set of "QSC Councils": one for each major department, chaired by the department head, and one at the division level chaired by me. Each council included a cross section of people ranging from rank-and-file workers to senior staff. The councils set the agenda for the units' quality programs and provided venues for quality teams, or departmental councils in the case of the division-level council, to report on their experiences. Where necessary, the councils would seek proactively to identify problems and suggest solutions, but mostly they provided a friendly and knowledgeable environment for the sharing of information. They also performed the critical tasks of dispensing recognition and suggesting rewards.

Teams, not councils, performed most QSC work. Sometimes a council would charter a team for a special purpose such as the controller's office team that developed our so-called RRI Toolbox. (RRI stood for rewards, recognition, and incentives.) Other teams were formed by the relevant line officers or in some cases the workers themselves in the normal course of their duties. Commitment to QSC principles and a desire for improvement represented the common thread, and the councils provided a cross-cutting venue for information sharing and reinforcement.

Leaders at all levels can create such councils without disrupting established work patterns or reporting relations. At Stanford, for example, department heads retained responsibility for planning, supervision, and performance. The QSC program improved awareness about quality, service, and productivity and enabled people to work more effectively, but it did not dilute individual responsibility or line authority. Key decisions continued to be made by the line officers, but because the line officers were members of the QSC councils their decisions were consonant with program goals and strategy. QSC was a "meta" program, just like education quality processes. It aimed to make the responsible parties' work easier and more effective, not to disempower them.

Education quality process councils should be created at the decanal and institutional levels. Most work teams operate at the department or program level, so decanal councils provide a good place for them to share results. The institution-level council, which generally should be chaired by the provost, provides a reinforcing venue for the decanal councils although on occasion it may invite department or program teams to participate in its meetings. All councils should meet frequently enough to maintain momentum and underscore the program's importance. At least two hours once a month appears necessary during the program's formative stage, although bimonthly meetings may prove sufficient once it has become established.

Paradigm-changing technology may be the best subject around which to build the initial council agendas. Technology's combination of intrinsic interest and tangible payoff provides an obvious reason for the discussions, and once the ice is broken there should be no lack of interesting ideas. Moreover, technology-based innovation leads naturally to consideration of education quality processes and cost—quality processes because the changes are process oriented and require assessment to gauge results, and cost because a broad array of resources must be deployed. The resulting program will reinforce the linkages among technology, cost, and quality, conserve scarce leadership and faculty time, and provide an ongoing impetus for change.

Step 4. Organize Workshops, Networks, and Consultation Services

Skill development, consultation, and networking are prerequisites for effective technology innovation. Faculty must be trained in the technologies and supported with deep expertise when they try to do something out of the ordinary. They need peer networks to which they can turn for guidance and support. I noted earlier that pilot projects should include skill development, networking, and consultation, and the need does not disappear once the pilot stage has passed. Universities have found that these functions should be well organized, well led, and funded on a long-term basis.

The same is true for education quality processes and cost analysis. Developing quality processes and cost consciousness requires professors to perform unfamiliar tasks. Education quality processes have not yet penetrated doctoral curricula and the examples of effective implementation still are too few to be widely known by faculty. Academic applications of activity-based costing are even newer—indeed, few professors have ever thought seriously about the cost of teaching and learning processes. Even when faculty have embraced these concepts, most are not at all clear about what they should do. Without readily available skill development and consultation services, the program will die at its inception. Without networking, progress is unlikely to be sustained.

Educational development units have become familiar parts of the college and university landscape. They can provide a good nucleus around which to build support for quality processes and cost analysis, but certain pitfalls must be avoided. First, such units sometimes carry a stigma—they may be perceived as serving only teaching assistants and faculty who have been identified as problem teachers. This is not a good foundation upon which to build a forward-looking program in which all faculty members are expected to participate.

Second, most educational development units lack expertise in quality process development and activity-based costing. Their staff can help people become better teachers, for example, by providing helpful tips or videotaping and critiquing performance, but they have no experience dealing with cost or the design of educational processes and assessment methods. A well-funded unit populated by smart and motivated people can climb the learning curve quickly, but the institution's leadership should not simply assign the new duties as a matter of convenience. In some cases it will prove better to create a new unit than to graft new tasks onto an existing educational development organization.

While no one has any experience in the matter, combining quality process development and cost analysis in the same unit strikes me as a good idea. Process design represents an important aspect of quality work, and good design requires consideration of costs as well as outcomes. Assessment also incurs costs, which should be considered at the design stage. Finally, implementation of quality assurance fits naturally with the analysis of activities. Often performance shortfalls result from failure to observe activity norms, as when professors skimp on preparation time or office hours. Support units can help faculty avoid these problems or identify mitigations if they occur.

Faculty support for activity-based costing should never be assigned to the university's finance and accounting department. Financial groups typically think in terms of cost allocations, not activities. They generally aspire to a greater level of precision than is appropriate for academic cost consciousness, and their demands for precision are likely to alienate faculty. Faculty support people should work closely with their financial colleagues, but the division of labor should be well understood. The financial people will determine the unit cost of resources, whereas the support people will work with faculty to define activities and construct models of resource usage.

The aforementioned support unit also may help faculty deploy paradigm-changing technology. They should work hand in hand with counterparts in the university's information technology organization, but the functions of the two groups are somewhat different. IT knows the technology, but in a mature system the quality and cost people understand educational processes and faculty work. The resulting collaboration will leverage the time of scarce and costly IT professionals while avoiding the tendency to let technology drive academic application.

I'll close this section with a note about skill development. Professors generally resist the idea of being "trained." They may view themselves as better than the trainers, and in any case "training" smacks of business rather than the noble profession of academe. Yet professors do need instruction in the principles and methods of quality process work and cost analysis. In my view, the best approach revolves around the pilot projects. Faculty participants should work closely with support people to achieve an agreed result, and in the process they will learn the things needed for success. That is, skills should be developed "just in time" instead of through "training" to accommodate expectations about future relevance. Workshops that address problems that faculty are currently encountering can be especially effective.

Once the pilot projects prove successful, it should be easier to extend the program to others. Eventually one may hope that developing skills in best-practice quality processes and cost analysis methods loses its stigma and becomes part of the faculty's regular repertoire of responsibilities, just like keeping up on the content in one's field.

Step 5. Broaden the Rewards, Recognition, and Incentives Environment

Awareness, pilot projects, venues, and support won't matter if rank-and-file professors have no incentive to change. Chapter 4 described how the built-in incentives in higher education have become skewed in the direction of research. Professors try to teach well out of a sense of professional pride and obligation to their students, but tangible rewards like promotion, tenure, and compensation tend to come disproportionately from research. Paradigm-changing technology offers the intrinsic rewards associated with creativity, but one can hardly expect them to compete with the tangible rewards of research. The situation is worse for quality processes and cost analysis, which few professors currently equate with creativity.

Accomplishing the strategic agenda will require significant change in the academic rewards, recognition, and incentives (RRI) environment. Improvement-focused RRIs need to be developed, discussed widely, and eventually adopted by all the relevant parties. Performance evaluation should be linked closely with RRI. Despite resistance from the academic hierarchy, meaningful evaluations that affect promotion, tenure, and salary setting will go a long way toward creating incentives for change. No formula can guarantee success, but some advice can be offered.

Including the RRI environment in the first four program steps is a prerequisite. The roundtables should address rewards and incentives as a central issue. Hopefully the participants will achieve a consensus that something needs to be done, and in any case the institution's leadership should stress the need at every opportunity. The pilot projects should test evaluation methods and criteria as well as the work on quality processes, technology, and cost analysis that represents their primary focus. The councils should discuss evaluation and incentives at every meeting. The skill development and consultation functions should contribute by offering expertise on evaluation. Last but not least, someone on the provost's staff should benchmark other institutions' RRI programs.

Institutions' academic RRI programs should key off the so-called annual faculty contract. More of a handshake than a formal contract, these agreements between department chair and professors describe what the latter is expected to work on during the next year and how it will be evaluated. Often the handshake is implicit, but good practice requires explicit discussion and documentation. The negotiation considers both departmental and individual needs—traditionally, teaching and service commitments and what the professor is expected to accomplish in research and scholarship. It should not be difficult to add work on education quality processes, paradigm-changing technology development, and cost analysis to the list of tasks the department needs to accomplish. No professor need participate in all activities every year, but somehow the bases have to be covered. Over time, most professors should contribute to all the areas on a rotating basis.

Clarity represents the essential condition for the annual contract. Chair and professor should leave the table with a common view of what is expected and what will constitute success. The view should be memorialized in writing and verified by both parties. There is an art to defining these agreements. One should describe outcomes as specifically as possible.

Chairs should link to the department's governance and planning processes when negotiating such agreements. For example, a quality work team might identify the aforementioned employer survey as an important need and ask the chair to find someone to take on the task. Better yet, a team member might volunteer for the work and ask the chair to make it part of his or her annual contract. Including the project in the contract allows tradeoffs against other activities. In a fully articulated system, the chair (probably aided by an executive committee) would consider the whole set of departmental needs and expectations before finalizing the year's contracts.

Follow up represents a key element of the contractual system. Without it, the contracts become empty gestures that no one takes seriously. In the example, the chair might ask colleagues for ex-post feedback: "Was the survey rigorous and comprehensive and did the person demonstrate leadership in considering its implications?" "If the work was not done or not done well, were there mitigating circumstances?" Such evaluations are no different in principle from those pertaining to research and scholarship, and they can easily be documented. They are easier than those pertaining to the quality of classroom teaching and advising.

Contractual follow up can form the basis for the professor's annual performance evaluation, and indeed that has become routine in some institutions. In fact, divorcing the contracts and follow up from decisions on salary, promotion, and tenure should be regarded as a breach of faith. How can a professor and chair agree on one set of criteria and then find the department, school, or institution applying different criteria after the fact? In effect, the chair binds the dean with the annual contract. Any disagreements should be resolved prospectively.

Tangible rewards aren't the only source of academic incentives. Chairs, deans, provosts, and presidents can recognize good work on the improvement agenda in other ways such as at the annual ceremony that honors outstanding teachers. Being asked to present one's work at council, or maybe even to the board of trustees, represents another kind of recognition. So does money to lead a workshop of one's peers or present one's accomplishments at a national conference.

Developing an RRI toolbox that goes beyond tangible rewards could be a good early task for an institutional or decanal council. Two things should be remembered. First, the reward or recognition should be clearly linked to the desired behavior and not be too long in coming. Ambiguous linkages and long delays sap effectiveness. Second, intangible rewards cannot substitute for the "big three" tangible ones: salary, promotion, and tenure. For example, our NCPI faculty interviews show clearly that recognition of outstanding teachers does not counterbalance the attraction of research. Building incentives for reform will require institutional leaders to tackle the big three as well as providing other kinds of rewards, recognition, and incentives.

Step 6. Adopt Performance-Based Resource Allocation

What the RRI program is to individuals, performance-based resource allocation is to organizational units. Chapter 10 described the details of the methodology, so I need focus only on the big picture here. The key requirements are as follows. First, schools and departments should be clear about what is expected of them. Second, their performance should be evaluated systematically using a combination of quantitative and qualitative measures. Third, something of consequence should ride on the results.

Figure 11.2 shows how an institution might implement performance-based resource allocation on a comprehensive basis. The system starts with quantitative performance indicators, as indicated in the diagram's uppermost box. They pull together all the information that can be garnered from the school's accounting and management information systems. We have seen, however, that even the best set of quantitative indicators fails to capture all the essential elements of performance. The indicators should be supplemented with the qualitative evaluations shown in the figure's next three boxes. Together, the four sets of indicators comprise the "balanced scorecard" discussed in Chapter 10.

Evaluation of education quality processes and research and scholarship follows the methodologies described in Chapter 8, informed where appropriate by the quantitative performance indicators. Provosts can evaluate schools' quality process maturity and deans can evaluate departmental maturity. The quality process indicators can include the maturity level itself, progress up the maturity curve since the last evaluation, and performance with respect to particular developmental targets. Research evaluations can include benchmarking the department's scholarly output against similar departments in peer institutions and testing it for consistency with mission and strategic plans.

Performance on institutional mission and priorities completes the scorecard. Testing the balance between teaching and research falls under mission. Other examples include evaluating public service and collaborations with other universities and with industry. Performance against special institutional priorities would be included here.

Figure 11.2

Performance-Based Funding at the Institutional Level

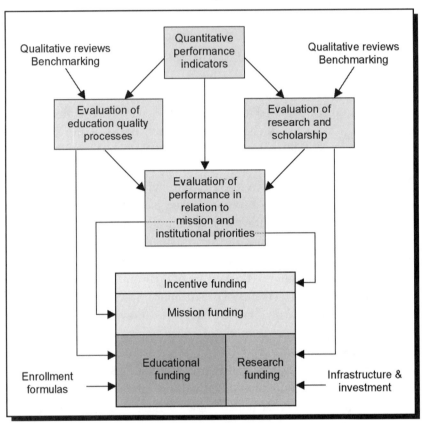

The remainder of Figure 11.2 shows how the evaluations can be linked to funding. According to the diagram, academic budgets are built up from four notional components.[5] (As discussed below, the notional components are used in budget development but not budget control.)

- An educational component: notionally related to teaching and its support activities, including education quality work. The allocation depends on credit-hour generation and other quantitative performance indicators.

- A research component: notionally related to departmental (that is, unsponsored) research and scholarship. The allocation depends on faculty FTEs and the qualitative evaluation of research performance.

- A mission component: supplemental funding that furthers the university's mission in ways not catered for by the education and research components. The allocation depends on cross-subsidy decisions like those discussed in Chapter 9 and on the assessment of future performance potential.

- An incentive component: supplemental funding that rewards good performance on university special priorities or penalizes lack of progress. The allocation depends on the qualitative evaluation of performance in relation to these priorities. For example, schools and departments that are making good progress on educational quality processes, paradigm-changing technology, and cost analysis would receive special rewards under this rubric, and those that fail to make adequate progress would be penalized.

One does not have to put large sums at risk in order to gain the advantages of incentive funding. Distributing even a few percent of the budget on an incentive basis raises the stakes to the point where people will pay attention. Using a small percentage mitigates worries about damaging educational programs if a unit gets penalized. In the long run, moreover, the better performance induced by using financial incentives will more than offset the penalty's short-term consequences.

The notional allocations refer to how the budget is related to performance, not to restrictions about how the money is spent. As noted in Chapter 3, institutional accounting systems cannot distinguish between expenditures for education and departmental research. (They can and should estimate the money spent on departmental research, but that is different from trying to track it in the accounting system.) Nor can they track expenditures for the mission and incentive components of funding. It is enough for deans and department chairs to know that their overall allocation depends on the four notional components of funding. Once academic units receive the funds, they are free to spend them as they see fit. However, they should not make long-term commitments from sums received under the incentive rubric, since these sums may not be forthcoming in the future.

Performance-based budgeting works at the level of system-wide administrations and higher education oversight bodies as well as on individual campuses. Jurisdictions such as the UK, Australia, and Hong Kong separate funding for education from funding for research. In Hong Kong, for example, 25% of government funding goes notionally for research; the rest goes for education. Chapter 10 described how some jurisdictions also set aside money for incentive allocations. There is no reason why mission funding cannot also be included.

Step 7. Develop an Internal Evaluation Capacity

The need for evaluation is inherent in performance-based resource alloca-tion and RRI. For example, presidents, provosts, deans, and chairs should accept responsibility for overseeing educational process development, technology deployment, and cost tradeoff decisions. This should include performance evaluation, since without evaluation there can be no rewards, recognition, or incentives. Institutions that have achieved steps 1 through 6 on the road to reform will have embedded oversight and review in their mainline administrative and academic processes. Experience shows that something more is needed, however.

The institutional and decanal councils described in step 3 provide opportunities for unobtrusive evaluation. The membership, which should include the senior leadership group, will gain significant visibility in the normal course of council business. The support units discussed in step 4 also provide visibility because they work closely with departments and professors. However, relying too much on the councils or support units for evaluation will subvert their primary function—working formatively to improve education quality processes, technology deployment, and cost consciousness.

Program review provides a better template for the evaluative compo-nent. The idea behind such reviews is that periodic arm's-length evaluation can benefit even the highest quality program or department. Local faculty, chairs, and even deans and provosts may be too close to the action to see the blemishes and opportunities for improvement. Third parties can develop insights and call them as they see them without being inhibited by local sensibilities and politics.

Some institutions have brought program review to a highly refined state of development. For example, the Yale University Council, on which I served for more than a decade, organizes external review committees for academic departments and programs on a regular basis. Then it discusses the reports and makes recommendations to the president and provost. Harvard's Board of Overseers functions in much the same way. North-western University has placed its program review function under a vice president whose main task is organize external evaluations of both academic and administrative units.

Internal audit provides another template. Accountability for good management and financial processes is embedded in a business or university's line organization, which strives to do the best job possible on an ongoing basis. Yet most organizations of significant size maintain an internal audit department. Such departments test financial controls and investigate allegations of malfeasance, but that is not all. They also perform management reviews, which are designed to improve operating effectiveness by offering third-party insight on a periodic basis.

Institutions that are truly serious about their education quality processes, technology deployment, and cost consciousness will create an "internal academic audit unit." The name derives from the academic audits performed by external quality agencies as described in Chapter 8, not from the traditional internal audit department. (Perhaps a name other than "audit" would make the idea more palatable.)

Depending on institutional size and preferences, the unit might develop an in-house capacity to perform academic audits or arrange for reviews by external parties. The unit's main focus would be on work at the departmental and program level, but it could look at school and institutional oversight processes when requested. The City University of Hong Kong has organized such a unit to help implement its education quality process agenda, for example, with reportedly good results.[6]

Internal academic audit helps institutional leaders assure the efficacy of education quality processes and related activities. According to the discussion in Chapter 8, the work should be unobtrusive and formative—unless, of course, significant problems are unearthed. Departments might be reviewed every three to five years unless a council or cognizant authority requests an interim review. The reviews would involve knowledgeable parties in conversations about the department's quality processes and the results it has been achieving. Experience shows that such conversations and the reports that stem from them can be beneficial to all concerned.

ACADEMIC AUDIT AS AN ENGINE OF CHANGE

The seven-step program envisions a linear action evolution, starting with the case for change and ending with evaluations of progress. This may indeed be the best approach. However, announcing evaluation early in the game can sometimes produce greater and faster progress. That is the method of choice for many quality oversight agencies, and it also can work within institutions.

At the University of Missouri, for instance, Vice President for Academic Affairs Steve Lehmkuhle decided to pilot test quality process audit in one department on each of the university's four campuses. In effect, this moved the introduction of audit from step 7 to step 2 of the change agenda. Finding an alternative for the state's mandatory program reviews provided the primary motivation. While useful in some respects, the review outcomes had become predictable and the process rather barren in its ability to improve education quality. Lehmkuhle saw audit as a way to boost education quality without setting aside his obligation to maintain accountability. The Missouri Coordinating Board for Higher Education agreed to the tryout, which was launched in the autumn of 2001.

The logic of starting with audit is simple: It provides a tangible event toward which departments can point as they begin their conversations about improving core educational competency. Putting audit first structures the conversations around the quality process domains and principles that will be considered by the site visitors and introduces the idea of quality process maturity. The cognizant academic leader begins the conversations by holding introductory sessions with involved faculty. Because the audit process is relatively unstructured, these conversations can reinforce the exercise's improvement orientation. For example, one can demonstrate flexibility in treatment of the quality principles and maturity language while making the case that all domains should be covered. Except for the domains, which represent the audit's essential corpus, everything can and should be in play. The only requirement is that the subsequent activities contain enough structure to effect improvement.

Once a structure has been agreed on, the departments prepare a self-evaluation and plan for improvement. This goes to the audit team, which uses it to guide its conversations during the audit visit. The first round of audits should be a purely formative exercise—it's not fair to hold people accountable for activities that have never before been considered important. Hence the audit reports should celebrate best practices and offer recommendations that can be shared across the institution. Including representatives of the pilot departments on the team, along with academic leaders and perhaps people from staff groups that provide training and consultation, further emphasizes that the first-round audits represent vehicles for spurring improvement rather than mechanisms for evaluation.

Getting started is the hardest part. The following, introduced originally in Chapter 8, represents some possible advice to departments' quality process advocates during the critical stage of formulating their self-study and improvement plans. The advocates would have been identified at an earlier stage of the pilot test. The strategy is to position them to build on the department's extant success stories. Whether impressive or paltry, these stories can bootstrap the needed conversations into being.

For each educational competency domain:

1) Identify one or a few exemplary accomplishments in the domain. For example, you may take pride in a well-formed statement of purpose for the major and the coherence of your curriculum relative to that purpose, your innovative use of technology or problem-based learning, your assessment of student learning and application of the results to program improvement, or an application of cost analysis.

The audit team wishes to include examples of good practice in its report, and also to use them as vehicles for understanding your department's quality processes. To further the latter objective, the team may ask the following kinds of questions in connection with each accomplishment.

a. What kinds of evidence led you to conclude that this accomplishment is in fact exemplary?

b. What key factors helped you make this accomplishment exemplary: for example, the seven quality principles presented earlier, other such principles, various data sources, and institutional or school policies, activities, or support services?

c. What could make this accomplishment even better: the application of additional quality principles or better use of institutional or school-level processes or services? Do you plan to improve in this way?

2) Identify policies or areas of activity within the domain that are most in need of improvement. For example, you might identify the adaptation of your curriculum to changing conditions, the introduction of

paradigm-changing technology, and the improvement of learning assessment as high priorities.

The above might stimulate the following questions during the audit visit.

a. What leads you to conclude that this area needs work?

b. How might you proceed: e.g., through the application of particular quality principles, use of institutional or school-level services? Do you plan to make this a priority?

c. What areas did you consider for improvement but did not include on the list?

3) Consider whether sufficient faculty time and other resources are being applied to education quality processes in the domain. What actions, and by whom, would be needed to increase your department's investment in quality processes if that is needed? What might the department do to substitute lower-cost for higher-cost resources or stimulate essential new resource commitments?

Departments might be encouraged to consider the self-improvement questions shown in the appendix when addressing points one and two. Similar questions might be prepared for other principles identified during the project's preparatory stage. While starting with examples helps focus one's thinking, to apply each question to each domain would cause the exercise to collapse from its own weight. Point three, on resources, offers the advocate an opportunity to address colleagues' attitudes about investment in quality processes as well as issues that are beyond the department's control. It also puts the audit team and the department on the same side of the table on the question of new resources.

Making audit a spur for improvement does not guarantee results, but it surely improves the change agent's chances. It puts a stake in the ground by which one can maintain leverage. If the conversations about education core competency occur frequently enough within the test departments, as well as with members of the audit team, interesting initiatives are likely to emerge. Because of audit's flexibility, the leverage can be attained at relatively low risk. Ideally, the test will generate enough enthusiasm so that audit, and the associated change agenda, can extended to other departments and organizational units.

Readers will notice that I have expanded the concept of academic audit to cover all three dimensions of education core competency. Institutions may wish to limit consideration to education quality processes, or the intersection of quality processes and technology, during the pilot project phase and early rollout. To realize the program's full potential, however, it eventually should be extended to include cost. I hope that quality oversight agencies will do the same.

ADDITIONAL ACTIONS

The improvement of education core competency will benefit from four additional actions: incorporation of these subjects in doctoral instruction; persistent questioning by governing boards; attention by the media and the public; and external reviews by accreditation agencies and higher education oversight bodies.

The development of doctoral instruction will be a natural outgrowth of faculty attention to the concepts and methods discussed in this book. What sense does it make to carefully teach research methodology and ignore the methodologies needed to produce value for money in education, where most professors spend the bulk of their time? Professors in doctoral institutions will find that providing such instruction is immediately helpful in clarifying their own thinking and enhancing their teaching assistants' ability to assist with the institution's improvement agenda. In the longer run, of course, doctoral instruction will propagate competency across the entire higher education sector.

Doctoral instruction might well start with special courses in education quality processes, paradigm-changing technology, and cost analysis. These courses would be open to students from across the university, and one may hope that all departments will require them for graduation. In the longer run, there should be specialized courses dealing with the disciplinary nuances of the improvement agenda. Faculties that have embraced the lessons of this book also will encourage dissertations on such subjects.

The actions I propose for trustees and regents are equally straightforward. Ask whether your institution endorses and is pursuing the change agenda. If so, inquire about the kinds of steps it is taking. If the answer is "no" or the steps are half-hearted, begin a dialog with the leadership. Your side of the dialog does not require academic knowledge and you should not defer to those who have it. While you can't design a program at the board level, let along micromanage its implementation, you can raise the question and keep raising it until people get the message. In my opinion, boards that fail to do so are derelict in their duty to the institution, its stakeholders, and the public. Someday, boards that fail to ask tough questions about their institutions' core educational competency may appear Enron-like—asleep at the switch.

My next word of advice goes to the media and people in public bodies concerned with higher education. If you buy the changes I have described, you have an obligation to take action. Governors, legislators, reporters, and those similarly positioned can take the tack I suggested for governing board members. Ask questions. Be persistent about getting education core competency on the public and institutional agendas. Insist that institutions, accreditors, and oversight bodies act within their respective purviews to further the agenda.

Accreditors and oversight bodies can do more than put these changes on the agenda; they can stimulate them directly. For example, academic audits can motivate an institution to use more of its resources to sustain and improve undergraduate education. Schools that have cost-conscious education quality programs will be able to demonstrate value for money more effectively than those who don't, and the successful deployment of paradigm-changing technology can provide further evidence of improvement. Audits also can stimulate the adoption of these subjects in doctoral curricula.

The academic audit framework fits nicely into accreditation's recent outcomes-oriented initiatives. Accreditors could develop standards for learning assessment methodologies and determine whether institutions are meeting the standards. Failure to establish meaningful indicators, or take appropriate action in the case of falling trend lines or adverse comparisons with benchmarks, might become grounds for putting an institution on probation or even for withdrawal of accreditation. Professional program accreditors could reinforce the regionals' institution-level programs by establishing discipline-specific assessment standards and reviewing quality processes and cost analysis at the departmental or program level.

Higher education oversight bodies could do all these things and more. In addition to embracing academic audit, state higher education executive officers (SHEEOs) could incorporate education quality processes, technology innovation, and cost consciousness into performance-based resource allocation. They could develop institutional balanced scorecards that include these activities as central elements. By so doing they would establish a dialog with institutions that, over time, could produce constructive change.

The quality literature says one can't improve something that can't be measured. Measurement is a necessary condition for closing the knowing-doing gap, and it provides the information that markets need to function effectively. Improved quality measurements depend on better education quality processes and more cost consciousness within institutions. Ideally, these improvements will occur spontaneously as a result of institutional self-interest. But if spontaneous improvement is not forthcoming, boards and oversight agencies should press for it on their own initiative. This can be done without disempowering institutions or faculty, or undermining the academy's essential values.

HONORING THE TRUST

I began this book with the proposition that colleges and universities can significantly improve the quality of undergraduate, master's, and professional education without boosting expenditures or dismantling the research enterprise. They can do this by rebuilding their core competency in education. Failure will do more than put one's own institution at risk. Honoring the trust placed in academe by the larger society requires solutions to the cost and quality problems addressed in this book.

Defenders of the status quo will argue that the quality of education in established colleges and universities is not all that bad. I accept that assessment, and indeed pointed out in Chapter 1 that it can be characterized as getting mostly a "B" grade. Academe's rhetoric claims that it produces A-level work, but the conclusion of this book is that "B" is more accurate. The problem goes beyond truth in advertising. Institutions and their faculty are not doing everything possible to produce A-level educational outcomes.

Should the academy be satisfied with a B? Should students and parents be willing to pay high prices to get B results? Should governments and donors allocate scarce resources for B-level work? Higher education's stakeholders deserve better, and the academy's own traditions demand the same. In the words of the quality movement, "Good enough isn't." Failure to use the available quality, technology, and costing tools in pursuit of educational excellence will be, and soon will be seen to be, a breach of trust that needs to be repaired.

The pursuit of true excellence in education, and especially undergraduate education, represents higher education's key strategic agenda. I've laid out the case for that agenda, described the kinds of changes that will be required, and offered an action plan for implementation. I hope this book will help colleges and universities become more responsive and, at the same time, protect essential academic values.

Appendix

SAMPLE SELF-IMPROVEMENT QUESTIONS

Domain 1: Determining Desired Learning Outcomes
What are the goals of the course or program and how do they relate to student needs?

1.1 *Define education quality in terms of student outcomes.* Have you consciously considered what students need in order to be successful in their chosen field and acquire meaningful values and social skills?

1.2 *Focus on the actual process of teaching, learning, and assessment.* Do your goals exploit the available process options? For example, have the development of desirable skills and work habits been included as explicit outcome goals?

1.3 *Substitute low-cost for high-cost resources where possible without hurting quality.* Have you asked whether your department or institution is the best place for students to gain certain knowledge levels and skills— e.g., whether some might better be obtained on the job?

1.4 *Strive for coherence in the department's curriculum and educational processes.* Do the various student outcome goals reinforce each other? Does they appear coherent to students and employers, or do they appear discreet and disconnected?

1.5 *Work collaboratively to achieve mutual involvement and support.* Do you collaborate effectively on the determination of student outcome goals?

1.6 *Base decisions on facts wherever possible.* Do you look beyond the standards of your discipline to seek input on goals? For example, do you use surveys or focus group interviews with employers or former students? Are the results documented so you can learn from its experience?

1.7 *Identify and learn from best practice.* Do you evaluate the student outcome goals of comparable departments in other institutions?

1.8 *Make improvement a top priority.* Do you reconsider your student outcome goals on a regular basis?

Domain 2. Designing Course Content and Department Curricula

What is to be taught, in what order, and from what perspective? What resources and resource materials will be used as content vehicles? How does the design relate to other courses the student will take as part of his or her program?

2.1 *Define education quality in terms of student outcomes.* How effectively does the curriculum reflect your student outcome goals?

2.2 *Focus on the actual process of teaching, learning, and assessment.* Does the curriculum exploit the available process options? For example, do assigned materials facilitate active learning, or do they mainly involve reading and listening?

2.3 *Substitute low-cost for high-cost resources where possible without hurting quality.* Do you consider cost in the selection of course materials? Do you go beyond cost to the student to include institutional and departmental costs like faculty time and infrastructure usage?

2.4 *Strive for coherence in the department's curriculum and educational processes.* Do the various parts of the curriculum reinforce each other? Does the curriculum appear coherent to students, or does it look like a smorgasbord or Chinese menu?

2.5 *Work collaboratively to achieve mutual involvement and support.* Do you collaborate effectively on curricular design? Are you able to reach agreement on the essential elements of design, or does the design represent a compromise of expediency?

2.6 *Base decisions on facts wherever possible.* Do you look beyond the standards of your discipline to seek input on curriculum? For example, do you consult systematically with colleagues at other institutions? Are the results documented so you can learn from the experience?

2.7 *Identify and learn from best practice.* Do you evaluate the curricula of comparable departments in other institutions?

2.8 *Make improvement a top priority.* Do you reconsider your curricular decisions systematically, on a regular basis?

Domain 3. Designing Teaching and Learning Processes
How are teaching and learning organized? What methods are used for first exposure to material, for answering questions and providing interpretation, for stimulating student interaction with the material, and for providing feedback on student work? What roles and responsibilities do various faculty members need to assume? What other resources are required?

3.1 *Define education quality in terms of student outcomes.* To what extent do you evaluate process options in terms of their effects on student learning and values as well as on your own workload and convenience? Do you analyze learning outcomes and use the results to revise educational processes?

3.2 *Focus on the actual process of teaching, learning, and assessment.* Do you analyze teaching and learning processes on a regular basis—e.g., by developing flowcharts and debating "what-if" options? Do you emphasize active learning? Do you ask whether the right people are doing the right things and address the tradeoffs between resource utilization and outcomes? Do you act promptly on good ideas?

3.3 *Substitute low-cost for high-cost resources where possible without hurting quality.* Do you test proposed process designs to see whether tasks can be eliminated or performed by TAs, support staff, technology, or the students themselves, instead of by high-cost faculty? Do you make sure that technology applications are worth their cost?

3.4 *Strive for coherence in the department's curriculum and educational processes.* Do the various process steps reinforce each other? Do teaching and learning processes appear coherent to students?

3.5 *Work collaboratively to achieve mutual involvement and support.* Do you collaborate effectively on process design? Do you readily reach agreement on the essential elements of design or does the design represent a compromise of expediency? Does the department accrue organizational learning from the experience of its members, or is process improvement a "lone wolf" activity?

3.6 *Base decisions on facts wherever possible.* Do you research the literature on process options and results in your discipline and related areas? Do you actively solicit inputs from students about their experience with various processes? Do you run tryouts or experiments to test process options and then document the results?

3.7 *Identify and learn from best practice.* Do you push beyond the familiar methods of your discipline to examine exemplary processes within and outside your institution?

3.8 *Make improvement a top priority.* Do you reconsider your teaching and learning processes systematically, on a regular basis?

Domain 4. Developing and Using Student Assessment

What measures and indicators are used to assess student learning? Do they assess value added, or only performance at the end of the program? How are the long-term outcomes of the educational experience determined? Are baseline and trend information available? Who is responsible for assessment?

4.1 *Define education quality in terms of student outcomes.* Have you defined "key quality indicators" based on your student outcomes goals? Do your assessment measures provide the data needed to track the indicators? Do they measure the learning that takes place on your watch, as opposed to measuring the quality and preparation of the student?

4.2 *Focus on the actual process of teaching, learning, and assessment.* Have you focused on the process of assessment? Do your assessment methods work smoothly and connect seamlessly with the processes of teaching and learning?

4.3 *Substitute low-cost for high-cost resources where possible without hurting quality.* Do you test proposed assessment designs to see whether tasks can be eliminated or performed by TAs, support staff, technology, or the students themselves, instead of by high-cost faculty? Do you make sure that technology applications are worth their cost?

4.4 *Strive for coherence in the department's curriculum and educational processes.* Do the various assessment measures and indicators reinforce each other? Does assessment appear coherent to students?

4.5 *Work collaboratively to achieve mutual involvement and support.* Do you collaborate effectively on the design of assessment processes and measures? Do you work together to interpret program-wide results and take appropriate actions based on assessment?

4.6 *Base decisions on facts wherever possible.* Are your assessment processes grounded in the literature wherever possible? Can you defend your choice of assessment measures by some appropriate combination of theory, experience, and experimentation?

4.7 *Identify and learn from best practice.* Do you evaluate the assessment practices of comparable departments in other institutions?

4.8 *Make improvement a top priority.* Do you reconsider your student assessment processes systematically, on a regular basis?

Domain 5. Resource Conservation

Do you consider cost in your pedagogical designs? Do you perform activity-based cost analyses? What tasks do you perform and what do you delegate to others? Is technology used to help contain costs or as an add-on?

5.1 *Define education quality in terms of student outcomes.* Not applicable.

5.2 *Focus on the actual process of teaching, learning, and assessment.* Do you perform activity-based cost analyses on proposed pedagogical designs?

5.3 *Substitute low-cost for high-cost resources where possible without hurting quality.* Do you use the analyses to identify cost-saving substitutions?

5.4 *Strive for coherence in the department's curriculum and educational processes.* Not applicable.

5.5 *Work collaboratively to achieve mutual involvement and support.* Do you work collaboratively on cost analysis and other aspects of resource conservation? Does your department expect this kind of activity and reward it appropriately?

5.6 *Base decisions on facts wherever possible.* Do you inform your cost analyses with real data? For example, do you collect data on time utilization and consult with the university's financial staff about unit costs?

5.7 *Identify and learn from best practice.* Do you evaluate the cost analysis practices of other departments inside and outside your institution? Do you identify and consider resource substitutions made by other departments?

5.8 *Make improvement a top priority.* Do you actively consider resource substitution on a continuous basis?

Domain 6. Implementing Quality Education

How are you organized to carry out your designs effectively, day in and day out, regardless of distractions? How can you assure yourself and others that content is delivered as intended, that teaching and learning processes are being implemented consistently, and that assessments are performed as planned and their results used effectively?

6.1 *Define education quality in terms of student outcomes.* Does quality assurance include a focus on student outcomes as determined by assessment as well as direct feedback from students?

6.2 *Focus on the actual process of teaching, learning, and assessment.* Have faculty focused on quality assurance? Do quality assurance processes connect seamlessly with the processes of teaching, learning, and assessment?

6.3 *Substitute low-cost for high-cost resources where possible without hurting quality.* Do you test proposed quality assurance initiatives to see whether tasks can be eliminated or performed by TAs, support staff, technology, or the students themselves, instead of by high-cost faculty? Do you make sure that technology applications are worth their cost?

6.4 *Strive for coherence in the department's curriculum and educational processes.* Do the various quality assurance methods reinforce each other? To what extent does implementation quality assurance appear coherent to students and faculty?

6.5 *Work collaboratively to achieve mutual involvement and support.* Do you collaborate effectively on the design of quality assurance methods? Do you work with colleagues to interpret the results and take appropriate actions based on quality assurance results?

6.6 *Base decisions on facts wherever possible.* Do quality assurance methods utilize factual inputs—e.g., peer evaluation of teaching, student course evaluations, and student-staff consultative committees? Can you defend your choice of quality assurance methods by some appropriate combination of theory, experience, and experimentation?

6.7 *Identify and learn from best practice.* Do you evaluate the quality assurance practices of comparable departments in other institutions?

6.8 *Make quality improvement a top priority.* Do you reconsider your quality assurance processes systematically, on a regular basis?

Endnotes

1. Institute for Research on Higher Education, University of Pennsylvania. The program was sponsored by the Pew Charitable Trusts, beginning in 1988, and the Knight Foundation beginning in the mid-1990s. The author facilitated roundtables on a number of campuses.

2. See Pfeffer and Sutton (2000) for an insightful discussion of the knowing-doing gap.

3. Massy (2000).

4. The project is described in Chapter 9.

5. Massy (1996), Chapter 12, divides academic budgets into two components: formula-driven and judgment-driven. In the present model, the education and research components are substantially formula-driven (the formulas are adjusted to take account of qualitative evaluations), while the mission and incentive components are driven entirely by judgment.

6. CityU's initiative was stimulated by the Hong Kong's first Teaching and Learning Quality Process Review, described in Chapter 7.

Bibliography

Ahn, T., Charnes, A., & Cooper, W. (1989). DEA and ratio efficiency analysis for public institutions of higher learning in Texas. In J. L. Chan (Ed.), *Research in government and non-profit accounting*. Greenwich, CT: JAI Press.

Association of American Colleges. (1985). *Integrity in the college curriculum: A report to the academic community*. Washington, DC: Association of American Colleges, Project on Redefining the Meaning and Purpose of Baccalaureate Degrees.

Ball, C. (1995). What the hell is quality? In D. Urwin (Ed.), *Fitness for purpose* (pp. 96–103). Guildford, England: The Society for Research into Higher Education and NFER-Nelson.

Barnett, R. (1992). *Improving higher education: Total quality care*. London, England: The Society for Research into Higher Education and The Open University Press.

Bartels, D. (1993). *The traditional liberal arts model: Persistence amid distress*. Unpublished doctoral dissertation, School of Education, Stanford University.

Bateman, G. R., & Roberts, H. V. (1993). TQM for professors and students (Paper No. PRFSTU.MSS). Chicago, IL: University of Chicago, Graduate School of Business.

Baumol, W. J., & Batey Blackman, S. A. (1983). Electronics, The cost disease, and the operation of libraries. *Journal of the American Society for Information Sciences, 34*, (3), 181–191.

Baumol, W. J., Batey Blackman, S. A., & Wolff, E. N. (1989). *Productivity and American leadership: The long view*. Cambridge, MA: MIT Press.

Beasley, J. E. (1995). Determining teaching and research efficiencies. *Journal of the Operations Research Society, 46,* 441–452.

Berman, J., & Skeff, K. (1988). Developing the motivation for improving university teaching. *Innovative Higher Education, 12* (2), 114–125.

Berry, T. H. (1991). *Managing the total quality transformation.* New York, NY: McGraw-Hill.

Bess, J. L. (1977). The motivation to teach. *Journal of Higher Education, 48* (3), 243–258.

Blasdell, S. W., McPherson, M. S., & Schapiro, M. O. (1993). Trends in revenues and expenditures in U.S. higher education: Where does the money come from? Where does it go? In M. S. McPherson, M. O. Schapiro, & G. C. Winston (Eds.), *Paying the piper: Productivity, incentives, and financing in U.S. higher education* (pp. 15–36.) Ann Arbor, MI: The University of Michigan Press.

Bloom, A. (1987). *The closing of the American mind.* New York, NY: Simon & Schuster.

Bogan, C., & English, M. J. (1994). *Benchmarking for best practices: Winning through innovative adaptation.* New York, NY: McGraw-Hill.

Bogue, E. G., & Saunders, R. L. (1992). *The evidence for quality.* San Francisco, CA: Jossey-Bass.

Bok, D. (1886). *Higher learning.* Cambridge, MA: Harvard University Press.

Bowen, H. (1980). *The cost of higher education: How much do universities and colleges spend per student and how much should they spend?* San Francisco, CA: Jossey-Bass.

Boxwell, R. J., Jr. (1994). *Benchmarking for competitive advantage.* New York, NY: McGraw-Hill.

Boyer, E. L. (1991). *Scholarship reconsidered: Priorities of the professoriate.* Princeton, NJ: Carnegie Foundation for the Advancement of Teaching.

Brennan, J., Dill, D., Shah, T., Verkleij, A., & Westerheijden, D. (1999). *A campaign for quality: Hong Kong teaching and learning quality process review.* Hong Kong: University Grants Committee.

Brewer, D. J., Gates, S. M., & Goldman, C. A. (2001). *In pursuit of prestige: Strategy and competition in U.S. higher education.* New Brunswick, NJ: Transaction Press.

Burke, J. C., & Serban, A. M. (Eds.). (1998). *Performance funding for public higher education: Fad or trend?* San Francisco, CA: Jossey-Bass.

Callan, P. M. (1993). *The California higher education policy vacuum: The example of student fees* (Policy Report). San Jose, CA: The California Higher Education Policy Center.

Camp, R. C. (1989). *Benchmarking: The search for industry best practices that lead to superior performance.* Milwaukee, WI: ASQC Quality Press.

Campbell, C., & van der Wende, M. (2000). *International initiatives and trends in quality assurance for European higher education.* Helsinki, Finland: European Network for Quality Assurance.

Cave, M., Hanney, S., Henkel, M., & Hogan, M. (1997). *The use of performance indicators in higher education: The challenge of the quality movement* (3rd ed.). London, England: Jessica Kingsley.

Center for Education Research and Innovation, OECD. (1992). *The OECD international education indicators: A framework for analysis.* Paris, France: OECD.

Cohen, M., March, J., & Olson, J. (1972). A garbage can model of organizational choice. *Administrative Science Quarterly, 17* (1), 1–25.

Cokins, G. (1994). What is activity-based costing … really? Retrieved December, 1998, from http://abctech.com/univ/abcanswer.htm

Cokins, G. (1996). *Activity-based cost management: Making it work.* Chicago, IL: Irwin Professional Publishing.

Cook, E. P., Kinnetz, P., Owens-Misner, N. (1990). Faculty perceptions of job rewards and instructional development activities. *Innovative Higher Education, 14,* 123–130.

Cook, P. J., & Frank, R. H. (1993). The growing concentration of top students at elite schools. In C. T. Clotfelter & M. Rothschild (Eds.), *Studies of supply and demand in higher education* (pp. 121–144). Chicago, IL: The University of Chicago Press.

Coopers & Lybrand (now PricewaterhouseCoopers). (1993). *Review of quality audit.* London, England: Higher Education Quality Council.

Cox, K. S., Downey, R., G., & Smith, L. G. (2001, Winter). Activity-based costing and higher education: Can it work? *The Department Chair, 11* (3), 15–18.

Creech, B. (1994). *The five pillars of TQM.* New York, NY: Truman Talley Books/Plume.

Cyert, R. M., & March, J. G. (1963). *A behavioral theory of the firm.* Englewood Cliffs, NJ: Prentice-Hall.

Csikszentmihalyi, M. (1982). Intrinsic motivation and effective teaching: A flow analysis. *New Directions for Teaching and Learning, No. 10.* San Francisco, CA: Jossey-Bass.

Damon, W., Csikszentmihalyi, M., & Gardner, H. (2000). *What does it mean to do good work in higher education today?* Paper presented at the Forum for the Future of Higher Education, Aspen Institute, Aspen, Colorado.

Davenport, T. H. (1993). *Process innovation: Reengineering work through information technology.* Cambridge, MA: Harvard Business School.

Dearing, R. (1997). *Higher education in the learning society: The Dearing report.* London, England: National Committee of Inquiry into Higher Education.

Deci, E. L., & Ryan, R. M. (1982). Intrinsic motivation to teach: Possibilities and obstacles in our colleges and universities. *New Directions for Teaching and Learning, No. 10.* San Francisco, CA: Jossey-Bass.

Deming, W. E. (1986). *Out of the crisis.* Cambridge, MA: MIT Center for Advanced Engineering Study.

Deming, W. E. (1993). *The new economics: For industry, government, education.* Cambridge, MA: MIT Center for Advanced Engineering Study.

Diamond, R. M. (1999). *Aligning faculty rewards with institutional mission: Statements, policies, and guidelines.* Bolton, MA: Anker.

Dill, D. D. (1992). Quality by design: Toward a framework for academic quality management. In J. Smart (Ed.), *Higher education: Handbook of theory and research* (pp. 37–83). New York, NY: Agathon Press.

Dill, D. D. (2000). Designing academic audit: Lessons learned in Europe and Asia. *Quality in Higher Education, 6* (3), 187–207.

Ehrenberg, R. G. (2000). *Tuition rising.* Cambridge, MA: Harvard University Press.

Ehrmann, S. C., & Milam, J. H., Jr. (1999). *Modeling resource use in teaching and learning with technology.* Washington, DC: The TLT Group.

El-Khawas, E., & Massy, W. F. (1996). Britain's 'performance-based' system. In W. F. Massy (Ed.), *Resource allocation in higher education* (pp. 223–342). Ann Arbor, MI: The University of Michigan Press.

Ewell, P. T. (1999). *A delicate balance: The role of evaluation in management.* Paper presented at the Fifth Conference of the International Network of Quality Assurance Agencies in Higher Education (INQAAHE), Santiago, Chile.

Fairweather, J. S. (1993). *Teaching, research, and faculty rewards: A summary of the research findings of the faculty profile project.* University Park, PA: Pennsylvania State University, National Center on Postsecondary Teaching, Learning, and Assessment.

Fairweather, J. S. (1996). *Faculty work and the public trust: Restoring the value of teaching and public service in American academic life.* Boston, MA: Allyn & Bacon.

Fenske, R. (1989). Evolution of the student services profession. In U. Delworth, G. R. Hanson, & Associates (Eds.), *Student services: A handbook for the profession* (pp. 25–56). San Francisco, CA: Jossey-Bass.

French, N. J., Ko, P. K., Massy, W. F., Siu, F. H., & Young, K. (1999, Spring). Research assessment in Hong Kong. *Journal of International Education, 10* (1), 46–53.

French, N. J., Massy, W. F., & Young, K. (2001, July). Research assessment in Hong Kong. *Higher Education, 42* (1).

Gaither G., Nedwek, B., & Neal, J. (1994). *Measuring up the promises and pitfalls of performance indicators in higher education.* Washington, DC: ERIC & George Washington University.

Gaudiani, C. (2000, July/August). The hidden costs of merit aid. *Change, 32* (4), 19.

Gilbert, S. W. (1996, March/April). Making the most of a slow revolution. *Change, 28* (2), 10–23.

Glassick, C. E., Huber, M. T., & Maeroff, G. I. (1997). *Scholarship assessed.* San Francisco. CA: Jossey-Bass.

Goldman, C. A., & Massy, W. F. (2001). *The PhD factory: Training and employment of science and engineering doctorates in the United States.* Bolton, MA: Anker.

Goldman, C. A., & Williams, T. (2000). *Paying for university research facilities and administration.* Santa Monica, CA: RAND Science and Technology Institute.

Graham, H. D., & Diamond, N. (1997). *The rise of American research universities.* Baltimore, MD: The Johns Hopkins University Press.

Graham, P. A., Lyman, R. W., & Trow, M. (1995). *Accountability of colleges and universities: An essay.* New York, NY: Columbia University, The Accountability Study.

Green, K. C., & Gilbert, S. W. (1995, March/April). Great expectations: Content, communications, productivity, and the role of information technology in higher education. *Change, 27* (2), 8–18.

Gross, P. R., & Levitt, N. (1994). *Higher superstition: The academic left and its quarrels with science.* Baltimore, MD: The Johns Hopkins University Press.

Hammer, M., & Champy, J. (1993). *Reengineering the corporation: A manifesto for business revolution.* New York, NY: HarperBusiness.

Hansmann, H. (1981, November). The rationale for exempting nonprofit organizations from corporate income taxation. *Yale Law Journal, 91,* 54–100.

Hansmann, H. (1986). The role of nonprofit enterprise. In S. Rose-Ackerman (Ed.), *The economics of nonprofit institutions* (pp. 57–84). New York, NY: Oxford University Press.

Hansmann, H. (2000). Higher education as an associative good. In M. E. Devlin & J. W. Meyerson (Eds.), *Forum futures 1999* (pp. 11–24). New Haven, CT: Yale University, Forum for the Future of Higher Education.

Harrington, H. J. (1991). *Business process improvement.* New York, NY: McGraw-Hill.

Hearth, M., Kaplan, R., & Waldron, J. (1991). New costing systems? *Journal of Accounting Historians, 4,* 6–22.

Hoenack, S. A. (1983). *Economic behavior within organizations.* New York, NY: Cambridge University Press.

Hood, A. B., & Arceneaux, C. (1990). *Key resources on student services: A guide to the field and its literature.* San Francisco, CA: Jossey-Bass.

Hopkins, D. S. P., & Massy, W. F. (1981). *Planning models for colleges and universities.* Stanford, CA: Stanford University Press.

Huber, R. M. (1992). *How professors play the cat guarding the cream: Why we're paying more and getting less in higher education.* Fairfax, VA: George Mason University Press.

Hughes, T. P. (2000). *Through a glass darkly: The future of technology-enabled education.* Paper presented at the Forum for the Future of Higher Education, Aspen Institute, Aspen, Colorado.

Hussain, K. M. (1971). *A resource requirements prediction model (RRPM-1): Guide for the project manager* (Tech. Rep. No. 20). Boulder, CO: National Center for Higher Education Management Systems at WICHE.

Hutchings, P., & Shulman, L. S. (1999, September/October). The scholarship of teaching: New elaborations, new developments. *Change, 31* (5), 11–15.

The Institute for Research on Higher Education. (1994, July/August). Discounting and its discontents. *Change, 26* (4), 33–36.

The Institute for Research on Higher Education. (1997, November/December). In search of strategic perspective: A tool for mapping the market in postsecondary education. *Change, 29* (6), 23–38.

The Institute for Research on Higher Education. (1999, September/October). Revolution or evolution? Gauging the impact of institutional student-assessment strategies. *Change, 31* (5), 53–57.

The Institute for Research on Higher Education. (2000, March/April). Why is research the rule? The impact of incentive systems on faculty behavior. *Change, 32* (2), 53–56.

The Institute for Research on Higher Education. (2001, September/October). A respectable B. *Change, 33* (5), 23–38.

James, E. (1986). How nonprofits grow: A model. In S. Rose-Ackerman, (Ed.), *The economics of nonprofit institutions* (pp. 185-195). New York, NY: Oxford University Press.

James, E. (1990). Decision processes and priorities in higher education. In S. A. Hoenack & E. L. Collins (Eds.), *The economics of American universities* (pp. 77–106). Albany, NY: State University of New York Press.

James, E., & Neuberger, E. (1981). The university department as a nonprofit labor cooperative. *Public Choice, 36,* 585–612.

Johnstone, D. B. (2000). *Higher education and those 'out of control costs'* (Working Paper). Buffalo, NY: State University of New York.

Joiner, B. L. (1994). *Fourth generation management: The new business consciousness.* New York, NY: McGraw-Hill.

Juran, J. M. (1989). *Juran on leadership for quality: An executive handbook.* New York, NY: The Free Press.

Juran, J. M., & Gryna, F. M. (1993). *Quality planning and analysis* (3rd ed.). New York, NY: McGraw-Hill

Kane, M. (2000). *Assessing the U.S. financial aid system: What we know, what we need to know.* Paper presented at the Forum for the Future of Higher Education, Aspen Institute, Aspen, Colorado.

Kaplan, R. S., & Norton, D. P. (1996). *The balanced scorecard.* Boston, MA: Harvard Business School Press.

Keller, G. (1983). *Academic strategy: The management revolution in American higher education.* Baltimore, MD: The Johns Hopkins University Press.

Kennedy, D. (1997). *Academic duty.* Cambridge, MA: Harvard University Press.

Kirstein, J. (1999). *Trends in learning structures in higher education.* Paper presented at the Confederation of European Rectors Conference, Geneva, Switzerland.

Knight Higher Education Collaborative. (1988, September). Seeing straight through a muddle. *Policy Perspectives, 1* (1).

Knight Higher Education Collaborative. (1989, May). The business of the business. *Policy Perspectives, 1* (3).

Knight Higher Education Collaborative. (1990, January). Breaking the mold. *Policy Perspectives, 2* (2).

Knight Higher Education Collaborative. (1990, June). The lattice and the ratchet. *Policy Perspectives, 2* (4).

Knight Higher Education Collaborative. (1990, September). Back to business. *Policy Perspectives, 3* (1).

Knight Higher Education Collaborative. (1991, September). An end to sanctuary. *Policy Perspectives, 3* (4).

Knight Higher Education Collaborative. (1992, September). Testimony from the belly of the whale. *Policy Perspectives, 4* (3).

Knight Higher Education Collaborative. (1993, September). A transatlantic dialog. *Policy Perspectives, 5* (3).

Knight Higher Education Collaborative. (2000, March). The data made me do it. *Policy Perspectives, 9* (2).

Kozma, R., & Johnston, J. (1991, January/February). The technology revolution comes to the classroom. *Change, 23* (1), 10–23.

Lareau, W. (1991). *American Samurai.* New York, NY: Warner Books.

Laurillard, D. (1993). *Rethinking university teaching.* New York, NY: Reutledge.

Lawler, E. E. (1981). *Pay and organization development.* Reading, MA: Addison-Wesley.

Leslie, L., & Brinkman, P. (1989). *The economic value of higher education.* New York, NY: McMillan.

Lovett, C. M. (2002, March/April). Cracks in the bedrock: Can U. S. higher education remain number one? *Change, 34* (2), 11–15.

Making quality work. (2001, July/August). *University Business, 4* (6), 44–48, 50, 78, 80, 85.

Manz, C. C., & Sims, H. P., Jr. (1993). *Business without bosses: How self-managing teams are building high-performing companies.* New York, NY: John Wiley & Sons.

March, J. G. (1981). Footnotes to organizational change. *Administrative Science Quarterly, 26,* 663–677.

Massy, W. F. (1990). *Endowment: Perspectives, policies, and management.* Washington, DC: Association of Governing Boards of Universities and Colleges.

Massy, W. F. (1996). *Resource allocation in higher education.* Ann Arbor, MI: The University of Michigan Press.

Massy, W. F. (1997a). Life on the wired campus: How information technology will shape institutional futures. In D. G. Oblinger & S. C. Rush (Eds.), *The learning revolution: The challenge of information technology in the academy* (pp. 195–210). Bolton, MA: Anker.

Massy, W. F. (1997b). Teaching learning quality process review: The Hong Kong programme. *Quality in Higher Education, 3* (3), 249–262.

Massy, W. F. (2000). *Energizing quality work: Higher education quality evaluation in Sweden and Denmark* (Tech. Rep). Stanford, CA: Stanford University, National Center for Postsecondary Improvement.

Massy, W. F., & French, N. J. (1997). *Teaching and learning quality process review: A review of the Hong Kong programme.* Paper presented at the Fourth Conference of the International Network for Quality Assurance Agencies in Higher Education (INQAAHE), South Africa.

Massy, W. F., & French, N. J. (1999, April). Teaching and learning quality process review: What the program has achieved in Hong Kong. *Quality in Higher Education, 7* (1), 33–45.

Massy, W. F., & Wilger, A. K. (1992). Productivity in postsecondary education: A new approach. *Educational Evaluation and Policy Analysis, 14* (4), 361–376.

Massy, W. F., & Wilger, A. K. (1995, July/August). Improving productivity. *Change, 27* (4), 10–20.

Massy, W. F., & Wilger, A. K. (1998). Technology's contribution to higher education productivity. In J. E. Groccia & J. E. Miller (Eds.), *Enhancing productivity: Administrative, instructional, and technological strategies* (pp. 49–60). San Francisco, CA: Jossey-Bass.

Massy, W. F., Wilger, A., & Colbeck, C. (1994, July/August). Overcoming 'hollowed collegiality'. *Change, 26* (4), 11–20.

Massy, W. F., & Zemsky, R. (1994). *Using information technology to enhance academic productivity.* Washington, DC: EDUCOM.

Mayadas, A. F. (1997). Asynchronous learning networks: New possibilities. In D. G. Oblinger & S. C. Rush (Eds.), *The learning revolution: The challenge of information technology in the academy* (pp. 211–230). Bolton, MA: Anker.

McKeachie, W. J. (1979). Student ratings of faculty: A reprise. *Academe,* 65, 384–397.

McMillin, L. A., & Berberet, W. G. (2002). *A new academic compact: Revisioning the relationship between faculty and their institutions.* Bolton, MA: Anker.

McPherson, M. S., & Schapiro, M. O. (1994a). *Merit aid: Students, institutions, and society* (Discussion Paper DP-25). Williamstown, MA: Williams College, Williams Project on the Economics of Higher Education College.

McPherson, M. S., & Schapiro, M. O. (1994b). *Expenditures and revenues in American higher education* (Discussion Paper DP-27). Williamstown, MA: Williams College, Williams Project on the Economics of Higher Education.

McPherson, M., & Schapiro, M. O. (1997). *The student aid game.* Princeton, NJ: Princeton University Press.

McPherson, M. S., Schapiro, M. O., & Winston, G. C. (1993). *Paying the piper: Productivity, incentives, and financing in U. S. higher education.* Ann Arbor, MI: The University of Michigan Press.

Meade, P., & Woodhouse, D. (2000, April). Evaluating the effectiveness of the New Zealand academic audit unit: Review and outcomes. *Quality in Higher Education,* 19–30.

Melan, E. H. (1993). *Process management: Methods for improving products and service.* New York, NY: McGraw-Hill.

Menchen, A. (2000). *The railroad passenger car.* Baltimore, MD: The Johns Hopkins University Press.

Meyer, J. W., & Rowan, B. (1977). Institutionalized organizations: Formal structure as myth and ceremony. *American Journal of Sociology,* 83, 440–463.

Meyer, K. A. (1998). *Faculty workload studies: Perspectives, needs, and future directions* (ASHE-ERIC Higher Education Report Volume 26, No. 1). Washington, DC: The George Washington University, Graduate School of Education and Human Development.

Milam, J. H., Jr. (2000). *Cost analysis of on-line courses.* Paper presented at the Forum of the Association for Institutional Research (AIR). Available: http://airweb.org

Milem, J. F., Berger, J. B., & Dey, E. L. (2000, July/August). Faculty time allocation: A study of change over twenty years. *The Journal of Higher Education, 71* (4), 454–475.

Miller, G. L., & Krumm, L. L. (1992). *The whats, whys & hows of quality improvement.* Milwaukee, WI: ASQC Quality Press.

Nadler, D. A., & Lawler, E. E. (1977). Motivation: A diagnostic approach. In J. R. Hackman, E. E. Lawler, & L. W. Porter (Eds.), *Perspectives on behavior in organizations* (pp. 67–78). New York, NY: McGraw-Hill.

National Association of College and University Business Officers (NACUBO). (2002). *Explaining college costs: NACUBO's methodology for identifying the costs of delivering undergraduate education.* Washington, DC: Author.

National Center for Higher Education Management Systems (NCHEMS). (2000). *Technology costing methodology (TCM) handbook.* Boulder, CO: National Center for Higher Education Management Systems, Western Cooperative for Educational Telecommunications, Western Interstate Commission for Higher Education.

National Commission on Responsibilities for Financing Postsecondary Education. (1993). *Making college affordable again.* Washington, DC: Author.

National Commission on the Cost of Higher Education. (1998). *Straight talk about college costs and prices.* Washington, DC: Author.

National Governors Association. (1991). *Time for results: The governor's 1991 report on education.* Washington, DC: Author.

Needham, D. (1982). Improving faculty evaluation and reward systems. *Journal of Economic Education, 13* (1), 6–18.

Nerlove, M. (1972). On tuition and the costs of higher education: Prolegomena to a conceptual framework. *Journal of Political Economy, Part II, 3,* S178–S218.

Nettles, M. T., & Cole, J. J. K. (1999). *State higher education assessment policy: Research findings from second and third years* (Tech. Rep.). Stanford, CA: Stanford University, National Center for Postsecondary Improvement.

Nettles, M. T., Cole, J. J. K., & Sharp, S. (1997). *Benchmarking assessment* (Tech. Rep.). Stanford, CA: Stanford University, National Center for Postsecondary Improvement.

Nilsson, K. A., & Whalen, S. (2000, April). Institutional response to the Swedish model of quality assurance. *Quality in Higher Education,* 7–18.

Northwest Missouri State University. (1996). *Guidelines for the implementation of the seven-step planning process.* Maryville, MO: Northwest Missouri State University, Office of the President.

Office of Technology Assessment (OTA). (1986). *The regulatory environment for science* (United States Congress, OTA-TM-SET-34). Springfield, VA: National Technical Information Service.

Orsburn, J. D., Moran, L., Musselwhite, E., & Zenger, J. H. (1990). *Self-directed work teams: The new American challenge.* Burr Ridge, IL: Irwin Professional Publishing.

Pfeffer, J., & Salancik, G. R. (1978). *The external control of organizations: A resource dependence perspective.* New York, NY: Harper and Row.

Pfeffer, J., & Sutton, R. I. (2000). *The knowing-doing gap.* Boston, MA: Harvard Business School Press.

Pitt, H. (1994). *SPC for the rest of us.* Reading, MA: Addison-Wesley.

Quinn, J. B. (2000). *Services and technology: Revolutionizing economics, business and education.* Paper presented at the Forum for the Future of Higher Education, Aspen Institute, Aspen, Colorado.

Randall, J. (2001). *Defining standards: Developing a global currency of higher education qualifications.* Proceedings of the sixth Biennial Conference of the International Network of Quality Assurance Agencies in Higher Education (INQAAHE), Bangalore, India.

Reisman, D. (1958). *Constraint and variety in American education.* Garden City, NY: Anchor Books.

Rogers, E. M. (1964). *Diffusion of innovations.* New York, NY: The Free Press.

Rosenbluth, H. F. & Peters, D. M. (1992). *The customer comes second: And other secrets of exceptional service.* New York, NY: Quill/William Morrow.

Rosovsky, H. (1990). *The university: An owner's manual.* New York, NY: W. W. Norton & Company.

Scholtes, P. R. (1988). *The team handbook.* Madison, WI: Joiner Associates.

Senge, P. M. (1990). *The fifth discipline: The art and practice of the learning organization.* New York, NY: Doubleday Currency.

Siegfried, J. (2000). *Developing infrastructure of policy-oriented research on the economics of higher education.* Paper presented at the Forum for the Future of Higher Education, Aspen Institute, Aspen, Colorado.

Smith, P. (1990). *Killing the spirit: Higher education in America.* New York, NY: Viking.

Sommers, N. (1982). Responding to student writing. *College Composition and Communication, 33* (2), 148–156.

Sonnenberg, F. K. (1994). *Managing with a conscience: How to improve performance through integrity, trust, and commitment.* New York, NY: McGraw-Hill.

Spence, L. D. (2001, November/December). The case against teaching. *Change, 33* (6), 11–19.

Spendolini, M. J. (1992). *The benchmarking book.* New York, NY: Amacom.

Stanford Forum for Higher Education Futures. (1995). *Leveraged learning: Technology's role in restructuring higher education.* Stanford, CA: Stanford University, Stanford Institute for Higher Education Research.

Stark, J. S., & Lattuca, L. R. (1997). *Shaping the college curriculum: Academic plans in action.* Boston, MA: Allyn and Bacon.

Staw, B. M. (1983). Motivation research versus the art of faculty management. *Review of Higher Education, 6* (4), 301–321.

Steinbruner, J. D. (1974). *The cybernetic theory of decision.* Princeton, NJ: Princeton University Press.

Stensaker, B. (1999a). *Quality as discourse: An analysis of external audit reports in Sweden: 1995–1998.* Paper presented to the 21st EAIR Forum, Lund, Sweden.

Stensaker, B. (1999b, October). External quality auditing in Sweden: Are departments affected? *Higher Education Quarterly, 353*–368.

Swan, J. (2001). *Transparency—an essential characteristic of the evaluation of higher education?* Proceedings of the sixth Biennial Conference of the International Network of Quality Assurance Agencies in Higher Education (INQAAHE), Bangalore, India.

Sykes, C. (1987). *Profscam: Professors and the demise of higher education.* Washington, DC: Regnery Gateway.

Tomkins, C., & Green, R. (1988). An experimental use of data envelopment analysis in evaluating efficiency of UK departments of accounting. *Financial Accountability and Management, 4,* 147–164.

Trow, M. (1994). *Academic reviews and the culture of excellence.* Stockholm, Sweden: Kanslersämbetet.

Twigg, C. (1999). *Improving learning and reducing cost: Redesigning large enrollment courses.* Troy, NY: Pew Learning and Technology Program.

Twigg, C. A., & Oblinger, D. (1996). *The virtual university* (Report from a Joint EDUCOM/IBM Roundtable). Washington, DC: EDUCOM.

United States Congress, Office of Technology Assessment (OTA). (1991). *Federally funded research: Decisions for a decade* (OTA-SET-490). Washington, DC: Government Printing Office.

van Vught, F. (1995). The new context for academic quality. In D. D. Dill & B. Sporn (Eds.), *Emerging social demands and university reform: Through a glass darkly* (pp. 194–211). New York, NY: Pergamon Press.

Vroom, V. H. (1964). *Work and motivation.* New York, NY: Wiley.

Wahlén, S. (1998). Is there a Scandinavian model of evaluation of higher education? *Higher Education Management and Policy, 10* (3), 18–33.

Walvoord, B. E., & Breilan, J. R. (1997). Helping faculty design assignment-centered courses. In D. DeZure (Ed.), *To improve the academy: Vol. 16. Resources for faculty, instructional, and organizational development* (pp. 349–372). Stillwater, OK: New Forums Press.

Walvoord, B. E., & Pool, K. J. (1998). Enhancing pedagogical productivity. In J. E. Groccia & J. E. Miller (Eds.), *Enhancing productivity: Administrative, instructional, and technological strategies* (pp. 35–48). San Francisco, CA: Jossey-Bass.

Warren, R. G. (1997). Engaging students in active learning. *About Campus, 2* (1), 16–20.

Watson, G. H. (1993). *Strategic benchmarking: How to rate your company's performance against the world's best.* New York, NY: John Wiley & Sons.

Weisman, D., & Mitchell, T. (1986, Spring). Texas Instruments recalculates their costing system. *Journal of Cost Management,* 63–68.

Westbury, D. B. (1997). *Management information for decision making: Costing guidelines for higher education institutions.* Bristol, England: Costing Study Steering Group.

Western Association of Schools and Colleges (WASC). (2002). *Evidence guide: A guide for using evidence in the accreditation process: A resource to support institutions and evaluation teams.* Alameda, CA: Accrediting Commission for Senior Colleges and Universities, Western Association of Schools and Colleges.

Whalen, E. L. (1991). *Responsibility center budgeting.* Bloomington, IN: Indiana University Press.

Whiteley, R. C. (1991). *The customer-driven company: Moving from talk to action.* Reading, MA: Addison-Wesley.

Williams, W. M., & Ceci, S. J. (1997, September/October). How'm I doing? *Change, 29* (5), 13–23.

Wilson, J. M. (1996). Reengineering the undergraduate curriculum. In D. G. Oblinger & S. C. Rush (Eds.), *The learning revolution: The challenge of information technology in the academy* (pp. 107–128). Bolton, MA: Anker.

Winston, G. C. (1997). *Why can't a college be more like a firm?* (Discussion Paper DP-42). Williamstown, MA: Williams College, Williams Project on the Economics of Higher Education.

Winston, G. C. (1999). *Do private colleges make big profits? Forum futures: 1998 papers.* Cambridge, MA: Forum for the Future of Higher Education.

Winston, G. C. (2000). *The positional arms race in higher education.* Paper presented at the Forum for the Future of Higher Education, Aspen Institute, Aspen, Colorado.

Winston, G. C., & Yen, I. C. (1995). *Costs, subsidies, and aid in U. S. higher education* (Discussion Paper DP-32). Williamstown, MA: Williams College, Williams Project on the Economics of Higher Education College.

Winston, G. C., & Zimmerman, D. J. (2000, July/August). Where is aggressive price competition taking higher education? *Change, 32* (4), 10–18.

Wood, R. (2001). Quality/activity-based costing: A compilation of academic modules in accounting, educational leadership, and theater communication. In R. A. Wood & D. L. Hubbard (Eds.), *Cost containment and continuous improvement* (pp. 48–57). Maryville, MO: Northwest Missouri State University in cooperation with Prescott Publishing Company.

Wood, R., & Hubbard, D. L. (2001). Quality, cost, and value added: A manual for integrating quality and activity-based costing in higher education. In R. A. Wood & D. L. Hubbard (Eds.), *Cost containment and continuous improvement* (pp. 1–22). Maryville, MO: Northwest Missouri State University in cooperation with Prescott Publishing Company.

Wood, R., & Wilson, M. (2001). Quality/activity-based costing: Comparison of synchronous and asynchronous delivery in finance, management, and philosophy. In R. A. Wood & D. L. Hubbard (Eds.), *Cost containment and continuous improvement* (pp. 58–69). Maryville, MO: Northwest Missouri State University in cooperation with Prescott Publishing Company.

Yuker, H. E. (1984). *Faculty workload: Research, theory, and interpretation* (ASHE-ERIC Higher Education Research Report No. 10). Washington, DC: Association for the Study of Higher Education.

Zeithaml, V. A., Parasuraman, A., & Berry, L. L. (1990). *Delivering quality service.* New York, NY: The Free Press.

Zemke, R., & Schaff, D. (1989). *The service edge.* New York, NY: New American Library.

Zemsky, R. (1989). *Structure and coherence: Measuring the undergraduate curriculum.* Washington, DC: Association of American Colleges.

Zemsky, R. & Massy, W. F. (1990, November/December). Cost containment: Committing to a new economic reality. *Change, 22* (6), 16–22.

Zemsky, R., & Massy, W. F. (1995, November/December). Expanding perimeters, melting cores, and sticky functions: Toward an understanding of our current predicaments. *Change, 27* (6), 40–49.

Zemsky R., Massy, W. F., Shapiro, D., Shaman, S., Dubrow, G., & Giancola, J. (1999). *Market, price, and margin: Determining the cost of an undergraduate education.* Philadelphia, PA: University of Pennsylvania, The Institute for Research on Higher Education.

Zhang, M. (1999). *An international perspective on performance indicators in higher education: A documentary study for the university grants committee.* Hong Kong: The University of Hong Kong, Comparative Education Research Center.

Index